STOCKWELL-MUDD LIBRARIES

3 5044 00066 8035

D1221912

MASSACHUSETTS AVENUE ARCHITECTURE
Volume II

issued by

THE COMMISSION OF FINE ARTS

prepared by

J. L. Sibley Jennings, Jr.
Architect

Sue A. Kohler
Historian

Jeffrey R. Carson
Architectural Historian

1975

THE COMMISSION OF FINE ARTS
708 Jackson Place N.W.
Washington, D.C., 20006
Established by Congress
17 May 1910

NA
735
.W3
U587
V.2

213665

Hon. J. Carter Brown, Chairman

Hon. Nicolas Arroyo   Hon. Edward D. Stone, Jr.
Hon. Jane O. Dart   Hon. Chloethiel Woodard Smith
Hon. E. Kevin Roche   Hon. George A. Weymouth

Charles H. Atherton
Secretary
Donald B. Myer
Assistant Secretary

For sale by the Superintendent of Documents, U.S. Government Printing Office
Washington, D.C. 20402—Price $4.45
Stock Number 010–000–00007–6

Foreword

When we began working on these two volumes of *Massachusetts Avenue Architecture* the intent was architectural documentation of existing structures, primarily of the style termed Beaux Arts. We recorded as fact the biographies of residents and architects, chain of title, recorded deeds, building permits, wills, and such architectural detail as was extant, or available in old photographs or drawings. But other areas of architectural history are less exact. Styles neither begin nor end with one building or one date; also, speculation on what determined the architect's design and assessments of the quality of that design are necessarily subjective.

The reader should be cautioned that we did not advance a theorem and then select buildings to prove it. Rather we selected those buildings that we felt were notable in design (agreed, this was subjective) and then began research. As material was ammassed and culled, patterns and correlations were first noted and then followed to conclusion. Our thought was that by advancing both the designer and the owner, the reader might then begin to appreciate the fact of the finished design.

And so Volume I, published in 1973, came into being. Shortcomings, however, were apparent before the manuscript went to press. The outline form, while easing the path for the researcher and architect, made a most unreadable format for the uninitiated. In the second volume we have drawn together the historical facts and introduced them as one statement, with the supporting documents as an appendix. Moreover, we are describing a visual art and only photography can approximate the actual object; so more photographs were in order for this second book. Also, as the buildings and major spaces are introduced in the architectural section, attention is focused on certain design elements which give the building its character. This last is based on opinion; whether the designer's intent was so premeditated is not known. Finally, I should point out that a considerable number of destroyed buildings have been included in Volume II. This was done for two reasons: because they were major examples of early structures in the Federal, Victorian and Beaux Arts manner that we felt should be brought to the attention of the public, and because most of them were built on Thomas, Scott or Dupont Circles and gave these circles a character they no longer have. We hope that a feeling for what has been lost will develop as the reader progresses through the books.

This editor would like to publicly acknowledge the talents and labors of the two finest associates possible—Sue A. Kohler, art historian, responsible for biographies of residents and architects, deeds, and wills; and Jeffrey R. Carson, architectural historian, responsible for architectural documentation. Jointly they seek out building permits and historical illustrative material, and dimension each building. In addition to other duties at the Commission of Fine Arts, they undertake these architectural surveys through strenuous, time consuming effort. This architect functions as photographer, draftsman, and editor, graphically documenting the buildings and coordinating the whole in preparation for the printer. All photographs and plans not otherwise credited come from this office.

J. L. Sibley Jennings, Jr.

1801 Massachusetts Avenue N.W.
1970/Jack E. Boucher

Postscript to Volume I

As always happens, additional material has come to light after publication. Often it is possible to disregard minor bits and pieces, but in the case of the Sulgrave Club, 1801 Massachusetts Avenue, we believe the discovery (by Dorothy Provine of the National Archives) of an original floor plan to be too important not to draw to the public's attention. As yet, the original permit itself eludes every researcher, and the architect is unknown. But although unsigned by an architect, the "Plan of First Floor" (we called it "ground floor") is dated "Jan. 16, 1900," and does give us more information than we possessed when Volume I went to press.

Of greatest interest is the realization that the location of the porte-cochère through the building was determined by the church previously on the site. We knew of the existence of Holy Cross Episcopal Church, but assumed that its demolition had occurred for the erection of Herbert Wadsworth's residence in 1900.

We do not know when the church was erected, although records in the Episcopal Diocese of Washington show that Holy Cross was established as a mission in 1873 and as a separate congregation in 1874. On 30 October 1882 a permit was issued to the church granting permission to "Build a brick tower and brick addition" for the sum of $2,000 (Permit No. 599). When the floor plan was found it showed especially thick walls from the "driveway" (porte-cochère) to Eighteenth Street, encompassing those areas known as "kitchen" and "back hall" (assumed to be the brick addition); and the "automobile room," "servants' hall," and "vestibule" (assumed to be the body of the original church). "Ghosted" in at the junction of the "vestibule," "smoking room," and "billiard room" is a rather suspicious rectangle that might be the 1882 brick tower.

Of interest to Washingtonians is the fact that the congregation of Holy Cross built a new church in 1893, just a few blocks away from the old building, at Eighteenth and Church Streets, N.W. The new church went through several changes of name: from Church of the Messiah to Calvary Protestant Episcopal Church to St. Thomas. The architect for the new church was T. P. Chandler, whose house for the Leiter family was under construction at 1500 New Hampshire Avenue in the same year. (See text.) St. Thomas became well-known as Franklin Roosevelt's church. Unfortunately, it was destroyed by fire in 1970, although services continue to be held in the Parish Hall.

At any rate, it is now possible to compare the original first floor plan and our second floor plan of 1973 (published as "First Floor Plan"). Moreover, if indeed the re-use of Holy Cross was responsible for the floor plans, as we now suspect, then we have gone a long way toward explaining the rather contorted arrangement of rooms.

Therefore, we now present you with the 1900 first floor plan:

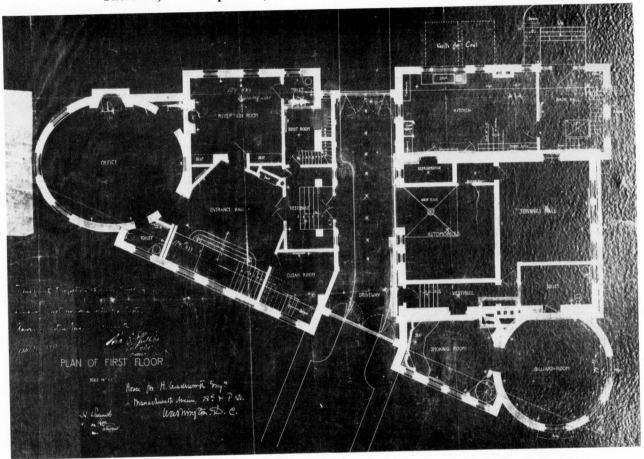

PLAN OF FIRST FLOOR

January 16, 1900
D.C. Permits, National Archives

to compare with our 1973 second floor plan:

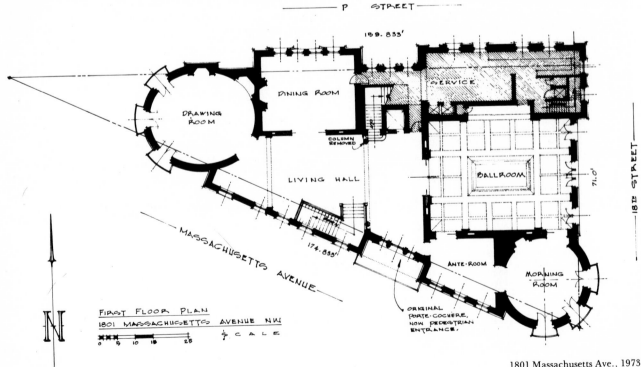

FIRST FLOOR PLAN
1801 MASSACHUSETTS AVENUE NW

1801 Massachusetts Ave., 1973
(Second Floor Plan)

A lesser, but interesting, discovery has been made regarding another house discussed in Volume I: the Patterson residence at 15 Dupont Circle designed by McKim, Mead and White. The decorative fruit swags, winged figures and escutcheons which are so prominent on the facade are strongly reminiscent of the stucco decorations on several sixteenth century Roman palaces: in particular the Palazzo Spada of 1550 (probably by Girolamo da Carpi) with its stuccos by Giulio Mazzoni, and the Palazzo Branconio dall'Aquila by Raphael, dated 1515.[1] This is not to imply that the Patterson house is a direct copy, only to point out that the source of inspiration was most likely from this period and this part of Italy.

[1] Corrado Ricci, *L'Architecture Italienne au Seizième Siècle,* Paris: Librairie Hachette, no date. Pls. 134–38.

15 Dupont Circle
The Patterson House
Photo by J. Alexander

Acknowledgements

The staff of the Commission of Fine Arts would like to express its gratitude to the many individuals, societies, and the District of Columbia and Federal agencies whose cooperation has aided in the completion of this book.

Personal thanks are extended to The Newport, Rhode Island, Historical Society; The Boston Public Library; The Henry E. Huntington Library and Art Gallery in San Marino, California, particularly Daniel Woodward, Alan Jutzi and Bruce Henry; the staffs of the Washingtoniana Room (especially Miss Betty Culpepper, Miss Barbara Hanley and Mr. Alexander W. Geyger) and History Department at the Martin Luther King Library; Miss Dorothy Provine, Archivist at the National Archives Building; Miss Hazel Dawson, Inter-Library Loan Assistant, Interior Department; Mrs. Cynthia Field, Smithsonian Fellow; The State Department, particularly Mrs. Helene De Long, Miss Penny Mac-Murtry and Miss Jane A. Guilbault; the Reverend Henry H. Breul (rector of St. Thomas Episcopal Church) and Mrs. Viola Leipold of the Episcopal Diocese of Washington; Mrs. Tanya Beauchamp, architectural historian for the Landmarks Committee, NCPC; Perry G. Fisher, Librarian, and Robert A. Truax, former Librarian, for the Columbia Historical Society; Margaret and Elden E. Billings; Donald J. Lehman, architectural historian; and John B. Earnshaw. Special note is made of the excellent initial research conducted by Mrs. Lynda Deming (nee Smith) for this second volume on Massachusetts Avenue. Credit is also given to the Government Printing Office staff, especially Robert M. Worley, Superintendent of Typography and Design, John L. Cooke, Chief of the Typographic Section, Clarence Alston, Printing Specialist, and James B. Watson, Jr., Visual Information Specialist.

Our special gratitude goes to Nancy N. Lusher, Administrative Assistant, whose help in so many capacities was invaluable in the production of this book.

This survey would not have been possible without the understanding and approval of the foreign governments and private citizens whose properties are included in this study. We are grateful to:

1013—15 L Street, N.W., The Soldiers, Sailors, Marines and Airmen's Club
    Mrs. William H. Beard, Executive Director
    Mrs. John O. Moench, former Chairman of the Publicity Committee

1107 Massachusetts Avenue, N.W., residence
    Miss Emily Nourse Steuart

1219 Massachusetts Avenue, N.W., rectory, Church of the Ascension and Saint Agnes
    Reverend Father Frederic Howard Meisel, Rector

1500 Rhode Island Avenue, N.W., The National Paint and Coatings Association
    Mr. Jerry L. Colness, Director, Communications Division NPCA
    Mr. William Cwiklo, Volta Bureau
    Mr. Keeler Bentley, Explorer's Hall, Nova Scotia
    Mr. Robert V. Bruce, Boston University History Department
    Mr. Raymond B. Clark, Jr., and Miss Stephany Jaramillo (both formerly with NPCA)

1732 Massachusetts Avenue, N.W., chancery, The Embassy of Chile
    Mrs. E. Morgan Pryse, Daughters of the American Revolution
       (On site information was gathered after the building passed to the Government of Chile. Refer to 2305 Massachusetts Avenue.)

1520 Twentieth Street, N.W., The Embassy of Colombia
His Excellency, Julio Cesar Turbay Ayala
    Ambassador Extraordinary and Plenipotentiary
Dr. Rodrigo Escobar, Chargé D' Affaires
Mrs. Luiz Estelle Mobin, Protocol Secretary (Civil Attaché)
Mr. J. Richard Abell, History and Literature Department,
    Cincinnati Public Library
Miss Jennifer De Remer, Humanities Reference, Boston Public Library

2000 Massachusetts Avenue, N.W., offices (Spencer, Whalen and Graham,
    Attorneys at Law)
Mr. Samuel Spencer
Mr. Frank Whalen, Jr.
Mr. Richard Derman, former graduate student at the University of
    Pennsylvania
Miss Olga T. Puspoki, Public Relations Assistant, Westinghouse

2025 Massachusetts Avenue, N.W., The Church of the Savior Ecumenical
Pastor N. Gordon Cosby
Miss Marjorie Pevey
Mr. L. S. Gum, American Telephone and Telegraph

2305 Massachusetts Avenue, N.W., The Embassy of Chile
His Excellency, Manuel Trucco
    Ambassador Extraordinary and Plenipotentiary
His Excellency, Walter Heitman, former
    Ambassador Extraordinary and Plenipotentiary
His Excellency, Orlando Letelier, former
    Ambassador Extraordinary and Plenipotentiary
Mrs. Maria Victoria Sanson, Social Secretary
Mrs. Hernan Labarca former Protocol Secretary (Civil Attaché)
Mrs. Amelia Orrego, former Protocol Secretary (Civil Attaché)
Mr. John T. Runk and Mr. Robert E. Scudder, Free Library,
    Philadelphia

2929 Massachusetts Avenue, N.W., residence
Countess Anthony (Sylvia) Szápáry
Mrs. Beatrice Bouchard

3000 Massachusetts Avenue, N.W., The Embassy of Brazil
His Excellency, João Augusto de Araujo Castro
    Ambassador Extraordinary and Plenipotentiary
Mr. Sergio de Queiroz Duarte, Counselor, Cultural Office
Mrs. Rachel Fowler Wahl, Social Secretary
Mr. Harold Hutchings, Archivist, Chicago Tribune

3100 Massachusetts Avenue, N.W., The Embassy of Great Britain
His Excellency, The Right Honorable, Sir Peter Ramsbotham
    Ambassador Extraordinary and Plenipotentiary
His Excellency, The Right Honorable, The Earl of Cromer, former
    Ambassador Extraordinary and Plenipotentiary
Mr. Thomas E. Colquhoun, Attachè, Property Service Agency
Miss Virginia Bailey, Social Secretary

RIVER

Contents

The original text and negatives for the illustrations in this publication are on file at the Prints and Photographs Division of the Library of Congress.

Sources and Abbreviations

Several sources are referred to frequently throughout the text and are documented here only:

Building permits: National Archives, Record Group 351 (17 February 1877–7 September 1949). Later permits are scattered among several agencies, are often filed only by number, and are therefore infrequently included in this text.

City directories: District of Columbia Public Library, Martin Luther King Branch, Washingtoniana Division; 901 G Street, N.W. (hereafter, MLKW). Directories from 1822–1973. These were not published annually until 1860, and none were published for the following years: 1944–47, 1949–53, 1955, 1957–59, 1961, 1963, 1966, 1968, 1970–72. Listings were by name only until 1914; therefore, gaps in listings for these early years indicate that names of tenants were not known and could not be checked.

Deeds: Office of the Recorder of Deeds, Sixth and D Streets, N.W.

Real estate maps of Washington: MLKW. Lloyd vanDerVeer (1851); Casimir Bohn (1854); A. Boschke (1857); G. M. Hopkins (1887; revised 1892–94); Sanborn Insurance Maps, 2 vols. (1903); Baist Real Estate Atlas, 3–4 vols. (1903–68), published in various years.

Social registers: MLKW. *The Elite List* (1888–1917); *The Blue Book* (1924–1973); *The Social Register* (1901–1972); *The Social List* (1932–1973).

Tax books: National Archives, Record Group 351 (1838–1879); MLKW (1886–1973).

Wills: Office of the Register of Wills, District of Columbia; 451 Indiana Avenue, N.W. Wills are filed by administration number and year of probate. If year of probate differs from year of death, this is so indicated in the text.

Abbreviations for frequently used sources are as follows:

ABD: *American Biographical Directories, District of Columbia,* 1908–09, Washington, D.C.: The Potomac Press, 1908.

AIA: The American Institute of Architects

BDAC: *Biographical Directory of the American Congress,* 1774–1971, Washington: The Government Printing Office, 1971.

CHS: The Columbia Historical Society

DAB: *Dictionary of American Biography,* New York: Charles Scribner's Sons, 1928–. At present, 20 volumes plus 4 supplements.

DLACB. *Dictionary of Latin American and Caribbean Biography,* London: Melrose Press, Ltd., 1971.

EB: *Encyclopedia Britannica,* London: William Benton, 1970.

EWB: *Encyclopedia of World Biography,* New York: McGraw-Hill, 1973. 12 volumes, including index.

H&M: Stilson Hutchins and Joseph West Moore, *The National Capital Past and Present,* Washington: The Post Publishing Company, 1884.

IWW: *International Who's Who,* London: Europa Publications, 1935–.

JWM: Joseph West Moore, *Picturesque Washington,* Providence, Rhode Island: J. A. and R. A. Reid, 1884.

MLKW: District of Columbia Public Library, Martin Luther King Branch, Washingtoniana Division.

NCAB: *The National Cyclopedia of American Biography,* New York: James T. White and Company, 1898–. At present, Volumes 1–54 and A–L plus index.

Proctor: John Clagett Proctor. References are either to his articles in the *Sunday Star,* 1928–1952, or to his book: *Washington Past and Present—A History,* New York: The Lewis Historical Publishing Company, 1930. 5 volumes.

WWA: *Who's Who in America,* Chicago: The A. N. Marquis Company, 1899–.

WWGB: *Who's Who* (Great Britain), London: A. and C. Black, 1849–.

WWLA: *Who's Who in Latin America,* Stanford University Press, California, second edition, 1940; third edition, 1945.

WWNC: *Who's Who in the Nation's Capital,* Washington: The Consolidated Publishing Company, 1921–22 edition; The W. W. Publishing Company, 1923–24 edition; Ransdell, Inc., 1926–27, 1929–30, 1934–35, 1938–39 editions.

WWW: *Who Was Who in America, A Component Volume to Who's Who in America,* Chicago: The A. N. Marquis Company; The Historical Volume (1607–1896), 1963; Volume 1 (1897–1942), 1943; Volume 2 (1943–50), 1950; Volume 3 (1951–60), 1963; Volume 4 (1961–68) 1968.

Withey: Henry F. Withey and Elsie R. Withey, *Biographical Dictionary of American Architects (Deceased),* Los Angeles: New Age Publishing Company, 1956.

Newspapers:

ES:	*Evening Star* (Washington)
NYT:	*New York Times*
SS:	*Sunday Star*
WDN:	*Washington Daily News*
WH:	*Washington Herald*
WP:	*Washington Post*
WSN:	*Washington Star-News*
WT:	*Washington Times*
WTH:	*Washington Times-Herald*

Residential Park
Scott Circle, c. 1900
Looking up 16th Street
Courtesy of Columbia Historical Society

Introduction

The Nation's Capital is an essay in idealism compromised by reality. Washington City has been a laboratory having special advantages unlike any other city. It is our misfortune that those advantages, and the dreams they have inspired, have been misunderstood, neglected and altered. One of our most important thoroughfares, Massachusetts Avenue, is a case in point.

It seems fruitless and perhaps irrelevant to blame any one source for the injustices visited upon this avenue. Rather, it should be understood that many factors play their part. It is unfortunate that our architectural heritage (no less important to us than the Old World masterpieces are to a European) must be compromised by building and zoning codes, and tax structures which discourage maintenance and good design. Few people realize that there are reasonable alternatives to destroying sound older structures. These alternatives can be economically viable, prudent, and aesthetically pleasing. Saving and utilizing our existing architecture does not mean an end to progress, but rather the beginning of a richer, more workable city. Already, citizens have become aware of the exciting possibilities and have begun to express concern, individually and in concert, over the destruction of their city. It is this concern which has prompted us to document the architecture of Massachusetts Avenue, including in this volume many of the resi-

Automobile Park
Scott Circle, 1974
Looking up Massachusetts Avenue

dences that have already been destroyed. The following pages contain a brief history of Washington, the meaning of Beaux Arts design in America and, finally, the character of the city we must face today.

Pierre Charles L'Enfant was well aware that soil, topography and climate affect the design and character of a city. He realized the advantages inherent in the site chosen for Washington and, with an eye to the stateliness and grandeur befitting the capital of a young nation, conceived a plan that was nearly ideal. He had not bargained for a recalcitrant government of powerful men, each with individual interests nor for a bankrupt treasury. For years the White House (then tan rather than white), the Capitol (seemingly never complete), and City Hall were lonely reminders of what had been intended.

According to H. P. Caemmerer,* the population was expected eventually to reach 800,000—the size of Paris in 1790. It was certainly a vast and noble dream. On paper Washington rivaled any European capital: as implemented, the effect was entirely different. Politically, the new city was in an ideal geographic position—midway between the North and South. This position also gave it what one would have thought a temperate climate, capable of supporting a wide range of planting material. In reality, the summers were too hot and humid for Northern lawns and the winters too cold for the Southern grasses. In addition, though the essentially low, flat topography seemed ideal for stately building, construction was unsuitable in many places due to malaria-infested swamps.

The creation of a new city for the sole purpose of government brought another problem: residents in Government were transient and not possessed of the civic interest and pride that a stable population develops. This milieu bred the speculator; houses were built as an investment for quick, inevitable and

* *Washington, the National Capital,* H. P. Caemmerer, 1932.

profitable sale. Benjamin Henry Latrobe, the architest responsible for some of the finer buildings of early Washington wrote on 12 August 1806:

> The City abounds in cases of extreme poverty and distress. The families of workmen whom the unhealthiness of the city, and idleness arising from the capricious manner in which the appropriations for the erection of the public buildings have been granted, give to them for a short time high wages and again for a whole season do not afford them a week's work. The result is distressing. Workmen who are ruined in circumstances and health are to be found in extreme indigence scattered in wretched huts over the waste which the law calls the American metropolis. They inhabit the half-finished houses, now tumbling to ruins, which the madness of speculation has created. . . (*Journal of Latrobe*, pub. 1905, p. 131)

The differences between the dream of L'Enfant and the reality that ensued during the early years of the Republic were great, but this is not to say that there were no fine public buildings and residences; rather, that they were few in number. In addition to the Capitol and White House, one must include among the finer structures George Hadfield's City Hall, Robert Mill's Treasury Building, Latrobe's Decatur House and St. John's Church, and William Thornton's Octagon and Tudor Place residences. Most Federal period and revival architecture was characterized by the use of ornamental detail copied from European pattern books and judiciously applied to facade and interior alike. Instead of Greek temples, there were fake front porticos applied to the real, rather mundane structures (1101 Massachusetts Avenue).

The Civil War further postponed the realization of a stately capital city; and, indeed, the city was such a disgrace in the early post-war period that Congress speculated on the possibilities of moving the Capital elsewhere. Conditions became even worse when, in 1872, a portion of the Mall, between Third and Fourth Streets, was ceded to the Pennsylvania Railroad.

The turning point came, however, with the administration of the appointed District of Columbia Governor, Alexander Robey Shepherd. A massive building program was initiated in the 1870's, and for the first time, Washington began to look like a capital city. The Shepherd administration came with mixed blessings. Much to the annoyance of the local citizens, he raised property taxes to pay for street paving, grading, lighting and the planting of thousands of trees. It was owing to his interest that Massachusetts Avenue became a very desirable street on which to live. The hills of Highland terrace (1400 block) and

Night Hawk Hill (1200 block) were flattened and graded, the tons of excavated material used as landfill for the south side of the future 2500 block of the Avenue. The improvements to Pacific Circle (Dupont Circle) caused a massive surge in property values. Encouraged by Shepherd, speculators became even more prolific than in the past—thus the "California Syndicate" (as they called themselves) bought up numerous lots on Dupont Circle for as little as ten to fifty cents a square foot. With the constant turnover of property, the value increased by 1885 to an average of $5.00 (*The National Capital, Past and Present,* Hutchins and Moore, 1885).

The great number of buildings that were erected in the last third of the nineteenth century gave Washington the appearance of a red brick city.

This was the common building material, and while the term Victorian architecture includes buildings of quite different stylistic origin, there are certain shared characteristics. The virtue of the Victorian house was its picturesque charm, reflected also in the parks and circles of the period. The "frantic essay in Queen Anne" (*The Century Magazine,* March 1886, p. 680) was a pastiche of detail applied to a whimsical arrangement of chambers. The "best" room of the house was a special chamber of cushioned furniture, palms, and bric-a-brac. The outdoor "parlors", such as Thomas Circle, mirrored this same character with their fussy gardens and statuary. The total effect of public space and house was not planned, and though the character was shared, there was actually no cohesion between one structure and its neighbor, or the park.

Around the turn of the century, major changes occurred in political, social and architectural realms which made Washington look with renewed interest at L'Enfant and his century old plan for the Capital. The United States was assuming its position as a world power; a new image and civic pride became manifest in the "City Beautiful" movement, and young architects were again turning to ancient Greece and Rome for inspiration. In 1898 the capital began a series of festivities to celebrate its centennial. Certain professionals, including Glenn Brown and Frederick Law Olmsted, Junior, joined with other interested parties to advocate the rebuilding of Washington according to L'Enfant's vision. They enlisted the help of Senator James McMillan of Michigan. Answerable to the Senator, a commission was formed by Congress in 1901. Established to draw up plans for the city, the Commission was sent to tour the capitals of Europe. The panel included Frederick Law Olmsted, Junior (landscape architect), Daniel H. Burnham (business leader and architect), and

The Parlor
Dupont Circle, c. 1890
    2000 Massachusetts Avenue (left)
    1913 Massachusetts Avenue (right)
Courtesy of the Columbia Historical Society

Charles F. McKim (architect). Their findings resulted not only in Washington as it exists today, but also in a new trend in domestic and public architecture.

By the end of the nineteenth century, American architects had traveled abroad and a few had studied in Paris at the Ecole des Beaux Arts, famous for its strict adherence to academic design. While in Europe, the student learned the disciplines required of classical architecture, adapting both classical and neo-classical styles to modern needs. He returned prepared to create his own Roman bath in the form of a railroad station, and the proliferation of historically inspired buildings that followed are grouped stylistically as "Beaux Arts".

The Beaux Arts "salon", whether indoors or as a public garden, was an expression of sublime elegance. Unlike the Victorian, the attempt was to produce a totality, a marriage between structure and adjacent public space (2234 Massachusetts Avenue, Vol. I; 2301 Massachusetts Avenue, Vol. I). A well-versed architect was one who understood and acknowledged the public space and designed his building so as to frame and complement it. Rather than whimsical, the designer was knowledgeable and sometimes shrewd. The client required of his architect an establishment that would be impressive. The result was a neo-classical residence which seemed self-consciously to aspire to greatness. Few of the great houses, however, pretended to be slavish copies of an earlier century. At their worst, they are only rich in detail and material. At their best they are works of art, designed as if by a seventeenth or eighteenth century architect accidentally transported in time. Their internal arrangements were such as were necessary for the residents' life styles, while their exteriors returned to the public an amenity, a delight to the eye, so frequently lacking to the contemporary street.

The Beaux Arts designer was aware that as cities grow provision must be made for more expansive streets and sites, introducing ever larger quantities of trees and shrubs to give scale, relief and a means of unifying diverse architectural forms. He perceived the need to clearly identify the three basic types of residence: the row house fronting the street and unified with its neighbors by similar street plantings (1520 Twentieth Street, N.W.; 2311 Massachusetts Avenue, Vol. I), the urban palace surrounded by a garden with outworks intended to marry it to the avenue (1606 Twenty-third Street, Vol. I; 1500 New Hampshire Avenue), and the country house situated in a park. The park, as opposed to the garden which is an adjunct of the residence, is a landscape which

The Salon
Dupont Circle, 1942
photo

normally reflects the natural characteristics of grasses, shrubs and trees. The desired effect of the country house, therefore, was of rurality with only those architectural provisions that were necessary. The difference might be explained by comparing the urban character of 2305 Massachusetts Avenue (now the Chilean Embassy) with the more rural aspect of 3000 Massachusetts Avenue (now the Brazilian Embassy).

The great period of Beaux Arts design on Massachusetts Avenue was short-lived. What had been the realm of the individual merchant prince was, by the 1920's, more the domain of the committee room; aesthetic principle, as with responsibility, became increasingly relegated to a group. Appropriate identity began to waver, the exceptional became common, and the corporate body began to assume the guise of both emperor and empire.

This does not mean that the late Beaux Arts period did not produce some fine buildings; the embassies of Japan and Great Britain are examples. In character, however, they are not likely to be confused with the earlier private palaces. The very arrangement of their parts indicates their function, with the chancery facilities as advance wings creating a fore-

court and protecting the central private pavilion beyond. Like the grand residences they are as one with the urban scheme; but unlike their antecedents, they are only reminiscent of the historical styles. By this time better designers had progressed from the re-creation of historical styles to the freedom of stylization and invention of detail for effect. Unlike the Victorians, where often details were applied indiscriminately, or the early Beaux Arts technicians who created historically correct chambers, details were now carefully devised to ornament space, to create a mood, but without copying an earlier structure.

Like any artistic endeavor, architectural and landscape design rely to some extent on intuition. This is also true of "good taste", or what has been called the "appropriate". The crucial elements involved in combining architecture with appropriate landscape are scale and balance. Not only must the building be in harmony with its landscape, but it should be compatible with its surroundings and reflect its purpose. This was frequently achieved during the height of the Beaux Arts period; later the sense of balance was lost. Expanding bureaucracy, increasingly heavy taxation and soaring land costs in urban areas forced the erection of ever larger buildings on sites too small

Residential Park
Sheridan Circle, 1970
Background: 2301 Massachusetts Ave. (left), Vol. 1
2253 R Street (right), Vol. 1
Jack Boucher, photograph

to allow the kind of planting needed to give the sense of scale and relief envisioned by the early Beaux Arts planners and architects.

Simultaneously with the decline of appropriate design came alteration to the existing city. One by one the residential palaces have been converted to embassy or chancery and commercial use. Those that have become ambassadorial residences have generally been well maintained, while their neighbors have succumbed to the indignities of harsh conversions. Deemed "economically unviable", countless numbers of houses have been bulldozed in favor of parking lots or replaced by ungainly office blocks, set in monotonous ranks along our avenues. Because of the direct relationship to the surrounding architectural envelope, the public space has also suffered. Decimated by planners, the grass, garden beds, and trees have silently fallen to concrete islands; the charm and visual pleasure guaranteed by these parks have been cheapened and hardened by bleak light poles and unnecessary street hardware. Swarms of automobiles hold victim a city where the pedestrian was to take comfort and ease. With the exception of Sheridan Circle, residential elegance and continuity have been swept away, the remaining monuments dwarfed and made frail.

Residential Park, Commercialized
Scott Circle, 1970
Background: Site of 1601 Massachusetts Avenue
J. Alexander, photograph

xxii

Massachusetts Avenue is only one of a series of avenues and streets which still retain proud reminders of Washington's past. As a group comprising the city, they are not unlike parts of other cities throughout the land. It is time that irresponsible destruction was halted. Perhaps the most eloquent plea for the preservation of our architectural heritage is that quoted by Douglas Haskell in the May 1975 issue of *Architectural Review*:

Architecture's masterpieces cannot be stored away like paintings and reproduced centuries later like poetry or music. The art lives on in used buildings; they alone can carry it. Without them we are perpetual juveniles, starting over and over, a people without a memory.

S.A.K.
J.R.C.
J.L.S.J.

Blaine Mansion
2000 Massachusetts Avenue, 1970
Corner 20th and P Streets
Jack Boucher, photograph

Blaine Mansion
2000 Massachusetts Avenue, c. 1905
Corner of 20th and P Streets
Courtesy of Martin Luther King Library

Thomas Circle, c. 1890
Looking South
Courtesy of Columbia Historical Society

Residential Park
Thomas Circle, ca. 1900
    Highland terrace (left)
    Luther Place Church (center)
    1205 Vermont Avenue (right)
Courtesy of Martin Luther King Library

Residential Park, Decimated
Thomas Circle, 1974
Background: Site of 1205 Vermont Avenue
Courtesy of International Inn

1013-1015 L Street, N.W.

This detached double house is on the north side of L Street between Tenth and Eleventh Streets. It is located in Square 341 on lots A, B, and C (part of original lot 2), now taxed as lots 800 and 801.

It is owned by the Soldiers, Sailors, Marines and Airmen's Club and is used as a service club and residence for transient enlisted men.

PREVIOUS STRUCTURES ON THE SITE

Tax records for the early 1850's show an improvement assessed at $400 somewhere on this property (at that time original lot 2), but it is not shown in 1857 when Caleb Cushing subdivided and sold the land. This is borne out by maps of Washington which show structures existing in 1851 and 1854 but not in 1857.

HISTORICAL INFORMATION

Because this house pre-dates the earliest available building permits, tax records have been used to fix a date for its construction. The first improvements shown on lots A, B, and C in Square 341 occurred in the tax book for 1865. At this time David L. Morrison owned lot A and the west one-half of lot B (Liber NCT-16 folio 292; Liber NCT-47 folio 340), and the improvement value which appeared on his property was $16,000. Reuben B. Clark owned the east one-half of lot B and all of lot C (Liber NCT-30 folio 30; Liber NCT-30 folio 33); in the same year (1865) an improvement value of $15,000 appeared on his property. As the style and the assessed values are not inconsistent with a date of 1865, this is the year in which these houses are assumed to have been built. Morrison and Clark had acquired the land in 1863 and 1864; in fact, it was Clark who had sold Morrison his one-half of lot B (Liber NCT-47 folio 340). The name of the architect is not known.

In 1876 the improvement value on Morrison's lots rose $5,000 while that on Clark's property remained the same. This was presumably the year in which the bays were added on the Eleventh Street side as they are of a later architectural style than the main house.

The first building permit indicating any alteration to either 1013 or 1015 L Street is from 1894 (No. 198). It was issued for 1013 L when this property was owned by Reuben Clark's daughter, Ida M. Wood, and was for repair of fire damage. Evidently

fire had destroyed the cupola on the 1015 side; the permit is for carrying the brick party wall up through the cupola, leaving only the 1013 side standing. It remains this way today.

In 1908 the dining room on the ground floor at 1015 was enlarged and a partition removed (No. 1734). It was owned at this time by Marie Byington, who had inherited it from David Morrison.

Perhaps the change which has affected the appearance of 1015 L most is the addition of the front porch with its "Shanghai" mansard roof. M. Frank Ruppert bought the house in 1916 (Liber 3923 folio 413) and added the porch in 1917 (Permit No. 3129). It was also Mr. Ruppert who, according to his son, changed the design of the stair at 1015 and replaced the wood stair with the present metal one. There are no permits for this alteration.

In 1923, 1015 L was purchased by the Woman's Army and Navy League, now the Soldiers, Sailors, Marines and Airmen's Club (Liber 5080 folio 42). Interior changes were made to convert the house to a servicemen's club, and a ground floor entrance on the Eleventh Street side under the existing first floor entrance was added (Permit No. 4181).

The League was also able to purchase 1013 L when it became available in 1930 (Liber 6503 folio 235). It was purchased from Ida M. Wood, the daughter of the original owner. Doors were cut to connect the two houses, but 1013 has not suffered such drastic changes as has 1015. After 1930 both houses are treated as one and known simply as 1015 L Street.

In 1943 a small one story brick addition was added to the Eleventh Street side, adjoining the main house (Permit No. 265674). In this year also, fire escapes were added to the L Street and the Eleventh Street sides (Permit No. 258453).

The small brick addition was razed in 1961 and a large two story addition erected which connects the main house with the old stable building at the rear of the property. No permit has been found for this work. It is known that Furman Builders, Inc. was the general contractor; and according to the Club, the architect was Harvey P. Baxter. This construction took away the last remnants of the 1015 section of the rear porch which had originally run across both houses. Part of it had already been removed when the small brick addition was built in 1943. The original porch can still be seen at the rear of 1013.

The building remained its original red brick color until 1965. According to the Club, the brick was painted grey and the trim white in that year.

KNOWN ARCHITECTURAL DRAWINGS

Front Porch: sections, elevations and plans.
Recorded on microfilm with Permit No. 3129, 5 January 1917. Sam'l R. Turner/Architect/807 Mt. Vernon Pla./Washington, D.C.

VIEWS

Exterior photographs:

Eleventh Street and L Street facades:
    ES, 3–29–31.
L Street facade:
    CHS, Proctor Collection. Same protograph reproduced in Proctor, SS, 3–1–42.

BIOGRAPHIES OF THE RESIDENTS— 1013 L STREET

Reuben B. Clark (–1894) was born in Ipswich, New Hampshire and came to Washington c. 1845. He had a grocery store at 4½ and M Streets, S.W. for many years. In 1858 the city directory also listed Clark and Dunn, brick manufacturers, at the same address; in 1867 the listing showed Clark selling hardware at 4½ and M Streets.

In addition to his business interests Clark was jail commissioner of the District of Columbia and a director of the Central Market Company and the Anacostia and Potomac Railroad. He was also an investor in land, owning numerous properties in Washington. In 1864 he sold David Morrison one half of lot B in Square 341, so that the two of them could build the double house on L Street. In 1880 he gave the 1013 L Street house to his daughter, Ida, (who had married William C. Wood, a patent attorney) and moved to 1501 Massachusetts Avenue, N.W. It was in this house that funeral services were held after his death at his summer residence near Providence, Rhode Island. (Obituary: ES, 9–12–94.)

Hon. Mason Summers Peters (1844–1914) lived at 1013 L Street in 1898 and was a representative from Kansas. He was a native of Missouri and practiced law in that state before moving to Wyandotte County, Kansas, in 1886. There he organized the Union Live Stock Commission Company in 1895 and in 1896 was elected to Congress as a Democrat-Populist. He was not re-elected and went back to Kansas to resume his law career and business activities in Kansas City. He died in Kansas City, Missouri, in 1914. (BDAC)

BIOGRAPHIES OF THE RESIDENTS— 1015 L STREET

David L. Morrison (1825–1887) was born in Emmitsburg, Maryland, and came to Washington as a young man. He was in the flour and feed business with a store at Twelfth and B Streets, N.W. which furnished government hospitals with flour during the Civil War. His company was at first called D. L. Morrison and Company, and his business partner was John P. Troxell. Later, in 1865, the firm name was changed to Morrison, Galt and Company, with the partners being Morrison, W. M. Galt and John W. Shaw. In 1866, only Morrison and Shaw remained, and it was not long before Morrison gave up the flour business and turned to real estate. He bought a considerable amount of land, built many houses, and was always willing to sell his property on monthly installments, in this way aiding persons of limited means to buy houses (Proctor, SS, 3–1–42). He died a widower with no children and distributed his large estate among his relatives and various churches and charitable organizations. His house at 1015 L Street and its furnishings were left to Marie E. Byington, whom he termed in his will "an attentive, considerate and faithful friend." (Admin. No. 2788, 1887) (Obituary: ES, 7–16–87)

Hon. William Craig Cooper (1832–1902) lived at 1015 L Street c. 1891 and was a representative from Ohio. A lawyer, he began practice in Mt. Vernon, Ohio, his native city. He became the prosecuting attorney of Knox County (1859–63), mayor of Mt. Vernon (1862–64), member of the state House of Representatives (1872–74), judge advocate of Ohio (1879–84) and was elected to Congress as a Republican in 1884. He served three terms, did not seek renomination in 1890 and returned to Mt. Vernon to practice law, where he died in 1902. (BDAC)

M. Frank Ruppert (1874–1950) was a native Washingtonian who attended St. Mary's Parochial School and St. John's High School in the District. When he was twenty years old he started in the hardware business. His store at 1021 Seventh Street, N.W. survives today and is owned by members of his family. Later in life Mr. Ruppert went into the real estate business. This business, like the hardware store, is still in the family. (Obituaries: WP, 7–18–50; ES, 7–19–50)

Soldiers, Sailors, Marines and Airmen's Club: 1013–1015 L Street. This organization had its beginnings back in 1872 in Albany, New York, when Mrs. E. Throop Martin, mother-in-law of General A. J. Alexander, organized a group of women to further the welfare of American men in arms. This group

Proctor Collection
Columbia Historical Society, ca. 1940

was called The Ladies' Union School Mission Association.

In 1877 Mrs. Martin moved to Washington and formed the Army and Navy Auxiliary, an outgrowth of the Albany society, which sent reading matter to service hospitals, furnished communion sets and provided money for Christmas parties for the children of soldiers.

In 1894 the name of the organization was changed again, this time to Woman's Army and Navy League, and incorporated in the District of Columbia. Mrs. Grover Cleveland was much interested in the work of the society. In 1895 the League took over a house for enlisted men at 38 I Street which was having financial difficulties; at this time the League actually became the servicemen's club that it is today. The League was able to acquire a better building at 317 C Street which had nine beds; transient enlisted men were given lodging, a cup of coffee and a roll for twenty-five cents.

The club continued to grow and to receive substantial contributions, including sums from the wife of Admiral Dewey and the widow of Admiral Sampson.

In 1906 President Roosevelt addressed the members and dined with them.

By 1923 the quarters of the club were again inadequate. With a contribution of $5,000 from the Naval Auxiliary of the Red Cross, a $500 legacy from Miss Margaret Ruff, and the proceeds from the Annual League Ball, the president of the League, Mrs. Emerson H. Liscum, and her co-workers were able to purchase the house at 1015 L Street. When the new clubhouse was formally opened, Mrs. Calvin Coolidge headed the receiving line.

Space was again a problem by 1930. Fortunately, the adjoining house at 1013 L Street was available. Funds for the purchase were very generously donated by Mrs. Jessie H. Metcalf, wife of the Senator from Rhode Island. She gave $17,500 for the purchase of the property and then $7,500 more to connect the two buildings and repair 1013 L Street, which was named The Metcalf Annex in her honor.

The war years saw a great increase in the activities of the club. More dormitory space was added in the old stable building at the rear, and during 1943 a total of 45,645 men were lodged and 84,877 meals were served. Years of fund raising had ended in 1942 when the club was included in the Community War Fund.

In 1950 the name of the club was formally changed to include the Air Force, and in 1954 the name of the organization was changed from Woman's Army and Navy League to the Soldiers, Sailors, Marines and Airmen's Club. During these years Mrs. Dwight Eisenhower was honorary president.

In 1962 the new wing connecting the main building with the annex in the rear was completed and named the Mary MacArthur Memorial Wing, after a past president of the League.

Women members of the armed forces were admitted in 1972, and at present the Club can accommodate 130 men and women overnight. Membership in the Club now numbers approximately 3,500. (*A History of the Soldiers, Sailors, Marines and Airmen's Club,* printed by the Club.)

Chain of Title: 1013 L Street, N.W.

1863   Deed 19 October ,recorded 19 March 1864; Liber NCT–30 folio 30
Robert S. Patterson to Reuben B. Clark
". . . Lot . . . lettered B in Caleb Cushing's recorded subdivision of original lots numbered . . (2) . . . (3) and . . . (4) in Square numbered . . . (341) . . ." For $2,015.

1863   Deed 19 October, recorded 19 March 1864; Liber NCT–30 folio 33
Robert C. Murphy et ux, Lannia H., to Reuben B. Clark
". . . Lot . . . lettered C in Caleb Cushing's recorded subdivision of original lots numbered . . . (2) . . . (3) and . . . (4) in Square numbered . . . (341) . . ." For $2,015

1879   According to the tax book for 1879, the ownership of lot C and the east one-half of lot B, Square 341 was transferred in that year from Reuben B. Clark to Ida M. Wood. No deed has been found to confirm this, but in his will Reuben Clark stated: ". . . Inasmuch as I have already given my daughter, Ida, my house 1013 L Street, N.W. . . . and the lot on which it stands . . ."; thereby confirming the transfer, if not the exact date. (Administration No. 6310)

1930   Deed 12 November, recorded 17 November; Liber 6503 folio 235
Ida M. C. Wood to Woman's Army and Navy League
". . . the East half of Lot "B" and all of Lot "C" in C. Cushing's subdivision of lots in Square . . . (341) . . . Beginning for the same on line of "L" Street North at a point distant . . . (37) feet . . . (6) inches East of the Southwest corner of said Square and running thence East along said Street . . . (37) feet . . . (6) inches, thence North . . . (124) feet to the line of an alley in the rear of said lots, thence West along said

alley . . . (37) feet . . . (6) inches and thence South . . . (124) feet to the line of said Street and the place of beginning . . ."

Chain of Title: 1015 L Street, N.W.

1863   Deed 19 October, recorded 30 October; Liber NCT–16 folio 292
Robert S. Patterson to David L. Morrison
". . . lot marked . . . A in Caleb Cushing's recorded Subdivision of original lots Numbered . . . (2) . . . (3) and . . . (4) in Square numbered . . . (341) . . ." For $2,700.

1864   Deed 1 October, recorded 12 October; Liber NCT–47 folio 340
Reuben B. Clark et ux, Margaret E., to David L. Morrison
". . . the West half of Lot B of Cushing's Subdivision of lots numbered . . . (2) . . . (3) and . . . (4) in Square Numbered . . . (341) . . ." For $1,364.

1887   Will of David L. Morrison. Administration No. 2788.
A codicil to the will states: ". . . I do hereby give . . . unto Marie E. Byington, who has been to me an attentive, considerate, and faithful friend, the real estate now owned and occupied by me situated at the North East corner of 11th and L Streets, N.W., in the City of Washington, D.C., together with all the goods, chattels, household furniture and personal effects therein and used in conjunction therewith . . ."

1916   Deed 17 October, recorded 19 October; Liber 3923 folio 413
Marie E. Byington to M. Frank Ruppert
". . . Lot A and West one-half Lot B in Caleb Cushing's subdivision of lots in Square 341 as per plat recorded in Book B page 106 of the records of the Office of the Surveyor of the District of Columbia . . ."

1923   Deed 1 August, recorded 2 August; Liber 5028 folio 319
M. Frank Ruppert et ux, Rose B., to Milton F. Ruppert

1923   Deed 1 August, recorded 2 August; Liber 5028 folio 323
Milton F. Ruppert to Liscum and Dorn, Trustees
". . . To have and to hold said land and premises . . . in trust for the sole use of such persons as have contributed to the purchase of the said property . . . as tenants in common, according to the amount contributed by each . . ."

1923   Deed 19 October, Liber 5080 folio 42
Liscum and Dorn, Trustees, to Woman's Army and Navy League, a Corporation
". . . Whereas the persons who have contributed to the purchase of said property have formed themselves into a body corporate of the District of Columbia . . . and . . . (said body) . . . has requested the parties of the first part to convey

11th Street Elevation
1973

the said property to it . . . the parties of the first part . . . do . . . convey . . . Lot lettered "A" and the West one-half of Lot lettered "B" . . . in Square . . . (341) . . ."

Building Permits:

No. 198, 1 August 1894. Permit to repair or alter.
Owner: W. C. Wood, 1013 L Street, N.W.
Estimated cost: $500
"To repair the damage caused by fire. Brick party wall to be carried through cupola."
No. 1730, 27 December 1905. Missing from government files.

Note: The preceding permits are the only ones issued for 1013 L Street. Those that follow, up through 1923, are for 1015 L. After both houses were purchased by the League (1930), permits were usually issued for just one address—1015 L.

No. 239, 7 August 1903. Permit to repair or alter.
Owner: M. E. Byington
Estimated cost: $1,544
"To renew roof and section of ceiling joist where damaged—new windows, doors and other interior wood work where damaged—renew plastering, painting, papering where damaged by fire—no alteration in design or dimensions in reconstructing work."

No. 1734, 30 October 1908. Permit to repair or alter.
Owner: Marie E. Byington
Estimated cost: $1,000
"To relay kitchen floor, remove cross wood partition, rear stairway—to enlarge dining room in basement and to install steam heating plant, change plumbing as per plan."
No. 3129, 9 January 1917. Permit to repair or alter.
Owner: Frank Ruppert
Architect: S. R. Turner
Estimated cost: $400
"Propose to remove present porch and rebuild new and make minor repairs, size of porch 12'–6″ x 40'–6″ double decked as per drawings submitted."
No. 4181, 10 November 1913. Permit to repair or alter.
Owner: May D. Liscum, President of Woman's Army and Navy League
Estimated cost: $4,884
New bath in basement. "Construct area steps to 11th St. entrance under existing entrance steps as per plan. Repair floors and columns of existing rear covered porch, no enlargement, no enclosure." Repairs and alterations to rear stable-garage. "Remove existing one story garage. Erect 9″ brick fence wall . . . on east party line to be 7'–0″ in height."
No. 4236, 13 November 1923. Permit to repair or alter.
Owner: May D. Liscum, President, Woman's Army and Navy League
An additional permit for area steps, 11th Street side.
No. 232976, 30 May 1940. Permit to repair or alter.
Owner: Woman's Army and Navy League
Estimated cost: $700
Repair front porch: replace wood columns, flooring . . .
No. 258453, 26 January 1943.
Permit to erect two standard fire escapes, 1013–1015 L.
No. 265544, 30 November 1943. Permit for sign.
No. 265674, 6 December 1943. Permit for addition.
Owner: Woman's Army and Navy League
Architect: Marcus Hallett
Builder: National Engineering Company
Estimated cost: $400
One story brick addition adjoining building on 11th Street side. Width: 17 feet; depth: 15'–6″; height: 18 feet
No. 267626, 24 March 1944. Permit to repair or alter.
Owner: Soldiers, Sailors and Marines Club
Architect: National Engineering Company
Contractor: Charles H. Tomkins Company
Repair front walk, steps, porch and cornice. Repairs to rear building.
The following permits are concerned solely with alterations to the buildings in the rear of 1013–1015 L Street, N.W.:
No. 2711, 20 December 1908
No. 1076, 6 October 1917
No. 2657, 2 April 1918
No. 154623, 17 June 1932
No. 241544, 17 March 1941
The following permits are for plumbing only:
No. 256231, 2 October 1942.

No. 256244, no exact date: c. September, 1942
No. 256463, no exact date: c. October 1942
No. 259310, no exact date: c. 1943
No. 753, 4 January 1945
No. 1178, 12 February 1945
No. 475, 17 January 1946
No. 44608, 21 July 1949
No. A19489, 18 December 1950
No. A20315, 11 January 1951
No. A22048, 5 March 1951
No. A58373, 26 February 1954

Listings of Residents: 1013 L Street, N.W.

City directories list the following tenants:

1866–1870 Reuben B. Clark (Listings before 1870 showed 476 L, the old street number.)
1871–1872 William C. Wood Note: Reuben B. Clark was listed at 1015 L in 1871 and not at any home address in 1872.
1873 Reuben B. Clark; William C. Wood
1874 William C. Wood; Clark listed at 1015 L.
1875–1879 Reuben B. Clark; William C. Wood
1880–1899 William C. Wood
1898 Mason S. Peters
1907–1914 Martha Stamper; clerk, patent office; or Miles Stamper, or Mattie F. Stamper.
1915 Mrs. Mildred E. Smith
1916 Craig Seymour
1928 Soldiers, Sailors and Marines' Club

Social registers list:

1888–1897 Mr. and Mrs. William C. Wood
1898 Hon. and Mrs. Mason Peters, Miss Peters

Listings of Residents: 1015 L Street, N.W.

City directories list the following tenants:

1866–1887 David L. Morrison (Listings before 1870 showed 474 L, the old street address.) Reuben B. Clark was also listed at 1015 in 1871 and 1874.
1888–1892 Marie E. Byington
1891 William C. Cooper
1893–1894 Max Georgii, patent attorney
1912–1917 Mrs. Adda V. Byrne, widow of Charles M., boarding
1918–1923 M. Frank Ruppert
1924 Soldiers, Sailors and Marines' Club

Social registers list:

1888–1889 Miss Marie Byington; Mr. and Mrs. Walter H. Smith
1892 Hon. and Mrs. William C. Cooper, Miss Cooper, Miss M. Cooper; The Misses Byington
1893–1894 Mrs. Frederica Georgii, Mr. Max Georgii

STATEMENT:

It is apparent that shortly after completion of this pair of mid–19th century row houses they were extended on 11th Street by an addition one chamber deep in the Italianate manner of Calvert Vaux.

SITE:

Orientation: The building is on the northeast corner of the intersection of 11th and L Streets and Massachusetts Avenue. The lot measures 75'–0" on the south (L Street); 124'–0" on the west (11th Street); 75'–0" on the north (alley); and 124'–0" on the east (party line).

Enclosures: At the street a stone base supports a decorative cast iron spike fence.

Outbuildings: To the north of number 1013 L Street is a carriage house which is connected to the recent three story addition at the northwest. Of the four bays facing onto the court, three are French doors with rectangular transom windows. The hipped tin roof has a square, louvered ventilator with hipped roof. The interior of the building was converted to a billiard room in 1963.

Paving: The court between 1013 and the carriage house is paved in brick.

Landscaping: On the west and south are clipped juniper, crabapple, pyrocanthus, magnolia and English ivy. The courtyard has dogwood, Chinese holly, climbing roses and wisteria.

EXTERIOR:

Dimensions: The three story rectangular building is 41'–8" from ground to cornice. The principal three bay facade on 11th Street measures 43'–6". The seven bay south facade is 65'–6".

Foundations: brick footings with concrete slab over brick. Sandstone stairs descend into segmentally-vaulted brick coal bin under the south bay on 11th Street.

Structure: 1'–8" brick bearing walls; wood joists and rafters.

Walls: The base has rusticated sandstone facing capped by a sandstone belt course which extends across the 11th Street addition. The walls are brick.

Doorways and doors: The 11th Street double door has raised wood panels and a segmentally-arched transom window flanked by scrolled consoles and rosette blocks on a raised ground which support a segmentally-arched cornice.

Jack E. Boucher, 1970

The double door at 1013 L Street has an applied roundel panel at the bottom; a flush rectangular panel at the middle; and a raised panel at the top with a curved head to conform to the segmental transom window. The surround is similar to the 11th Street entrance.

The double door at 1015 is not original. The surround is similar to the 11th Street entrance.

Windows: double and triple-hung; two panes.

The windows on the 11th Street elevation are double-hung. The central entrance is flanked by narrow semicircular-headed windows. The second and third floors above the entrance each have a pair of segmentally-headed windows.

Below both gables flanking the central bay on 11th Street are two stories of bay windows. The segmentally-headed windows are separated by pedestals with single story pilasters which support pairs of scrolled consoles (between brackets), and corona and ovolo cornices. The second floor bay window cornices are capped by decorative wrought iron railings behind which are semicircular-headed third floor windows with side lights.

All windows on L Street have segmental heads. The first floor triple-hung windows have shallow, cast iron balcony guards of lattice panels with anthemion modillions.

Stoops: There are three wide sandstone risers from 11th Street to a narrower flight of nine risers and the first floor stoop. The three original risers allow for access to the basement areaway below the stoop. The railings and newels are cast iron.

At 1013 L Street three sandstone risers and a landing give access to eight sandstone risers and the entrance stoop. The stair is flanked by octagonal newels (the balustrades have been replaced by pipe railings). The landing also gives access to the basement areaway.

Porches: The two story, three bay porch (41'–6" wide by 12'–4" deep) is a 1917 addition to the west end of the L Street facade. It has seven central risers. The rock-faced sandstone base has first floor sandstone pedestals which support wood Tuscan columns. Between the pedestals are railings in the Chinese Chippendale manner. The second floor is similar to the first excepting wood pedestals. The red tile roof has exposed rafters forming a hip on the west.

The two and one half story porch (27'–0" wide by 7'–3" deep) at the north elevation has wood posts with cast iron railings and steel stairs which are a recent alteration. A retaining wall for the

Detail 11th Street entrance
1973

Detail eave and cornice
1973

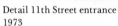

basement areaway supports short, cast iron, fluted columns as base for the wood floor of the porch.

Cornice: Consoles divide the bargeboard on the L Street facade into segmentally-arched bays below modillions capped by a corona and cyma cornice.

Roof: Over the original double dwelling is a low-pitched gable roof. Beginning at the juncture of the two chimneys at the west, the early addition on 11th Street has two parallel ridges with gables (separated by a shallow pent roof) over either bay window.

Lantern: The attic at 1013 L Street is ventilated and lighted by a lantern with a bracket and modillion-supported hipped metal roof, terminated at the west by the brick party wall. The west half of the lantern over 1015 was removed after the 1894 fire.

Skylight: A skylight ventilates the attic at 1015.

Chimneys: There are six brick chimneys; two over the east gable, two over the brick party wall (reduced and sealed below the roof line) and two over the early addition on 11th Street.

PLANS:

The two side hall row houses facing L Street had first floor front and rear vestibules, the halls flanked by a parlor with paired chimneys. The 11th Street elevation is an early addition one room in depth. The addition has a center hall flanked by chambers with bay windows. This hall intersects the original side hall as a short "T."

The second floor has small chambers over the vestibules and two bedrooms separated by closets and connecting doors, over the parlors.

The third floor is similar to the second with the exception that within the bedroom passageway there is a steep stair to the attic.

INTERIOR:

The recent renovations have altered the original effect. Pale yellow walls, high ceilings and floor length windows at opposite ends of the parlors help make the chambers light and airy. Spacial rigidity is further

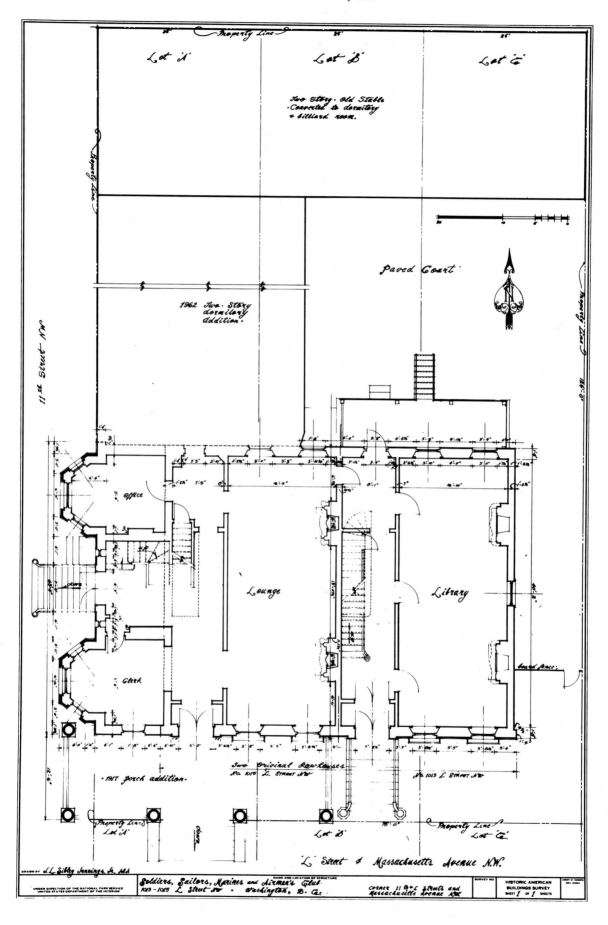

Lot *A*

Lot *B*

Lot *C*

Property Line

Two Story Old Stable Converted to dormitory & billiard room.

Paved Court

1962 Two Story dormitory addition.

11 th Street N.W.

Property Line

Office

Lounge

Library

Clerk

board fence

1917 porch addition

Two Original Row Houses
No. 1015 L Street N.W.

No. 1013 L Street N.W.

Property Line
Lot *A*

Property Line
Lot *B*

Property Line
Lot *C*

L Street & Massachusetts Avenue N.W.

DRAWN BY J. L. Sibley Jennings, Jr., AIA

UNDER DIRECTION OF THE NATIONAL PARK SERVICE
UNITED STATES DEPARTMENT OF THE INTERIOR

NAME AND LOCATION OF STRUCTURE

Soldiers, Sailors, Marines and Airmen's Club
1013 – 1015 L Street N.W. · Washington, D. C.

Corner 11th & L Streets and
Massachusetts Avenue N.W.

SURVEY NO.

HISTORIC AMERICAN
BUILDINGS SURVEY
SHEET 1 OF 1 SHEETS

Library Mantel
Jack E. Boucher, 1970

lessened by the softness of curves as seen in the stair and its niche at 1013, chimney openings, window valances and ceiling coves.

All spaces have similar details. The items below are common throughout the first floor. A description of those elements individual to each chamber follows.

Height: 12'–0"
Flooring: asbestos travertine squares over original hardwood.
Baseboard: 11", wood with cyma cap.
Chairrail: The lounge and library have 2'–10" high wood chairrails (not original).
Walls: plaster.
Ceiling: plaster.
Doorways: The 7'–6" high doorways have double, fascia and cyma architraves.
Windows: The windows on the north and south are triple-hung and had panelled shutters which folded into the reveal. (The lounge shutters still exist.)
Heating: Ventilators pierce the marble panels which seal the chimney fireboxes in all spaces but the lounge. Additional radiators are camouflaged within wood cabinets.

STAIR: (1015 L Street)

The present stair is a replacement. The risers ascend north, turn south to a landing which extends from the 11th Street hall into the original side hall, and continue north to the second floor. The structure is metal and is covered in veneered plywood from floor to stringer. The risers, treads and landings are asbestos tile. The stair to the basement (below the risers within the west hall) has been replaced.

LOUNGE: (1015)

Depth: 40'–2"
Width: 16'–9"

Doorways and doors: The 5'–7" wide cased opening to the south end of the entrance hall is not original. Its fascia architrave (with bull's eye corner blocks) is capped by an overdoor raised panel. The panel and architrave are surrounded by fascia and cyma mouldings.
Chimneys: projects 1'–1½".
  Hearth: 5'–0" by 1'–2"; white marble.
  Firebox: 2'–6" wide by 2'–7"; cast iron fleur-de-lis panels, convex coal grate, brass and cast iron surround.
  Mantels: white marble. Clustered plinths support bundled roll mouldings which are designed to form a semicircular-headed fire opening. Plain spandrels and a female bust keystone support a molded shelf, 6'–5½" wide by 4'–0" high.
  Overmantels: gilded Victorian baroque mirrors.

HALL: (1013)

Depth (with vestibules): 40'–2"
Width: 8'–1"

Cornice: plaster, beaded cove.
Doorways and doors: The three, black-enamelled doors to the library have raised panels in an ogee moulding.
Hardware: The entrance and first two library doors have brass door knobs, mortise locks (keyholes sealed), and finial and pendant hinges. The north door to the library has faceted glass knobs.
Lighting: An opaque glass fixture hangs over the foot of the stair from a cast iron, diamond-shaped acanthus medallion.
Stair: The wood stair ascends twenty-four risers north, the last four turning to the east. The fluted, tapered and turned balusters and molded handrail terminate at a 10" diameter octagonal newel. At the turn of the stair is a semicircular-headed wall niche.

LIBRARY: (1013)

Depth: 40'–2"
Width: 16'–9½"

Cornice: The full entablature has a diminutive architrave, plain frieze, and cyma, corona and ogee cornice.

1013 L Street N.W., Library
Jack E. Boucher, 1970

Lighting: Centered in the ceiling is a 3'–0" diameter, cast iron acanthus medallion, the lighting fixture removed.

Chimneys: project 1'–1½".

Hearth: 5'–0" by 1'–2"; white marble.

Fireboxes: sealed by marble slabs.

Mantels: white marble. The semicircular-headed fire opening is flanked by plinths which support an ogee surround and a molded shelf, 6'–5" wide by 4'–1" high. The ornamentation differs between the two mantels, the north mantel having birds and the south mantel having cornucopia.

1101 Massachusetts Avenue, N.W. "Wisteria House"

This house was located in Square 315, on part of original lot 1. Part of original lot 11 was also included in the property. "Wisteria House" was demolished in 1924 and an apartment building erected on the site.

STATEMENT

The free standing clapboard residence faced south at the northwest intersection of Eleventh Street and Massachusetts Avenue. According to tax records, the two story side hall Greek revival building was constructed c. 1863. Considering the style and similarity of detail, it is assumed the improvements of 1869 (tax records) included the two story porch and the semioctagonal bays which faced Eleventh Street. The awkward joinery is evidence that the porch was an alteration. In 1882 a permit was issued for the removal of the gable roof and the addition of the flat-roofed third story. Note from the illustrations the difference in third floor siding, louvered shutters (which have mid-rails), and later window sash.

It is conceivable (but not probable) that the front elevation corner pilasters originally supported a tympanum gable. The pilasters would ordinarily have continued around the corner as "piers." The brackets above the Roman revival, fluted lotus columns were possibly added at the same time as the third story. Attention is directed to the eagle centering each bay of the cast iron balcony railing, which may suggest the railing is not contemporary but pre-dates the house.

HISTORICAL INFORMATION

As there are no building permits extant for Washington buildings erected before 1877, tax assessment records provide the best clue to the date of an early

c. 1900
Washingtoniana Room
Martin Luther King Library

13

structure unless other factual data are available. In the case of the house at 1101 Massachusetts Avenue, N.W., deed and tax records show that the two eastern sections of lot 1 (along with parts of lot 11), which would include the houses at both 1101 and 1107 Massachusetts Avenue, were always sold together until 1878. The first year in which any improvements were shown on the two eastern sections of lot 1 in the tax books was 1840, when an improvement of $1,500 appeared. From the architectural styles of the two houses on the lot (in later years) it is presumed that this improvement was the house at 1107 (See text for this house.).

The next year in which there was a significant change in the value of the improvements on this part of lot 1 was 1863, when the assessed value jumped from $3,000 to $4,700. As $1,700 is a reasonable assessed value for a two story frame house at that time, and as the architectural style is suitable for a date in the early 1860's (though perhaps one would suppose an earlier date), it is assumed that the house at 1101 was built c. 1863.

The improvement value on the eastern parts of lot 1 rose sharply again in 1869, from $4,700 to $6,000. This was probably the year in which the two story portico was added to the front and the two bay windows added to the Eleventh Street side, as both elements seem to be quite definitely of a later style.

The owner of the property at the time the house was built was William Thomas. He purchased it in 1852 from John Nourse, who had presumably already built the house on the part of the property known as 1107 Massachusetts Avenue. The price was $4,100 (Liber JAS–45 folio 101). Thomas was listed in the city directories as living at 1101 from 1871–74 and may have lived there earlier. The old street address numbering system in effect before 1870 maks it difficult to be sure whether the street address given for Thomas (sometimes 468 L, other times 368 Massachusetts) corresponds to 1101 or 1107.

It was during Thomas's ownership that the famous wisteria vine was planted which gave the house the name, "Wisteria House." Mrs. John Binckley, an old Washington resident who was born about 1837, made this comment on the house sometime prior to 1927:

> At the other end of the block, Massachusetts Avenue and Eleventh Street, was the old Thomas place, famous in Washington for its wonderful wisteria vine, one of the lovely sights of spring until very recently. This vine was originally brought from China and given to my mother by one of the young naval officer cousins—either Edwin Denby (uncle of the Secretary) or Nick Van Zant, who lived in the block. As they brought many presents to us from

their trips I cannot remember now to which young man we (and all Washington) were indebted for this beautiful vine which my mother and Mrs. Thomas planted. (Proctor, SS, 3–1–42)

William Thomas moved to Saint Louis and in 1878 sold the part of lot 1 on which "Wisteria House" stood to Gustavus Ricker for $16,000 (Liber 886 folio 489). It was during Ricker's ownership that the only documented alterations were made to the building. In 1882 a permit for repairs and alterations was issued. It read:

> To raise story on main building of frame house, take off pitch roof and replace with flat, top covered with tin, also a summer kitchen 10 x 12 on 120 sq. ft. of ground surface and bath room 8 x 8 on 64 sq. ft. of ground surface and an additional story on back building in place of pitch roof.

The estimated cost was $1,300. This alteration gave the house the appearance it has in all known photographs. (Permit No. 74, 7–17–82)

After Ricker's death in 1886 his widow, Elizabeth M. Ricker, continued to live in the house until her death in 1922. She willed the house to Raymond Worsham, her great-nephew (Admin. No. 29227). He died in 1924; his brothers and sisters, who were his heirs, sold the house in that year to Abraham and Barney Liebman and Sydney C. and Joseph C. Kaufman for $57,500 (Liber 5387 folio 12). This was in September; in November the Liebmans and the Kaufmans received two permits: one to raze "Wisteria House" (No. 4664, 11–10–24) and another to build an apartment house on the site (No. 5192, 11–25–24). The apartment house is known as "Wisteria Mansions."

VIEWS

Exterior photographs:

Massachusetts Avenue facade:
MLKW; *National Geographic*, Vol. XXVII, No. 3 (March 1915), p. 270 (color).
West elevation and Massachusetts Avenue facade:
MLKW, E. B. Thompson purchase.

BIOGRAPHIES OF THE RESIDENTS

Of **William Thomas** practically nothing is known. He was never listed in the city directories with both a home and business address, and so it is uncertain what his occupation was. There is a possibility that he was a partner in a firm which sold stoves and tinware called Eberly, Thomas and Company, with a store at 718 Seventh Street, N.W. The partners were listed as Anton Eberly and William Thomas. In 1873 the firm no longer showed the name of Thomas, and by 1875 Thomas was no longer listed in the Washington city directories. It is known that he moved to Missouri sometime in the 1870's, as the deed by which he sold his house to Gustavus Ricker showed him living in St. Louis. Evidently he was a man of some means; he owned the houses at both 1101 and 1107 Massachusetts Avenue as well as other property in Washington. Also, the area around Eleventh Street and Massachusetts Avenue was a fashionable one at the time. In the same block with Thomas lived John Binckley, an Assistant Attorney General in Andrew Johnson's Administration and an editor of the *National Intelligencer*. Nicholas Vedder, Sherman's paymaster general, lived two doors away, at 1111 Massachusetts Avenue.

Gustavus Ricker, to whom Thomas sold the house, also remains an enigma. The newspapers seem to have taken no notice of his death; he left no will and the only known information about him is what can be deduced from the papers filed with the Register of Wills relative to the settlement of his estate.

It appears that he was a businessman, actively engaged in the affairs of the Florence and Wakefield Marble Company of Rutland, Vermont and the Standard Nail and Iron Company of Middleport, Ohio. He owned a considerable number of securities, principally railroad bonds, and particularly those of the Chesapeake and Ohio Railroad Company. He lent money frequently—mostly unsecured loans to people who, at the time of his death, had either left the city and could not be traced or who were insolvent. He also borrowed a great deal of money— $102,000 from one New York bank and $24,000 from another. He left his business affairs in such a state of confusion that lawyers were sent to New York, Ohio, and Vermont in an effort to straighten them out. In the end, his estate of some $255,000 had been reduced by disbursements of nearly $183,000.

Ricker and his wife, Elizabeth, had only one child: a daughter, Elizabeth, who married a man named Sawyer. She was thirty years old at the time of her father's death and mentally ill. She lived with her mother and was listed in the city directories until 1915; she was not living at the time of Mrs. Ricker's death in 1922. She, too, had just one child: a daughter, Marguerite, who was also afflicted with mental illness. Marguerite Sawyer was confined to Chestnut Lodge sanitarium in Rockville, Maryland, after her mother's death. (Estate of Gustavus Ricker, Admin. No. 2498)

Washingtoniana Room
Martin Luther King Library

LISTINGS OF RESIDENTS

City directories list the following tenants:

1863–1868 William Thomas: 468 L north, L corner Mass. or 368 Mass., depending on year. Thomas could have lived at either 1101 or 1107 during these years; the old numbering system makes it difficult to be sure which address is meant.
1869–1870 No listing for William Thomas.
1871–1874 William Thomas: 1101 11th or 1101 L.
1879–1886 Gustavus Ricker
1887 No listing for Ricker or his widow.
1888–1915 Elizabeth M. Ricker. Mrs. Elizabeth Sawyer and Miss Marguerite Sawyer also were listed in various years during this period.
1916–1919 Elizabeth M. Ricker
1920–1923 Elizabeth M. Ricker, Raymond Worsham
1924 Mary A. Mullin

Social registers list:

1891–1916 Mrs. Elizabeth M. Ricker. Mrs. Elizabeth Sawyer and Miss Margaret (or Marguerite) Sawyer also listed through 1911.

1107 Massachusetts Avenue N.W.

This house is on the north side of Massachusetts Avenue between Eleventh and Twelfth Streets, N.W. It is located in Square 315, on part of original lot 1, now designated for tax purposes as lot 801.

It is owned by Dr. William Chin-Lee and used as a residence.

STATEMENT

The John Nourse residence was designed as a row house on a lot 22'–8" wide. It is likely one of the last surviving of the earlier antebellum homes on Massachusetts Avenue. Though built apparently in 1840, its style is perhaps more reminiscent of the Federal era. The ogee front is more popularly associated with similar (if "grander") row houses in Boston. The undulation is elegant though seemingly incomplete without mates. The common-laid brick is light grey, the facade obviously painted far more often than the west elevation. It should be noted that of the windows (all of which curve to the facade) the most tall (six-over-nine as compared to six-over-six) are on the second floor (again suggesting a Federal period reference).

According to permits, the front porch was designed to incorporate the original "brownstone" steps. The completed porch is not as rich, however, as the elevation drawing indicates; wrought iron is not introduced, the columns are Tuscan not Ionic, and the second floor balustrade is now a "bow-knot" railing rather than urn-balustered. The cornice may not be original, although it is realized that similar designs were available in 1840. The brackets, however, are particularly fine which might indicate they are not contemporary with the more restrained decorative elements of the house.

HISTORICAL INFORMATION

Tax assessment records show that the first improvement on lot 1 occurred c. 1840. The amount of assessed valuation in that year was $1,500. John Nourse owned the entire lot (Liber WB–74 folio 298); and as the western part of the lot which he sold to Jared Eliot in 1842 did not show any improvements until 1843, it is reasonable to suppose that the 1840 improvement was on the eastern part of the lot and that it was the brick house at 1107 Massachusetts Avenue. This is because of its architectural style, and because an improvement of that date assessed at $1,500 would probably mean a brick rather than a frame dwelling. The architect is not known.

John Nourse, therefore, is assumed to be the builder of this house. In fact, the city directory of 1843 showed him living at "North side L St. North, between 11th and 12th North, near 11th." (As L Street merges into Massachusetts Avenue at this location, addresses are sometimes given as L Street and at other times as Massachusetts Avenue.) Nourse owned the property until 1852. In that year he sold it to William Thomas (Liber JAS–45 folio 101). Thomas owned it until 1883, and there are no documented alterations or additions from the period of his ownership.

The house passed through the hands of several owners who did not live in it and made no changes that are apparent. In 1904 it was sold to Jacob Moser (Liber 2807 folio 44), and it was while he owned it that the first documented alterations and additions were made. In 1907 new porches were put on the front and the rear of the house and an areaway in the rear was bricked up (Permit No. 857). In 1915 the rear porch was enclosed and converted to a kitchen, and a lavatory was installed where the old pantry had been (Permit No. 876).

In 1920 the house was sold by Moser's family to Percy Mays (Liber 4427 folio 44). He added a two story frame sleeping porch at the rear of the house (Permit No. 3896). In 1938, when the house was owned by Louise Engels (Liber 7222 folio 142), this addition was covered with asbestos shingles (Permit No. 214623). Since that time no building permits have been found for work which has significantly altered either the exterior appearance or the plan of the house.

From the early thirties until 1950 the house was in the hands of a succession of owners who used it as a rooming house. In 1950 it was purchased by Yee Sin Foung Ho (Liber 9141 folio 344) and held by her and her husband until 1967, when it was sold to Dr. William Chin-Lee (Liber 12823 folio 56) who presently holds title. Dr. Chin-Lee denied the Commission of Fine Arts permission to inspect the building, thus making it impossible to obtain an architectural description or photographic record of the interior.

No photographs or illustrations of this house have been found.

Jack E. Boucher, 1970

KNOWN ARCHITECTURAL DRAWINGS

Front porch: projection plan. Ink on linen.
Filed with permit No. 857, 9 September 1907.
   Projection Plan for Porch/House 1107 Mass. Ave.,
   N.W./Part of Lot 1, Sq. 31/T. S. Moser, Owner

Front porch: elevation. Blueprint.
Filed with permit No. 857, 9 September 1907.

Sleeping porch: east, north, and west elevations: first
and second floor plans. Scale: 3/16″–1′. Recorded on
microfilm with permit No. 3896, 2 November 1923.

BIOGRAPHIES OF THE RESIDENTS

John Nourse was a member of a prominent (and prolific) Washington family. His grandfather, James Nourse, came to America in 1769 from England, hoping to make a better living for his wife and nine children. They settled in Virginia, first at Hampton and then at Berkeley Springs. Nine more children were born to them in this country. The oldest child, Joseph, fought in the Revolution and was secretary to General Charles Lee. He came to Wash-

1973.

ington with the Government and was Register of the Treasury until 1829. The names of several other members of the Nourse family appeared over the years on the Treasury rolls, including that of John Nourse, who was a clerk in the Register's office.

John's father was Gabriel Nourse, brother of Joseph and the fourteenth child of James Nourse. He was a Baptist preacher, publisher of religious tracts, and at one time a postmaster.

John Nourse married Araminta Dickens (or Dickson) in 1838. They had no children. He remained a clerk in the Treasury Department until he moved from Washington to Frankfort, Kentucky, c. 1852. Other members of the Nourse family had settled in that state at an early date. It is said that John Nourse became a major in the Military Institute of Farmdale, near Frankfort. He died in Kentucky and his widow remarried. (Maria Catherine Nourse Lyle, compiler, *James Nourse and His Descendants,* Lexington, Ky.: Transylvania Printing Co., 1897. Lent by Miss Emily Nourse Steuart, Georgetown.)

The Nourse family name is associated with two of Washington's historic houses: Joseph Nourse lived in Georgetown at "Bellevue," now known as "Dumbarton House," from 1805–13. It was he who commissioned Benjamin Latrobe to remodel it. Major Charles Nourse, his son, built "The Highlands" on Wisconsin Avenue, now owned by the Sidwell Friends School.

William Thomas: See text, 1101 Massachusetts Avenue, N.W.

Henry D. Barr was a native of Boston who came to Washington in 1866 and established a tailoring business. In 1879 he opened a shop at 1111 Pennsylvania Avenue, N.W. which was evidently very successful; in the mid–1880's he was employing approximately thirty people. An entry in one of the Washington commercial guide books compares him with fashionable tailors in New York and London, and another comments on the fact that his customers included Senators, Representatives and other prominent people. Mr. Barr lived at 1107 Massachusetts Avenue from 1888–92. (John P. Coffine, ed., *Washington: Historical Sketches of the Capital City of Our Country,* 1887, p. 312; E. E. Barton, ed., *Historical and Commercial Sketches of Washington and Environs,* Washington: E. E. Barton, 1884, p. 71.)

APPENDIX

Chain of Title:

1839   Deed 20 August, recorded 10 September; Liber WB–74 folio 298
Lewis Johnson to John Nourse
". . . lots number . . . (1) and . . . (11) in Square three hundred and fifteen . . ." For $1,220.

1852   Deed 9 August, recorded 6 September; Liber JAS–45 folio 101
John Nourse et ux, Araminta (of Kentucky) to William Thomas
". . . parts of lots . . . (1) and . . . (11) in Square numbered . . . (315) . . . beginning at a point on Massachusetts Avenue, forty three feet from the West, Northwest corner of Lot number One, and running Southeasterly with the line of said Avenue, sixty two feet eight inches, thence East, with the line of L Street thirty-three feet three inches, to the Southeast corner of said lot, thence North with the line of Eleventh Street, one hundred and sixty nine feet, two inches to the North boundary of lot number eleven, thence West, with said North boundary Eighty nine feet, one inch, thence South one hundred and forty three feet, to the place of beginning . . ." For $4,100.

1883   Deed 10 July, recorded 20 July; Liber 1044 folio 474

William Thomas et ux, Jane (of St. Louis), to Albanus L. Johnson

". . . part of original lot . . . (1) in Square . . . (315) Beginning on Massachusetts Avenue . . . (40) feet Northwesterly from the intersection of said Avenue with L Street, and running thence North . . . (82) feet, thence West . . . (18) feet, thence North . . . (8) feet . . . (8) inches, thence West . . . (3) feet, then South . . . (83) feet to Massachusetts Avenue and thence Southeasterly on said Avenue . . . (22) feet . . . (8) inches to the beginning . . ." For $7,000.

1883   Deed 20 July, Liber 1044 folio 477
Albanus Johnson et ux, Mary M., to Olive A. Fitzgerald (of Baltimore) For $7,500.

1884   Deed 15 February, recorded 18 February; Liber 1069 folio 491
Albanus L. Johnson to Olive A. Fitzgerald
A deed made to correct error in recording name of Olive Fitzgerald's husband in preceding deed.

1904   Deed 13 April, recorded 21 April; Liber 2807 folio 44
Olive A. Fitzgerald, widow (of New York), to Jacob S. Moser

1919   Deed in Trust 2 October, recorded 29 June 1920; Liber 4394 folio 21
Jacob S. Moser et ux, Sarah E. V. to James M. Moser et al, Trustees

1920   Deed 13 August, recorded 1 September; Liber 4427 folio 44
James M. Moser et al, Trustees to Percy R. Mays et ux, Nellie W.
$8 in Internal Revenue Stamps affixed. The rate before 1 July 1940 was $.50 per $500, making the price approximately $8,000.

1931   Deed 18 March, recorded 21 March; Liber 6538 folio 362
Percy R. Mays et ux, Nellie W., to Mary E. Seabridge
". . . subject to a first deed of trust for . . . ($11,000) and a second deed of trust for . . . ($1,500) which the party of the second part hereby assumes and agrees to pay . . ."

1933   Trustees' Deed 19 April, recorded 2 May; Liber 6728 folio 541
Watson F. Clark to T. H. Reynolds
". . . Whereas Percy R. Mays and Nellie W. Mays . . . made . . . a certain Deed of Trust . . . on the 12th day of April, 1926 (Liber 5743, folio 144) . . . unto Louis R. Peak (now deceased) and Watson F. Clark . . . upon default . . . the party of the first part . . . on the 28th day of March 1933 . . . did sell at public auction unto J. Clarence Welch, acting therein for the said party of the second part, who as the highest bidder . . . became the purchaser . . . for . . . ($7,500) . . . part of original lot . . . (1) in Square 315 . . ."

1938   Deed 28 April, recorded 2 May; Liber 7222, folio 142

Thomas H. Reynolds et ux, Anne A. to Louise Engel
$9 in Internal Revenue Stamps affixed, making the price approximately $9,000.

1946   Deed 15 July, recorded 18 July; Liber 8303 folio 40
Louise Engel to Hazel McMurray
$25.30 in Internal Revenue Stamps affixed. The rate after 1 July 1940 was $.55 per $500, making price approximately $23,000.

1947   Deed 26 August, recorded 15 September; Liber 8575 folio 274
Hazel M. McMurray to J. Arthur McMurray et ux, Lucile W.

1950   Deed 8 February, recorded 9 February; Liber 9141 folio 344
J. Arthur McMurray et ux, Lucile W., to Yee Sin Foung Ho
$12 in Internal Revenue Stamps affixed, making the price approximately $11,000.

1954   Deed 24 March, Liber 10161 folio 244
Yee Sin Foung Ho to Blanche P. Puckett

1954   Deed 24 March, Liber 10161 folio 247
Blanche P. Puckett to Ng Ho et ux, Yee Sin Foung Ho

1957   Deed 26 July, recorded 29 July; Liber 10892 folio 601
Ho Ng (ng Ho) et ux, Yee Sin Foung Ng, to M. Cecilia Green

1957   Deed 26 July, recorded 29 July; Liber 10892 folio 603
M. Cecilia Green to Yee Sin Foung Ho

1967   Deed 31 October, recorded 21 November; Liber 12823 folio 56
Yee Sin Foung Ho et vir, Ho Ng, to William Chin-Lee et ux, Nancy
$37.40 in Internal Revenue Stamps affixed, making the price approximately $34,000.

1967   Deed 7 November, recorded 21 November; Liber 12823 folio 62
William Chin-Lee et ux, Nancy, and Lee Ngon Win Chin, joint tenants to Armand I. Robinson, Trustee
For the purpose of reconveyance.

1967   Deed 7 November, recorded 21 November; Liber 12823 folio 64
Armand I. Robinson to William Chin-Lee et ux, Nancy, as tenants by the entirety as to a . . . (2/3rds) undivided interest; as tenants in common with Lee Ngon Win Chin, as the remaining . . . (1/3rd) interest.

Building Permits:

No. 857, 9 September 1907. Permit to repair or alter.
Owner: J. S. Moser
Architect: A. H. Beers
Contractor: J. W. Hobbs
Estimated cost: $1,000

"New porch on front and back. Bricking up area-way in rear. Repairing fence in back yard." Also plumbing changes.

Filed with permit No. 857: Special application for projections beyond the building line, No. 67523, 31 August 1907.

Porch, covered: 5'–0" projection; 20'–0" width
Steps to main entrance: 8'–6" projection; 6'–0" width
Steps to basement: 10'–0" projection; 2'–6" width

No. 876, 24 August 1915. Permit to repair or alter.
Owner: Jacob S. Moser
"To enclose the present porch by enclosing two open sides with brick wall, 6 x 8 one story." Kitchen appliances are to be moved to this area and a lavatory is to be installed in the present pantry. The house is to be wired for electric lights.

No. 3896, 2 November 1923. Permit to repair or alter.
Owner: Mr. N. P. Mays (Percy R. Mays?)
Mechanic: James P. Brumbaugh
Estimated cost: $600
"To construct a sleeping porch on rear of dwelling. West side to be covered with wire lath and plaster."

No. 214623, 12 July 1938. Permit to repair or alter.
Owner: Louise Engel
Estimated cost: $1,000
"Repair joistings, apply asbestos shingles over wood construction in rear."

No. 11506, 16 August 1946. Plumbing permit.

No. A32588, 8 January 1952. Plumbing permit (missing from government files)

Listings of Residents:

City directories list the following tenants:

1843, 1850 John Nourse. 1843: "north side L north, between 11th and 12th north, near 11th." 1850: "corner 11th west and L north."

1858, 1860 William Thomas, 468 L north. This is the old street address numbering system in effect until 1870. 468 L north would mean a location on or near the corner of L and 11th.

1861–1862 No listing for William Thomas.

1863–1868 William Thomas: 468 L North, L corner Mass. or 368 Mass., depending on year. Thomas could have lived at either 1101 or 1107 during these years; the old numbering system makes it difficult to be sure which address is meant.

1888–1892 Henry D. Barr. 1888 directory also listed Franklin Langstaff: mantels, tiles, and leaded, stained and plate glass.

1908–1920 Reverend Jacob Moser, Dr. James Moser, and John J. Moser. 1920 directory also listed Dr. W. J. Lally.

1921–1931 Percival R. Mays; except for 1925 and 1927 when the house was vacant, and 1926, when only Mrs. Lydia Zimmer was listed.

1932 Bennie Morgan; Ruby Riker, nurse

1933 Ruby Riker

1934 Mrs. Esther Ogush; Frank N. Cummins

1935 Mrs. Esther Ogush

1936 Carl Dessi

1937 Mary L. Tallman, nurse

1938 Frank M. Beck; C. G. Carnahan; Jacob Bostick; L. G. Woody

1939 Vacant

1940 Louis (Louise?) Engel; Madame Harrison Astor, clairvoyant

1941 Louis Astor(?); Madame Harrison Astor

1942–1943 Louis Engel; Madame Harrison Astor

1948 Joseph H. McMurray

1949–1969 Stanley Ho

1970 Roger C. Wiley

1973 Mrs. Mildred A. Helms

1974 Herbert Chin; Frank H. Lee (These listings from Addressokey Directory)

Social registers list:

1891–1892 Mr. and Mrs. Henry D. Barr and daughter (1892: "Miss Barr")

1916 Dr. and Mrs. James M. Moser

1917–1918 Dr. James M. Moser

1219 Massachusetts Avenue, N.W.

This house is on the north side of Massachusetts Avenue between Twelfth and Thirteenth Streets, N.W. It is located in Square 282 on lot 5.

It is owned by the Church of the Ascension and St. Agnes and used as a parish house.

PREVIOUS STRUCTURES ON THE SITE

The Hopkins map of 1887 shows a sizeable frame building on lot 5, but the tax book for 1886–87 shows an improvement with a valuation of only $100; therefore, it is assumed that the structure was of no significance.

HISTORICAL INFORMATION

Lot 5 in Square 282 was sold to Avarilla Lambert, wife of Tallmadge Lambert, in 1886 (Liber 1203 folio 5). In 1887 Lambert received a permit to build the house (No. 2060). Phelps and Atkinson were the architects. In 1890 he enlarged it by adding a third story to the back building (Permit No. 363). No architect was listed for this work.

Sometime between 1890 and 1896 further alterations were made for which there is no permit. Indications as to what these alterations were come from two sources: a building permit dated 1896 and the Hopkins map of 1892. The building permit states the depth of the buliding to be seventy feet, which is eighteen feet longer than the depth stated on the original permit for the house plus its back building. The Hopkins map of 1892 shows a building already of a greater depth and different configuration than described on the original permit, so it is assumed that the eighteen foot addition was added sometime before 1892. If the 1892 map is correct, this 1890–92 addition was not as wide as the back building, which was twenty feet.

The permit issued in 1896 (No. 40) was for both additions and alterations. The building was to be extended six feet to the rear, although it appears that it was extended along the west side as well: The Sanborn map of 1903 shows this back section covering the entire width of the lot, which was not the case of the 1892 map. At this time, also, a two story addition, approximately twelve by thirteen feet, was added to the rear on the west side of the lot. The first floor was to be used as a pantry.

The alterations included in the 1896 permit were to the facade of the building; windows were put between the columns on the third story of the bay. Interior repairs were also mentioned in this permit. No architect was listed.

The house went to Somerset Waters and his wife in 1907 (Liber 3084 folio 465), and there are no permits for any additions or alterations during the time that they owned it.

Hyman Zirkin bought the house in 1919 (Liber 4189 folio 237); in 1922 he had a room at the rear of the house fireproofed for use as a garage (Permit No. 7614). Zirkin's son, Schley, sold the house in 1954 to Margaret Bradshaw (Liber 10166 folio 439); she sold it to the Church of the Ascension and St. Agnes in 1962 (Liber 11813 folio 332). No permits have been found for any work after the 1922 garage alteration. The church has done some remodeling, including new entrance doors and interior changes to convert the building to parish house use.

No photographs or illustrations of the house have been found, and there is only one known architectural drawing: a plan of sewers and projections, filed with permit No. 2060, 14 April 1887. The drawing is stamped: "Geo. B. Phelps, R. H. Atkinson, Architects."

ARCHITECTS

The original building permit lists Phelps and Atkinson as the architects, and from the stamp on the projections drawing filed with this permit (see above) it is known more specifically that they were George B. Phelps and R. H. Atkinson. The firm of Phelps and Atkinson was never listed under the "Architects" heading in the city directory, and nothing is known about this firm as such. The following information has been found on the two partners:

George B. Phelps (1857–1890) was born in North Andover, Massachusetts. His first architectural experience was in an office in Salem. Late in 1875 he was appointed a draftsman in the Office of the Supervising Architect of the Treasury, a position he held for eleven years. He was first listed in the Washington city directory in 1877; in 1888 an office address, 1427 F Street, N.W., was given. A Washington commercial guide book, published in 1887, indicates that he had his own practice by that time. A listing of work in his office in that year includes the following buildings: House for T. A. Lambert on Massachusetts Avenue between Twelfth and Thirteenth Streets (1219), three houses for Captain George W. Shears at Rhode Island Avenue and Iowa Circle (now Logan Circle), two houses for John Savary on M Street between New Hampshire Avenue and Twenty-second Street, N.W., and a house for Dr. J. T. Johnson on K Street, between Seventeenth and Eighteenth Streets, N.W. Completed work at that time included: Commodore Sicard's house on Highland Terrace; Plymouth Church, corner Seventeenth and P Streets, N.W.; and R. B. Taylor's house on Stoughton Street. (John P. Coffine, ed., *Washington: Historical Sketches of the Capital City of Our Country,* 1887, p. 280.)

George B. Phelps died of typhoid fever while still a young man. His obituary in the *Evening Star* (8–4–90) gives the following information:

> He had just begun his career in the city as an architect and had succeeded in building up a good business. He was engaged in completing plans for 146 houses, which it is proposed to erect on Carroll Square. Mr. Phelps was for several years employed in the Supervising Architect's office and resigned his place to go into business.

Papers filed with the Register of Wills state that Phelps died at his home, 810 Rhode Island Avenue, N.W. He was survived by his widow, Mary, and a son Reuel (or Ruel), age one year. (Estate of George B. Phelps, Admin. No. 4060)

Robert Harbottle Atkinson was in all probability the R. H. Atkinson who worked with George Phelps on the house at 1219 Massachusetts Avenue. Like Phelps, he was first listed in the city directory in 1877. He was listed as an architect, but no place of employment was given. The entries for 1888–90 did not give a business address at 1427 F Street for R. H. Atkinson as they did for George Phelps, so it is not possible to be certain that this was the man who was George Phelps' business partner. However, he was the only R. H. Atkinson listed in the city directories over a period of many years, and he was an architect. Later entries gave his occupation as "draftsman, treasury." Phelps was employed at the Treasury Department early in his career; and it is entirely possible that Atkinson was also, even though the directories do not give this information. The conjecture could be made that the two men met at the Treasury and collaborated on the Massachusetts Avenue house after Phelps had left to open his own practice. Atkinson was still listed as a draftsman at the Treasury in 1922. Papers filed with the Register of Wills state

that he was employed by the United States Government at the time of his death, 15 May 1924. He left a son, R. Bruce Atkinson. (Estate of Robert H. Atkinson, Admin. No. 32016)

BIOGRAPHIES OF THE RESIDENTS

Tallmadge A. Lambert (1842–1915) was born in Wisconsin, the son of David and Frederica Renata (Preuss) Lambert. The family moved to Washington, D.C. where young Lambert attended the public schools and graduated from Georgetown University with a Bachelor of Arts degree. Shortly after graduation he went to work for a law firm in New York. There is some confusion in the biographical sources as to where he went to law school, but it is agreed that he became a member of the bar in the District of Columbia in 1869.[*] He received a Doctor of Laws degree from Georgetown in 1893, and from that year until 1900 was a professor of civil law there.

Lambert was involved in many leading cases before the Supreme Court and received national recognition. He was one of the organizers of the Bar Association in the District of Columbia, was a director of the Lincoln Bank of Washington and one of the founders and directors of the Union Savings Bank. He was interested in education and served as a trustee of the District of Columbia public schools. He was a member of the National Geographic Society and the Columbia Historical Society.

Mr. Lambert married Avarilla van Riswick, daughter of John and Mary (Fenwick) van Riswick, in 1870. They had three children: Wilton John, Maud C. and Mildred B. Lambert.

Wilton John Lambert (1871–1935) was Tallmadge Lambert's son and was also a lawyer. He graduated from the Emerson Institute in Washington and then went to Princeton where he received his Bachelor of Arts degree in 1892. He received his law degree from his father's alma mater, Georgetown, and practiced law in Washington, where he was involved in several historic cases. One of his famous cases was the contest over the will of John R. McLean, involving several million dollars. He was also the chief counsel for Albert J. Fall, the former Secretary of the Interior, when he was acquitted in the conspiracy trial which grew out of the Teapot Dome Scandal.

---

[*] Proctor (*Washington, Past and Present,* vol. IV, p. 486) says it was the Columbia University Law School in New York; the ABD says the Columbian University Law School (now George Washington) in Washington.

April 1970/Jack E. Boucher

Lambert was vice president and general counsel for the Munsey Trust Company, president of the Washington Times Company and of the Washington and Old Dominion Railroad Company, and a director of the Federal American National Bank, Washington Post Company and Washington Gas Light Company.

Mr. Lambert was a member of the American Bar Association, Board of Trade and Chamber of Commerce. He belonged to several social clubs in New York, and in Washington was a member of the Chevy Chase Club, University Club and Racquet Club. He was also the president of the Brightwood Citizens' Association.

He was married to Elizabeth Gorman, daughter of Senator Arthur Gorman of Maryland. They had two children, Elizabeth and Arthur. (WWW, Vol. 1; WWNC, 1929–30; Proctor, *Washington, Past and Present,* Vol. IV, p. 485.)

Somerset R. Waters (1856–1926) was born in Carroll County, Maryland. He was a wholesale grocer, a director of the O Street Market Company and of the Schneider Baking Company in Washington; however, he is remembered primarily as a banker. He was president of the Seventh Street Savings Bank, a dirctor of the Second National Bank and a member of the Board of Trade and the American Bankers' Association.

In 1883 he married Mary Lillian Spignul. They had a son, Somerset R., Jr. and a daughter, Rosalie. (Obituaries: WP, 1–24–26, 3:2; ES, 1–23-26, 2:1. Obituary for Mary L. Waters: ES, 1–23-23, 7:8.)

Hyman Zirkin (1862–1932) was a prominent furrier in Washington and lived in the city for nearly half a century. He was born in Russia and came to the United States as a boy. He became an apprentice in the fur business in New York, and after moving to Washington was the manager of B. H. Steinmetz on Pennsylvania Avenue before opening his own store in 1885. At the time of his death the store was located at 821 Fourteenth Street, N.W. (Obituary: ES, 10–14–32, 9:8 & 16:3)

Mr. Zirkin married Sarah Harris of New York. She died at the age of ninety in 1958. (Obituary: ES, 4–23-58) They had six children: three sons, Schley, Dewey and Harold; and three daughters, Ida, Estelle and Lizbeth. The Zirkin children were all active in their father's business. Dewey became head of the firm when his father died. Schley was treasurer, Harold was secretary and Estelle second vice-president of the firm. Both Schley and Harold Zirkin died in the late 1950's; Dewey Zirkin died in 1966. In 1963 the family business had been merged with Saks of Washington. (Obituaries: Schley Zirkin, ES, 2–24–58; Harold Zirkin, WP, 12–29–59; Dewey Zirkin, WP, 9–7–66)

The Church of the Ascension and St. Agnes

The Episcopal church which now owns the house at 1219 Massachusetts Avenue and uses it as a parish house has a long history in the city of Washington. Ascension Parish was organized in 1845 and moved into its present building at the corner of Twelfth and Massachusetts in 1875. The ground for the church was donated by the Corcoran family. At the turn of the century it was known as Washington Pro-Cathedral, as it provided the Episcopal Seat for the bishops of Washington. In 1948 St. Agnes Parish was incorporated with Ascension Parish, and the church assumed its present name.

The parish has been active in community life, sponsoring a neighborhood preschool play group program and a family housing project. It has also become a center for the performance of music, particularly organ music; its Bach festivals have been especially noteworthy. (Literature from the Church of the Ascension and St. Agnes.)

APPENDIX

Chain of Title:

1886   Deed 2 August, recorded 18 August; Liber 1203 folio 5
Laura A. Morse (of Vineland, New Jersey) to Avarilla Lambert
" . . . Lot . . . (5) in Heirs of John Davidson's subdivision of Lots . . . (1) . . . (2) et al in Square . . . (282) as . . . recorded in Liber N. K. folios 77 and 78 of the Records of the Surveyor's Office of the District of Columbia . . ." For $6,000.

1907   Deed 12 July, recorded 25 July; Liber 3092 folio 83
Avarilla Lambert to John L. Warren
". . . Lot . . . (5) . . . in Square . . . (282) . . " This deed also includes transfer of land in Square 140.

1907   Deed 19 July, recorded 20 July; Liber 3084 folio 465
John L. Warren et ux, Annie K., to Mary Lillian Waters

1919   Deed 7 May, recorded 31 May; Liber 4189 folio 237
Mary L. Waters et vir, Somerset R., to Hyman Zirkin
$20 in Internal Revenue Stamps affixed. The rate before 1 July 1940 was $.50 per $500, making the price approximately $20,000.

1932 Will of Hyman Zirkin. Administration No. 44085. Mr. Zirkin left the premises known as 1219 Massachusetts Avenue, together with the contents of the house, to his wife, Sarah.

1953 Deed 21 September, recorded 22 September; Liber 10054 folio 298
Sarah Zirkin, widow and devisee under the will of her husband Hyman Zirkin, deceased, to Schley Zirkin

1954 Deed 25 February, recorded 1 April; Liber 10166 folio 439
Schley Zirkin to Margaret L. Bradshaw
$36.30 in Internal Revenue Stamps affixed. The rate after 1 July 1940 was $.55 per $500, making the price approximately $33,000.

1962 Contract 5 February, recorded 8 February; Liber 11749 folio 381
Margaret L. Bradshaw to The Vestry of Ascension and St. Agnes Parish of the Protestant Episcopal Church of the Diocese of Washington
". . . seller . . . hereby acknowledges to have received from purchaser . . . a deposit of . . . ($1,000) to be applied as part payment of the purchase of lot 5 in Square 282, with improvements thereon, known as premises Number 1219 Massachusetts Avenue, N.W. . . . The total price of the property is . . . ($40,000) which the purchaser agrees to pay in cash at the date of conveyance of which sum the deposit shall be a part . . ."

1962 Deed 5 June 1962, recorded 7 June; Liber 11813 folio 332
Margaret L. Bradshaw to The Vestry of Ascension and St. Agnes Parish of the Protestant Episcopal Church of the Diocese of Washington

Building Permits:

No. 2060, 14 April 1887. Permit to build.
Owner: T. A. Lambert
Architect: Phelps and Atkinson
Builder: J. H. Grant
Estimated cost: $11,000
No. 363, 14 August 1890. Permit to repair or alter.
Owner: J. H. Grant (This is not correct. T. A. Lambert was the owner; J. H. Grant was a builder.)
Estimated cost: $1,300
"To build a 2nd story to the brick back building, 18 x 20, tin roof." (This should read *3rd* story. Original building permit indicated a two story back building.)
No. 40, 9 July 1896. Permit to repair or alter.
Owner: T. A. Lambert
Mechanic: J. H. Grant
Estimated cost: $8,000
"To extend back building six feet toward rear of lot and build rear addition of brick 13'–3″ x 12–'9″—2 stories plus basement—tin roof—for pantry and c. (?) Repair servants' bath in basement and alter bay window on 3 story or mansard by putting windows between the columns and minor interior repairs."

No. 7614, 22 April 1922. Permit to repair or alter.
Owner: H. Zirkin
Contractor: Frank L. Wagner
"Work consists in fireproofing ceiling of rear room for use as a garage . . . Also includes installing a ramp with concrete roof accessible from alley level by stairway shown—changing present brick fence as indicated."

Listings of Residents:
City directories list the following tenants:

1888–1906 Tallmadge A. Lambert
1908–1919 Somerset R. Waters
1920–1948 Hyman Zirkin through 1931; afterward, Mrs. Sarah Zirkin
1954–1956 vacant
1960–1962 Mrs. Margaret L. Bradshaw
There are no directory listings for the Church of the Ascension and St. Agnes at 1219 Massachusetts Avenue, N.W.

Social registers list:

1888–1906 Mr. and Mrs. T. A. Lambert. Mr. Wilton Lambert listed from 1894–98.
1907 Dr. Ollie J. Prescott

STATEMENT:

The original semidetached building of 1887 was extensively enlarged and altered in 1896. In 1960's the west elevation became the party wall of a new apartment building. The neo-Romanesque facade of brick, sandstone and terra cotta is representative of similar houses throughout the city. The side hall plan has the unusual feature of two principal staircases back to back.

The Victorian interiors are typically eclectic, often combining several styles which cover a multitude of conflicting fashions. On the first floor, where there are many common elements, most plaster is painted white and all wood dark brown-enamelled except for the floors and stair treads which have been sanded.

SITE:

Orientation: The building faces south on a lot measuring 25'–3″ on Massachusetts Avenue; 99'–2″ on the west (party wall); 25'–3″ on the north (public alley); and 100'–1″ on the east (party wall).
Enclosures: a low iron fence on stone base at sidewalk.
Outbuildings: none.
Paving: There are three risers from the sidewalk to a concrete walk which leads to the front stoop.
Landscaping: The flat front lawn is bordered at the sidewalk by ivy and at the house by shrubbery. The public sidewalk is lined by trees.

EXTERIOR:

Dimensions: This raised basement, two and one half story building measures 56'–0" from sidewalk to roof-crest. The west bay of the two bay 25'–0" facade is a tower bow. The original 1887 structure was 34'–8" deep. In 1896 it was joined by a 17'–8" addition to a back building 17'–4" deep. The bay window of the addition forms the east side of a light well. Also in 1896, the back building was extended north by 6'–0", west by 5'–0" and received a northwest pantry 12'–1" wide by 12'–9" deep.

Foundation: concrete footings and slab.

Structure: brick bearing walls and wood joists and rafters.

Walls: The base of rusticated sandstone facing supports common bond brick. A sandstone belt course acts as basement window lintel. Several molded string courses break the facade. The first acts as a first floor sandstone window sill. The second breaks upward over the entrance to form a molded brick drip course and to frame a frieze of terra cotta plaques. The third acts as a second floor sandstone window sill. Between the second and third string courses at the bow is a frieze of terra cotta plaques. Capping the second floor windows is a plain sandstone band.

Doorways and doors: The original entrance door has been replaced by a glass-panelled double door. Molded brick impost blocks support a semicircular arch of brick voussoirs framed by a pressed brick drip moulding.

Windows: double-hung. At the bow the glazing is convex. The basement has wrought iron grilles. The first floor has lead came transom windows.

Stoop: sandstone. From the walk to the stoop are six risers with closed stringers and iron railings. The balustrade is trabeated. On the right there are six risers from the basement areaway beneath the stoop.

Stair: From the brick enclosed rear court to the pantry door are single flights of five and six concrete risers divided by a landing. There are four additional risers from the pantry landing to the terrace over the garage.

Cornice: brick. Block course, plain frieze, dentil course and cavetto moulding capped by second plain frieze and copper gutter.

Roof: A hipped slate roof with crenelated tin cresting faces onto the avenue. At the rear is a metal, low-slope roof.

Dormers: Over the entrance is a wood dormer, the paired sash divided by a mullion. The slate dormer has a gable (centered by a raised circular panel) with a slate roof and tin cresting.

Tower: The tower bow has a third floor porch of paired columnettes (infilled in 1896 by double-hung windows), capped by a plain frieze and an ovolo cornice. The slate, semiconical roof has cresting.

Chimneys: brick, sealed, not visible from the avenue.

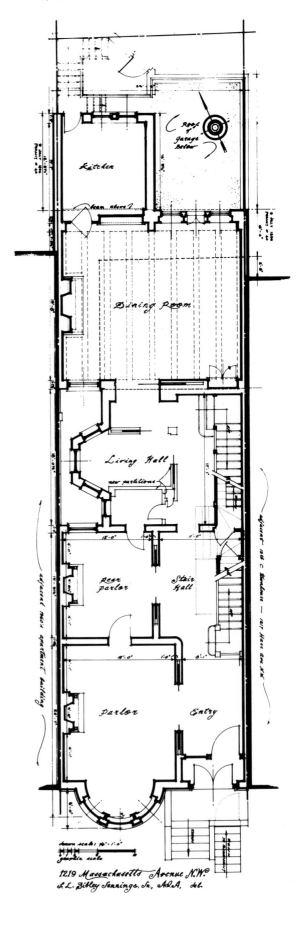

1219 Massachusetts Avenue N.W.
L.L. Sibley Jennings, Jr., A.I.A., del.

Entrance Hall
Jack E. Boucher, 1970

PLANS:

The side hall structure with vestibule has a front parlor on Massachusetts Avenue. The hall widens to accommodate the stair and allow access to the back parlor. (This constitutes the original structure.) The bay-windowed living hall (presently partitioned for a chapel and a lavatory) has the second principal stair (rising in the oppposite direction to the first) and connects the front hall to the dining room (part of the original back building) and northwest pantry (present kitchen) addition.

VESTIBULE:

Depth: 3'–0"
Width: 8'–3"

Flooring: blue and yellow patterned encaustic tiles.
Dado: brick.
Chairrail: 2'–0½" high, sandstone, flush.
Walls: brick.
Ceiling: 11'–6" high, plaster.
Doorways and doors: The upper half of the off-center door to the hall is bevelled glass. Left of the door is an opaque glass side light. The transom window has a turquoise and yellow floral motif.

ENTRANCE HALL:

Depth: 29'–2"
Width: 8'–1" (at entrance)

The hall is a pastiche of several fashions. The staircase has ornamental architectural details on a diminuitive scale; the dividing screen at the ceiling is "arts and crafts" spool work; and the floral wall frieze and newel lamp are art-nouveau.

The living hall staircase is the result of the later alteration of 1896 and is more classically defined by pilasters and rinceau carving.

Flooring: 2" hardwood.
Baseboard: 10½", wood; base with cyma cap.
Wainscot: 3'–7" high; two rows of raised wood panels with chamfered cap.
Walls: plaster.
Cornice: Above a plain wood moulding is a plaster low relief frieze and a chamfered wood cornice. Dividing the hall and stair is a spool and raised panel screen on brackets.
Ceiling: 11'–6" high, plaster.
Doorways and doors: The 8'–5½" high doors are divided by three rows of raised panels. Jambs, fluted to chair-rail height, support a lintel with bead, plain frieze and cyma cap.
Hardware: brass door pulls and knobs.
Lighting: gilded newel lamp of pierced cast metal with an opaque glass, tulip petal chimney.
Stair: wood. Two risers east to the landing, eleven risers north to two risers which turn west, and four risers west to the second floor. The treads are linoleum. The stair carriage and east wall dado have raised panels. The turned balusters support a molded handrail. The newels are pedestals ornamented with architectural devices.

FRONT PARLOR:

Depth: 22'–7" (including bow)
Width: 15'–0"

The front and back parlors are a combination of classical and medieval detail, envariably stylized. Special emphasis is placed on tile fire surrounds and unusual cast iron fireboxes.

Flooring: 2" hardwood.
Baseboard: 11", wood; base with cyma cap.
Walls: plaster; applied mouldings with rocaille corner embellishment. The north doorway and part of the wall are recent additions.
Cornice: plaster with ogee, corona, cove and bead mouldings.
Ceiling: 11'–6" high, plaster.
Doorways and doors: The 8'–5½" high doors are divided by three rows of raised panels. Jambs support a lintel with bead, plain frieze and cyma cap. The reproduction door to the back parlor has a beaded architrave with bull's-eye corner blocks.

Front Parlor
Jack E. Boucher, 1970

reproduction door to the lavatory has a beaded architrave and bull's-eye corner blocks.
Hardware: brass door pulls and knobs.
Chimney: projects 9½".
   Hearth: 5'–0", tile.
   Firebox: 2'–4" wide by 2'–6", cast iron; scene of Renaissance dancers.
   Surround: Shakespearean scenes in blue and crimson tiles.
   Mantel: 5'–0" wide by 5'–7", wood. A frieze, centered by lion mask, supports a shelf flanked by Ionic stylized columns below a second shelf. A mirror separates the shelves.

LIVING HALL:

Depth: 17'–1"
Width: 17'–7"

Flooring: 2" hardwood.
Baseboard: 1'–0", wood; base with cyma cap.
Wainscot: (at north wall) 3'–8½" high, plaster painted brown. There are three rows of flat panels in stiles and rails with wood cap.
Walls: plaster. Originally decoratively molded in low relief.
Cornice: plaster with ogee, corona, cove and bead mouldings.

Back Parlor, 1973

Hardware: brass door pulls and knobs.
Chimney: projects 8½".
   Hearth: 5'–0", olive green tile in floral surround.
   Firebox: 2'–4", wide by 2'–6", cast iron; embossed pattern.
   Surround: green tile with non-repeat floral pattern.
   Mantel: 5'–0" wide by 4'–6", spiral columns support consoles at diaper frieze below shelf.
   Overmantel: mirror in gilded frame of columnettes, cornice and ante-fixa.

BACK PARLOR:

Depth: 13'–9½"
Width: 12'–0"

Flooring: 2" hardwood.
Baseboard: 9½", wood; base with cyma cap.
Walls: plaster; applied mouldings with rocaille corner embellishment.
Cornice: plaster with ogee, corona, cove and bead mouldings.
Ceiling: 11'–6" high, plaster.
Doorways and doors: The 8'–5½" high doors are divided by three rows of raised panels. Jambs support a lintel with bead, plain frieze and cyma cap. The

Dining Room 1973

Ceiling: 11'–6" high, plaster.

Doorways and doors: The 8'–5½" high doors are divided by three rows of raised panels. Jambs support a lintel with bead, plain frieze and cyma cap.

Windows: The bay has stained glass and lead came transom windows of flowers and fruit.

Hardware: brass door pulls and knobs.

Lighting: a newel cap lamp of gilded metal with bulbous base.

Stair: wood. Three risers east to landing, fourteen risers south to two winders which turn west and four risers west to second floor. The balustrade of raised panels is divided by panelled stiles. The stiles (except for the first bay) support pedestals with pilasters. Secondary pilasters flank frosted glass and lead came panels. Over the first landing and the first panelled bay, acanthus consoles support a wood, semicircular screen of rinceau.

DINING ROOM:

Depth: 20'–8½"
Width: 24'–0"

The lapse of nine years between the building of the original structure (1887) and the addition of this chamber has resulted in a change of expression. Late Tudor or Jacobean is exemplified by the wainscot, the strapwork panelling, the tapered overmantel pedestals, the wood-beamed and ornamented plaster ceiling, and especially the early 17th century figures on the warming cabinet doors. The use of Roman brick for the severely detailed mantel is an anamoly characteristics of neither style.

Flooring: basket weave parquetry over original flooring.

Baseboard: (The height has been reduced by the new flooring.) wood with quarter-round cap.

Wainscot: 5'–3" high, raised panels.

Walls: rough plaster. The north wall is divided by three stylized pedestals which support strapwork pilasters and Ionic capitals.

Cabinet: built-in at southeast below a cupboard with lead came and glass doors.

Buffet: The built-in buffet, between the pantry door and the central pilaster, has cabinets below two horizontal, beveled mirrors separated by shelves. Over the top mirror and the pantry door is a row of semicircular-headed, opaque, and stained glass openings between fluted columnettes.

Cornice: plaster, bead moulding.

Ceiling: 11'–6" high; beams divide the decorative plaster ceiling into long panels.

Doorways and doors: The door to the living hall has a crossette architrave of fascia and cyma.

Windows: The three openings at the north wall have lead came transom windows and louvered shutters

Living Hall
Jack E. Boucher, 1970

which fold into the jamb. The central opening is now a French door approached by two removable risers. The window at the southwest has louvered shutters and a crossette architrave.

Lighting: There are two, two-light, brass sconces at the east wall and one, four-light, crystal arm and bead chandelier.

Heating: At the northwest is a gilded hot water radiator on feet cast as doves. The ornamented pipes are separated by a warming cabinet of three shelves concealed behind a cast iron double door. The two panels have male figures in decorative Renaissance clothing.

Chimney: projects 7½".

Hearth: 7'–0" wide, brick.

Firebox: 2'–1" wide by 5'–3", brick.

Mantel: 7'–0" wide by 5'–3". Roman brick; five plain niches below modillions which support the wood shelf.

Overmantel: wood. Three, beveled mirrors separated by strapwork pedestals, with stylized Ionic capitals, support a plain entablature with an egg and dart cornice.

1205 Vermont Avenue, N.W.
"Judge Andrew Wylie House"

The Wylie house was located in Square 245 on lot E. Lot O was also included in the property. The house was demolished in 1947; the site is now occupied by a motel.

STATEMENT

The Wylie residence faced southwest on the northeast corner of M Street and Vermont Avenue. Built on axis with Thomas Circle, the center hall structure had a raised basement, three floors, a hipped roof with snow guard and central lantern. At the circle the property was enclosed by a fine cast iron fence of spiked bays divided by bundled reed posts.

c. 1920
Columbia Historical Society

As with other residences built in Washington prior to 1877, dates of construction are deduced from tax records, observation and knowledge of historical trends. The slate and red brick residence was an anachronism for its time. The classical proportion of the 1840's and 50's was combined with Italianate details (entrance stoop railings, facade window sash, brick cornice). Only on the street were the double-hung windows designed to mimic casements, a conceit evident in Washington (Blair-Lee House, Pennsylvania Avenue).*

Available photographs for the Wylie house point out with accuracy (which does not necessarily mean understanding) three apparent changes in the brick work not accounted for in permits. At the southeast elevation, the basement wall thickness had been increased by one brick course (note the prominent joints) perhaps as additional buttress for the chimney wall (?). Referring again to the same elevation, the brick used for the third story was lighter in tone than elsewhere, the significance of which is unknown. All photographs show the chimneys as having been "Victorianized," likely during the 1870's, but prior to 1877.

HISTORICAL INFORMATION

Charles L. Coltman bought lots 5 and 7 in Square 245 in 1827 (Liber WB–20 folio 184). He had purchased lot 4 in 1825 and lot 6 in another transaction in 1827. In the tax book for 1843 an improvement with an assessed valuation of $2,500 appeared on lot 5. This was the site of the building later known as the Wylie house, and as its architectural style was consistent with a date in the 1840's, 1843 is assumed to be the approximate date of its construction. The name of the architect is not known.

The improvement valuation on lot 5 had risen to $3,000 by 1852. In 1853 it was reduced to $150 and a $3,000 valuation placed on lot 4. Perhaps this was simply a mistake; it is also possible that the building on lot 5 had been severely damaged by fire. In any case, the low valuation remained on lot 5 through

---

* This detail became popular during the Beaux-Arts period. Also take note of the six-over-six sash used for the southeast elevation.

1862. Lots 4 through 7 in Square 245 were subdivided into lots A through O in 1859. When this subdivision finally appeared on the tax book in 1863, the improvement on lot E (formerly lot 5) had inexplicably risen to $12,600. Possibly this reflected a complete rebuilding of the house, though certainly the exterior remained closer in style to the 1840's than to the 1860's.

Columbia Historical Society

It is not known when, or even whether, Charles Coltman lived in this house. City directories of this period were vague as to street addresses and replete with errors. It is clear from Coltman's will that he was not living in this house at the time of his death in 1860. He left his wife Rebecca ". . . the house in which I now reside and lots . . . C and D in Square numbered Two hundred and forty-five. . ." The house at 1205 Vermont was on lot E in Square 245. Also, in the contract which Coltman's children made with Thomas B. Bryan when they sold him their interest in the house on lot E, they referred to this house as being

in ". . . so much of Square 245 . . . as is not specifically devised to the widow . . . being the brick mansion and grounds adjoining the same inclosed by a brick wall on three sides and an iron railing in front and also the brick stable and the lot adjoining thereto, being lots E and O in said Block 245 and the same formerly rented and occupied by the Brazilian minister. . ." (Liber NCT–49 folio 11). Moreover, the inventory of household furnishings in Coltman's residence at the time of his death (contained in papers filed with his estate, Admin. No. O.S. 4330, 1861) describes a smaller house with only a basement, second story and attic; and with a plan different from the house on lot E.

The Brazilian Legation was listed in the city directories of 1860–62 at "Coltman's house, 14th and L." In 1864 three of the four Coltman children sold their interests in the house to Thomas B. Bryan (Liber NCT–49 folios 16 and 24). He never lived in the house, and no deeds have ever been found whereby he transferred his interest to the next owner, his brother-in-law, Judge Andrew Wylie. The 1874 tax book indicates a transfer to Wylie in that year, and it is known that he bought the last quarter interest in the house from Coltman's daughter, Rebecca, in November 1873 (Liber 738 folio 198). Some sources have Wylie living in the house as early as 1865 (ES, 4–20–47; 4–6–48; WP, 2–2–64) when he delivered the writ of *habeas corpus* for Mrs. Surratt, although directories for 1864–65 show him living at "422 N North." By 1867 he was listed at "M north corner Vermont Ave."

The first building permit available for the house was dated 1 July 1893 (No. 6). It was for a two story brick addition, 14 by 30 feet, with an estimated cost of $2000. In 1894 an open porch, 7 by 28 feet, was added (Permit No. 1807, 6–7–94). Other permits were for minor repairs and additions: a window cut into the second floor, east side (Permit No. 573¾, 9–30–01) and a lavatory addition, 13 by 7 feet and area to the basement on the north side (Permit No. 767, 8–5–09). There is no permit for the Victorian chimney caps, which were probably added sometime during the 1870's.

The house remained in the Wylie family until approximately one year before it was demolished. Horace Wylie, Andrew's son, received it upon the death of his father in 1905 (Estate of Andrew Wylie, Admin. No. 13174). Horace deeded it to his wife, Katherine, in 1911 when he left her for Elinor Hichborn (Liber 3456 folio 207). In 1941, by Katherine Wylie's will, the house was placed in trust until her youngest child, Craig, reached the age of thirty years (Will of Katherine Wylie, Admin. No. 59,553). At that time, September 1946, it went to her three remaining children: Katherine, Margaret and Craig (Liber 8341 folio 329). A fourth child, Andrew, had died in 1945. The Wylie children (along with their father, Horace, who was the only heir of his son, Andrew) sold it immediately to Helen Loughlin (Liber 8341 folio 329). In April 1947 she sold it to the Chesapeake and Potomac Telephone Company (Liber 8475 folio 328) four days after it had been damaged by fire (ES, 4–20–47). The telephone company demolished it in August, planning to build an administration building on the site (WTH, 8–24–47). Plans for this never materialized; the property is now occupied by a motel.

The only known architectural drawing of the Wylie house is a plat with drawing of the 1909 and earlier additions, and some measurements; filed with permit No. 767, 5 August 1909.

VIEWS

Exterior photographs:

Thomas Circle facade: *Records of the CHS,* Vol. 27 (1925), facing p. 157, c. 1920.
Thomas Circle and M Street elevations: Collection of the CHS.
From above, southeast of Thomas Circle, showing Circle and M Street elevations at time of fire, April 1947. ES, 4–20–47. A print from this negative is in the collection of the CHS.

BIOGRAPHIES OF THE RESIDENTS

Charles Lilly Coltman (c. 1800–1862). The Coltman family came to Washington from Philadelphia with the government, according to J. Harry Shannon in one of his "Rambler" articles on Washington history in the *Evening Star* (7–8–17, 2:99). Charles Coltman was first listed in the city directory in 1834. His occupation was given as "brick layer." By 1853 he was called a "brick maker," and in 1858 the entry showed the firm of "C. L. Coltman and Son, brick makers, Vermont Ave. corner 2nd." At this time Coltman also had a flour mill. The firm's name was Coltman and Duncanson, and the mill was located at Ohio Avenue and Twelfth Street. Later directories listed it as the "Metropolitan Mill." After Coltman's death, his son Robert ran the mill. Robert was not listed in the city directory after 1863; a note on a paper filed with his father's estate, dated 1866, noted that he had moved to Philadelphia (Admin. No. O.S. 4330).

Coltman's wife Rebecca continued to be listed at the Coltman house at 420 M Street for several years, but then apparently went to live with her daughter Rebecca, who at some time married a man named Chandler. This is mentioned in Mrs. Coltman's will (Admin. No. 6054). Mrs. Coltman died in 1894.

The Shannon article also mentions that Coltman was superintendent of buildings and grounds during the Jackson Administration. He owned a considerable amount of property at the time of his death, including the old glass works buildings between Twenty-second and Twenty-third Streets N.W. This was a center for the manufacture of glass during the first half of the nineteenth century, but was used for other manufacturing purposes during the time Coltman owned it. (Robert H. Harkness, "The Old Glass-House," *Records of the CHS,* Vol. 18 (1915), pp. 209–238.)

Thomas Barbour Bryan (1828–1906) was born in Alexandria, Virginia. He was the son of Daniel and Mary (Barbour) Bryan, and was related to the prominent Barbour family of Virginia: his mother was a sister of Governor James Barbour, and his uncle was Supreme Court Justice Philip Pendleton Barbour.

Thomas B. Bryan was graduated from Harvard Law School in 1849. He practiced law in Cincinnati and then in Chicago, where he was also engaged in the real estate business. He became prominent in Chicago civic affairs, ran for mayor twice and was instrumental in bringing the World's Fair to Chicago in 1893.

During the Civil War Bryan was a strong supporter of the Union. He was an author (*Stephen A. Douglas on the Cause and Effect of the Rebellion,* 1863) and a linguist. He was known for his frequent and elaborate entertaining, and the *Dictionary of American Biography* mentions that he had "several palatial residences." He was married to Jane Byrd Page, daughter of an army chaplain. They had two children. One of Bryan's sisters married Judge Andrew Wylie; another married J. H. Lathrop, also of Washington; she was the mother of Mrs. Thomas Nelson Page, wife of the noted author and diplomat. Bryan was a member of the first District of Columbia Board of Commissioners (1875–78), and for many years owned a considerable amount of real estate in Washington. (Obituary: ES, 1–26–06)

Andrew Wylie (1814–1905) was born in Washington County, Pennsylvania, the son of Andrew and Margaret (Ritchie) Wylie. The elder Wylie was an ordained minister in the Episcopal Church, but is remembered primarily as an educator. He was the first president of Indiana University.

Young Wylie received his degree from his father's university in 1832, managed the family farm for several years, and then studied law; first at Transylvania University in Lexington, Kentucky, and then with Walter Forward in Pittsburgh. Forward was Secretary of the Treasury under Tyler.

Wylie opened his practice in Pittsburgh, but sometime in the late 1840's or early 1850's moved to Alexandria, Virginia, where in 1860 he cast the only vote in the city for Lincoln. In 1863 the President appointed him a judge of the newly established Supreme Court of the District of Columbia. It was Judge Wylie who issued the writ of *habeas corpus* in the conspiracy case of Mary Surratt, a writ which was superseded by President Johnson, thus bringing about her death by hanging. Wylie remained on the bench until 1885, and on the occasion of his retirement, the *Washington Post* (4–26–85) described the man in this way:

> He was always firm and impressed with the fact that it was for him to do his official duty regardless of consequences, and whether it affected rich or poor he always did it . . .
> He is as honest a man judicially as ever sat upon the bench of a Federal court, and has always been particularly watchful of the rights of private citizens as against prosecutions in the name of the United States . . .
> In character Judge Wylie, though excitable and apt to show temper at trickery or fraud, is nevertheless the first to discover his mistakes and to acknowledge his wrong. In private life he is always the urbane, elegant and accomplished gentleman. His domestic life has been one of almost unalloyed bliss, and it has been frequently remarked by his friends that "he is as much in love with his wife now as if he was a boy in love with his first girl."

His wife was Mary Caroline Bryan of Alexandria, a sister of Thomas B. Bryan. (See above.) They were married in 1845 and had one son, Horace. Mrs. Wylie died c. 1898. (DAB, WWW; Obituary: WT, 8–2–05)

Horace Wylie (c. 1865–1950) led a domestic life which was anything but unalloyed bliss. An attorney by profession, he is remembered primarily as the man who left his wife, Katherine, and their four children for poet Elinor Morton Hoyt Hichborn. The two fled to England early in 1911 when Wylie's wife refused to give him a divorce. In 1912 Philip Hichborn, Elinor's husband, committed suicide. The Wylies, Hoyts and Hichborns were prominent in Washington and Philadelphia society, and the scandal created was intensified by its dramatization in the newspapers.

By 1915 war had made England less than a pleasant place in which to live. Horace Wylie's wife had finally granted him a divorce, and so he and Elinor returned to the United States. They were married in

Boston the next year. In 1919 the Wylies returned to Washington, where Elinor wrote poetry and Horace worked at a minor job with the Government. Elinor became more and more involved with the literary world, and in 1921 she left Washington and her husband for New York. In 1923 she divorced Wylie and married poet William Rose Benet.

Elinor Wylie (she continued to use this name professionally) died of a stroke in 1928 at the age of forty-three. Horace Wylie never returned to the social world of his family and old friends in Washington. A newspaper article in 1938, re-telling the story of the scandal, mentioned that he was living in an apartment in Greenwich Village then (WT, 3–19–38). His former wife, *Katherine Virginia Hopkins Wylie,* to whom he had deeded the Thomas Circle house in 1911, continued to keep the Wylie name alive in Washington society until her death in 1941. Her Christmas night dances at the house were a Washington tradition for over thirty years. Some two hundred people—leaders of society and friends of the Wylie children—made up the guest list. (WP, 12–19–36; 12–36–39)

There were four Wylie children: Andrew, Katherine Virginia, Margaret, and Craig. *Andrew Wylie,* a scientist, explorer and big game hunter, died in 1945. He was a colonel in the Marine Corps during World War II; while on assignment in Warsaw he apparently fell off a bridge and drowned. His body was not recovered until several years later, and in 1949 he was buried in Arlington Cemetery. Colonel Wylie had also served in World War I and had received the the Belgian Croix de Guerre with Palm. After the war he worked with the Hoover Relief Mission and as an overseas correspondent for the Chicago Tribune before returning to Washington to enter the real estate business. In 1937 Wylie was commissioned a captain in the Marine Corps. Called to active duty in 1940 he headed the Eastern European section of the office of Naval Intelligence and became United States naval attache for Poland in 1945. He was awarded the Officer's Cross of the Order of Polonia Restituta. (TH, 10–18–47; ES, 5–31–49; WDN, 6–1–49)

The two Wylie daughters married. *Katherine* became Mrs. Frederick Lawrence, and at the time of Andrew Wylie's burial (1949) was living in Brookline, Massachusetts. *Margaret* was married to Hugh F. Sawbridge of Corsham, Wiltshire, England. He was active in the Toc H religious movement, which Mrs. Katherine Wylie had been instrumental in starting here in 1929. *Craig* was an instructor in a New England preparatory school at the time of his brother's funeral.

Columbia Historical Society

LISTINGS OF RESIDENTS

City directories list the following tenants:

Note: Street addresses in the early directories were often given as only approximate locations, typographical errors were frequent, and until 1870 the numbering system for addresses was different from the one in use today. Therefore, all entries for Charles Coltman in the approximate area are given, as it is not certain which, if any, refer to the house at 1205 Vermont.

1843,1850 Charles Coltman, north side M north, between 13th and 14th.

1855–1860 Charles Coltman, 420 M north.

1860–1862 Brazilian Legation, Coltman's house, corner 14th and L (M?)

1863 Rebecca Coltman, widow Charles L., 420 M north

1864–1865 Rebecca Coltman, 420 M north
Andrew Wylie, 422 N

1866–1870 Andrew Wylie, M north, corner Vermont (or, corner Vermont, M and 14th)

Note: From 1871–1905, the address is given as 1205 Vermont, 1205 Thomas Circle or 1205 14th. After 1905, 1205 Vermont is used.

1871–1894 Andrew Wylie

1895–1905 Andrew Wylie; Horace Wylie, lawyer

1906–1916 Horace Wylie

1918 Andrew Wylie, 2nd Lieut., USA

1919–1920 Katherine V. H. Wylie

1921–1935 Katherine V. H. Wylie (sometimes listed as "widow, Horace"). Andrew Wylie was also listed through 1933; Craig, Katherine and Margaret Wylie were listed at various times during this period.

1936 vacant

1937–1941 Katherine V. H. Wylie, Andrew Wylie

1942–1943 Andrew Wylie, USMC; Craig Wylie, instructor (1942); USN (1943)

Social registers list:

1888–1894 Hon. and Mrs. Andrew Wylie

1896–1898 Hon. and Mrs. Andrew Wylie, Mr. and Mrs. Horace Wylie

1899–1905 Judge Andrew Wylie, Mr. and Mrs. Horace Wylie

1906–1911 Mr. and Mrs. Horace Wylie

1916–1917 Mrs. Horace Wylie

1927 Mrs. Katherine V. H. Wylie; Dr. and Mrs. G. Wythe Cook (Listed at No 3 Thomas Circle—is this Wylie house?)

1929–1942 Mrs. Katherine V. H. Wylie. Wylie children also listed at various times during this period.

1943 Major Andrew Wylie, USMC; Lieut. and Mrs. Craig Wylie

1944–1945 Andrew Wylie

1400-1402 Massachusetts Avenue, N.W., Mrs. Annie A. Cole residence

These houses were located at the convergence of Massachusetts Avenue and M Street, N.W. at Thomas Circle, in Square 213 on parts of lot 1. They were demolished in 1971, and the site is now occupied by the headquarters of the National Association of Home Builders.

1970, Jack E. Boucher

STATEMENT

Number 1400, an 1888 addition to number 1402, became a separate property only in 1895. Though the structures would seem to have had little in common, a comparative statement will prove otherwise.

The structural and ornamental elements were either similar or opposite by contrast. (Contrasting motifs can unify as effectually as those of similar style and composition.) To conform to the lot the buildings

both had trapezoidal plans, rounded at the corner. For the addition the corners nearest the circle converged to make a single tower. Near the center of the facades on Massachusetts Avenue and M Street, 1402 (the earlier structure) had projecting bays and 1400 had recessed semihexagonal bays.

The attic stories had the most in common, both buildings having had a mansard roof, surfaced in a nearly identical slate pattern, pierced by dormers with segmentally-headed and denticulated pediments. Though the dormers were similar, a subtle difference was achieved in ornamental "weight," where the heavier proportions at 1402 caused the facade ornamentation to seem more delicate by contrast.

Brick, another means of comparison, was used essentially as structure at 1402 (other material delineating ornament), whereas for the addition it was the source of both structure and ornament. Though a paint or plaster coating was appropriate for the original building, a similar coating would have been aesthetically incompatible to the essential character and ornament of the addition. Unlike 1402, where ornament is used as decoration for its own sake, the patterned and molded brick courses for the addition were a contrast to the verticalities of recesses and turrets as well as a means of transmitting the horizontal lines of the more decorative neighbor. The type of ornament, especially the curious Mayan chain motif for the upper story of the tower, is of great interest.*

HISTORICAL INFORMATION

The houses were built at different times, but at one period were used as a single residence. The one formerly at 1402 was built c. 1874 by Peter J. Lauritzen, who was also the architect. He built it on land purchased in 1873 from Thomas B. Bryan for $8,147

* One of the first scientific journals on Mayan architecture and related arts was compiled in 1880 by A. P. Maudslay (*Biologia Centrali-Americana,* Archeology, 4 vols., London, 1889), though Brasseur de Bourbourg published in 1866 *Monuments Anciens du Mexique* (Paris), and, most important to this commentary, W. H. Holmes' *Ancient Art of the Province of Chiriqui,* in 1888 (Sixth Annual Report, Bureau of American Ethnology, Washington).

1402 Massachusetts Ave. N.W.
ca. 1875, before Mrs. Cole's addition
Proctor Collection, Columbia Historical Society
(Scott Circle and Stewart's Castle beyond.)

(Liber 737 folio 456). The house first appeared on the tax book in 1876 with an assessed valuation of $12,000. Lauritzen was never listed in the directories at this address, and in 1876 he sold the house to B. Edward J. Eils (Liber 834 folio 180). In 1877, upon default of a trust from Lauritzen to R. H. J. Leipold (Liber 811 folio 347), the house was sold at auction for $5,000 to Theodore N. Gill (Liber 855 folio 287). In 1879 Gill sold it to Annie A. Cole for $25,000 (Liber 917 folio 151).

In 1888 Mrs. Cole decided that she wanted to build an addition to the house. She commissioned the well-known architect Alfred B. Mullett, and the building permit was issued 7 September 1888 (No. 468).

The site was small and triangular in shape; and, apparently in an attempt to provide as large a building as possible, Mullett took advantage of the long established right of property owners to build bays, porches and other projections beyond the building line onto public space. The limitation was 5 feet in depth and 14 feet in length, though it should be noted that exceptions were sometimes granted—notably in the case of the Portland apartment house which had recently been completed near Mrs. Cole's house on Thomas Circle; and in that of the National Safe Deposit Company at Fifteenth Street and New York Avenue (ES, 10-2-88, 4:2).

Mullett's first drawing submitted for the building permit shows nearly the entire Massachusetts Avenue and M Street facades projecting beyond the building line: The Massachusetts Avenue projection was approximately 37 feet, the M Street projection approximately 39 feet (plus a rectangular tower at the apex). The drawing is stamped approved on 7 September; but filed with the permit is another drawing on tracing paper showing a revised design, with a penciled notation: "Substitute for the original—approved Sept. 12, 1888." This drawing shows a recess cut into each facade, back to the building line, to reduce the length of the projections. Each projection is still longer than the 14 feet allowed—they range from 16 to 49 feet. This drawing also varies from the original in that the rectangular tower and entrance at the convergence of Massachusetts Avenue and M Street have been eliminated, and the entrance placed in the recess on the Massachusetts Avenue facade. Instead of the tower, there is a simple rounding off of the facades as they converge at this point, reflecting the shape of the site and repeating the rounded corners seen in the original building and elsewhere in the addition. In elevation, the rounded form was expressed as a tower at the mansard level.

This revised design appears in another drawing, on linen, stamped: "eng'r. Dep't. D.C., Oct. 3, 1888." But this drawing shows something else: The recess on the M Street side is now filled in with a semi-hexagonal bay, in effect increasing the length of the projections again. Still another drawing, identical to the preceding, gives dimensions for this bay and indicates that it was approved 7 September 1889, exactly one year after the original permit was issued. Filed with this permit are numerous letters from Mrs. Cole, the Inspector of Buildings and the District Commissioners regarding the legality of this M Street bay.

All this is visual evidence of the dispute which ended in a court case involving the projection of "Mrs. Cole's bay window," as the addition came to be called. Evidently Mrs. Cole's neighbors in the fashionable Thomas Circle area, especially those on Highland Terrace, objected to her additions. It was the United States, however, which brought suit in November 1888 against Mrs. Cole, the District Commissioners and the Inspector of Buildings, alleging that the District of Columbia building regulations had been violated. While the case was pending in the District of Columbia Supreme Court, Mrs. Cole pressed on with her attempt to get her M Street bay approved, and the building continued to rise. At one point the Assistant Attorney of the District of Columbia said in a letter to the Commissioners:

Mrs. Cole is at liberty to proceed with her work, subject to the liability of having to undo it should the General Term so decide . . .

I do not see why the Commissioners should interfere with her if she is willing to take the risk involved. If she is hereafter required to undo her work so will everyone be who is doing similar work. (Letter, 8–17–89, filed with permit No. 468, 9–7–88)

The case was decided against Mrs. Cole, but it is said that she hired a surveyor to survey all the buildings around Thomas Circle in order to prove her point that there were numerous other violations existing. In any case, she was not ordered to tear down the building. To bring the matter to an end, Congress added to the District deficiency bill of 1891 a paragraph stating:

That the action of the Commissioners of the District of Columbia in heretofore granting permits for the extension of any building or buildings . . . beyond the building line . . . is hereby ratified . . . And hereafter no such permit shall be granted except upon special application and with the concurrence of all of said Commissioners and the approval of the Secretary of War. (Proctor, SS, 1–2–38)

This got to be a rather cumbersome procedure, and the act was amended in 1906 to make the Secretary's approval necessary only in cases where the building site was adjacent to a public reservation.

In 1895 Mrs. Cole deeded the original part of her house (1402 Massachusetts Avenue) to the Reverend Thomas DeWitt Talmage in exchange for a house in Brooklyn, New York (Liber 2061 folio 264). In 1894 they were parties to a quit-claim deed, whereby the wall separating the two houses became a party wall (Liber 2417 folio 107). No permit has been found for converting the Cole house into two separate dwellings.

In 1903 Mrs. Cole sold the newer house (1400) to William H. Walker (Liber 2754 folio 343). He made no changes except in the heating system. (Permit No. 1757, 5–14–04).

In 1911 the house at 1402 underwent some rather extensive interior remodeling. Some partitions were removed, others added; plumbing fixtures were replaced, floors in the kitchen and baths were replaced, and the house wired for electricity. Philip S. Henry was listed as the owner on the permit, although deeds indicate that Eleanor Talmage (widow of Thomas DeWitt) owned the house until 1922. Boal and Brown were the architects for this work. Estimated cost was $3,000 (Permit No. 27, 7–13–11).

1400 Massachusetts Avenue was sold to Emilie C. Riley in 1907 (Liber 3043 folio 466) and then again in the same year to Alonzo C. Mather of Chicago (Liber 3121 folio 128). He did not live in the house and made no documented changes. He sold the house for $20,000 in 1920 to Rachel Notes, wife of Marcus

Notes (Liber 4387 folio 423). Notes converted a basement room to a garage the year the house was purchased (Permit No. 2547, 11–21–20).

Marcus Notes also bought 1402 Massachusetts Avenue. He purchased it from Eleanor Talmage in 1922 for $30,000 (Liber 4713 folio 36). Both houses stayed in the Notes family until they were sold to the National Association of Home Builders in 1970 (Liber 13155 folio 37). They were demolished in 1971 to make way for the new headquarters building of that organization.

KNOWN ARCHITECTURAL DRAWINGS

Filed with Permit No. 468, 7 September 1888 (1400 Massachusetts Avenue)
Addition: original plan. Ink on linen.
   Signed: A. B. Mullett, Architect
Addition: revised plan, with recesses but no M Street bay. Pencil on tracing paper. On this drawing are the following notes: "Substitute for the original—approved Sept. 12, 1888." Also: "Copy made for exhibit in case"

1402 Massachusetts Avenue (1400 beyond)
April 1970, Jack E. Boucher

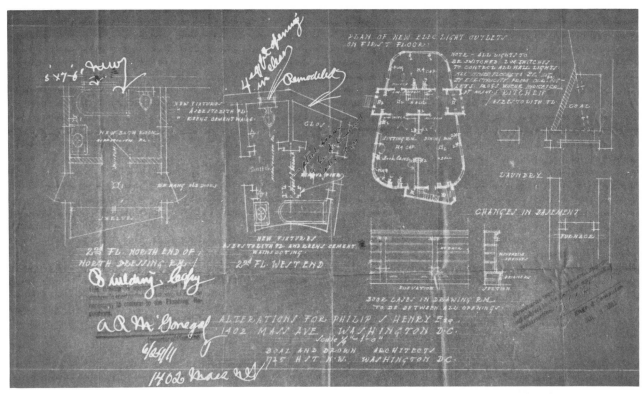

1911 Alteration
D.C. Permits, National Archives

Addition: revised plan, showing M Street bay. Ink on linen. Eng'r. Dep't. D. C. / Oct. 3, 1888

Addition: revised plan; same as above but with dimensions of bay given and note, with arrow to bay: "App. Sept. 7/89"

Massachusetts Avenue arch: elevation and plan. Pencil sketch.

Massachusetts Avenue arch: elevation and plan. Pencil and ink sketch (another version)

M Street bay: elevation and plan. Pencil sketch.

Alterations (1911) to 1402 Massachusetts Avenue: plans. Blueprint.

Filed with Permit No. 27, 3 July 1911.
ALTERATIONS FOR PHILIP S. HENRY, ESQ. / 1402 MASS. AVE. WASHINGTON, D.C. / Scale: ¼"=1'–0" / Boal and Brown, Architects / 1725 H St. N.W., Washington, D. C.

VIEWS

Exterior:

Lauritzen house, before Mrs. Cole's addition: CHS, Proctor Collection; print, c. 1875. Same view is in the 1875 Washington city directory, facing page 321.

From apex of Massachusetts Avenue and M Street, showing Mrs. Cole's tower and foreshortened view of M Street facade: CHS, photograph, c. 1928.

ARCHITECTS

Peter J. Lauritzen (original house, 1402 Massachusetts Avenue, N.W.)

Very little is known about Peter J. Lauritzen He was first listed in the city directory in 1870, with his occupation given as, "draftsman, Treasury." By 1874 he was listed as an architect with an office at 615 Fifteenth Street, N.W. In 1875 he placed a full page advertisement in the directory with an illustration of the house at 1402 Massachusetts Avenue and a list of names of prominent persons as references. Presumably he had performed some kind of architectural service for these men; because there are no building permits for the period before 1877, however, it would be difficult to substantiate this. Among the names were those of the Danish Minister and the Consul General of Switzerland, Thomas B. Bryan and Justice Andrew Wylie (see text, 1205 Vermont Avenue), Chief Justice Waite and Attorney General George H. Williams.

In 1877 the entry in the "Architects" section of the directory read, "Lauritzen and Didden." This was in all probability C. A. Didden, an architect who later practiced by himself. In 1878 Lauritzen was listed as the Danish Vice-Consul and as an architect, while from 1880–82 the entry read, "Assistant Superintendent of Buildings and architect." Evidently he was

Original drawing, 7 Sept. 1888
D.C. Permits, National Archives

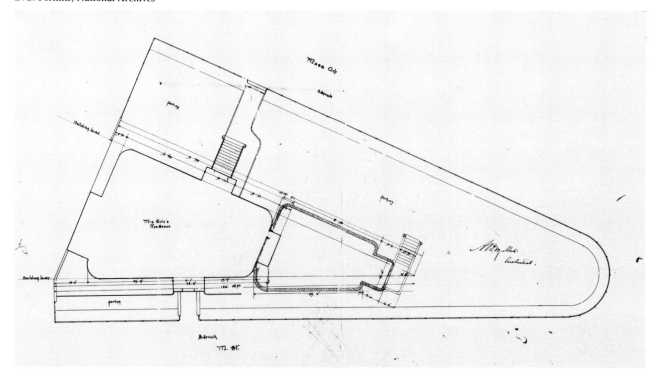

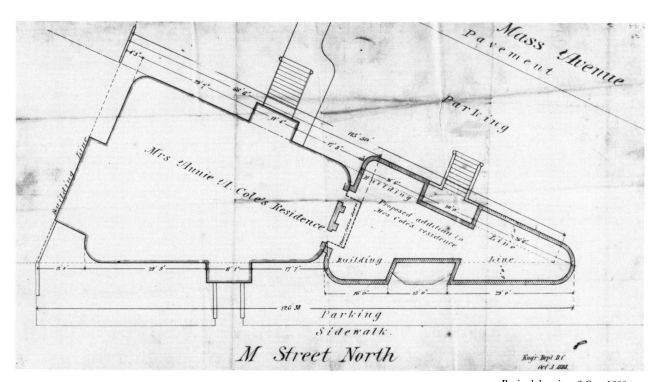

Revised drawing, 3 Oct. 1888
D.C. Permits, National Archives

doing work for the District Government at this time, as there are in existence drawings for the remodeling of a Hook and Ladder Company at 438 Massachusetts Avenue, N.W. for use as an Engine House (No. 6) stamped, "P. J. Lauritzen, First Assistant Inspector of Buildings." This work was done c. 1879. (Drawings are in the files of Engine House No. 6.)

The last listing for Lauritzen in the directory was in 1884, when he was listed as an architect with an office at 701 Fifteenth Street, N.W. Apparently he left Washington after this, as there is no record of his death in the Office of the Register of Wills of the District of Columbia.

Alfred Bult Mullett (addition, 1400 Massachusetts Avenue, N.W.)

In contrast to Lauritzen, the career of Alfred B. Mullett (1834–1890) has been well documented. Born in England, he was the son of Augustin Aish and Hannah (Bult) Mullett, who came to the United States in 1845 and settled in Glendale, Ohio; now a suburb of Cincinnati. Mullett acquired some knowledge of architecture in an Ohio college (which one is not known) and later travelled and possibly studied in Europe.

After returning to the United States Mullet went to work in the Cincinnati office of Isaiah Rogers (c. 1860) and later became a partner in the firm. He opened his own office after Rogers had dissolved the partnership.

In 1863 Mullett received an appointment as a clerk in the office of the Supervising Architect of the Treasury, an appointment which may have been due to the influence of Isaiah Rogers, who had been appointed Supervising Architect in 1862. Feeling that the clerk's position was not really commensurate with his experience and ability, Mullett applied for and received the position of chief clerk; soon afterward he was appointed Acting Supervising Architect in the absence of Rogers. When Rogers resigned in 1865, Mullett was appointed Supervising Architect (May 1866).

In this same year Mullett married Pacific Pearl Myrick, daughter of a sea captain and shipowner from San Francisco, Joseph Myrick. They had six children: Josephine, Thomas Augustine, Frederick William, William Hanson, Richard Myrick and Daisy. Thomas and Frederick both became architects; Daisy married Lawrence F. Schmeckebier of Washington.

As Supervising Architect Mullett was in charge of the design and construction of a large number of Federal buildings. The post-war period was one of expansion, and it saw the proliferation of large and expensive courthouses, post offices, and other Government facilities. Mullett produced the present day equivalent of about 300 million dollars worth of buildings before he resigned in 1874. (Wodehouse, p. 24*) All indications are that he kept a tight rein on the design of the projects under his supervision; and that he was indeed the architect to the fullest extent possible, considering the vast amount of work in his office. A listing of some of Mullett's Government work follows:

> Post offices, courthouses or customs houses (or combinations thereof) in New York City; St. Louis; Philadelphia; Boston; Cincinnati; St. Paul; Hartford, Connecticut; Cairo, Illinois; and Portland, Maine.
> Branch mints at San Francisco and Carson City, Nevada.
> Marine hospital in Chicago.

Mullett's most important Government building was the State, War and Navy Building in Washington, now the Old Executive Office Building. It took close to twenty years to build and cost over ten million dollars.

The enormous amount of construction for which Mullett was responsible, the sums of money involved and the competition and intrigue over contracts inevitably brought charges of wrongdoing against him, none of which was ever substantiated. His Annual Reports began to show his dissatisfaction and frustration, and his many recommendations regarding contracts and prevention of corruption went unanswered.

Mullett resigned his post in 1874; from 1875–90 he was in private practice with his two sons, Thomas and Frederick, and another architect, J. F. Denson. The Central National Bank (now the Apex Liquor Store) on Pennsylvania Avenue and Seventh Street, N.W., and several houses near the northwest corner of Pennsylvania Avenue and Twenty-fifth Street, N.W. are about all that remain from this period. Larger buildings, including two office buildings on F Street, N.W. have been demolished, as has his Mexican Legation at 1413 I Street, N.W. While he was in private practice, Mullett served on the Naval Yards Commission and on the Board of Public Works for the District of Columbia under Governor Shepherd.

In 1889 Mullett filed suit against the Government for professional fees in connection with several build-

---

* There are biographies of Mullett in Withey and the NCAB; the major sources for his architectural career are Donald Lehman, *The Executive Office Building*, General Services Administration Historical Study No. 3, Washington: Government Printing Office, 1970; and Lawrence Wodehouse, "Alfred B. Mullett and His French Style Government Buildings," *Journal of the Society of Architectural Historians*, Vol. XXXI, No. 1 (March 1972), pp. 22–37. Obituaries for Mullett: ES, 10–21–90; WP, 10–21–90.

1400 Massachusetts Ave. N.W.
c. 1928
Columbia Historical Society

ings, including the State, War and Navy Building. Because of his delay in filing his claim, however, he received nothing. In 1890 he filed another suit, this time against a client for whom he had designed a house. He could not sell the houses he had built next to his own at 2501 Pennsylvania Avenue, N.W. Plagued by financial worries and failing health, Mullett shot himself in October 1890. His obituary in *American Architect and Building News* (Vol. XXX (1890), p. 25) said of him: " . . . although en-

trusted, in a way in which no other official of the United States ever was trusted, with the expenditure of almost countless millions of public money, he lived modestly, on a very meagre salary, and died poor."

BIOGRAPHIES OF THE RESIDENTS

Annie A. Cole (1836–1913) was the daughter of Horatio and Anne (Collins) King of Maine. King was long associated with the Post Office Department and became Postmaster General during Buchanan's Administration. He was a lawyer, and his practice brought him both wealth and a reputation as one of Washington's foremost citizens. He was a leader of the Saturday Evening Literary Society, which met in his home; he was also an author. It was in this environment that his daughter, Annie, grew up. She was prominent in Washington society during Buchanan's Administration, and was later married to George E. Cole, at one time lieutenant governor of Oregon and postmaster at Portland. He died sometime in the 1880's. Mrs. Cole died in 1913 at the Toronto Apartments, Twentieth and P Streets, N.W., while visiting a friend. (Obituaries: NYT, 1-4-13, 9:3; WP, 1-4-13. Biography, Hortatio King: DAB.)

Charles S. Hamlin (1861–1938) lived in one of Mrs. Cole's houses from 1894–1896. (Perhaps the two houses were still one at the time.) Hamlin was born in Boston and was the son of Edward Sumner and Anna Gertrude (Conroy) Hamlin. Hannibal Hamlin, Lincoln's Vice-President, and Cyrus Hamlin, the noted educator and missionary, were members of the same family.

Charles S. Hamlin was educated at Harvard, where he received his A.B., A.M. and L.L.B. degrees. Later he received L.L.D. degrees from Washington and Lee and Columbia universities. He opened his law practice in Boston, and in 1893 was appointed Assistant Secretary of the Treasury. He served until 1897 and then again from 1913 to 1914. During his first term he changed the entire accounting system of the Treasury. At this time also, he was much concerned with the question of seal fishing in the Bering Sea, which had also been of interest to James G. Blaine (see text 2000 Massachusetts Avenue). Hamlin was appointed the first governor of the newly established Federal Reserve Board in 1914 and served until 1916. He was a member of the Board from 1916–26 and again from 1926–36. From 1936 until his death he was the special counsel of the Federal Reserve System. Hamlin was a member of many special commissions and conferences called to settle differences between the United States and other countries, and acted as an arbitrator in a number of industrial disputes.

In 1898 Charles Hamlin married Huybertie Lansing Pruyn. They had one daughter, Anna. Mrs. Hamlin was the daughter of John Van Schaick Lansing Pruyn, a lawyer and railroad man who drew up the consolidation agreement which merged ten railroad companies into the New York Central Railroad. Later he became the company's secretary, treasurer and general counsel. Pruyn was also a regent of the Smithsonian Institution.

Hamlin was a member of the American and Boston bar associations and a trustee of the Carnegie Endowment for International Peace. He was a member of the Cosmos and Metropolitan Clubs in Washington. (NCAB, WWW. Biography, John Pruyn: DAB)

Thomas DeWitt Talmage (1832–1902) was born in Bound Brook, New Jersey, the youngest of twelve children of David T. Talmage, a farmer and an official in the Dutch Reformed Church. DeWitt was educated at the University of the City of New York, and it was there that he gave the first of his dramatic speeches (later sermons) that so inspired audiences of his day. The subject of the speech was "The Moral Effects of Sculpture and Architecture," and it was printed in full in one of the New York papers.

After a period of studying law, Talmage decided that the ministry was his true calling, and following the path of three brothers, two uncles and one brother-in-law, he was ordained a minister in 1856 upon graduation from the Reformed Dutch Theological Seminary in New Brunswick, New Jersey. In the same year he married Mary R. Avery of Brooklyn. They had two children. His sermons began to attract attention while he was pastor of a church in Syracuse, New York, and in 1862 he accepted a call to the Second Dutch Reformed Church in Philadelphia. He began to draw crowds to a church previously conservative and relatively unknown. While he was in Philadelphia Talmage's wife was drowned in a boating accident; a year later he married Sarah Whittemore, a well-to-do young woman from Long Island.

In 1869 Talmage went to the Central Presbyterian Church in Brooklyn, after being offered a salary of $7,000. The church had been torn by dissension, but he was immediately successful in increasing the congregation. He was instrumental in getting a new church built, but it had been in use less than two years when it was burned to the ground in 1872. By 1874 another building had been erected. It provided seats for 4,650 people, but at times 7,000 persons crowded in to hear Dr. Talmage preach. In 1878 his salary was increased to $12,000, but in 1879 the Brooklyn Presbytery accused him of "falsehood and deceit, and . . . using improper methods of preaching, which tend to bring religion into contempt." (DAB. p. 288) He was acquitted, but the vote on some counts was close. In 1889 Talmage's second church was destroyed by fire, and again, another building took its place. This, too burned in 1894.

Talmage was only momentarily discouraged by this latest disaster. He left Brooklyn and accepted a call to the First Presbyterian Church in Washington. It was at this time that Annie Cole deeded him 1402

Massachusetts Avenue in exchange for a house in Brooklyn. Talmage preached at the Washington church until 1897. He then devoted the rest of his life to the *Christian Herald,* of which he had been editor since 1890. He had also been the editor of *Frank Leslie's Sunday Magazine.* Soon after he came to Washington Talmage's second wife died, leaving him $200,000. In 1898 he married another well-to-do women, Eleanor Collier, a widow.

The publication of Talmage's sermons was widespread; at one time they appeared in 3,500 newspapers. He also published numerous other works, among them *The Abominations of Modern Society* (1872); *Every-Day Religion* (1875); *The Masque Torn Off;* (1880); *Rum, the Worst Enemy of the Working Class* (1886); *Social Dynamite* (1887); *The Marriage Tie* (1890); and *From Manger to Throne* (1890). An autobiography, *T. DeWitt Talmage As I Knew Him,* was published in 1912, with the last chapters written by his widow. (NCAB, DAB, WWW)

William H. Walker (c. 1868–1941) was a prominent Washington builder and real estate man. He bought Mrs. Cole's "bay window" (1400 Massachusetts Avenue) in 1903. He was an 1890 graduate of Georgetown University Law School and went into the real estate business with his father, Redford W. Walker. From that time on he was a leader in furthering the residential development of Washington. He was also involved in commercial real estate; his last building was the Walker Building, 734 Fifteenth Street, N.W., adjacent to the American Security and Trust Company.

Mr. Walker was a director of the Second National Bank and of the National Savings and Trust Company. He was a member of the Chevy Chase, Metropolitan and University clubs. (Obituaries: ES, 10–17–41; WP, 10–22–41)

Alonzo Clark Mather (1848–1941) owned 1400 Massachusetts Avenue from 1907–20 but never lived in the house. In fact, he was not listed in the city directories at any address during this period. Deeds show him residing in Chicago in 1907 and in 1920. He was born in Fairfield, New York, the son of William and Mary Ann (Buell) Mather. He was a member of the distinguished Mather family, a descendant of Richard and Cotton Mather. His father was a noted geologist, and a professor of both geology and chemistry. When Mather sold the property at 1400, it was with this stipulation: ". . . that in the event it is decided to take up with the United States Government the matter of the erection of a Memorial Fountain to the memory of Cotton Mather said

Fountain to be located in Reservation 65, adjoining the easterly point of said part of lot . . . one, the grantee will offer no objections . . ." (Liber 4387 folio 423). Apparently the fountain was never erected.

After graduating from Fairfield Preparatory School and while still in his twenties, Mather moved West. He settled in Chicago in 1875 and for five years ran the mercantile firm of Alonzo Mather and Company. Then he became aware of the problem of caring for livestock in transit, and designed a railroad car in which cattle could be transported without being unloaded periodically for feeding and watering. The Mather Humane Stock Transportation Company was organized in 1881 with Mather as president. It developed into a large enterprise; at one time it was estimated that five million cattle were transported annually in Mather cars. The car had another advantage. The cattle were on the average twenty pounds heavier when they arrived at market because of adequate feeding en route. Because of the significant improvement in the treatment of cattle effected by the Mather car, the American Humane Society presented Mather with its gold medal in 1883. Mather also designed and manufactured refrigerator cars for the transportation of meat products.

Another project which interested Mather was that of the construction of an international bridge over the Niagara River connecting Buffalo and Fort Erie, Ontario. He had a plan as early as 1893 which included a harbor at Fort Erie and a scheme for harnessing the water flowing between the bridge abutments to produce electricity. The plan was approved by the Canadian Government, but Congress at that time passed a law prohibiting the construction of international bridges without its consent, and the project was abandoned until 1927, when the Peace Bridge was built. In 1926 Mather presented six acres of parkland at the Canadian side of the bridge to the park commission of Ontario, to be named Mather Park in his honor.

Mather was married three times; in 1878 to Martha C. Johnson, who died in 1879; in 1880 to Louise Eames; and in 1914 to Irene Argyle Ward. He had one child, by his first marriage, Martha J. Mather. (NCAB)

Marcus Notes (c. 1864–1951) owned both 1400 and 1402 Massachusetts Avenue. He was a native of Lithuania who came to Washington at the age of sixteen. He started out in the second hand furniture business and at one time owned an auction gallery where Garfinckel's department store now stands.

He was best known as a theater operator and real estate man. He owned the Empress, Plaza, Criterion,

Roosevelt and Strand Theaters. His real estate holdings were centered on Georgia Avenue, in Brookland and in Anacostia. He also owned real estate in Atlantic City, New Jersey.

Marcus Notes and his wife, Rachel, had six children: Mrs. Carrie Dorman of Baltimore; and Mrs. Augusta Brandon, Mrs. Sadie Schwartz, Isaac, Sylvan and Louis Notes—all of Washington at the time of Mr. Notes's death in 1951. (Obituaries: ES, WP, 1–15–51)

Alexander Robey Shepherd was listed in the *Elite List* for 1896 as residing at 1402 Massachusetts Avenut. While it is more likely that he lived in the house later known as 1404, his biography is included here because he was of such importance in the development of the city of Washington.

Shepherd (1835–1902) was the man almost single-handedly responsible for turning Washington from a backward village with unpaved streets, poor lighting and open sewers into a capital city worthy of the name. He was born in Washington, the eldest of the seven children of Alexander and Susan Davidson (Robey) Shepherd. He began his adult life as a clerk in a plumbing firm, branched out into real estate and building operations, and by 1862 was far enough along in his public service career to be elected president of the Common Council. Five years later he and Crosby Noyes and three other friends purchased the *Evening Star,* which he used as his organ. In the late 1860's he served on the Levy Court, and in 1870 was chosen president of the Citizens' Reform Association, as well as alderman.

Shepherd's idea of what Washington needed at the time was a centralized government, closely tied to Congress, which could carry out a broad program of urban improvement and thus thwart the attempts to remove the capital of the nation to a more prestigious city. His ideas were adopted by Congress with the passage of the law of February 1871 which created a territorial government for the District; and, of utmost importance, a Board of Public Works with wide powers. Shepherd became vice-president of this board and took over control of it to the extent that he received the name "Boss Shepherd" from his colleagues. He began his monumental improvement program, proceding on the basis that the end justifies the means. There were reports of contracts awarded casually to friends, and millions were spent beyond what had been authorized; but, despite increasing opposition, Grant appointed him governor in 1873 when Henry D. Cooke resigned. Washington was, indeed, transformed; but Shepherd's alleged unscrupulous methods led to an investigation by Congress and the passage of an act in 1874 which replaced terri-

torial government by commission rule. Grant promptly appointed Shepherd a commissioner; but although found innocent of any personal dishonesty, he was not confirmed by the Senate.

Shepherd turned to other things after this. He left the country in 1880 with his wife (the former Mary Grice Young) and seven children and settled in Mexico, where he managed a silver mine and proceeded to turn it into a very valuable piece of property. He stayed in Mexico longer than he had expected, and in the meantime his accomplishments in Washington had begun to be appreciated. On a trip back to Washington in 1887 he was given a parade and treated as a benefactor. Shepherd continued to spend most of his time in Mexico, however, and died there in 1902. (DAB: Mrs. Elden Billings, "Alexander Robey Shepherd and His Unpublished Diaries and Correspondence," *Records of the CHS,* Vol. 60–62 (1960–62), pp. 150–166.

LISTINGS OF RESIDENTS

Note: 1400 Massachusetts Avenue was the address given for both houses until approximately 1904; therefore, people who lived at 1402 were listed at 1400, causing much confusion. Similarly, listings for 1402 before 1904 probably refer to the house later known as 1404. Therefore, all doubtful listings in both directories and social registers have been marked with an asterisk.

1400 Massachusetts Avenue, N.W.

City directories list the following tenants:

1880 George E. Cole
1881, 1885 Annie A Cole
1887, 1889 Annie A. Cole, widow George E.
1887 Senor Don Ricardo Becerra, attaché Columbian Legation
1890–1891 Hon. and Mrs. William J. Connell, State Representative
1893 Senor Don Manuel Multado, attaché Columbian Legation
1894–1896 Mr. and Mrs. Charles S. Hamlin
1897–1903 Rev. T. DeWitt Talmadge* (sic) (Talmage owned 1402 at this time)
1904–1906 Mr. and Mrs. William H. Walker
1914 vacant
1915–1916 Jose T. Godoy
1917 Marcus Notes, real estate
1918 National Education Association; James W. Crabtree
1919–1920 National Education Association

1921–1939 Marcus Notes, real estate
1940 James Gray
1941–1943 Walter R. Landers (1400-1404)
1948 Mrs. Tommie G. Rossen, Rossen Company, Inc., Furnished Rooms
1954 Walter R. Landers; Elaine Bake
1956 Louis Keller, economist; Henry C. Flynn
1960–1971 Apartments

Social registers list:

1886 Senor Don Ricardo Becerra
1890–1892 Hon. and Mrs. W. J. Connell
1893 Senor Don Manuel Multedo
1894–1896 Mr. and Mrs. Charles S. Hamlin
1897–1902 Rev. T. DeWitt Talmadge* (sic)
1904–1907 Mr. and Mrs. William H. Walker

1402 Massachusetts Avenue, N.W.

City directories list the following tenants:

1889 Hon. and Mrs. Carroll Wright, Commissioner of Labor*
1890–1891 Dr. and Mrs. Henry Krogstad*
1892–1896 Commodore and Mrs. William R. McCann, USN*

1897–1905 Dr. T. L. MacDonald*
1914 Philip S. Henry
1915–1917 vacant
1918 Mrs. Harry Treat
1919 Charles B. Howry
1920 J. F. Webster
1921 vacant
1922 Dr. Robert J. Conlon; Margaret G. McDonough
1923 vacant
1924–1925 Delta Chi Fraternity
1927 Mario Otero
1928–1940 apartments
1941 J. Robert Hoff
1942–1943 Walter R. Landers (1400-1404)
1948 Mrs. Tommie G. Rossen, Rossen Company, Inc., Furnished Rooms
1956–1971 apartments

Social registers list:

1889 Hon. and Mrs. Carroll D. Wright*
1891 Mrs. C. P. Bacon; Dr. and Mrs. Henry Krogstad*
1892–1895 Commodore and Mrs. W. P. McCann*
1896 Gov. and Mrs. Alexander P. (R.?) Shepherd*
1897–1905 Dr. T. L. MacDonald*
1906–1908 Mrs. T. DeWitt Talmage

1500 Rhode Island Avenue, N.W., Brodhead-Bell-Morton residence

The building is located in Square South of Square 195. The property comprises the whole square, and is bounded on the north by Rhode Island Avenue, on the east by Fifteenth Street, on the south by N Street, and on the west by Scott Circle. It is taxed as lot 800.

Originally a private residence, the building is now owned by the National Paint and Coatings Association, Inc., and used as its headquarters.

HISTORICAL INFORMATION

The original house was built for John T. and Jessie Willis Brodhead on land purchased by Mrs. Brodhead in 1879 (Liber 910 folio 293). The building permit was issued in the same year, with John Fraser as the architect (No. 2491).

c. 1884
National Capital Past and Present
Hutchins and Moore, p. 301

RESIDENCE OF ALEXANDER GRAHAM BELL.

It is not known if the Brodheads ever lived in the house. The only listings for them in the city directories were in 1878–79 when they lived at 1311 Fourteenth Street, N.W. When they sold the house in October 1882 they were living in Detroit (Liber 1020 folio 211). The house was purchased by Gardiner Hubbard for his daughter, Mabel, who was married to Alexander Graham Bell. While the Bells lived in the house two permits were issued for additions. The first (1883) described an addition to the mansard

roof and a two story brick addition on the northeast corner (No. 115). C. A. Didden was the architect. In 1887 another permit was issued (No. 2224). It said: "To build an additional story and put on steep slated roof." Whether this story was to be added to the whole building or only part of it was not stated. Also, there was a fire in the house sometime in the winter of 1887: Was this work done to repair the damage? The permit did not indicate that it was. A comparison of two early views of the house, one before the fire (c. 1884) and one after (c. 1889), makes evident distinct differences in the third story, roof and chimneys. The conical termination of the tower is also different. (See "Views of Original House," below, H&M print and CHS photograph.) It is possible that the 1889 photograph shows the changes mentioned in the 1887 permit. Evidently the damage from the fire and water was extensive; Proctor says that the house was insured for $25,000 and the damage was estimated at $30,-000 (SS, 6–9–40). Estimated cost for the 1887 work was $20,000. James G. Hill was the architect.

In 1889 the house was sold to Levi P. Morton, the newly-elected Vice President (Liber 1369 folio 366). Two months after he bought it a building permit was issued to "enlarge the building" (No. 1942). Nothing more specific was mentioned, but a projection plan drawing shows a "Bay Window for New Dining Room." Morton went back to the original architect, John Fraser, for this work.

While the Russian Embassy was occupying the building (1903–07), two heating boilers were installed (Permit No. 2061); and Marsh and Peter were hired to cut a new window in the second floor, the location not specified (Permit No. 1803½).

When Morton moved back to the house in 1912, he hired John Russell Pope to carry out a major remodeling (Permit No. 4214). The Victorian bays, tower, mansard and chimneys were removed or wrapped in a cloak of Italian Renaissance design; red brick was replaced by pale limestone—the ugly duckling was transformed into a swan! (Or, depending on one's taste, the original house was lost forever; covered by a Beaux Arts adaptation of Renaissance design.)

The house stayed in the Morton family until 1936. After being passed back and forth between owners several times and leased for a short period to the National Democratic Club of America, it was sold in 1939 to the National Paint, Varnish and Lacquer

c. 1905
Washington News Co. Postcard
Washingtoniana, M. L. King Library
(Note change in tower roof, chimneys, and elimination of mansard attic.)
(Similar to, but more distinct than 1889 photo.)

Association (Liber 7430 folio 94). It is interesting to note that the price was the same as it was in 1889 when Levi P. Morton bought it from Gardiner Hubbard—$95,000. The Association made some interior changes to convert the building as their headquarters (Permit No. 229516), and also removed a two story garage and service wing. No permit has been found for this work.

KNOWN ARCHITECTURAL DRAWINGS

Bay window: projection plan. Ink on linen.
Filed with permit No. 1942, 8 May 1889.
  Outline of Bay Window/For New Dining Room/For House of Hon. Levi P. Morton/Rhode Island Av. 15th and "N" Sts./Washington, D.C./John Fraser, Architect/Corcoran Building/Washington, D.C.

Plat: outline of original building and proposed remodeling. Filed with permit No. 4214, 25 March 1912.

Porte-cochere: plan and elevation. Ink on linen.
Filed with permit No. 4214, 25 March 1912.

PORTION OF PORTE COCHERE BEYOND THE/BUILDING LINE IN PROPOSED ALTERATION/1500 RHODE ISLAND AVE./WASHINGTON, DIST. COL/John Russell Pope, Archt./527 Fifth Ave. N.Y./Scale ¼" equals 1 ft./March 19, 1912

Freight elevator: standard layout sheet. Blueprint.
Filed with permit No. 3122, 28 December 1912

Passenger elevator: standard layout sheet. Blueprint.
Filed with permit No. 3140, 31 December 1912.

West elevation. Black line print.
Archives of the National Paint and Coatings Association, Inc.
  RESIDENCE FOR/HON. LEVI P. MORTON/ WASHINGTON, D.C./John Russell Pope, Architect, New York/WEST ELEVATION

East elevation. Blueprint.
Archives of the National Paint and Coatings Association, Inc.
  RESIDENCE FOR/HON. LEVI P. MORTON/ WASHINGTON, D.C./John Russell Pope, Architect,

c. 1906
"Rambler", Columbia Historical Society
Showing Fraser's Dining Room Bay Window behind tree at center of photo. Carriage House to right.

N Street Elevation, 1912
National Paint and Coatings Assn., Inc. Compare with 1906 photo.

Scott Circle Elevation
National Paint and Coatings Assn., Inc. Compare with 1905 photo.

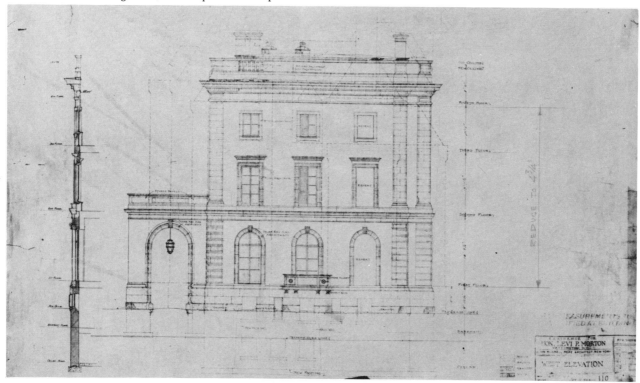

15th Street Elevation, 1912
National Paint and Coatings Assn., Inc.

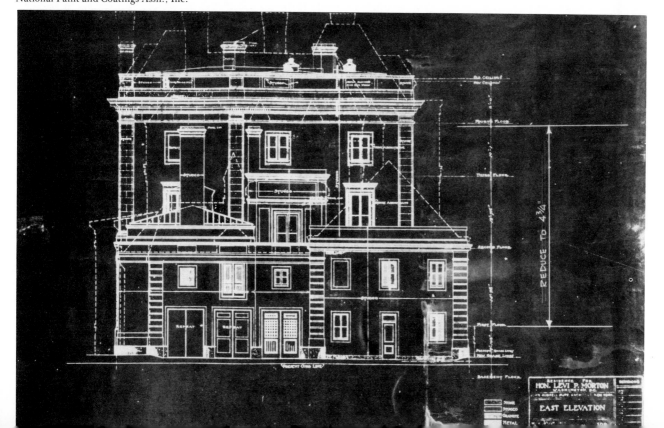

April 1970, Jack E. Boucher
Compare with 1905 photo.

New York/EAST ELEVATION
South elevation. Blueprint.
Archives of the National Paint and Coatings Association, Inc.
    RESIDENCE FOR/ HON. LEVI P. MORTON/
WASHINGTON, D.C./John Russell Pope, Architect,
New York/SOUTH ELEVATION
North elevation and main floor plan.
The Architecture of John Russell Pope, Vol. II, introd.
    by Royal Cortissoz, New York: William Helburn, Inc.,
    1928. Pls. 94, 95.

VIEWS OF ORIGINAL HOUSE
Exterior

Scott Circle facade:
    H&M, p. 301, print, c. 1884; CHS, Proctor Collection,

W. H. Seaman photograph, c. 1889; Archives of the
National Paint and Coatings Association, photograph,
c. 1900; NCAB, print, c. 1896.
Scott Circle facade and partial view of Rhode Island
    Avenue facade:
    MLKW, photograph (post card), dated 1905; Marguerite Cassini, *Never A Dull Moment,* New York:
    Harper & Brothers, 1956; undated photograph, between pp. 150–51.
N Street facade, from southeast:
    CHS, photograph, 1906(?).

Interior

Frances Benjamin Johnston photographs in the Henry
E. Huntington Library and Art Gallery, San Marino,
California, c. 1903:

Photo #1912, Huntington Library
c. 1903, F. B. Johnston

Entrance hall and stair (No. 1911); view from southwest chamber (library?) through anteroom and southeast drawing room to dining room (No. 1912); view
from anteroom through southeast drawing room to
dining room (No. 1913); dining room fireplace and
mantel, banked with palms and flowers (No. 1910).

These interior photographs were taken c. 1903,
when the Russian Embassy was occuping the building. The house is being decorated for some festive occasion—a ladder is visible in the dining room in
photograph No. 1912, and the unfinished mantel
decorations in that photograph are shown completed
in photograph No. 1910. Perhaps the occasion was
the wedding in February 1903 of Irene Desplanques
to Alexander Pavlov, the Russian minister to Korea.
Irene was the cousin of Marguerite Cassini, daughter
of the Russian ambassador; in her book, *Never A
Dull Moment* (*op. cit.,* p. 185). Marguerite describes
the downstairs rooms as being "transformed into a
garden of white roses and lilies." Calla lilies are con-

Photo #1910, Huntington Library
c. 1903, F. B. Johnston

Photo #1913, Huntington Library
c. 1903, F. B. Johnston

spicious in the photographs, and suggestions of a wedding can be seen in the bows of white tulle tied to the stairway candelabra, festooned around the chandeliers, and fastened to the floral arrangements which almost completely cover the dining room fireplace and mantel.

These photographs also give some idea of what the Blaine house may have been like originally (see text 2000 Massachusetts Avenue.) The houses were built by the same architect within two years of each other. Similarities in the treatment of architraves and other moldings are apparent—especially the frequent use of routed parallel lines. (Compare the architrave at 1500 Rhode Island, photograph 1912, and the basement moldings, with the window architrave in the northwest chamber of the Blaine mansion.) Also, both houses have similar Corinthian pilasters on pedestals: flanking the entrance hall arch in 1500 Rhode Island and on either side of the entrance hall in the Blaine

mansion (though it should be noted that the pedestals in the Blaine mansion may not be the original ones).

In spite of the many similarities in detail, however, it is interesting to note the stylistic differences in the treatment of the Corinthian capitals on the pilasters in the two houses. The Blaine mansion capitals are stiff, rather heavy, stylized—typical of Fraser's ornament of the period—while those in the Morton house are more free and delicate in design. While some of this delicacy can be seen on the fireplace mantel in the living hall of the Blaine mansion, the ornament there is rather static and lacks the exuberance of that on the Morton house capitals and particularly in the spandrels of the entrance hall arch. The flowing, curvilinear quality and the design of the flowers brings to mind similar elements in the Art Nouveau style of the next decades.

This type of ornament can also be seen over the

fireplace mantel in the dining room of the Morton house (photograph 1910). This room was an addition by Fraser ten years after the original house was built (1889) and is the latest example of Fraser's work in Washington for which there are any known photographs. Possibly the ornament over the entrance hall arch was replaced or added at this time, as it is so different from the incised, geometric quality of the trim seen in the rest of the original part of the house. A comparison with details in the surrounding area —the newels and balusters of the stair and the bookcases in the library—make the contrast evident.

ARCHITECTS

John Fraser, original house: See text, 2000 Massachusetts Avenue.

John Russell Pope, 1912 remodeling: See text, 3000 Massachusetts Avenue.

Typical Fraser millwork remaining in basement. 1973

BIOGRAPHIES OF THE RESIDENTS

John T. Brodhead (1851–1904), the builder of the house, was born in Detroit. His father was a military man, General Thornton Flemings Brodhead, who was also the owner and editor of the *Detroit Free Press*. His mother was Archange (Macomb) Brodhead, granddaughter of Commodore Macomb, the original owner of Grosse Ile, Detroit.

John T. Brodhead came to Washington at the age of eleven with his father, who was taking the First Michigan Cavalry to the Capital on orders from President Lincoln. Lincoln and Brodhead were friends. The young boy rode with his father at Harper's Ferry, but two weeks later, at the second battle of Bull Run, General Brodhead was killed. John stayed in Washington with his uncle, John M. Brodhead, a controller in the Treasury Department. He went through the public school system, graduated from the Polytechnic School in New York, and then entered the Marine Corps with the rank of lieutenant. He joined the Mediterranean fleet, and while his ship was stationed in Nice met his future wife, *Jessie Willis* of Detroit. She was the daughter of Richard Storrs Willis, formerly of Boston and a member of one of the first families to settle in Massachusetts. Willis was a well-known writer and editor, particularly in the field of music; he also taught German at Yale. Jessie Willis was educated in Europe and inherited her father's interest in literature. She contributed both poetry and prose to numerous periodicals.

Photo #1911, Huntington Library
c. 1903 F. B. Johnston

The Brodheads were married in New York and settled in Washington, but when Lieutenant Brodhead was asked to take a three year assignment in China he declined, not wanting to leave his wife and three children. He resigned his post, returned to Detroit, and established himself in the real estate business. (Clarence M. Burton, ed., *The City of Detroit, Michigan,* 1701–1922, Vol. V, Detroit: The S. J. Clarke Publishing Co., 1922, pp. 600–605.)

Brodhead was evidently financially independent when he left Washington (c. 1882). His uncle stated in his will: "I also bequeath to him (John T.) and his wife Jessie, Five hundred dollars . . . I should leave a much larger sum to them, were they not already wealthy." (Will of John M. Brodhead, Admin. No. 352, 1880). The entry in the Detroit city directory for 1886 read, "John T. Brodhead, capitalist."

John Brodhead remained in Detroit until his death in 1904. He was survived by his wife and six children. Mrs. Brodhead died in 1929. (Obituaries for Jessie Brodhead: *The Detroit News,* 8–12–29, 13:1; *The Detroit Free Press,* 8–13–29, 5:6)

Gardiner Greene Hubbard (1822–1897), born in Boston, was a lawyer and a member of a family which came to Massachusetts in the 1630's. His father was Samuel Hubbard, a justice of the Massachusetts Supreme Court. His mother was Mary Greene, daughter of Gardiner Greene of Boston, one of the three wealthiest men in America in the early 1800's. (NCAB)

Gardiner Hubbard graduated from Dartmouth in 1841, then studied law at Harvard and in the law office of Charles and Benjamin Curtis in Boston. He practiced law for many years in Cambridge and Washington, but is known primarily for his promotion of policies and institutions dedicated to improving the public welfare, and particularly for his organization of the telephone industry. While still in Cambridge he brought about an improvement in the city's water supply, introduced gas for lighting, and built a street railway line between Cambridge and Boston— one of the first in the country.

Hubbard was married to Gertrude Mercer McCurdy in 1846. They had a daughter, Mabel, who suffered a loss of hearing after a childhood attack of scarlet fever. His daughter's plight led to Hubbard's interest in the education of the deaf and to his participation in the establishment of the Clarke School for the Deaf at Northampton. It also brought about his first meeting with Alexander Graham Bell, who was working with the students at the Horace Mann School for the Deaf. Bell was later married to Hubbard's daughter.

Hubbard was much interested in Bell's work with the telephone and, typically, saw in this invention a chance to use his organizational abilities. It was he who took Bell's invention and built from it the powerful public utility which is the Bell System today. The policy of renting telephones, instead of selling them, still in use, was Hubbard's idea.

In 1876 President Grant asked Hubbard to make suggestions for the improvement of mail transportation by railroad. He also made studies of the telegraph system and strongly advocated its control by the government.

Hubbard moved to Washington sometime in the 1870's: either in 1873 (NCAB), 1878 (Washington city directories) or 1879 (DAB). He became deeply involved in Washington affairs: He was a trustee of George Washington University and a regent of the Smithsonian; three times president of the forerunner of the Washington Academy of Sciences; a member of the Columbia Historical Society; and of greatest importance, the founder and first president of the National Geographic Society (1888–97). He was associated with Bell in the founding of *Science,* the publication of the American Association for the Advancement of Science; and in the establishment of the American Association to Promote the Teaching of Speech to the Deaf. (Obituaries: *National Geographic* Feb. 1898; ES, 12–11–97)

Alexander Graham Bell (1847–1922) was born in Edinburgh, Scotland, the son of Alexander Melville Bell, an educator and inventor of "visible speech" method of teaching deaf mutes to speak. His mother was Eliza Grace Symonds, a musician and painter who taught him at home during his early years. He received his formal education in Edinburgh schools and at the University of Edinburgh; later, after his family moved to London, he attended the University there. He became his father's assistant and worked with him until the Bells left England for America in 1870.

Young Alexander taught his father's "visible speech" to students in a school for the deaf in Boston and soon became much in demand as a teacher and lecturer in this field. He also taught vocal physiology at Boston University. At the same time he was pursuing an interest in scientific invention which had absorbed him for a number of years, an interest centered primarily on the electrical transmission of speech. In 1875–76 he received patents for telegraphic transmitters and receivers, but it was the concept of the telephone which most intrigued Bell. While working on one of his telegraphic experiments he found the answer to transmitting the human voice, and in 1876—

77 received the first patents on his invention. These produced a flood of lawsuits contesting Bell's rights (approximately six hundred cases), but the Supreme Court upheld all Bell's claims. He demonstrated the telephone at the Centennial Exhibition in Philadelphia in 1876, and with the help of Gardiner Hubbard the Bell Telephone Company was organized in 1877.

In the same year Bell married Hubbard's daughter, Mabel. She had been deaf since childhood and was one of Bell's students. After their marriage the couple sailed for Europe where Bell introduced the telephone. They returned in 1878 and moved to Washington that winter.

In 1880 Bell was awarded the Volta prize by the French Government for his invention of the telephone. He used the money to establish the Volta Laboratory so that he could carry on his research for the deaf and work on his inventions. He was associated in this endeavor with Sumner Taintor and with his cousin, Chicester Bell. In this laboratory Bell invented the photophone, by which speech was transmitted over a ray of light; the induction balance for locating metallic objects in the human body; and an audiometer, which facilitated his work with the deaf. Bell was also interested in Edison's phonograph and improving the original tinfoil record. He and his associates developed both flat and cylindrical wax records as well as an improved recorder and reproducer. These inventions were patented and sold to the American Graphophone Company in 1886. After this the Volta Laboratory became the Volta Bureau and was devoted exclusively to research relating to the deaf.

Bell's major interest during the latter part of his life was aviation. As early as 1891 he was encouraging and financing Samuel Langley, Secretary of the Smithsonian, in his study of flight. His own experiments led to the invention of the tetrahedral kite and then to the application of this type of construction to other uses. He was the founder of the Aerial Experiment Association, to which he contributed fifty thousand dollars.

From 1896–1904 Bell was president of the National Geographic Society, following Gardiner Hubbard. He served as a regent of the Smithsonian from 1891 until his death, and his financial assistance made possible the establishment of the Astrophysical Observatory of that institution. Also of interest in relation to Bell's association with the Smithsonian is the fact that in 1904 he had the body of James Smithson, its founder, brought from Genoa to Washington for burial.

Bell received honors, awards and medals too numerous to mention. When he was buried at his Cape Breton, Nova Scotia home, "every telephone in the continent of North America remained silent." (DAB) (Obituary: NYT, 8–3–22, 1:1)

Mrs. Bell lived only a few months longer than her husband. She died in January 1923. (Obituary: NYT, 1–4–23, 19:4) The Bells had two daughters: Marian Hubbard, who married David G. Fairchild of Washington; and Elsie, wife of Gilbert Grosvenor, president of the National Geographic Society.

Levi Parsons Morton (1824–1920), merchant, banker, Congressman, diplomat, Vice President and Governor, was a native of Vermont. He was a descendant, on both sides of his family, from early Massachusetts settlers. His father was the Reverend Daniel Morton and his mother Lucretia (Parsons) Morton. Levi Morton did not attend college and at the age of fifteen went to work in a country store. (NCAB) He was engaged in the mercantile business in Hanover, New Hampshire, Boston, and New York until 1861, when his business failed after Southern debts became worthless. He switched his career to banking and in 1863 opened the firm of L. P. Morton and Company in New York. He was very successful in this venture and soon had reorganized the firm into Morton, Bliss and Company in New York and Morton, Rose and Company in London. It was not long before Morton found himself competing with Jay Cooke for dominance in American finance.

Morton began to have political aspirations after his London firm had participated in the Geneva arbitration sessions of the Joint High Commission of 1871, and he was in frequent contact with President Grant and Secretary of State Fish. He ran for Congress as a Republican in 1876, was defeated, but was elected for the two following terms. During his second term, however, he was appointed minister to France, after having declined offers of the Vice Presidential nomination and the position of Secretary of Navy. Morton enjoyed Paris and entertained lavishly.

When he returned to the United States, Morton aspired to a seat in the Senate but had to settle for the Vice Presidency, which he achieved when Benjamin Harrison was elected in 1888. It was at this time that Morton bought the house on Scott Circle. He also had a country estate, "Ellerslie," at Rhinecliff-on-Hudson. Much to his disappointment he was not renominated in 1892. His interest in politics continued, however, and in 1895 he became Governor of New York. He was an advocate of civil service reform and of the consolidation of greater New York. As a banker he was a strong supporter of the gold standard. He was a favorite son in 1896, but nothing came of this; in 1897 he returned to his banking house. The Morton Trust Company was formed in

1899 when Morton was seventy-six and in 1909 was amalgamated with the Guaranty Trust Company. After this Morton retired from active business life and spent much of his time traveling. He was a benefactor of the Cathedral of St. John the Divine and of Dartmouth and Middlebury colleges. He died at the age of ninety-six at "Ellerslie." (DAB: obituaries: NYT, 5–17–20, 1:6; WP, 5–17–20, 1:5)

Morton was married twice: first in 1856 to Lucy Young Kimball; then after her death to *Anna Livingston Read Street* in 1873. Anna Street was from Poughkeepsie, and was the daughter of William I. Street, a literary man and poet. She was socially prominent before she married Mr. Morton, and was a descendant of the Livingstons, Van Rensslaers and Schuylers. Her grandfather was General Randolph S. Street. She enjoyed being a social leader, and was responsible for the social brilliance of the American Legation in Paris while her husband was minister. She played much the same role in Washington when Morton became Vice President, and after the death of Mrs. Benjamin Harrison took over the duties of First Lady. She and Levi Morton had five daughters, three of whom were living when Mrs. Morton died in 1918. They were: Helen Morton, Mary Morton, and Edith Livingston Morton Eustis. (Obituary: NYT, 8–15–18, 11:6)

Edith Livingston Morton Eustis (c. 1874–1964) was born in Newport, Rhode Island and educated there and in New York. As a young girl she undoubtedly lived at 1500 Rhode Island Avenue with her parents. She married William Corcoran Eustis in 1900 and lived in the old Corcoran house on Lafayette Square. Her husband was a grandson of William W. Corcoran, Washington banker and philanthropist. During World War I he was General Pershing's personal secretary; he was also a director of the American Security and Trust Company. (Obituaries: NYT, 11–25–21, 15:4; WP, 11–25–21, 1:7)

Edith Eustis bought the house at 1500 Rhode Island from her mother's estate in 1920, and she and Mr. Eustis lived there until he died in 1921. Mrs. Eustis lived in the house off and on during the twenties and thirties, and spent the rest of the time at "Oatlands," her house in Leesburg, Virginia, now a property of the National Trust for Historic Preservation. Later she lived at 1534 Twenty-eighth Street, N.W.

Edith Eustis was active in charitable work in both Washington and Loudon County. She was a Red Cross worker, president of the Washington Visiting Nurses, and was on the board of the Loudon County Hospital. She gave the Chapel of St. Francis of Assisi to St. Matthew's Cathedral in memory of her daughter, Edith Celestine, who died at the age of twenty-three. She lost another child: her only son, Morton, was killed in action in France during World War II. Edith Eustis died at the age of ninety and was survived by three daughters: Helen Eustis of New York, Mrs. Eustis Emmet of Washington, and Mrs. David E. Finley, wife of the former director of the National Gallery of Art. (Obituaries: ES & WP, 11–13–64; NYT, 11–14–64, 29:4)

Charles Franklin Sprague (1857–1902) was born in Boston and graduated from Harvard Law School and Boston University. During the 1890's he served in the Boston Common Council and Massachusetts House of Representatives, was a chairman of the State Board of Park Commissioners for Boston and a member of the Massachusetts Senate.

He was elected to Congress and served from 1897–1901. It was at this time that he lived at 1100 Rhode Island Avenue. He did not run again and died a year after his second term expired, at the age of 45. His home was in Brookline, Massachusetts. (BDAC; WWW)

Count Arturo Cassini (c. 1835–1919) was the ambassador from Russia during the time that Levi Morton leased his house to the Russian Embassy. He was born in St. Petersburg and educated at the Imperial Alexander Lyceum there. (WWA, 1903–05) Cassini was of Italian-Russian ancestry with the imposing full name of Arthur Paul Nicholas, Marquis de Capizzucchi de Bologna, Count de Cassini. His daughter described him as "arrogant and self-centered . . . ruled all his life by his passions." (Marguerite Cassini, *op. cit.*, p. 5)

From an early age the Count displayed a penchant for gambling and women which, while not unusual, affected his life in such a way as to make it read like a popular romantic novel.

His first notable escapade involved his attentions to a lady-in-waiting at the court. The outcome of this was the lasting and violent disapproval of the wife of Czar Alexander II. In 1862, at the age of twenty-seven, he was appointed secretary of the Legation in Dresden; and in the same year he made a proper marriage. Julia Nierod Mortsew, a niece of the Foreign Minister, Prince Gorchakov, became his bride. The marriage lasted six years; then, tired of Arturo's infidelities and the loss of her fortune through his gambling, Julia took their two children and went back to St. Petersburg. When the Czarina heard what had happened she made sure that Cassini received only minor diplomatic posts.

After his divorce from Julia in 1869 Cassini married one of the "other women" in a civil ceremony and kept it a secret. As a diplomat he had to have the Czar's consent to marry, and he knew he would never get it in this case. This marriage was not a success, either; it ended a year later in divorce. But, alas, the lady felt the need for some kind of remuneration if she were to keep the story of the marriage to herself; thus the Count was obliged to send her large sums of money throughout his diplomatic career.

Unfortunately, Cassini compounded his troubles by falling in love again, this time with a Dutch woman, Stephanie Van Betz. She was a singer, a member of a family of entertainers known throughout Europe. She met Cassini when she was singing for the Czar in St. Petersburg. The two fell in love and were secretly married in London. Again, Cassini knew that the Czar would not approve of the marriage. They had a daughter, Marguerite, and lived in Hamburg until Cassini was appointed ambassador to China. (Alexander III was now Czar and Cassini's "punishment" had ended.) Stephanie went to China as "Mme. Scheele," Marguerite's governess, and Marguerite was introduced as the child of Cassini's dead brother.

Count Cassini was appointed the first Russian ambassador to the United States in 1898. In 1900, to put an end to the whispers making the rounds in Washington, he went to the Czar and confessed that Marguerite was his daughter. The Czar, who had already guessed this, decreed that Marguerite was Cassini's adopted daughter and gave her the title of Countess. Although still unmarried, she was now more acceptable to the diplomatic wives of Washington in her role as her father's hostess.

From Washington Cassini went to Madrid as ambassador (1905) and then retired from the diplomatic service. He was able at last to marry Stephanie in a religious ceremony, with the Czar's blessing, and the two lived outside Paris until he died in 1919, at the age of eighty-four. His wife died in 1924.

Marguerite Cassini (1882–1961) was the daughter of Count Arturo Cassini and Stephanie Van Betz. Her childhood was spent in Hamburg and in Peking, where she learned to speak Chinese, a knowledge she used later when she served as her father's translator. When Marguerite was sixteen, Count Cassini was appointed ambassador to Washington. Beautiful, intelligent and high-spirited, she was the source of much gossip, jealousy and adoration in Washington's social and diplomatic circles. (*Saturday Evening Post*, 12–22–1900) She loved clothes, jewels, and dogs—it was said that at one time she kept twenty wolfhounds at the Embassy. (ES, 3–12–22) She was adventuresome: She bought one of the first automobiles in

Washington and drove it herself; was one of the first women to play golf; and with her bosom friend, Alice Roosevelt, enjoyed doing shocking things such as smoking cigarettes. The friendship cooled when Marguerite told Alice that Nicholas Longworth had proposed to her. (Cassini, *op. cit.*, p. 200.)

Marguerite left Washington in 1905. Although her father was transferred to Madrid she spent little time there. In Paris she met a young Russian, Count Alexander Loiewski, whom she married. They had two sons and the prospect of an interesting life in the diplomatic corps ahead of them, when the Russian revolution put an end to the old way of life. Marguerite sold her jewels and other possessions to support the family. She opened a dressmaking shop in Florence, eventually became very successful, and spent her money as fast as she made it. The depression and a dishonest accountant brought her close to ruin, but by 1937 she had recovered to the point where the family could return to the United States. They decided to use the name of Cassini from then on as it was better known here than Loiewski. When she returned to Washington Marguerite noted that one thing had not changed: The Patten sisters were still giving their Sunday afternoon teas. (See text, 2122 Massachusetts Avenue) The family stayed in Washington for a number of years and then moved to New York, where Countess Cassini died in 1961 at the age of seventy-nine. She was survived by her husband and two sons: Igor, a gossip columnist who used the name "Cholly Knickerbocker," and Oleg, a well-known dress designer. (Obituaries: NYT, 9–26–61, 39:2; ES, 9–26–61, B5:1)

Elihu Root (1845–1937) lived at 1500 Rhode Island Avenue from 1907-09, when he was Secretary of State. This was only one of the many important positions held by this man, who was certainly one of the more distinguished figures in American history during the first quarter of the century.

Elihu Root was born in Clinton, Oneida County, New York. His father was Oren Root, professor of mathematics and astronomy at Hamilton College for forty years. Elihu Root graduated from Hamilton and then studied law at the University of the City of New York. He graduated in 1867 and began the practice of law in New York City. His ability to grasp complex legal problems made his rise in the profession a rapid one. He specialized in corporation law and was the personal counsel of such men as Jay Gould, Chester A. Arthur and Edward H. Harriman. After a number of years of involvement in municipal and state affairs in New York, Root was appointed Secretary of War by McKinley in 1899. Although he had no background in military affairs, Root became one of the most able Secretaries the country had seen. He completely reorganized the department, set up a general staff and created the staff college at Leavenworth, Kansas and the Army War College in Washington. One of his most important achievements was outlining American policy in the Philippines and setting up what was virtually a constitution and code of laws for a republican form of government.

Root resigned his post in the cabinet in 1904, but by 1905 he was back again at the request of Theodore Roosevelt, this time as Secretary of State, succeeding John Hay. Again, he reorganized the department; he enforced strict rules governing promotions and appointments in the diplomatic service and set about to allay the fear and mistrust felt in Latin America toward the United States. Root worked tirelessly for world peace, and his skill as a negotiator and an arbitrator resulted in the alleviation of many international disputes.

Root left the State Department in 1909 after being elected to the Senate as a Republican from New York. He served one term and was a member of the foreign relations committee; he did not run again. In 1910 he had been elected a member of the Hague Permanent Court of Arbitration; and after World War I, although a Republican, he was a strong supporter of Wilson and the League of Nations. He was the chief architect of the new Permanent Court of International Justice, established at The Hague in 1921. He was a delegate to the Conference on the Limitation of Armaments of 1921–22, and in 1923 was one of the organizers of the American Law Institute, which undertook a complete restatement of the law.

The honors and awards accorded Root were endless. They included the Nobel Peace Prize in 1912 and the Woodrow Wilson Foundation medal and prize for his role in creating the Permanent Court of International Justice. Outside his field, he was honored in the fine arts; he received the international award of the National Academy of Design for distinguished service to the fine arts in 1929 and was given an honorary membership in the American Institute of Architects. He was influential in bringing about the erection of the Lincoln Memorial on the site selected by the Park Commission in 1901,*[1] and as a Senator he introduced the bill which created the National Commission of Fine Arts. He was chairman of the board of trustees of the Carnegie Institution in Washington from 1913 until death, a trustee of the Metropolitan Museum of Art and the New York Public Library, to mention only a few of the many organizations of which he was an officer or member.

Root was married in 1898 to Clara Wales, daughter of Salem Howe Wales, one of the publishers of *Scientific American.* (See text, 1601 Massachusetts Avenue, for another publisher of *Scientific American:* Charles A. Munn.) The Roots had two sons, Elihu and Edward Wales; and a daughter, Edith, who married Ulysses S. Grant III. Mrs. Root died in 1928. (NCAB, WWW.)

* For Root and the Lincoln Memorial, see Glenn Brown, *Memories,* Washington: W. F. Roberts Company, 1931, pp. 65–74.

John Hays Hammond (1855–1936) was a well-known mining engineer who lived at 1500 Rhode Island Avenue in 1911. His father was a native of Maryland and a major in the Mexican war. His mother was from a prominent Tennessee family. They moved to San Francisco, where John Hammond was born. The child was fascinated by the mining activity around him and showed an early interest in mineralogy. He went to Yale, graduating in 1876, then to Frieburg, Saxony to study at the Royal School of Mines. Returning to the United States, he opened his office as a gold assayer and then was employed by the United States Geological Survey as an expert examining California gold mines. His subsequent move to the unknown west coast of Mexico resulted in harrowing tales of bandits and revolutionaries, but no gold. He worked as a consulting engineer for several firms, and his expertise in judging mining properties eventually took him to South Africa as a highly paid consultant to "Barney" Barnato, the exploiter of that country's rich gold deposits. He became a close friend of Cecil Rhodes, advising him on his investments in gold. He then became involved in the "Jameson Raid" against the Boer Government and narrowly escaped being hanged. Back in this country he became associated with wealthy financiers such as William C. Whitney and Daniel Guggenheim and developed rich mining property for them. Hammond was also interested in various hydro-electric, irrigation and oil projects.

John Hammond was president of the American Institute of Mining Engineers, a member of many clubs and organizations both in England and the United States, and a prolific writer on scientific subjects. In 1911 President Taft, who was a friend, appointed him special ambassador and personal representative at the coronation of George V. In 1912 he was president of the Panama-Pacific Exposition, and in 1915–16 chairman of the World Court Congress. President Harding appointed him to the United States Coal Commission in 1923 to investigate the coal mining industry. He was a strong supporter of a Pan-American union.

Hammond had palatial residences in Washington and in Gloucester, Massachusetts. His Washington home at 2221 Kalorama Road was sold before his death to the French Government for use as an Embassy. (NCAB; WWNC, 1934–35; Obituaries: NYT, 6-9-36, 23:1; WP, 6-9-36, 1:2)

Hammond was married in 1880 to Natalie Harris, daughter of Judge Harris of Vicksburg. They met in Germany where he was studying engineering and she music. She traveled with him to Mexico and South Africa and wrote two books about her experiences. The Hammonds had four children: John Hays, Jr,. an inventor of a number of radio and telegraphy devices; Richard Pindell, a composer; Harris; and Natalie Hays. Mrs. Hammond died in 1931. (Obituaries: NYT, 6-19-31, 23:1; WP, 6-19-31, 3:4)

Ogden Livingston Mills (1884–1937) was Under Secretary of the Treasury when he lived at 1500 Rhode Island Avenue in 1929–30. He was born in Newport, Rhode Island, the son of Ogden and Ruth (Livingston) Mills. He was the grandson of Ogden Darius Mills, a financier and philanthropist who made a fortune in gold mining. Thus Mills joins other prominent men discussed in this book whose money came from mining: John Hays Hammond (see above), Edmond Patten (2122 Massachusetts Avenue) and Senators Stewart and Clark (1913 Massachusetts Avenue).

Ogden L. Mills, who did not need to work for a living, nevertheless spent the greater part of his life in public service. After graduating from Harvard Law School in 1907, he practiced law in New York with the prestigious firm of Stetson, Jennings and Russell, and involved himself immediately in Republican politics. He was a tireless worker, but his aristocratic manner often worked against him politically. He was defeated as a candidate for Congress in 1912 but was successful in being elected to the New York state senate for two terms (1914–17). In 1926 he ran against Alfred E. Smith for Governor of New York, but he was no match as a politician for the "Happy Warrior." He lost the election.

Near the end of his term in the House, Mills was appointed Under Secretary of the Treasury by President Coolidge, to serve under Andrew Mellon. When Mellon retired and was made ambassador to Great Britain, Hoover appointed Mills to succeed him (1932); he held this Cabinet post until the end of the Hoover Administration.

Mills had a great deal of experience in the field of taxation and in budget matters, and he exerted a strong influence on the fiscal policy of both the Coolidge and Hoover Administrations. He was a staunch conservative, and after Hoover's defeat spent much of his time talking and writing against the policies of the New Deal and trying to revitalize the Republican Party.

Mills was active as a director of several large businesses, including the Atchison, Topeka and Sante Fe Railroad, the National Biscuit Company, the International Paper Company, and the Chase National Bank. He was a trustee of the Metropolitan Museum of Art and the American Museum of Natural History, and president of the Home for Incurables in Washington. He was a member of the Metropolitan Club here.

Ogden Mills married twice: in 1911 to Margaret Stuyvesant Rutherford, daughter of Lewis Morris Rutherford of New Jersey, followed by a divorce in 1920; and in 1924 to Dorothy (Randolph) Fell, former wife of John R. Fell. She was the daughter of Philip S. P. Randolph, a sportsman of Lakewood, New Jersey. Mills had no children. (NCAB; Obituaries: NYT, 10-12-37, 1:2; WP, 10-12-37, 1:2)

The National Paint and Coatings Association, formerly the National Paint, Varnish and Lacquer Association, was officially organized in 1933. It grew out of the desire of a number of local and regional paint and varnish associations (some of them still in existence) to form a national organization. It is one of the oldest trade associations in the United States.

According to the Association's literature, the purpose of the organization is "to promote the welfare of the industry, to strengthen business and fraternal relations among its members, to remove evils and customs contrary to sound business principles and ethics, and to safeguard the interests of the public."

The Association is divided into a number of divisions and subdivisions; some deal with the scientific and technical aspects of the coatings themselves while others are concerned with sales, legal matters, education and research. The organization represents more than 1,500 paint, varnish and lacquer manufacturers, employing over 77,000 people.

APPENDIX

Chain of Title

1879 Deed 26 April, Liber 910 folio 293
Charlotte A. Weed to Jessie Willis Brodhead
". . . all of Square South of Square numbered . . . (195). (Plus other real estate.) For $14,625.

1882 Deed 5 October, recorded 17 October; Liber 1020 folio 211
Jessie Willis Brodhead et vir, John T. (of Detroit to Gardiner Hubbard, Trustee (of Cam-

bridge, Massachusetts)

". . . for Mabel G. Bell, wife of Alexander Graham Bell of Boston, Massachusetts . . . all of Square South of Square . . . (195) containing . . . (11,700) square feet of ground more or less . . ."

1889 Deed 28 February, recorded 1 March; Liber 1369 folio 366

Gardiner G. Hubbard, Trustee to Levi P. Morton For $95,000.

1910 Deed 25 April, recorded 5 October; Liber 3571 folio 229

Levi P. Morton (of Rhinecliff, New York) to Anna L. Morton, his wife

". . . the property deeded . . . to party of the first part . . . in Liber 1369 folio 366 . . ."

1918 Will of Anna Livingston Morton. Administration No. 24970. The house at 1500 Rhode Island Avenue was left to Levi P. Morton. Upon his death it was to be added to the remainder of her estate, which was held in trust for her children, in equal shares.

1920 Deed 1 September, recorded 21 September; Liber 4387 folio 429

American Security and Trust Company, Executor and Trustee, to Edith Morton Eustis et vir, William Corcoran

". . . Executor and Trustee under the last Will of Anna Livingston Morton, deceased, . . . and with the consent of the majority of the children . . . namely; Helen Morton and Mary Morton . . ." For $200,000.

1936 Deed 17 August, recorded 4 September; Liber 7027 folio 587

Edith Morton Eustis (surviving joint tenant) to H. Rozier Dulany, Jr.

$50 in Internal Revenue Stamps affixed. The rate before 1 July 1940 was $.50 per $500, making the price approximately $50,000.

1936 Deed 3 September, recorded 9 October; Liber 7038 folio 525

H. Rozier Dulany, Jr. et ux, Kate A. W., to Edward O. Keller

1936 Deed 5 October, recorded 9 October; Liber 7038 folio 526

Edward O. Keller et ux, Miriam J., to Willoughby T. Lammond

1936 Deed 5 October, recorded 9 October; Liber 7038 folio 529

Willoughby T. Lammond to Edward O. Keller et ux, Miriam J.

1937 Agreement 23 November, recorded 1 December; Liber 7177 folio 105

Miriam J. and Edward O. Keller to National Democratic Club of America

". . . agree to lease . . . and give . . . the right and option . . . to purchase . . . for the sum . . . of . . . ($150,000) . . ."

1938 Deed 16 September, recorded 20 September; Liber 7269 folio 185

Edward O. Keller et ux, Miriam J., to William F. Strouse

1938 Deed 16 September, recorded 20 September; Liber 7269 folio 186

William F. Strouse et ux, Harriet E., to Miriam J. Keller

1939 Deed 9 December, recorded 9 January 1940; Liber 7430 folio 94

Miriam J. Keller et vir, Edward O., to National Paint, Varnish and Lacquer Association, Inc.

$95 in Internal Revenue Stamps affixed. The rate before 1 July 1940 was $.50 per $500, making the price approximately $95,000.

Building Permits:

No. 2491, 14 June 1879. Permit to build.

Owner: Lieut. John T. Brodhead, U.S.N.

Architect: John Fraser

Builder: Robert I. Fleming

Estimated cost: $25,000

Material: brick and stone; Number of stories: 3

Size of building: front 60 feet; rear 60 feet; depth: 50 feet.

Height: to highest point of roof: 52 feet; to highest part of wall: 52 feet; to eaves: 36 feet.

Material of foundation: brick and stone, 18 inches thick.

Thickness of external and party walls: 14 inches.

Materials of front: pressed brick and brownstone.

Roof: mansard; slate and metal.

Cornice: metal and brick.

Ornamental projections: conservatory and porte-cochere.

Bay windows: 2 stories; width: 14 feet; projection: 5 feet; form: octagonal and square.

Tower: height: 64 feet; width: 11 feet.

Projection of steps from building line: porte-cochere: 14 feet.

Permit signed by John Fraser.

Filed with No. 2491 is a document signed by owners and residents in the immediate area giving their permission to build "an ornamental brick stable."

No. 115, 24 July 1883. Permit to repair or alter.

Owner: A. G. Bell

Architect: C. A. Didden

Estimated cost: $12,000

"To build an addition to the mansard roof provided the same shall not exceed 20 ft. for the entire height (new and old), also a brick addition two stories high, on the NE corner."

No. 2224, 29 April 1887. Permit to repair or alter.

Owner: A. Graham Bell

Architect: James G. Hill

Mechanic: W. C. Morrison

Estimated cost: $20,000

"To build additional story in brick and put on steep slated roof."

No. 1942, 8 May 1889. Permit to repair or alter.

Owner: Levi P. Morton

Architect: John Fraser

Estimated cost: $18,000

"To enlarge building as per plan approved." Projection drawing indicates that this was a new dining room with bay window.

No. 2061, 30 June 1904. Permit to build ovens, furnaces, etc.

Owner: Levi P. Morton
Occupant: Russian Embassy
Estimated cost: $1,700

"To install two low pressure cast iron heating boilers."

No. 1803½, 9 June 1906. Permit to alter or repair.

Owner: L. P. Morton
Architect: Marsh and Peter
Contractor: Louis N. Emmet (sp.?)

"To cut opening in second story brick wall and put in window frame."

No. 4214, 25 March 1912. Permit to repair or alter.

Owner: Levi P. Morton
Architect: John Russell Pope
Contractor: D. C. Weeks and Son, New York
Estimated cost: $60,000

"Remodel present building as per plans and specifications filed herewith."

No. 4430, 5 April 1912. Permit for temporary bridge (roof over sidewalk)

No. 4978, 30 April 1912. Permit for temporary sidewalk.

No. 634, 7 August 1912. Permit for hoisting engine.

No. 2071, 21 October 1912. Permit for hoisting engine.

No. 3122, 28 December 1912. Permit to erect freight elevator.

Owner: Anna L. Morton
Contractor: Otis Elevator Company
Estimated cost: $400

"To install one hand power freight elevator, 2′–11½″ x 2′–11″

No. 3140, 31 December 1912. Permit to erect passenger elevator.

Owner: Levi P. Morton
Contractor: Otis Elevator Company
Estimated cost: $3000
Size of car: 5′–2″ x 3′–8½″

No. 229516, 1 February 1940. Permit to repair or alter.

Owner: National Paint and Varnish Association
Estimated cost: $1000

"Remove non-bearing partitions on first and second floors—enlarge 2 windows on north side to 5′–0″—install." "Cut necessary doors for fire stair."

No. B133295; B14575(3?)5, 19 August 1966. Permits for air conditioning.

Listing of Residents

City directories list the following tenants:

1883–1887 Alexander Graham Bell
1890–1894 Levi P. Morton
1898–1901 Charles F. Sprague
1904–1906 Russian Embassy
1907–1909 Elihu Root

1911 John Hays Hammond
1912–1920 Levi P. Morton
1921 William C. Eustis
1922–1928 Edith Eustis. 1927–1928 listings also include Margaret and Morton Eustis.
1929–1930 Ogden L. Mills
1931–1936 Edith Eustis
1937 vacant
1938–1939 National Democratic Club of America
1940 vacant
1941–National Paint, Varnish and Lacquer Association, Inc.

Social registers list:

1891–1894 Hon. and Mrs. Levi P. Morton and daughters
1898–1901 Hon. and Mrs. Charles F. Sprague
1904–1905 Comte Cassini and Comtesse Marguerite Cassini
1913 Hon. and Mrs. Levi P. Morton
1927 Mrs. William Corcoran Eustis
1929–1935 Mrs. William Corcoran Eustis, Misses Helen and Margaret and Mr. Morton C.

STATEMENT:

Fifteen hundred Rhode Island Avenue is a drastic remodeling which incorporates portions of a larger, turreted structure by John Fraser. There is evidence that much of the basement and certain exterior and interior walls as well as window and door openings of the earlier brick building still exist. (See plan.) The present limestone facade by John Russell Pope is characteristic of northern Italy in the mid-sixteenth century. The fact that the plan is not rectangular but trapezoidal is reason for the awkward spaces on the northeast overlooking the avenue. Certain major chambers (notably the salon and dining room) are strained by a false symmetry which is the product of enlarging or incorporating existing spaces and either utilizing elements or overlaying the structure with ornamental pastiche.

SITE:

Orientation: The building faces northwest on Rhode Island Avenue on a trapezoidal lot measuring 144′–0″ on N Street; 133′–6″ on 15th Street; 157′–11″ on Rhode Island Avenue; and 49′–0″ on the west overlooking the Hahnemann Memorial and Scott Circle.

Outbuildings: none. The original attached carriage and utility wing has been demolished for the east parking lot.

Paving: Paving includes a concrete areaway to the basement entrance below the west bay of the dining room on N Street. Asphalt paving has replaced the garage wing. The entrance drive to the carriage porch is

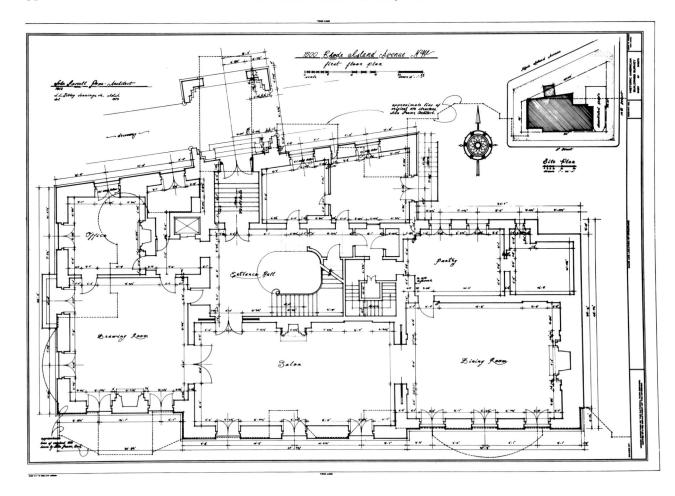

concrete.

Landscaping: Oak, maple and butternut trees border on the streets with perimeter boxwood hedges and grass dotted by juniper, yews, azaleas, southern magnolia and dogwood on the north, south and west.

EXTERIOR:

Dimensions: The plan of this detached three and one half story plus basement structure is trapezoidal. The elevation drawing indicate 52'–4'' from ground to parapet cap. The dimensions include the 78'–0'' five bay northwest entrance facade; the 46'–2'' three bay west elevation; the 110'–11'' eight bay south elevation on N Street; the 42'–7'' east elevation, the party wall of the garage wing; and the 34'–7'' three bay north elevation which breaks back one bay, 17'–9½''.

Foundations: Where the original building walls remain the footings are brick. The new construction has concrete footings and slab.

Structure: brick bearing walls with steel roof members.

Mechanical: The original elevators and heating system have been replaced.

Walls: The walls are smooth limestone except for stucco at the east service wing. A raised basement with ogee cap supports the first floor which has quoins and a Tuscan belt course cap. The basement and first floor act as pedestal for the two story corner pilasters of the second and third floors.

Windows: casement throughout. The second and third floor shutters were removed during the 1940's.

The basement windows which lack architraves have cast iron web grilles. The first floor semicircular-headed windows have fascia and bead architraves with scroll keystones and flush balcony rails. The second floor windows have fascia and cyma architraves on a raised ground with a plain frieze and cornice cap. Flush railings have been installed to conceal air-conditioning grilles. The third floor windows have fillet and roll sills and a raised fascia and cyma ground. The horizontal third floor window above the carriage porch centers a cartouche having bell-flower pendants and shell mount.

Carriage porch: The limestone carriage porch is approximately 18'–8'' wide by 17'–9'' deep. The three exposed walls each have a semicircular-headed archway in a fascia and roll architrave with scroll keystone. The first floor belt course continues around the porch and is capped by a stuccoed parapet. The interior walls and vault are stucco. There are four granite ris-

April 1970, Jack E. Boucher

ers to the entrance. Ornamental cast iron pedestals and columnettes flank the plate glass and cast iron double door to the vestibule. The entrance door and semicircular transom light have a fascia and cyma limestone architrave.

Balconies: The first floor central bay at the west elevation and the second floor central bay over the south salon have scrolled brackets which support a limestone balcony with cyma base, panelled dado and block cap.

Areaways: the southwest basement areaway at N Street is covered by a fixed grating.

Cornice: fillet and roll architrave, plain frieze, and dentil, corona and cyma cornice. The cornice is capped by a stuccoed parapet interrupted by vase balusters over each bay.

Roof: hipped slate roof.

Dormers: The fourth floor windows are concealed be-

hind the parapet balusters. The skylight over the central stair has been replaced by flooring.

Chimneys. There are five stuccoed chimneys with moulded limestone caps.

PLANS:

The building is a central hall and stair with peripheral chambers. The first floor hall is entered from the carriage porch vestibule. The dining room, salon and present boardroom are at the south on N Street; the service rooms are at the northeast via a service passage; and the office is at the northwest via the elevator corridor.

The second floor contains bedrooms and family rooms. The principal suites are at the south and the library is at the west overlooking Scott Circle.

VESTIBULE:

Depth: 10′–4″
Width: 9′–6″

The vestibule is oppressive. The space is high and confining, with risers which start abruptly at the entrance and end between columns before the central hall door. This together with a mixture of plaster and variegated marbles in muted colors seems more pretentious than elegant.

Vestibule.

Flooring: tan marble, seven risers to first floor.
Baseboard: 6½″, tan marble.
Dado: flat panels, tan marble to 1′–11″ height of pedestal dados at head of stairs.
Chairrail: 5′–7½″ high; cavetto.
Walls: plaster painted tan with raised panels painted cream in cyma moulding. Single tan marble pedestals and grey-veined yellow marble columns with white marble bases and Ionic capitals flank the entrance hall door.
Cornice: fascia and decorated cyma architrave; plain frieze; dentil, egg and dart, corona and cyma cornice.

Ceiling: plaster painted cream with centered patera painted tan.
Doorways and doors: plate glass double door to hall in iron sash with transom light; decorative grille; fascia and decorated cyma architrave.
Lighting: two, two-light, escutcheon and cornucopia sconces with alabaster bowls; applied to columns.
Heating: register panel in dado.

ENTRANCE HALL:

Depth: 28′–8½″
Width: 17′–10″
Height: 12′–11½″

The three story stair was originally a dramatic feature when in combination with natural light from an overhead skylight. The removal of that element resulted in an attempt to lighten the space by introducing contrasting paint and gilding to the large scale frieze and heavy overdoor enrichments.

Flooring: carpeted.
Baseboard: 8½″, wood painted cream; fascia and ovolo cap.

Vestibule.

Stairhall — Second Floor,
c. 1940's, Del Ankers.

Walls: plaster painted cream; applied cyma and ovolo
   mouldings.
Cornice: plaster painted cream with ornament painted
   grey. Fascia and cyma architrave, palmette and anthemion frieze; cyma, corona and cyma cornice.
Ceiling: plaster painted cream; cyma border moulding.
Doorways and doors: four 7'–3¼" high single doorways
   with flat-panelled reveals (excluding door under
   stair); cyma, fascia and decorated ovolo architraves;
   capped by friezes with egg and dart, corona and cyma
   cornices. Frieze and cornice overlaid by gilded escutcheon, cornucopia and ribbon. The 9'–0" high double
   door to the salon (pocket doors replaced by hinged)
   and the entrance door have decorated ovolo architraves.
Lighting: six, three-light, metal flambeau and drape
   sconces. One, two-tier, eighteen-light, brass and glass
   chandelier in stair well.
Stair: rises to third floor. There are eleven 6" risers east
   to the first landing, nine risers north to the second
   landing and eight risers west to the second floor. The
   closed stringer curves at the landings. The decorative
   gilded metal balustrade has rinceau monogram panels
   and a wood handrail. Each rise of the stair is empha-
   sized by a soffit patera.

OFFICE:

Depth: 16'–3"
Width: 15'–10"
Height: 12'–11½"

The smallest of the public spaces is also the most

crisply detailed. The possibility of femininity however is
cancelled by the antique mantel which is masculine in
character. The combination therefore is intimate, though
neuter in effect.

Office.

Flooring: basket weave, oak.
Baseboard 9¼", wood; ogee and bead cap.
Walls: plaster painted pale green; applied fascia and ovolo mouldings.
Cornice: fascia architrave with dentil, ovolo, corona and cyma cornice.
Ceiling: plaster painted white.
Doorways and doors: two, single 7'–3¼" high doors, wood; flat panels in ovolo moulding; fascia and decorated cyma architrave; overdoor tablet flanked by scrolls and capped by egg and dart, corona and cyma cornice.
Windows: 10'–11" high semicircular-headed casement windows in flat-headed fascia and decorated cyma architrave; flat-panelled shutters.
Hardware: faceted glass knobs and brass mortise locks, cremorne window bolts with bundled reed knobs.
Lighting: four, two-light, escutcheon sconces. One, two-tier, twelve-light brass chandelier.
Chimney: projects 5½".
　　Hearth: 5'–10" by 1'–4¼", grey marble.
　　Firebox: 2'–11" wide by 3'–7" cast iron; ribbon and escutcheon backpanel.
　　Mantel: 6'–2" wide by 5'–7", cream marble; composite candelabra pilasters support full entablature with floriate frieze.

Board Room.

BOARDROOM:

Depth: 25'–0½"
Width: 25'-0½"
Height: 12'–11½"

The chamber is large scale, both in size and detailing. Though the walnut panelling is warm in character it is not necessarily intimate. In effect the room is potently masculine.

Flooring: basket weave, oak.
Baseboard: 7", wood; ogee cap.
Dado: raised panels in ovolo moulding.
Chairrail: 3'–1" high; fascia.
Walls: raised panels in fascia and cyma mouldings.
Cornice: decorated gouge and patera frieze; dentil, co-

rona and cyma cornice painted white.
Ceiling: plaster painted white.
Doorways and doors: three, single 7'–3¼" high doors, wood painted to simulate walnut graining; flat panels in ovolo moulding; fascia, cyma and backband architrave. One double, 9'–0" high door with mirror panes; flat panel overdoor and reveal; fascia and cyma architrave, 10'–10" to soffit.
Windows: semicircular-headed, 10'–10" high casement windows in flat-headed fascia and cyma architrave; flat-panelled and louvered shutters.
Hardware: All hardware is brass. Decorative round knobs and rectangular escutcheons, cremorne window bolts with bundled reed knobs.
Lighting: four, three-light, metal, flambeau and drape sconces. One, two-tier, eighteen-light, brass chandelier.
Chimney: projects 6½".
　　Hearth: 5'–9" by 1'–5¾", grey marble.
　　Firebox: 3'–9½" wide by 2'–10½", cast iron; escutcheon and spray backpanel.
　　Mantel: 6'–1" wide by 5'–0", grey-veined yellow marble; ovolo surround capped by tablet with end scrolls and shelf.

SALON:

Depth: 42'–1"
Width: 20'–11"
Height: 12'–11½"

The largest and most elaborate of the spaces is the least effective. This may be explained by the fact that the salon was originally two chambers (see plan). The ornamentation is more awkward than complementary.

Flooring: carpeted.
Baseboard: 6", wood; ovolo cap.
Dado: wood painted cream; raised panels in ovolo moulding.
Chairrail: 3'–0½" high; ovolo.
Walls: wood painted cream; recessed plaster panels in ovolo, fascia and bundled reed mouldings with plaster escutcheon, shell and floriate embellishment.
Cornice: cavetto, egg and dart.
Ceiling: plaster painted cream; cove terminated by bundled reeding.
Doorways and doors: three (a fourth door to the right of the mantel is false) 9'–0" high double doors. Pocket doors to hall replaced by hinged. Mirror-paned doors to boardroom and pocket dining room doors, segmental panel overdoor of plaster musical instruments painted tan; decorated cyma, scotia, ovolo and backband architrave.
Windows: semicircular-headed, 10'–11" high casement windows in flat-headed decorated cyma, scotia, ovolo and backband architrave; louvered and flat-panelled shutters.
Hardware: All hardware is brass. Decorative oval knobs and escutcheons, cremorne window bolts with bundled reed knobs.

Salon.

Dining Room

Lighting: applied fluourescent ceiling panels.
Chimney: projects 1'–2".
Hearth: 5'–6" by 1'–4", marble; grey-veined yellow insets in grey ground.
Firebox: 2'–3" wide by 2'–1", cast iron; lattice and escutcheon concave surround and Trophy-of-the-Hunt backpanel.
Mantel: 5'–6½" wide by 4'–0", grey-veined yellow marble; consoles, brass embellishment with mask and spray key.
Overmantel: mirror in gilded fern, ribbon and wreath frame on raised ground.

DINING ROOM:

Depth: 32'–7"
Width: 23'–6"
Height: 15'–8"

The dining room is an 1889 addition enlarged by Pope for the present building. That the chamber is not quite symmetrical may indicate the retention of several original elements including the pocket doors to the sa-

lon. The circular ceiling fan with its elaborate grille is the most unusual device in the house.

Flooring: carpeted.
Baseboard: 8½", wood painted yellow; ovolo and fascia cap.
Dado: wood painted cream; raised panels in ovolo moulding.
Chairrail: 3'–5" high; bead, fascia, bead and cyma backband.
Walls: wood painted cream; applied fascia and cyma mouldings.
Cornice: fascia and cyma talon architrave; plain frieze; fascia, egg and dart, corona and cyma cornice.
Ceiling: plaster painted white; high cove recessed behind cornice and terminated by Greek-key moulding. Central roundel of cyma and bound bay-leaf pulvination surrounds perforated iron medallion for fan.
Doorways and doors: All doorways and windows have fascia and decorated cyma architraves. The 9'–0" high doors are mirror-paned and have overdoor panels. Door at northeast is false. Only part of door at northwest opens, remainder of mirror panels are fixed. Pocket doors to salon flanked by fluted Ionic pilasters.

Dining Room
c. 1940's, Del Ankers.

Windows: semicircular-headed, 8'–7½" high casement
   windows, 2'–2" from floor, in flat-headed architraves.
Hardware: All hardware is brass. Handles and pocket
   door pulls. Cremorne window bolts with bound reed
   knobs. A pull to the right of the northwest service
   door may have been intended to call servants.
Lighting: applied fluorescent ceiling panels.
Chimney: projects 3". Fluted Ionic pilasters on a raised
   ground flank mantel.
   Hearth: 6'–2" by 2'–1", black, grey and green-veined
      marble.
   Firebox: 4'–0" wide by 3'–3½", glazed fire tile; black,
      green and grey marble surround.
   Mantel: 8'–5½" wide by 5'–3½", wood painted
      yellow; lion-footed terms, plain frieze and ovolo,
      dentil and decorated cyma shelf break forward over
      terms.
   Overmantel: mirror in decorative cyma frame flanked
      by candelabra panels, capped by plain frieze and
      ovolo escutcheon cornice.

1601 Massachusetts Avenue, N.W., the Windom-Munn residence

The house was situated to the northwest of Scott Circle in Square 181 on lot 141. It was demolished in 1964 and the Australian Embassy building erected on the site.

STATEMENT

As designed for Secretary Windom, the residence faced south on Scott Circle, bordered by Sixteenth Street, Massachusetts Avenue and a garden at north and west. The style is associated with a school of design illustrated by examples which include 2000 and 2122 Massachusetts Avenue. The characteristic severity was without specific generic origin, though the occasional ornament often had mixed antecedents. The several sympathetic alterations and additions made for Munn greatly enlarged the house, eliminated the garden and generally improved the design.

The building of stone and red brick with slate, mansard and hipped roof was somber, bulky and, as originally designed, lacked proper focus. Details increased with each floor, which concentrated attention at the cornice and seemed to make the building top-heavy. Though the first floor was oddly deficient in respect to pedestrian interest, it is possible the intended visual point-of-view was from the opposite side of the circle with trees obscuring the lower floor. Whatever the architect's intention, however, the original structure lacked balance.

The alterations made by James G. Hill sympathized with the stone and molded brick ornament, though by no means were details exactly copied. What is more important, the richer quality of the carriage porch and the Sixteenth Street entrance additions refocused attention properly on the first floor, correcting to a degree the earlier distortions.

HISTORICAL INFORMATION

This house was built by Secretary of the Treasury William Windom. He purchased the land in May 1881 from John F. Olmstead (Liber 973 folio 10) for $10,051.80. The building permit was issued the next month (No. 1362, 6–6–81) with the architects listed as Dearing and Johnson. The house was to be three stories plus basement, 48'–6" front, 52 feet deep, with a three story back building 20 feet long

and 10 feet wide. There were to be two octagonal bay windows, 14 feet wide and 5 feet deep. The estimated cost was $25,000.

The only year in which Windom was listed in the city directory at 1601 Massachusetts Avenue was 1883. In 1885 he leased the house to the James G. Blaine family.

On 18 April 1888 Windom and his wife sold the house to Carrie B. Munn, wife of Charles A. Munn of Chicago (Liber 1310 folio 415) for $70,000. Munn received a permit on 9 October 1888 to make general repairs and to build a porte-cochere, 14 by 24 feet, at the Massachusetts Avenue entrance (Permit No. 752). The estimated cost was $3,000 and there was an architect named: James G. Hill, who was to do a great deal of work on this house.

In 1890 Munn added a one story brick addition, 14 by 28 feet. The location was not specified. In 1893 the pantry was enlarged, 4 by 10 feet (Permit No. 2726, 6–26–93), and in 1894, there was a permit for a two story addition, 12 by 21 feet, with a glass roof (Permit No. 1202, 3–8–94). Again, no location is specified, although these additions, of necessity, must have been on the north and west sides of the house. No architect was listed for this addition; F. L. Harvey was the contractor. In 1897 Harvey built an oriel window, approximately 4 by 11 feet, on the third floor overlooking the back yard (Permit No. 673, 10–28–97).

c. 1884
Picturesque Washington

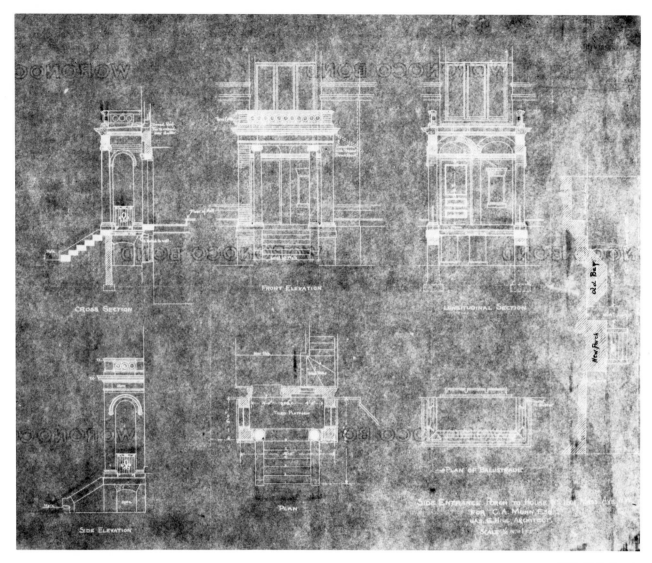

1901, D.C. Permits

In 1901 Mr. Munn commissioned James G. Hill "to enlarge main hall, cut door through on 16th Street . . . also to build one covered porch, 5'–0" projection, 12'–0" long. . ." (Permit No. 1526, 4–23–01).

More changes occurred in 1902. Two walls were removed in the first floor ballroom and steel beams and columns inserted (Permit No. 2068, 6–10–02). Hill was again the architect. The next month a permit was issued for Hill to build a three story and basement addition on the west side: 12'–6" by 25 feet. The roof was to be similar to that on the main structure and there was to be one bay window, 1'–8" by 8 feet. Cost was $3,000, and William P. Lipscomb was the builder (Permit No. 202, 7–29–02).

Mr. Munn died in 1903, but the family lived in the house until 1925. In 1904 two windows were cut into the west rear wall facing a light shaft (Permit

No. 2023½, 6–24–04). In 1906 Mrs. Munn had some finished rooms made in the attic and two dormer windows cut (Permit No. 1789, 1–6–06). Hill (now Hill and Kendall) was the architect, as he was for the last major exterior change, the addition of a copper roofed oriel window, 3 feet by 7 feet, on the second story in the rear (Permit No. 2080, 2–13–06).

The house was leased to a succession of tenants from 1925–31, and then to the Peruvian Embassy from 1932–44. There are no documented changes during this period.

The Munn family sold the house in 1945 to Cate R. Caperton for $52,000 (Liber 8065 folios 381, 383). She sold it on the same day (2 February) to Henry C. Reiner and Irving Moscowitz for $60,000 (Liber 8065 folio 380). The Red Cross occupied the building until 1946, when Reiner and Moscowitz sold it to the Court District of Columbia Club, Inc.

for $100,000 (Liber 8352 folio 359). The Club made some interior changes in 1947 to meet code requirements for their use (Permit No. 295180, 5–20–47). Estimated cost was $10,000.

The house was sold again in 1963 to the Commonwealth of Australia for $300,000 (Liber 12052 folio 401). It was razed in 1964 and the new Australian Embassy erected on the site.

KNOWN ARCHITECTURAL DRAWINGS

Porte-cochere: block plan. Ink on linen.
Filed with permit No. 752, 9 October 1888.
> Block Plan / of Porte-cochere and Drive-way / for / House, 1601 Mass. Ave., N.W. / Washington D.C. / Scale ⅛ inch = 1 foot
> Drawing stamped: James G. Hill, Architect

Entrance porch: cross section, front elevation, longitudinal section, side elevation, plan, and plan of balustrade. Blueprint.

Filed with Permit 1526, 23 April 1901.
> SIDE ENTRANCE PORCH TO HOUSE NO. 1601 MASS. AVE. N.W./FOR C. A. MUNN, ESQ./Jas. G Hill, Architect/Scale ¼″ = 1′

Partial first floor plan: showing 1902 addition, ballroom

walls to be removed.
Blueprint Filed with Permit No. 2068, 6 June 1902.
> Addition to/HOUSE NO. 1601 MASS. AVE. N.W./ FOR/MR. C. A. MUNN/Jas. G. Hill, Arch't.

Details of steel work. Blueprint. Filed with permit No. 2068, 6 June 1902.

West side addition, 1902: front elevation. Blueprint. Filed with permit No. 202, 29 July 1902.
> ADDITION TO/HOUSE NO. 1601 MASS. AVE. N.W./FOR/MR. CHAS. A. MUNN/Jas. G. Hill, Arch't.

West side addition, 1902: block plan, with some measurements, showing outline of entire house. Ink on paper. Filed with permit No. 202, 29 July 1902.
> Additions to No. 1601 Mass. Ave./for/Mr. C. A. Munn/Washington D.C./Jas. G. Hill, Arch't./ BLOCK PLAN/Scale: ⅛ in. = 1 foot.

VIEWS

Exterior

Massachusetts Avenue facade and partial view of Sixteenth Street facade: JWM, p. 257, print, c. 1884; CHS, Proctor Collection, photograph, c. 1888, attributed to W. H. Seaman. Both views show the house before addition of porte-cochere.

Sixteenth Street and Massachusetts Avenue facades:

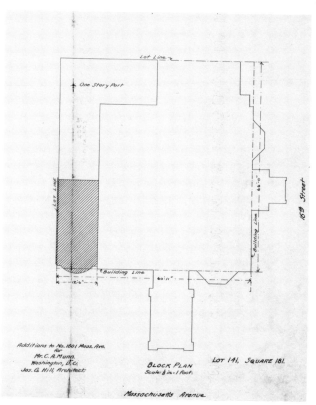

1902, D.C. Permits

1902, D.C. Permits

Evening Star, c. 1946
M. L. King Library

MLKW, *Evening Star* photograph, c. 1946. This appeared in the *Star*, 9–7–46.

Interior

Frances Benjamin Johnston photographs in the Henry E. Huntington Library and Art Gallery, San Marino, California:

> Two adjoining parlors, location unknown; photographs Nos. 2060 and 2061. Note the elaborate stencilled designs on the upper part of walls, cornices and ceilings, reminiscent of the work produced by the English Arts and Crafts Movement.

ARCHITECT

Original house: Dearing and Johnson. No information has been found on this firm.
Additions: James G. Hill

James G. Hill (1839 or 1841–1913) was born in Malden, Massachusetts, and at the age of sixteen began his architectural career in the office of a Boston architect. He came to Washington at the age of twenty-three. Evidently he worked here for awhile,

applied for a job as a draftsman in the office of the Supervising Architect of the Treasury, then left the city and returned in 1867 when he received his appointment as draftsman. He continued working in the Treasury Department and in 1876 was appointed Supervising Architect.*

As Supervising Architect Hill designed the Bureau of Printing and Engraving building (1880) in Washington, the custom house and post office in Albany (1877), the post office in Baltimore (1881) and the post office in Minneapolis, among many other buildings. He also designed an archives building in 1882 which was never built.

In 1883 Hill resigned his post following a Treasury Department investigation which resulted from charges of various improper dealings with suppliers. The evidence was strong that he was part of the notorious "Granite Ring," although the investigating committee

* Information on Hill's early career and his investigation provided by Donald Lehman, Washington architectural historian. See also: Withey (birth date and date of appointment as Supervising Architect are incorrect) and obituaries: *American Art Annual*, Vol. II (1914), p. 393; ES, 12–21–13.

c. 1888-9
F. B. Johnston
Huntington Library

came to no definite conclusions and his resignation was not requested.

After leaving the post of Supervising Architect, Hill entered private practice and designed a number of buildings in Washington, among them the Stoneleigh Court Apartments, Connecticut Avenue and L Street, N.W. (demolished), and the Mendota Apartments, 2118 Twentieth Street, N.W. (1901); the National Bank of Washington at Seventh Street and Market Space (1889), and the Riggs National Bank Branch at Ninth and F Streets, N.W. (1891); the Atlantic Building, F Street between Ninth and Tenth Streets, N.W., the Columbian Law Building, E Street between Fifth and Sixth Streets, N.W. (demolished), and the Government Printing Office (1900). A house for Calderon Carlisle which formerly stood at 1722 I Street, N.W., and the additions to 1500 Rhode Island Avenue, N.W. (see text) and 1601 Massachusetts Avenue are undoubtedly only a few examples of Hill's residential work, but at present no research has been done on this aspect of his career.

James G. Hill was member of the American Institute of Architects and was vice president of the Washington chapter in 1897.

BIOGRAPHIES OF THE RESIDENTS

William Windom (1827–1891) was both a Representative and Senator from Minnesota and also Secretary of the Treasury. He was born in Ohio, the son of early Quaker settlers in that state, Hezekiah and Mercy (Spencer) Windom. He studied at Martinsburg Academy and then read law with Judge R. C. Hurd of Mount Vernon, Ohio. He was admitted to the bar at the age of twenty-three, began practice and entered Whig politics.

In 1855 he moved to Minnesota, practiced law and was elected to Congress as a Republican when Minnesota was granted statehood in 1858. He was a Representative until 1869. During this time he was a friend and supporter of Lincoln and for a time chairman of the committee on Indian affairs. While generally unbiased in his dealings with the Indians, he had no sympathy for the Sioux, and after the uprising of that tribe was one of those who urged the President to have all the captured Indians hanged.

Windom was elected to the Senate in 1871, resigned in 1881 to become Secretary of the Treasury, but returned to the Senate after Garfield's death to finish out his term. While in the Senate his most important work was as chairman of a committee on transportation routes to the seaboard, which published a two-volume report advocating competitive routes controlled by the government, as well as the development of waterways. He was a strong supporter of railroads and of homestead legislation.

Windom fully expected to be re-elected in 1883 but was not; he was so disappointed he took a year's vacation in Europe, settled in the East upon his return and never went back to Minnesota. For the next six years he devoted himself to law, his real estate holdings and his railroad securities. In 1889 he was again appointed Secretary of the Treasury and held this post until his unexpected death on a speech-making trip to New York in 1891. While he did not make any outstanding contributions as Secretary of the Treasury, Windom was widely respected; and unlike many of his contemporaries in the Government his name was never tinged with scandal. (DAB)

James G. Blaine See text 2000 Massachusetts Avenue, N.W.

Charles A. Munn is an elusive figure. Very little biographical information has been found, although the house he and his wife purchased from William Windom and the additions he made to it would indicate that he was both prominent and well-to-do. The deed by which William Windom sold his house to Munn's wife, Carrie, stated that the Munns were living in Chicago at that time (1888). Chicago sources have yielded little except for the fact that Munn was listed in the city directories from 1875–90. During this time his occupation seems to have varied. At times he was listed simply as "agent." From 1878–79 he was vice president of the Union National Bank, and from 1880–81 the name David Dows and Company was entered after his name.

Washington directories gave an occupation for Munn only once: in 1899 he was listed as a patent attorney. The directories do provide evidence that he died c. 1904, as the listings thereafter are in Mrs. Munn's name and she is referred to as a widow. The building permits substantiate this; they are issued in Mrs. Munn's name from 1904 on. The District of Columbia Register of Wills has on file the estate of a Charles A. Munn who died in Phoenix, Arizona, on 27 November 1903 (Admin. No. 11,887), but there are no obituaries in the local papers.

Recourse to the usual biographical sources yields information on two men with the name of Munn: Orson Desaix Munn (DAB; WWA, 1906–07) who died in 1907, and Charles Allen Munn (WWW)

who died in 1924. Orson Desaix Munn was one of the founders (1846), along with Alfred E. Beach and Salem Howe Wales, of *Scientific American,* published by the firm of Munn and Company in New York. The firm began to receive numerous requests from inventors for information on obtaining patents, as there were few patent attorneys in those days. Eventually a Washington office was opened under Judge Charles Mason, former Patent Commissioner, with the name of Munn and Company, Patent Examiners.

Charles Allen Munn was the son of Orson Desaix Munn and was listed in *Who's Who in America, 1906–07,* as treasurer and director of Munn and Company and in *Who Was Who* as editor, president and director of *Scientific American.* He died in New York in 1924, and no references to him, either in *Who's Who* or in his obituary in the *New York Times* (4-4-24, 19:5), mention that he lived in Washington at any time. As his date of death does not correspond with city directory and building permit information on the death of the C. A. Munn who lived at 1601 Massachusetts Avenue, it is assumed that this was not the Washington Charles A. Munn. The assumption at present is that our Charles A. Munn died in 1903, that he was most likely associated with the Washington office of Munn and Company, Patent Examiners, and that he was very possibly a brother or other relative of Orson Desaix Munn who came from Chicago to manage the Washington office.

Richard Steere Aldrich (1884–1941) lived at 1601 Massachusetts Avenue from 1928–30. He was born in Washington, D. C., but moved with his parents to Providence, Rhode Island, as a child. His father was Nelson Wilmarth Aldrich, financier, businessman, Representative and Senator from Rhode Island. His mother was Abby (Chapman) Aldrich.

Richard Aldrich graduated from Yale in 1906 and from Harvard Law School in 1909. In 1911 he was admitted to the bar and began practice in New York City. He returned to Providence in 1913, continued his practice, and also entered politics, serving in both the State House of Representatives and the Senate. In 1923 he was elected to Congress as a Republican and served in the House until 1933. He had not been a candidate in 1932, preferring to return to his law practice in Providence. He died in that city in 1941. While in Congress, Aldrich served on the Foreign Affairs and Ways and Means committees. He was also a director of the *Providence Journal,* the Providence National Bank and the Providence Washington Insurance Company.

Richard Aldrich was married to Janet White. They

c. 1888-9
F. B. Johnston
Huntington Library

had one son, Richard Steere Aldrich, Jr. Mr. Aldrich also had two stepdaughters, Mrs. C. Tracy Barnes of Arlington, Virginia (at the time of his death) and Mrs. Samuel Spencer. Mrs. Spencer (nee Dora White) is the wife of one of the owners of the James G. Blaine house, 2000 Massachusetts Avenue (see text).

Mr. Aldrich was an uncle of Vice President Nelson Aldrich Rockefeller. (BDAC; WTH, 12-26-41)

LISTINGS OF RESIDENTS

City directories list the following tenants:

1883 William Windom
1885 James G. Blaine
1890–1903 Charles A. Munn
1904–1905 Carrie L. Munn, widow Charles
1909–1918 Carrie L. Munn and various family members: Gurnee, Charles A., Jr., Gladys and Ector Munn.
1923–1924 Gurnee Munn
1925 Frederick Lewis
1926 Herman Dierks
1927 vacant
1928–1930 Richard S. Aldrich

1931 vacant
1932–1943 Peruvian Embassy
1948 vacant
1954–1956 All Nation Club
1960 Catholic Daughters of America

Social registers list:

1888–1889 Mr. and Mrs. George R. Pyne*
1891 Mr. and Mrs. Charles A. Munn
1893–1894 Mr. and Mrs. Charles A. Munn; Mrs. Louise Gurnee
1896–1903 Mr. and Mrs. Charles A. Munn
1904–1907 Mrs. Charles A. Munn, Miss Carrie L. Munn. 1907 listing also included a Miss G. M. Munn.
1909 Mrs. C. A. Munn, Mr. C. A. Munn, Mr. Gurnee Munn, Miss C. L. Munn.
1931 Mr. and Mrs. Richard S. Aldrich; Misses Dora I. and Janet White and Mr. William W. White.

* This is very possibly the George R. Pyne who was a partner of Eugene C. Gardner, a Springfield, Massachusetts architect who had an office in Washington at the time. Pyne is listed in the city directories of 1887–1888 as a draftsman. He is not listed at 1601 Massachusetts Avenue; however, the address given may be business addresses.

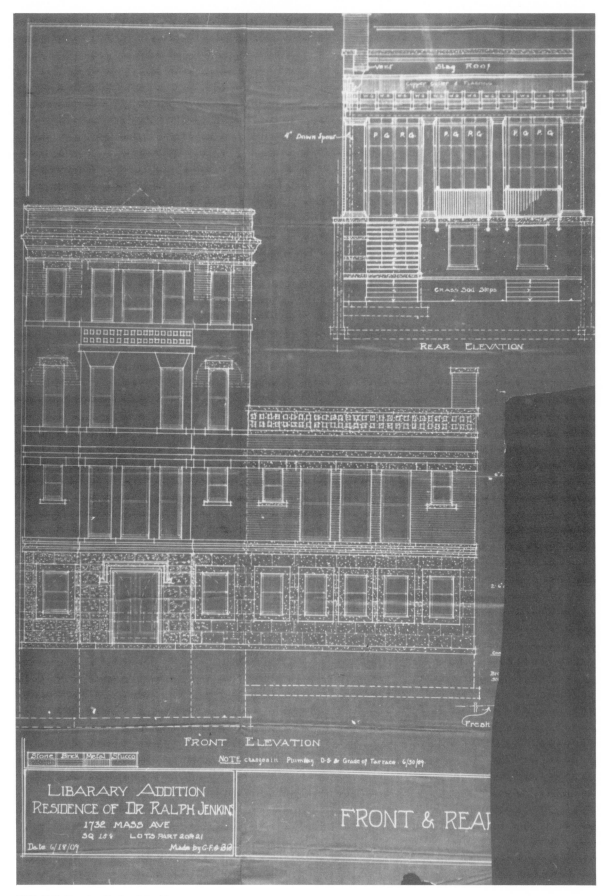

1732 Massachusetts Avenue, N.W.

The building is on the south side of Massachusetts Avenue between Seventeenth and Eighteenth Streets. It is located in Square 158 on parts of lots 20 and 21, now taxed as lot 824.

Originally a residence, it is owned by the Government of Chile and used for offices.

PREVIOUS STRUCTURES ON THE SITE

The only structure on the site previously was a frame building where the present library addition is situated. It is shown on the Hopkins map of 1887 and had an assessed valuation of only $400.

HISTORICAL INFORMATION

The house at 1732 Massachusetts Avenue, N.W. was built by Dr. J. C. McGuire on the west twenty four feet of lot 21, Square 158, which his wife, Mary, purchased in February 1889 from Peter H. Hooe (Liber 1375 folio 52). The building permit was issued the next month, with Glenn Brown as architect, for a four story brick dwelling with a two story back building (No. 1487). The permit for the brick stable fronting on the alley behind the lot was issued at approximately the same time (No. 1456).

The McGuires had been in the house about one year when they sold it in 1890 to Maria Jenkins (Liber 1550 folio 24). Mrs. Jenkins's husband, Dr. Ralph Jenkins, was an associate of Dr. McGuire; in fact, the city directory and the *Elite List* showed the McGuires and the Jenkins both residing at 1732 Massachusetts Avenue in 1891. By 1892 Dr. McGuire had moved elsewhere (1527 Sixteenth Street, N.W.) and Dr. Jenkins alone was listed. 1732 Massachusetts Avenue was given as both his house and office address, as it was during all the years he owned the house.

In 1892 Dr. Jenkins received a permit to enlarge his house by adding a four story brick addition at the rear (No. 2317). Presumably the two story back building mentioned in the original building permit was destroyed or incorporated at this time. The name of the architect for the new addition is not known.

Alterations to the house occurred in 1906 when two window openings were cut into the west wall, one existing window closed up, and a bathroom added (Permit No. 3358). There are no drawings with this permit to clarify just where all this happened. In 1907 another window was cut into the west wall (Permit No. 1337½).

A major change took place in 1909 when a two story addition was added to the west side of the house. The land for this addition, which is the east one-half of lot 20, had been purchased by Maria Jenkins in 1901 from James L. Mathews (Liber 2555 folio 218). The architect of the original house, Glenn Brown, was commissioned to do this addition, which is referred to on the permit as the library addition. Glenn Brown was by this time practicing with his son, Bedford Brown. At the time the library addition was built, the facade of the house was changed quite drastically. Round arched door and window openings were removed, the roof line was changed and the present three story bay added. Openings were cut to connect the old and new sections of the house, and some interior changes were made (Permit No. 434).

Dr. Jenkins died in 1927, but the house remained in the hands of his wife until 1940. Only minor changes were made to the house between 1909 and 1940.

Mrs. Jenkins sold 1732 Massachusetts Avenue in 1940 to the Washington Chapter of the Daughters of the American Revolution (Liber 7430 folio 594). The chapter made changes in the conservatory behind the library, removing the glazed partition which separated it from the library and replacing the original windows at the rear with a bow window. Decorative Adamesque details were also added to the parlor walls, below the cornice. There are no building permits for this work.

The house was sold by the Daughters of the American Revolution to the People's Republic of Bangladesh in 1973 (Liber 13471 folio 156) when soaring property taxes made it economically unfeasible for them to keep it. Changes in the political scene plus financial difficulties forced Bangladesh to sell it only a few months after purchase to the Government of Chile (Liber 13510 folio 246).

In 1974 the Government of Chile made some exterior changes. The steps at the front entrance were removed, as was the driveway, and the whole area was regraded.

KNOWN ARCHITECTURAL DRAWINGS

Library addition: front and rear elevations. Blueprint. Filed with permit No. 434, 22 July 1909.

> LIBRARY ADDITION/RESIDENCE OF DR. RALPH JENKINS/1732 Mass. Ave./6/18/09

Library addition: details of entrance: projection plans, sections, and entrance elevation. Blueprint. Filed with permit No. 3199, 11 November 1909

> LIBRARY ADDITION/Residence of Dr. Ralph Jenkins/1732 Mass. Ave./July 20/09/Glenn Brown and Bedford Brown, Architects/806 Seventeenth Street

VIEWS

Exterior and interior photographs: Lillian Chenoweth, "Vision to Victory," *National Historical Magazine,* May 1940, pp. 26–29.
> Dining room, library, facade.

ARCHITECT

Glenn Brown (1854–1932) was born in Fauquier County, Virginia, the son of Bedford Brown and Mary E. (Simpson) Brown. His grandfather was Bedford Brown, United States Senator from North Carolina. He was educated at Washington and Lee University, worked for a short time in the architectural office of N. G. Starkweather in Washington, and then attended the Massachusetts Institute of Technology, where he took the special course in architecture. After finishing his studies he felt that he needed some experience in actual construction; he applied for a job with O. W. Norcross, H. H. Richardson's master builder, who was erecting Richardson's Cheney Building in Hartford at the time. Hired as a carpenter, Brown was soon appointed clerk of the works, a job he held for two years. He learned a great deal about Richardson's work from this experience; in his *Memories* (Washington: 1931) he remarked: "The office (clerk of the works) was in reality a working branch of the architect's office." (p. 24) Brown developed a strong admiration for Richardson as well as a conviction that he was the only man who could design successfully in the Romanesque style.

Glenn Brown opened his office in Washington in 1880. In 1882 he became a member of the American Institute of Architects, helped to organize the local chapter, and in 1887 was made a Fellow. From 1899–1913 he served as secretary-treasurer of the organization. During this period he was active in the Institute's efforts to encourage the Federal Government to employ distinguished private architects to design Federal buildings. He was responsible for focusing the A.I.A. convention of 1900 on the development and growth of the city of Washington. This convention and the ideas presented there aroused the interest of Senator James McMillan and led, with the help and encouragement of Glenn Brown and the Institute, to the establishment of the Park Commission and the development of its Plan for Washington in 1901. Brown was also secretary of the A.I.A. committee which in 1909 asked President Roosevelt to establish a Council of Fine Arts to advise on plans and designs for future public buildings, bridges, parks, sculpture, painting and other work in which design played a key role. This was the predecessor of the National Commission of Fine Arts.

Glenn Brown was also an author. His writings varied from technical treatises on plumbing to lengthy historical volumes and included: *History of the United States Capitol,* 2 volumes (1900); *Papers Relating to the Improvement of the City of Washington,* compiled by Glenn Brown (1901); *The Octagon* (1915); *Personal Recollections of Charles F. McKim* (1916); *Roosevelt and the Fine Arts* (1919); *Memories of Washington City, 1860–1930; European and Japanese Gardens,* Glenn Brown, editor (1902); *Frank D. Millet and Augustus Saint Gaudens,* memorial volume, Glenn Brown, editor (1913).

Brown's architectural practice was a varied one and included: the restoration of old Pohick Church and Gunston Hall in Fairfax County, Virginia; the National Union Insurance Building, 918 F Street, N.W. (1890); Dumbarton Bridge, which carries Q Street across Rock Creek (with his son, Bedford Brown, 1914); and undoubtedly many other buildings in Washington. The following residences are known to have been designed by him: 927 Massachusetts Avenue, N.W. (1881); 1732 Massachusetts Avenue, N.W. (1889 and 1909); and two houses for Joseph Beale: 2012 Massachusetts Avenue, N.W. (1898) and 2301 Massachusetts Avenue, N.W. (1909). From 1921–26 Brown was architect for the U.S. Marine Corps, Quantico, Virginia.

Glenn Brown married Mary Ella Chapman in 1876. They had two sons: Glenn Madison, a painter and etcher; and Bedford, an architect who worked with his father. In addition to his membership in the A.I.A., Glenn Brown was an associate in the National Academy of Design, president of the Washington Society of Fine Arts, a member of the Institute of Arts and Letters and the Cosmos Club, and a director of the Chamber of Commerce. (H. Paul Caemmerer, *Washington, The National Capital,* Washington: U.S. Government Printing Office, 1932, p. 105; Withey, WWW. Obituaries: *American Architect,* Vol. 141 (June 1932), p. 44; WP, 4–23–32, A5:5; NYT, 4–24–32; *AIA Octagon,* June 1932.)

BIOGRAPHIES OF THE RESIDENTS

Dr. James Clark McGuire (1854–1931) was a native of Washington. He was the son of James Clark McGuire, who had been a bookbinder and then had gone into real estate and auctioneering. The elder McGuire had a fine collection of books and paintings and was considered one of the leading citizens of Washington. One son, Frederick McGuire, was for many years the director of the Corcoran Gallery of Art.

Dr. McGuire attended St. John's College in Annapolis and received his degree in medicine from Georgetown University, where he later taught; he specialized in dermatology. Later in life Dr. McGuire worked for the *Evening Star.* He was a member of the Cosmos Club. (Obituary: ES, 1–21–31)

Dr. Ralph Jenkins (1864–1927) was born in New York City and graduated from Cornell University in 1885. After graduation he went to Europe, where he practiced medicine and surgery for several years. In 1887 Dr. Jenkins returned to the United States and opened his practice in Washington. He was much involved with the Homeopathic Hospital here, and remained a trustee and adviser even after his retirement from active practice. He was the chairman of the District of Columbia Chapter of the American Red Cross during World War I. He was also a director of the Federal National Bank.

Dr. Jenkins was a member and governor of the Metropolitan and Chevy Chase clubs and a member of the Cosmos Club, Patuxent Club and the Sons of the Revolution. (ABD, WWNC, 1921–22. Obituaries: ES, 2–10–27, 5:4; WP, 2–11–27, 2:2)

Dr. Jenkins married *Maria Brewerton Williams,* a native of Newburgh, New York, who had come to Washington as a girl. She had been presented to Washington society by her uncle and aunt, Rear Admiral and Mrs. Augustus Case. She was a member of the Chevy Chase Club, Sulgrave Club, Women's National Republican Club and the Colonial Dames. She was interested in several charitable organizations here, among them the Washington Home for Incurables and St. John's Orphanage. She lived at 1732 Massachusetts Avenue from 1895 until 1935, according to her obituary in the *Evening Star* (9–8–42). After 1935 she lived at 2400 Sixteenth Street, N.W. She died in 1942. (Obituary also in WP, 9–8–42).

The Jenkins's had one son, *Ralph B. Jenkins.* He was a graduate of St. Alban's School in Washington, St. George's in Newport and of Harvard University (1919). He was trained as an architect and engineer and was a veteran of both world wars. At the time of his death as a suicide in 1956, he was a retired Lieutenant in the Marine Corps; he was also associated with the architectural firm of Mills, Petticord and Mills in Washington. In 1949 he had married the Baroness Irene Mary Ungern-Sternberg. (Obituaries: WP, 7–4–56, 24:6; NYT, 7–4–56, 19:5).

The National Society of the **Daughters of the American Revolution** was founded in Washington in 1890, with Mrs. Benjamin Harrison, then First Lady, as the first President General. By 1907 the District of Columbia chapters were beginning to think about the purchase of a chapter house. A committee was formed, but it was unable to generate much enthusiasm; its last report was issued in 1913. Red Cross and war relief work during World War I diverted attention from the purchase of a house, but in 1919 the committee again began the work of collecting funds and reviving interest. In 1924 the committee became the Chapter House Corporation. By 1936 it could report that all chapters had contributed to the Chapter House fund; by 1940 the fund had grown to the point where the purchase of the house at 1732 Massachusetts Avenue was possible. Mrs. Lillian Chenoweth, State Regent, received the deed for Mrs. Jenkins's house in January of that year. At that time there were 5,000 District Daughters and sixty chapters.

The purchase of this twenty-three room house gave the growing number of members adequate space for large chapter and committee meetings and for the chapters' many social events, especially those associated with the annual Continental Congresses of the national organization, held each April in Washington.

With the house went a considerable number of furnishings which had belonged to the Jenkins family —the library furniture, a large mahogany dining room table and twenty-two chairs, a concert grand piano, floor coverings, lamps and several bronze vases. (Lillian Chenoweth, "Vision to Victory," *National Historical Magazine,* May 1940, pp. 26–29; ES & WP, 1–14–40; ES, 10–13–40)

By 1965 the chapters were beginning to feel the pressure of skyrocketing real estate taxes. The organization tried unsuccessfully to secure tax exempt status from the District of Columbia Government. In 1968 taxes were almost double what they had been in 1965, and even additional dues failed to solve the problem. In 1973 the Daughters felt that it was no longer possible to keep the house, and it was reluctantly sold to the People's Republic of Bangladesh. The chapters are now housed at 3000 Tilden Street, N.W. (WDN, 7–1–65; WP, 9–14–68, E–1)

APPENDIX

Chain of Title

1889 Deed 15 February, recorded 18 February; Liber 1375 folio 52
 Peter H. Hooe et ux, Augusta, (of Maryland), to Mary E. McGuire
". . . the west. . . (24 feet wide, front to rear, of original Lot . . . (21) in Square . . . (158) . . . For $7,850.25.

1890 Deed 1 December, recorded 4 December; Liber 1550 folio 24
 Mary Elizabeth McGuire et vir, James C., to Maria B. W. Jenkins
". . . Part of Original Lot . . . (21) in Square . . . (158), Beginning on Massachusetts Avenue at the North West corner of said lot and running thence Southeastwardly along the line of said Avenue . . . (24) feet; thence South Westwardly and South parallel to the Westerly lines of said lot to the public alley in said Square, as laid down in Liber J.H.K., folio 193 of the records of the Office of the Surveyor of the District of Columbia, thence Westwardly along the North line of said alley to the West line of said lot and thence North and North Eastwardly along the Westerly lines of said lot to the place of beginning . . ."

1901 Deed 4 May, Liber 2555 folio 218
 James L. Mathews et ux, Sophia A., et al, John S. Butler to Maria B. W. Jenkins
In this deed James L. Mathews and John S. Butler are acting as trustees under two deeds in trust (Liber 2392 folio 335 and Liber 2392 folio 341). The land conveyed is described as: ". . . the east one half of Original Lot . . . (20) in Square . . . (158); fronting . . . 30 feet . . . 7 inches on Massachusetts Avenue and running back of even width to the alley laid out upon the plat recorded in J.H.K., folio 193 of the Records of the Office of the Surveyor of the District of Columbia . . ." For $16,880.80.

1908 Deed 3 June, recorded 23 June; Liber 3163 folio 131
 Maria B. W. Jenkins to Mary E. Scully
". . . the West 5 feet front by the full depth thereof of the East one half of original lot . . . (20) in Square . . . (158) . . ."

1940 Deed 6 January, recorded 11 January; Liber 7430 folio 594

 Maria B. W. Jenkins to The Chapter House Corporation, Daughters of the American Revolution of the District of Columbia
". . . Parts of Original Lots . . . (20) and . . . (21) in Square . . . (158) described as follows: Beginning on Massachusetts Avenue at the Northeasterly corner of Lot . . . (71) in said Square, as per plat recorded in the Office of the Surveyor for the District of Columbia in Liber 33 at folio 195, and running thence Southeasterly along the line of said avenue, 49.58 feet to the Northwesterly corner of Lot . . . (65) in said square, as per plat recorded in said Surveyor's Office in Liber 27 at folio 72; thence Southwesterly along the Westerly line of said lot . . . (65), 135.60 feet; thence still with said line of said lot, South 4.84 feet to the Northerly line of an alley; thence Westerly along said alley, to the Southeasterly corner of the aforesaid lot . . . (71); thence Northeasterly along the Easterly line of said lot, 153.45 feet to Massachusetts Avenue and the point of beginning; All of said property being now known for purposes of assessment and taxation as Lot . . . (824) in Square . . . (158) . . ."
$33 in Internal Revenue Stamps affixed. The rate before 1 July 1940 was $.50 per $500, making the price approximately $33,000.

1970 Deed 10 July, recorded 22 July; Liber 13122 folio 170
 Chapter House Corporation of the Daughters of the American Revolution of the District of Columbia to District of Columbia Daughters of the American Revolution, Inc.

1973 Deed 21 March, recorded 5 April; Liber 13471 folio 156
 District of Columbia Daughters of the American Revolution, Inc. to Government of People's Republic of Bangladesh

1973 Deed 9 July, recorded 11 July; Liber 13510 folio 246
 Government of the People's Republic of Bangladesh to The Republic of Chile

Building Permits

No. 1456, 13 March 1889, Permit to build.
Owner: J. C. McGuire
Estimated cost: $1,000
Permit to build a private brick stable at rear of lot fronting alley.
Front: 18½ feet; depth: 36 feet; height: 23 feet; 2 stories.
No. 1487, 16 March 1889. Permit to build.
Owner: Dr. J. C. McGuire
Architect: Glenn Brown
Estimated cost: $10,000
A four story plus cellar brick dwelling. Pressed stone front, brick cornice and brick oriel.
No. 2317, 10 May 1892. Permit to repair or alter.
Owner: Dr. Ralph Jenkins

Mechanic: George W. Corbett
Estimated cost: $10,000
A four story brick addition, 16 feet by 50 feet.
No. 3358, 5 June 1906. Permit to repair or alter.
Owner: Ralph Jenkins
Contractor: John McGregor
Estimated cost: $300
"Build bathroom 6 x 10 feet over present one story building—all brick—two window openings cut through west wall, one window opening bricked up and part of wall removed."
No. 1337½, 18 October 1907. Permit to repair or alter.
Owner: Ralph Jenkins
Estimated cost: $15
". . . to put one window in west wall on ground floor . . ."
No. 434, 22 July 1909. Permit to repair or alter.
Owner: Ralph Jenkins
Architect: Glenn Brown and Bedford Brown
Estimated cost: addition: $10,000; repairs: $2,500
"Build two story addition on west side of 1732, 55'–3" x 25'–1". Remove present front first story and change front on 3rd and 4th floors, remove partition on 1st floor and insert channel irons and columns, cut openings through from new addition to present house, remove chimney in 1st and 2nd floors . . ." (Work completed 27 December 1909.)
Filed with No. 434: special application for projections beyond building line, No. 80565, 12 July 1909.
"One bay window, 2'–0" projection, 12'–0" wide (door entrance)"
No. 3199, 11 November 1909. Permit to repair or alter.
Owner: Dr. Ralph Jenkins
Architect: Glenn Brown and Bedford Brown
Contractor: John McGregor
Estimated cost: $500
". . . to construct open porch 10' x 30', steps 11' wide x 12'–6" projection."
No. 5821, 4 December 1924.
Permit to install rotary fuel oil burner.
No. 5822, 16 December 1924.
Permit to install motors for oil burner.
No. 166301, 19 September 1933. Permit to repair or alter.
Owner: Mrs. Ralph Jenkins
Permit to add three clothes closets, one linen closet, new bathroom and slop sink on fourth floor and a new bath on the first floor.
No. 231240, 11 April 1940. Permit for sign.
No. 5557, 29 November 1945. Plumbing permit.
No. 22258, 12 August 1947. Plumbing permit.
No. A33320, 7 July 1952.
Permit to repair or alter: missing from government files.

The following permits are concerned solely with repairs and alterations to the stable-garage at the rear of 1732.
No. 1709, 9 May 1904
No. 5275, 13 May 1912
No. 3356, 7 February 1916
No. 146263, 2 September 1931

Listings of Residents

City directories list the following tenants:

1890 James C. McGuire, physician
1891 James C. McGuire, physician; Ralph Jenkins, physician
1892–1927 Ralph Jenkins, physician and surgeon, sometimes listed as orthopedic surgeon. Listings from 1903–1906 read, "Shepherd and Jenkins, real estate; and those for 1912–1913, "Ralph Jenkins, president, 808 17th, N.W." The listings from 1917–1923 show some confusion between Ralph Jenkins, physician, and his son, Ralph B. Jenkins, who was not a physician.
1928–1930 Mrs. Maria B. Jenkins or Mrs. Ralph Jenkins
1931 Mrs. Brice Allen
1932 Ralph Jenkins; Mrs. Bryce Allen
1933–1934 Ralph Jenkins (probably Mrs. or perhaps her son)
1935–1937 vacant
1938–1940 Mrs. Maria Jenkins
1941–1973 Daughters of the American Revolution, The Washington Chapter

Social registers list:

1891 Dr. and Mrs. J. C. McGuire; Dr. Ralph Jenkins
1894 Mrs. Ernest Lord Kinney, Miss Kinney, Miss Ethel Kinney; Miss Catlin, Miss Clara Catlin
1896–1915 Dr. and Mrs. Ralph Jenkins
1916–1918 Dr. and Mrs. Ralph (B.?) Jenkins
1927 Dr. and Mrs. Ralph Jenkins
1929–1931 Mrs. Ralph Jenkins
1932–1935 Mrs. Ralph Jenkins, 135 E. 74th Street, New York City

STATEMENT:

The dark brick and sandstone structure is austere Art Nouveau (rather than whimsical, sinuous or organic) though many interior elements are related to the Arts and Crafts movement especially as seen in the work of Arthur Little, and McKim, Mead and White in the 1880's, and Frank Lloyd Wright just after 1900.

SITE:

Orientation: The building faces north on a lot measuring 49'–7" on Massachusetts Avenue; approximately 135'–8" along the east party wall; approximately 55'–0" on the south alley; and 153'–6" along the west party line.
Enclosures: 7'–0" high wooden alley fence; a brick wall between the service areaway and the garden of the library wing.

June, 1974

Paving: an elliptical concrete driveway with limestone
curbing to the entrance terrace (raised and paved level
with terrace in 1974). A drive connects the south
alley to the paved area between the house and the
back building.

Outbuildings: At the southeast corner of the lot is a
brick, tin-roofed, two story garage and apartment, 20'–
0'' by 40'–0''.

Landscaping: front yard (now paved): hemlocks and
English ivy. Rear yard: overgrown with scrub, remains of privet hedge and lawn (likely destroyed May
1974).

May, 1974

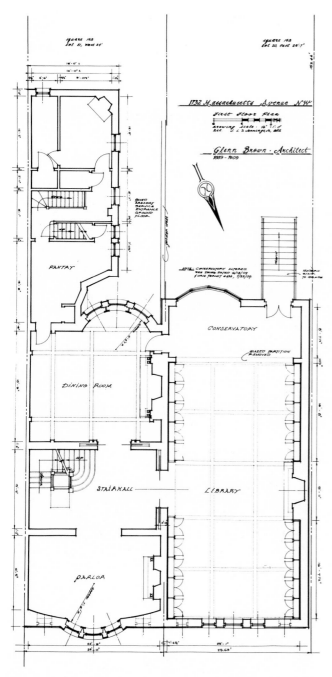

EXTERIOR:

Dimensions: The four story structure with basement is 44′–0″ high, 24′–0″ wide and approximately 50′–5″ deep (including the 4′–9″ addition (1892) to the dining room). The southeast service wing (1892) is 16′–0″ wide by 39′–5″. The two story library addition (1909) is 25′–1″ wide by approximately 55′–4″, including the rebuilt conservatory. (See plan.)

Foundations: brick.

Structure: brick bearing walls and steel beams.

Walls: The ground floor has range-coursed sandstone facing and the upper stories are brick divided by sandstone string courses acting as window sill. The first floor is accentuated by belt courses at both window sill and lintel.

Doorways and doors: The Massachusetts Avenue entrance has a glazed double door, wood frame, and sandstone architrave with drip mould and label stops.

Windows: single-light, double-hung, wood sash. The ground floor windows have unadorned block architraves.

Areaway: An areaway divides the east service addition from the grounds.

Terrace: The 10′–0″ by 30′–0″ brick entrance terrace has sandstone balustrade and treads. The 11′–0″ wide treads are centered on the property.

Cornice: The four story structure has a sandstone entablature with a diminutive architrave, plain frieze and cove cornice surmounted by a brick parapet and sandstone cap. The two story west wing is capped by a sandstone block balustrade.

Roof: asphalt and gravel roofing except the rear addition which has tin.

Chimneys: There are five brick chimneys with sandstone caps.

PLANS:

The ground floor vestibule bow is centered on the asymmetrical entrance hall. On the east, beneath the main stair, is a corridor through to the service wing. West of the stair is a door to the breakfast room. West of the hall is the billiard room.

From the stairhall on the first floor is the parlor to the front, the library to west (above the billiard room) and the dining room on the rear beyond which is the pantry, service stair, and a bedroom and bath. (See plan.)

Several of the bedrooms on the second and third floors are connected by baths.

ENTRANCE HALL:

Width: 22′–9″
Depth: 28′–2″
Height: 7′–11″

The dark, intimate space has a wood wainscot and beamed ceiling which contrast with the small amount of white plaster walls, making the room seem darker and smaller than in reality. The low ceiling forces the eye down and the transverse beams seem to bring the stair forward. The stair has direction and movement, catching the eye with wider treads at the base and drawing it to the light filtering down from the skylit stair well.

Entrance Hall

Flooring: 2″, oak.

Baseboard: 5″, walnut.

Wainscot: 6′–0″ high, walnut; raised panels, fluted Tuscan pilasters.

Walls: plaster painted white.

Cornice: wood, denticulated.

Ceiling: plaster painted white; divided by transverse beams.

Doorways and doors: 7′–0″ high; raised walnut panels.

Hardware: brass doorknobs and pulls, rectangular escutcheons.

Lighting: entrance and billiard room doorways flanked by two-light pewter sconces converted from gas.

Chimney:

    Hearth: 5′–10″ by 2′–0″; olive-green glazed tile.

    Firebox: 3′–0½″ wide by 2′–5″; cast iron, late Gothic scenes of richly dressed people.

    Mantel: flanked by pilasters, glazed ochre tile surround, flat frieze flanked by decorative scrolls below acanthus modillions which support a corona and cyma shelf 5′–10″ wide by 5′–3½″ by 10½″.

Stair: The stair is walnut. The typical 3′–4½″ wide step has a 7½″ riser and 10½″ tread.

Entrance Hall

First Floor Hall

Parlor

BILLIARD ROOM:

Width: 23'–1"
Depth: 43'–2½"
Height: 7'–11"

The room has characteristics similar to the entrance hall. The lack of decorative distractions, the maintenance of dark intimacy, and the central focus of attention achieves an informal masculinity. Each detail is functional to the extent that the mantel is reduced to pegged stiles and rails. Since the predominant wall material is plaster painted white, the ceiling with its dark wood beams looks lower than in reality. This, together with the great length and width of the room and the abnormally high chairrail apparently lower the ceiling height. The bank of high windows at the north wall prevents sufficient light from reflecting off the plaster. The resultant dimness, the difficulty in looking out, and the seemingly low ceiling force the eye down.

Floor: 2", oak.
Baseboard 10½", walnut; chamfered cap.
Chairrail: 3'–7½" high, walnut; acts as window sill.
Walls: plaster painted white.
Ceiling: plaster painted white; panelled wood beams.
Doorways and doors: 7'–0" high, raised panels, fascia and chamfer architraves. The hall door has a raised panel jamb.
Hardware: brass; knobs and pulls, mortise locks, rectangular escutcheons.

Lighting: seven, two-light, brass sconces converted from gas.
Chimney, projects 1'–0".
   Hearth: (with peripheral 1'–10" high seat) 8'–3½" by 2'–2½", olive-green, glazed tile.
   Firebox: 3'–5" wide by 2'–6" high, fire tile.
   Mantel carriage: 6'–9½" wide by 6½" deep, olive-green tile surround, plinths support wood stiles and rails.
   Mantel shelf: 7'–7" wide by 4'–6" by 1'–1", wood; chamfered and supported by brackets.

FIRST FLOOR HALL:

Width: 21'–9"
Depth: 13'–3"
Height: 10'–10½"

From the ground floor approach to the stark central hall, attention is directed counterclockwise to the parlor (the only space without doors), the library and the dining room. The white walls and ceiling contrast sharply with the wood staircase; the dark color and sweep of the treads is accentuated by the skylight two floors above.

Floor: herringbone, oak.
Baseboard: 10", walnut; ogee cap.
Chairrail: 3'–8½" high, walnut.
Walls: plaster painted white.
Cornice: (similar to parlor) cove between mouldings.
Ceiling: plaster painted white.
Lighting: five-light candelabrum, gilded metal.

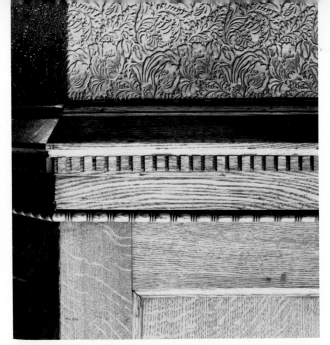

Dining Room

PARLOR:

Width: 22'–9"
Depth: 15'–6" (includes bow)
Height: 10'–10"

The parlor (or reception room), painted light pink, is a pastiche of details without stylistic unity. The firebox is Gothic, the mantel Romanesque, the frieze late Georgian, the cornice Victorian and the ceiling Adamesque. The curved north wall and the side windows which are too high from the floor are without apparent purpose.

Floor: herringbone, oak.
Baseboard: 10", wood, cyma cap.
Walls: plaster painted pink.
Cornice: 1'–8" high frieze, cove between mouldings.
Ceiling: plaster, central oval of applied ornament.
Doorways and doors: 9'–4½" high plaster archway to hall.
Windows: raised panels below shuttered windows of bow. The window architrave flanking the bow have patera corner blocks.
Lighting: two sconces have been removed. The exposed outlets show adaption from gas to electricity.
Chimney: projects 1'–1½".
  Hearth: 6'–10½" by 1'–8½", glazed yellow tile.
  Firebox: 2'–9¼" wide by 2'–2¼", cast iron, late French Gothic scenes of richly dressed people.
  Mantel: 6'–10" wide by 5'–6½", tile surround, detached 5½" square plinths support fluted composite columns and oak leaf cushion frieze 11¼" deep.

DINING ROOM:

Width: 22'–9"
Depth: 22'–9" (includes bow)
Height: 10'–11"

The present space is the result of a 4'–9" addition (1892) to the depth of the original room. The design is both rich and dark. Intimate masculinity was achieved with a gilded high relief plaster frieze; pressed leather (painted ochre); and natural oak for the wainscot, ceiling, fluted pilasters and door and window architraves.

Flooring: herringbone, oak.
Baseboard: 11", oak, torus and scotia cap.
Wainscot: 5'–0" high, flat panels, astragal and dentil rail.
Walls: pressed leather, peony pattern, painted ochre.
Cornice: 10" plaster frieze painted gold, floriate.
Ceiling: oak panels and beams with astragal.
Doorways and doors: hidden door to pantry at southeast. Glazed door to conservatory at southwest. Pocket double door to hall 5'–9½" by 8'–0", flanked by paired pilasters.

Dining Room

Windows: panelled and louvered shutters at bow with architraves having patera corner blocks.
Hardware: brass. Door pulls and ornamented conservatory door handle for cremone bolt.
Lighting: three, two-light, brass sconces converted from gas.
Chimney: projects 1'–8".
  Hearth: 9'–10" by 2'–2¼", glazed brown brick.
  Firebox: 4'–2" by 2'–6", fire brick.
  Mantel: 10'–7½" wide; 4¼" square plinths support paired columns 4'–2" high for a fascia architrave and a denticulated shelf 1'–1½" deep over the columns and 9½" at the center.
Overmantel: beveled mirror in astragal.

Dining Room

Library

Library

LIBRARY:

Width: 23′–1″
Depth: 43′–2½″
Height: 12′–2″

The library is a large, masculine room which is made airy by the high ceiling, white walls, and windows at opposite ends. Counterpoints of chimney wall opposite doorway opening and white plaster walls

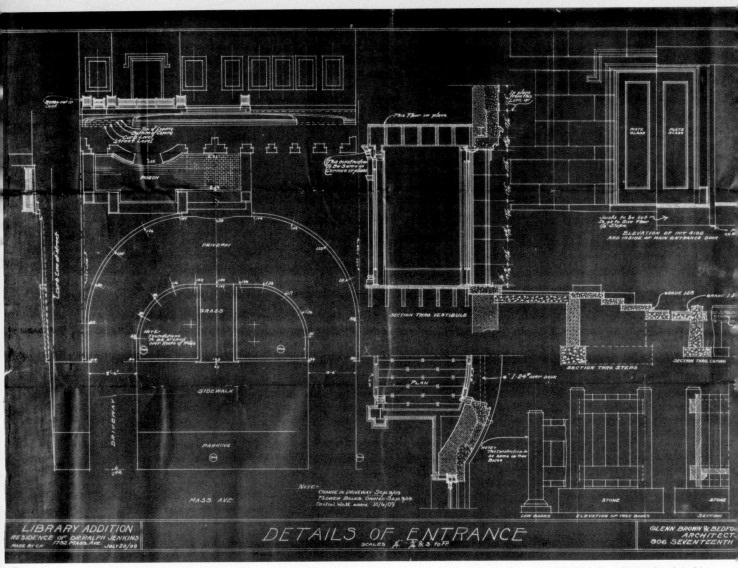

1909, D.C. Permits, National Archives

versus walnut cabinets below are the important factors rather than any applied ornamentation. The beams achieve a subtle balance by drawing the design together and breaking up the expanse of ceiling which would otherwise overpower the room.

Flooring: 2″, oak.
Baseboard: 9½″, walnut, ogee cap.
Bookcabinets: 4′–6¼″ high, built-in, walnut, burled walnut veneer counters, glazed doors.
Walls: plaster painted white.
Cornice: walnut, fascia.
Ceiling: plaster painted white, 7″ deep beams with flat burled walnut soffit panels.
Lighting: two sconces at chimney and two at door, removed.

Chimney: projects 1′–3″.
  Hearth: 9′–9″ by 1′–6″, slate.
  Firebox: 4′–4″ wide by 3′–½″, fire tile.
  Fire surround: 5′–10″ wide by 4′–6½″, cast stone, fascia and cyma.
  Mantel: 7′–4″ wide by 5′–5½″, walnut, Tuscan semi-pilasters supporting glyph frieze and denticulated shelf 9½″ deep.
Heating: The north central bay has window sill and dado brass registers.
Doorways and doors: pocket double door to hall, 7′–3″ wide by 9′–4″, wanut; panelled burled walnut jamb, sides and overdoor.
Windows: louvered shutters at windows flanking north bay.
Hardware: brass door pulls.

1826 Massachusetts Avenue, N.W. and 1347 Connecticut Avenue, N.W.
The Hopkins-Miller House

The Hopkins-Miller double house was situated to the southeast of Dupont Circle, at the intersection of Connecticut and Massachusetts Avenues. It was located in Square 137; the Miller house on lot 12 and the Hopkins house on lot 13. The Miller house was demolished in 1912 and a bank, now the Guardian Federal Savings and Loan, built on the site. The Hopkins house was not razed until 1948; the site is also part of the bank property.

STATEMENT

The mirror-image residences were designed as one structure. The raised basement, two and one-half story building had hip, mansard and gable roofs. The attic terraces, balconies and oversized windows made this an unusually important floor. Certain of the details which most readily defined the character have various antecedents, such as sixteenth century Belgium (gables with fractables), seventeenth century England (fenestration and balustrades) and Islam (second floor corner balconies with cusped arches). Construction was of common bond red brick with brick and stone coping, fishscale tile roof, wood balconies and porches, louvered shutters and copper gutters. Brick string courses delineated floors and window sills.

Of greatest importance was the facade overlooking the circle. Openings from both residences were set in diagonal walls and recessed behind shared archways. A very careful balance was achieved by using the first floor balcony as a brick base for the more elaborate balconies directly above. Acting as a bridge, the attic balcony linked the flanking chimneys with the result that chimneys and balconies became one related design (rather than separate elements) and verticality was reduced by increasing the "weight" of the elements with each higher floor.

HISTORICAL INFORMATION

The double house at 1826 Massachusetts Avenue and 1347 Connecticut Avenue was built in 1880 on land purchased in March of that year from Robert I. Fleming. Lot 12 was sold to Katherine Miller

(Liber 933 folio 331) and lot 13 to Charlotte E. Hopkins (Liber 933 folio 333). The price of each lot was $3,500. Katherine was married to Jacob W. Miller and Charlotte to Archibald Hopkins. They were sisters, according to *Harper's New Monthly Magazine* (Vol. LXX (March 1885), p. 528), and desired separate but adjoining houses.

J. Cleveland Cady of New York was selected as the architect, and building permits were issued 29 March 1880 (No. 1154 for Hopkins; No. 1155 for Miller). The permits described each house as being brick, three stories, 25 feet long by 55 feet deep. The estimated cost for each was $9,000. The builder was Robert I. Fleming, who had sold the land to Hopkins and Miller.

The Millers seem never to have lived in their house. There are no listings in the city directories for them at that address, or at any other address. The *Harper's* article refers to Miller as "Lieutenant Miller," and the building permit gives the owner's name as "Lieut. J. W. Miller, U.S.N." Possibly Jacob Miller was transferred to another post soon after the house was built and never returned to Washington.

In 1895 the house was sold by Katherine Miller (then of New York City) to Mary T. Aldis (Liber 2014 folio 87). Mrs. Aldis (and later her son, Owen) made several changes in the house. In 1903 the old

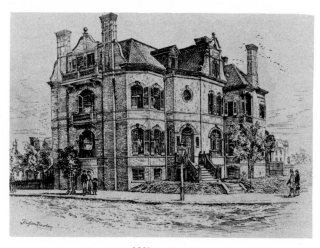

c. 1885
Harpers' New Monthly Magazine, Vol. LXX

wood steps were replaced by a brick and stone porch and steps (Permit No. 414, 9–4–03). Hornblower and Marshall were the architects. Minor interior repairs and alterations were made a few years later (Permits Nos. 1166, 10–20–05 and 1632, 11–10–06). In 1907 a permit was issued for a three story brick addition, 24 by 42 feet, to be added at the rear of the house. There was to be a bay 5 by 16 feet. Again, Hornblower and Marshall were the architects. William P. Lipscomb was the builder, and the estimated cost was $14,000 (Permit No. 3390, 4–27–07). In 1908 Hornblower and Marshall built "an additional story on the south portion." The permit states that "there will be no brickwork" on the addition and also that "the mansard roof will be covered with tiles." Estimated cost was $2,500 (Permit No. 5, 7–1–08). The balcony on the Dupont Circle facade was repaired and the original balustrade replaced in 1911 (Permit No. 2307, 11–1–11).

By early 1912, however, Owen Aldis decided to sell the house. It was sold in March to E. Olivia Johnson (Liber 3503 folio 449) and then by her to the United States Trust Company (Liber 3520 folio 276). The Trust Company razed the house in order to erect a bank on the site (Permit No. 847, 8–9–12). The building is now owned by the Guardian Federal Savings and Loan.

The Hopkins' occupied their house until he died in 1926 and she in 1935. The only documented alteration to the house while they owned it was the construction of an areaway, approximately 4 by 29 feet, to keep dampness from the wall. This was done in 1899 (Permit No. 441, 9–7–99). Mrs. Hopkins willed the house to her children, Amos and Charlotte (Patterson). (Will of Charlotte E. Hopkins, Admin. No. 48, 853) After 1935 only minor changes were made, primarily when the basement was converted to a flower shop in 1936. The Hopkins children did not live in the house and sold it in 1945 to Jerry Maiatico (Liber 8067 folio 31). He bought the Patten house at 2122 Massachusetts Avenue at about the same time. Maiatico razed the Hopkins house in 1948 (Permit No. 313271, 11–10–48). The site is now owned by the Guardian Federal Savings and Loan.

KNOWN ARCHITECTURAL DRAWINGS

Porch: plan and elevations. Blueprint. Filed with permit No. 414, 4 September 1903.

> Sketch for porch for/MR. OWEN F. ALDIS/1347 Connecticut Ave./Scale: ½ inch = 1 foot July 14, 1903/Hornblower and Marshall, Architects

Plat, showing configuration of 1347 Connecticut Avenue with 1907 addition and some measurements. Filed with permit No. 3390, 29 April 1907.

Addition: front elevation. Blueprint. Filed with permit No. 3390, 29 April 1907.

> ADDITIONS AND ALTERATIONS/HOUSE OF MR. OWEN F. ALDIS/No. 1347 Conn. Ave./Hornblower and Marshall, Architects/Drawing No. 5A/Scale: ¼″ = 1′–0″/Date: Dec. 15, 1906

Addition: projections, section and plan. Ink on linen. Filed with permit No. 3390, 29 April 1907.

> ADDITIONS AND ALTERATIONS/HOUSE OF MR. OWEN F. ALDIS/No. 1347 Conn. Ave., N.W./Hornblower and Marshall, Architects/Drawing No. 8A/Scale: ¼″ = 1 ft./Dec. 17, 1906

VIEWS

Exterior

Connecticut Avenue and Dupont Circle facades (1347 Connecticut Avenue):

> *Harper's New Monthly Magazine,* Vol. LXX (March 1885), p. 528; print.

Dupont Circle and Connecticut Avenue facades (primarily 1347 Connecticut Avenue):

> CHS, Proctor Collection, photograph attributed to W. H. Seaman, c. 1889.

Massachusetts Avenue and Dupont Circle facades (1826 Massachusetts Avenue):

> WDN, 3–28–46, photograph.

ARCHITECT

J. Cleveland Cady (1837–1919) was born in Providence, Rhode Island. He graduated from Trinity College and studied architecture in New York City. He worked as a draftsman with several leading architectural firms, one of which was Town and Davis.

In 1870 he opened his own practice. His first partner was William S. Gregory. This partnership produced a number of college buildings: Dwight Hall, the Chittenden Library and several dormitories (all at Yale) among others. Later in his career Cady designed buildings for Williams and Wesleyan colleges, and for his alma mater, Trinity. It was to Trinity that he left his architectural library, consisting of 375 volumes and 2,000 photographs, one of the most important in the country.

In the 1880's Cady's firm was known as Cady, Berg and See. This firm designed many public and religious structures in the New York City area, including: The Brooklyn Academy of Design (with Henry M. Congdon); The American Museum of Natural History (the first building of the group facing 77th Street); Hudson Street Hospital; Skin and Cancer Hospital, Bellevue Medical School; Madison Avenue Hospital (the rebuilding after a fire); St.

c. 1889
Columbia Historical Society
W. H. Seaman

Andrews Methodist Church, West 76th Street; Park Avenue Methodist Church at 85th Street; South Presbyterian Church, Morristown, New Jersey; Webb Memorial Chapel, Madison, New Jersey.

Probably the most outstanding example of his work was the old Metropolitan Opera House, opened in 1883. It was destroyed by fire and rebuilt in 1903 by Carrère and Hastings.

In Washington Cady is best known for his Presbyterian Church of the Covenant, now demolished, which stood at Connecticut Avenue and N Street. Cady was a devoted member of the Presbyterian Church and held the position of Superintendent of the Sunday School at the Church of the Covenant in New York for fifty-three years. He was a governor of the Presbyterian Hospital (New York), a trustee of Berea College in Kentucky, vice-president of the New York City Mission, and president of the National Federation of Churches. He was a member of the American Institute of Architects and elected a Fellow in 1865.

In 1881 Cady was married to Emma M. Bulkley of Orange, New Jersey. They had five children. (Withey,

WWW; Obituaries in *Journal of the AIA,* Vol. VII (May 1919), p. 226; NYT, 4–18–19, 13:3).

BIOGRAPHIES OF THE RESIDENTS

Archibald Hopkins (1842–1926) was born in Williamstown, Massachusetts, the son of Dr. Mark and Mary (Hubbell) Hopkins. Dr. Mark Hopkins was both a physician and a minister, but his career was centered primarily in teaching (moral philosophy and rhetoric), and he was for many years president of Williams College. (DAB) Archibald, one of the Hopkins's ten children, graduated from Williams College in 1862, received a captain's commission in the army, and saw active service until the end of the Civil War. He held the rank of colonel at this time.

After the war, Colonel Hopkins studied law at Columbia University and graduated in 1868. He practiced for several years in New York City, and in 1873 accepted a position in Washington as clerk of the Court of Claims, a position he held for many years.

Hopkins was president of the District of Columbia

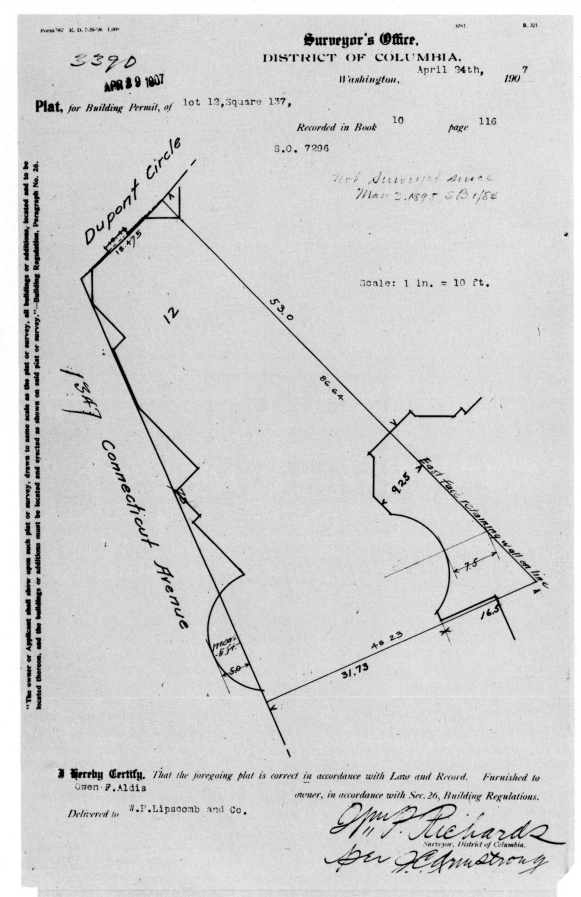

Form 907 E. D. 7-20-'06 1,000

8881   R. 321

Surveyor's Office,
DISTRICT OF COLUMBIA,

3390

APR 29 1907

Plat, *for Building Permit, of* lot 12, Square 137,

Washington,   April 24th,   190 7

Recorded in Book   10   *page*   116

S. O. 7296

*not Surveyed since
Mar 3, 1895 S B 1/84*

Scale: 1 in. = 10 ft.

Dupont Circle

18.475

12

53.0

86.64

1347 Connecticut Avenue

9.25

East face retaining wall on line

7.5

16.5

48.23

50

31.73

"The owner or Applicant shall show upon such plat or survey, drawn to same scale as the plat or survey, all buildings or additions, located and to be located thereon, and the buildings or additions must be located and erected as shown on said plat or survey."—Building Regulation, Paragraph No. 26.

I Hereby Certify. *That the foregoing plat is correct in accordance with Law and Record. Furnished to*

Owen F. Aldis

owner, in accordance with Sec. 26, Building Regulations.

Delivered to   W. P. Lipscomb and Co.

Wm. P. Richards
Surveyor, District of Columbia.

per H. Armstrong

Sons of the Revolution, a governor and vice-president of the Metropolitan Club, and a member of the executive committee of Garfield Hospital and the Associated Charities. (NCAB)

Charlotte Wise Hopkins (1851–1935) was born in Cambridge, Massachusetts, but moved to Washington with her family at the age of one year. She was the granddaughter of Edward Everett, Massachusetts orator, clergyman, teacher, statesman and president of Harvard. (DAB) Her father was Henry A. Wise, a naval officer from Virginia; her mother was Charlotte Brooks (Everett) Wise.

An article in the *Washington Post* (6–3–34) relates the story of Mrs. Hopkins's lifetime work with Washington charities. In 1878 she married Archibald Hopkins, and in the early years of her marriage devoted most of her time to the Home for Incurables, which had been founded by her uncle, Sidney Everett. In 1912 Mrs. Hopkins became president of the woman's welfare department of the National Civic Federation and began the campaign to clean up the alley slums with which her name was associated until her death in 1935. She spoke about the filth, the crime and the wretched existence of the alley dwellers to anyone who would listen. She sought the aid of Mrs. Woodrow Wilson, and in 1914 Congress passed a bill permitting the condemnation of alley houses, only to have the courts upset its legality in 1922, when it had finally been put into effect. In 1932, when Eleanor Roosevelt became First Lady, Mrs. Hopkins knew she had found a sympathetic listener. She took Mrs. Roosevelt on a tour of the alley slums. The time was ripe; the agitation for slum clearance—born of the depression and the public works programs—was gathering momentum. In 1934 Congress passed a law setting up a District housing authority and providing for a ten year slum clearance program. President Roosevelt presented Mrs. Hopkins with the pen he used to sign the bill. She died one year later at the age of eighty-four at her summer home in Annisquam, Massachusetts.

In addition to her interest in slum clearance and the Home for Incurables, Mrs. Hopkins was a member of the Boards of St. Elizabeth's Hospital and the United States Hospital for the Insane.

Charlotte and Archibald Hopkins had two children: Amos L. Hopkins of Cambridge, Massachusetts (at the time of his mother's death) and Charlotte Wise Patterson, the wife of Dr. Henry Patterson of New York. (Obituaries: ES, 9–7–35, 9–9–35; WP, 9–7–35, 9–8–35, 9–9–35.)

Owen F. Aldis (1852–1925) was born in St. Albans, Vermont. His father was Asa Owen Aldis, a judge of the United States Court of Claims in Washington. His mother was born Mary Taylor. Owen Aldis graduated from Yale in 1874, studied law at the Columbian Law School in Washington (now the law school of George Washington University), and in the office of Beckwith, Ayer and Kiles in Chicago. He was admitted to the Illinois bar in 1876.

Aldis settled in Chicago and practiced law; his firm was Paddock, Aldis and Wright. The real estate business had a growing attraction for him, and in 1887 he gave up his law practice in order to devote his full time to real estate. His brother, Arthur T. Aldis, joined him; in 1903 their firm took the name of Aldis and Company. The firm expanded until it was the largest of its kind in Chicago. Aldis was trustee for a number of large estates and agent for several Scottish and English insurance and investment companies. Of interest to students of the Chicago school of architecture is the fact that Aldis's name is associated with the development of the steel frame office building in that city; an association shared with another part-time Washingtonian, Levi Leiter (See text, 1500 New Hampshire Avenue.)

Aldis was a director of the Chicago World's Fair of 1893 and a member of its building and grounds committee. Again, he shared this association with other builders or owners of houses discussed in this book: Thomas B. Bryan (1205 Vermont Avenue) and Robert R. Hitt (1511 New Hampshire Avenue).

Aldis retired in 1908, and in his later years divided his time between Washington and France. His first wife was Leila Russell De Zeng Houghteling of Chicago, by whom he had a son, Owen. She died in 1885. In 1912 Aldis married Marie Madeline, daughter of Comte Gaston du Mas of Paris.

Mr. Aldis was a collector of American manuscripts, letters, and first editions; in 1911 he gave his collection to Yale University. He was a member of many clubs in Chicago and New York and was a trustee of the Chicago Museum of Natural History. In Washington he was a member of the Metropolitan Club. Owen Aldis died in Paris in 1925. (NCAB)

LISTINGS OF RESIDENTS

The Hopkins House

City directory listings are not included for this house as Archibald Hopkins and his wife, Charlotte, were the only owner/occupants from 1881 until his

1907 Plat, 1347 Connecticut Ave., N.W.
(mirror-image of 1826 Massachusetts Ave., N.W.)
D.C. Permits, National Archives

death in 1926 and hers in 1935. From 1936–48 the house was occupied by roomers and a florist's shop.

Social registers list:

1888–1927 Mr. and Mrs. Archibald Hopkins. From 1898–1911, Miss Mary Hopkins was listed, and from 1898–1900, a Miss Hopkins. Mrs. Lawrence Hopkins, 2nd, was listed in 1900.
1929–1935 Mrs. Archibald Hopkins

The Miller House

City directories list the following tenants:

1888–1889 Winthrop A. Chandler

1896–1901 Mary T. Aldis (Mrs. Asa O. Aldis)
1903–1906 Mary T. Aldis, Cornelia Aldis
1907 Mary T. Aldis
1908–1909 Mary T., Cornelia and Owen F. Aldis
1910 Cornelia and Owen F. Aldis
1911 Owen F. Aldis

Social registers list:

1888 Mr. and Mrs. Winthrop A. Chandler
1889 Mr. and Mrs. Charles Carroll
1899–1906 Mrs. Asa O. Aldis, Miss Cornelia Aldis
1909 Mrs. Asa O. Aldis, Miss Cornelia Aldis, Mr. Owen F. Aldis
1911 Mr. Owen F. Aldis, Miss Aldis

1328 Connecticut Avenue, N.W.
Edson Bradley Residence

The Edson Bradley house was located at the convergence of Nineteenth Street and Connecticut Avenue, in Square 138 on lot 5 (old lots 4 and 5). It was demolished in 1923. The Dupont Circle Building now occupies the site.

STATEMENT

The original house occupied a large triangular site with excellent opportunity for enlargement and embellishment. As viewed in the Connecticut Avenue elevation drawing, the alterations and additions of 1907 resulted in a large sprawl of red brick, stone trim, terra cotta ornament, stained glass and lead came windows and slate roof. The residence was built on a podium approximately six feet higher than the surrounding sidewalks. As though fear that this higher elevation would not produce the desired baronial effect, a "medieval" chapel wing was added for extra measure.

The architect apparently chose a style which, in massing and romantic character, was akin to certain Victorian England residential and public buildings. It would seem, however, to be more elaborate, the pro-lific detail ranging from late medieval to Stuart. Certainly windows of every description were used including oriels, dormers and semi-dormers. The building silhouette is one of gables, mansards, hips and towers all of which sprout either fractables, crockets, finials or weather vanes, the whole embellished with terraces, balconies and parapets.

PREVIOUS STRUCTURES ON THE SITE

On the site of the Bradley house was the Gardiner Hubbard residence, which was incorporated into the new structure. Hubbard, "First organizer of the telephone industry, promoter of education of the deaf, founder of the National Geographic Society," (DAB) moved to Washington from Cambridge, Massachusetts c. 1878. It is not known whether Hubbard built the house at 1328 or bought it; no building permit has been found. Illustrations of the house show it to be typical of other Washington houses of the late 1870's or early 1880's (H&M, p. 310). The Hubbards were first listed at 1328 in the city directory for 1883. (See text, 1500 Rhode Island Avenue, for Hubbard biography.)

1907, D.C. Permits, National Archives.

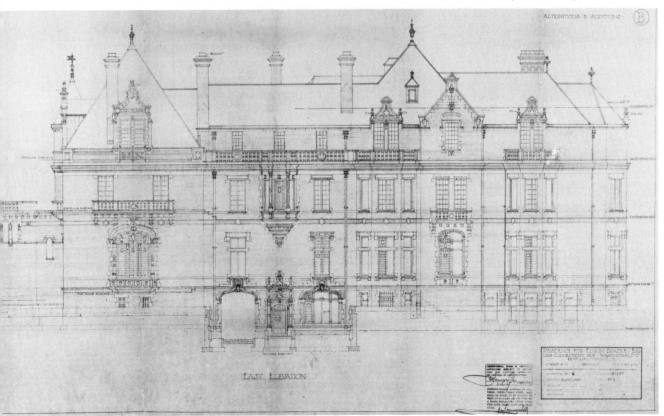

EAST ELEVATION

HISTORICAL INFORMATION

Edson Bradley bought the Gardiner Hubbard house (on part of original lot 4 and lot 5) in March 1907 (Liber 3060 folio 230). In June he bought another part of lot 4 from American Security and Trust, trustees under the will of Teunis Hamlin (Liber 3088 folio 391). He then combined the two pieces of property to make new lot 5 (Office of the Surveyor, Liber 43 folio 65).

There is a story which says that Bradley was dissatisfied with the house as he bought it and decided to tear it down. Learning that if he did this, zoning regulations would require him to build a house smaller in size than he desired, he applied for a permit to remodel the old house and build an addition, and then proceeded to replace the old house brick by brick. (WH, 6–22–35)

Bradley commissioned Howard Greenley of New York as the architect and built a house which, from descriptions, surpassed anything Washington had yet seen. It was referred to as "Alladin's Palace." Unfortunately, and almost unbelievably, no exterior photographs have yet been found; although the architect's drawing of the Connecticut Avenue elevation has been preserved with the original building permit (No. 36, 7–3–07).

The building permit gave permission to build "one (building) and remodel existing building." The house was described as two stories plus attic, brick with limestone and granite trim, with a pitched slate roof and dormers. The size was to be: front, 33 feet; depth, 65 feet 8 inches. A back building was to be 33 feet 2 inches wide, 20 feet long and 24 feet high. The height of the main building from the sidewalk to the highest part of the roof at the front was to be 60 feet; to the eaves at the back, 37 feet. There was to be an elevator, for which a separate permit was granted (No. 759, 8–30–07). Estimated cost for the house was $100,000; the builder was George Hill.

The interior was sumptuous beyond belief. There was a private chapel filled with Spanish Gothic antiques and a theater panelled in wood supposedly taken from an old English house. There was also a music room with what was termed "the finest electric organ in Washington." (WH, 5–29–10), as well as many other musical instruments in the Bradley collection. The picture gallery housed the collection of paintings and sculpture, and there were innumerable china cases to display Mrs. Bradley's collection of Chinese porcelain.

Despite such luxury, Bradley tired of Washington and decided to move to Newport. Sixteen years after he built his house he was granted a permit to raze it (No. 8030, 3–20–23). Howard Greenley, the architect, signed the permit and began the three year task of dismantling the house and moving it, piece by piece, to Newport. There it was incorporated into a villa with over one hundred rooms, designed by Greenley, and called "Seaview Terrace." It is now used as a private school and called "Burnham-by-the-Sea."

In 1926 Bradley sold his Washington property to Joseph J. Moebs for $300,000 (Liber 5691 folio 430). The Dupont Circle Building was erected on the site.

KNOWN ARCHITECTURAL DRAWINGS

Plat, showing configuration of old house and new addition. Filed with permit No. 36, 3 July 1907.

Connecticut Avenue elevation. Black line print. Filed with permit No. 36, 3 July 1907.
RESIDENCE FOR EDSON BRADLEY, ESQ./1328 Connecticut Ave., Washington, D. C./Howard Greenley, Architect/12 West 40 St. New York City/Drawing No. 6/Drawn May 1907/ Scale: ¼′ = 1 ft./By H .G.

Present and proposed projections beyond building line, Connecticut Avenue elevation; plan through first story wall; plan through second story wall. Ink on linen. Filed with permit No. 36, 3 July 1907.
HOUSE FOR EDSON BRADLEY, ESQ. WASHINGTON, D. C./Howard Greenley, Architect/12 West 40 St. New York City.

Passenger elevator: plan, section and elevation. Blueprint Filed with permit No. 759, 30 August 1907.
Howard Greenley, Architect, New York

VIEWS

Interior

Photographs in SS, 12–24–22, Rotogravure section:
Chapel, west gallery, main entrance, Spanish altar in chapel, entrance to chapel.
Photographs in WP; no date, but probably late 1922 (in MLKW, house clipping file):
Music room, dining room, east gallery of the main hallway, conservatory, altar, theater, bed in a guest room, china cases.
M. Stapley, "Interior Decoration," *The American Architect,* Vol. C, No. 1858 (2 Aug. 1911):
Library ceiling, music room, wood ceiling (room not identified).

ARCHITECT

Howard Greenley (1874–1963) was born in Ithaca, New York. His parents were Frederick A. and Lucy R. Greenley. He received his education at the Holderness School in Plymouth, New Hampshire, and at Trinity College in Hartford, where he received his

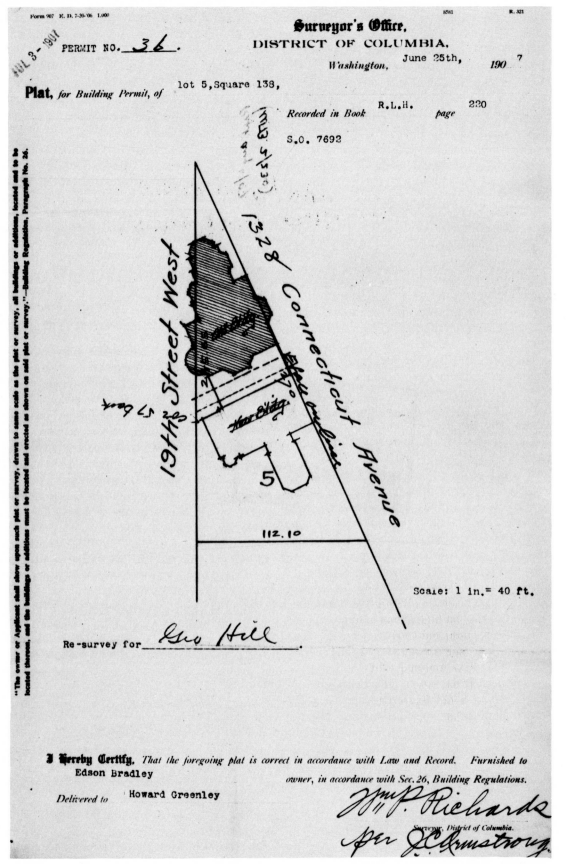

Form 907 E. D. 7-20-'06 1,000   8581   R. 321

PERMIT NO. **36**.

Surveyor's Office,
DISTRICT OF COLUMBIA,
Washington,   June 25th,   190 7

Plat, *for Building Permit, of*   lot 5, Square 138,

Recorded in Book   R.L.H.   page   230

S.O. 7692

19th Street West

1328 Connecticut Avenue

5

112.10

Scale: 1 in. = 40 ft.

Re-survey for   *Geo Hill*

I hereby Certify, That the foregoing plat is correct in accordance with Law and Record. Furnished to
Edson Bradley   *owner, in accordance with Sec. 26, Building Regulations.*

Delivered to   Howard Greenley

Wm P. Richards
Surveyor, District of Columbia.
Per J.C. Armstrong

1907, D.C. Permits, National Archives.

Bachelor of Science degree in 1894. After graduating from Trinity, Greenley began his architectural career in the office of Carrere and Hastings in New York City. Then he returned to school, studying at the Ecole des Beaux Arts in Paris, where he was awarded a diploma in architecture in 1901. Following this he was associated with Arnold Brunner in New York.

Greenley opened his own practice in New York in 1903. The firm remained in existence until 1932 and was responsible for the design of the Prince George Hotel (1905) and the interiors of the Lord Duveen mansion, both in New York; a house for Alanson B. Houghton (former ambassador to Germany and England) in Corning, New York; residences for Edson Bradley in Washington and Newport, Rhode Island; the Charles A. Coffin house in Locust Valley, Long Island; and Joseph Widener's picture galleries at Elkin Park, Philadelphia.

In addition to his architectural practice Greenley was president of the Architectural League of New York (1921–23), a member of the New York Art Commission (1953–55), and of the American Institute of Architects, which elected him a Fellow in 1926. He was a lecturer at the Metropolitan Museum in New York, the Department of French of Middlebury College, and the Boston and Chicago chapters of the American Institute of Architects. He was also an instructor in fine arts at Trinity College.

Greenley was a reserve officer in the United States Naval Air Force during World War I, and a trustee of Holderness School (1935–36), the French Institute of New York (1952–53), and the Sheldon Museum, Middlebury, from 1956 until the time of his death. Of interest to Washingtonians is the fact that Greenley directed the pageant dedicating the Lincoln Memorial.

In 1947 Mr. Greenley was given a testimonial dinner in honor of the twenty-fifth anniversary of his presidency of the Architectural League of New York. At this dinner he was awarded the League's President's Medal.

Mr. Greenley was married to Elizabeth Inness in 1903. They had two children: Howard Greenley, Jr. and Mrs. Bettina Greenley Champlain. Howard Greenley died at Mrs. Champlain's home in Santa Barbara, California in 1963. (Files of the AIA Library, Washington; *Architectural Record*, March 1947, p. 130)

BIOGRAPHIES OF THE RESIDENTS

Edson Bradley (c. 1852–1935) was a native of New Canaan, Connecticut and was educated in Germany, at Munich and Heidelberg. He made his money in the distilling business, and through him the brands of "Old Crow" and "Old Hermitage" became famous. He was for many years president of the "whiskey trust," the organization of distillers formed to control the nation's liquor supply.

Bradley was an avid art collector and filled several houses with paintings, tapestries, musical instruments and Chinese porcelain. The Bradley villa at Alexandria Bay, Thousand Islands, New York burned in 1922, destroying many works of art. In 1927 Bradley began to dispose of his art collection. In that year he sold part of it in New York at the American Art Galleries for $155,000. In 1934 he sold one Gothic tapestry at Christie's in London for 3,465 pounds. The Chinese porcelain collection was to have been sold at auction in England in 1935, the year of his death. (ES, 6–21–35) (Other obituaries and descriptions of the house: WP, 6–21–35; WH, 6–22–35; WDN, 6–21–35; Newport, R.I. *News,* 6–21–35.)

Julia Wentworth Williams Bradley (c. 1852–1929) was a descendant of Roger Williams on her father's side, and of the old Dutch families of Van Rensselaer, Van Arnim and Van der Huyden on her mother's side. Nothing is known of her early life, but after she married Edson Bradley she gained a reputation as a hostess in both Washington and New York. When she gave a party in her Washington house special trains would bring cars full of guests from New York. She was especially remembered for her musicales and other performances in the theater-ballroom, said to have accommodated one thousand persons comfortably (NYT, 8–23–29). Stars from the Metropolitan Opera sang in the Bradley theater, and it was there that the first jazz was played in Washington (WDN, 6–21–35).

Julia and Edson Bradley had one child, a daughter, Julie Fay. She married Herbert Shipman, Episcopal Suffragan Bishop of New York. He died in 1930. (Obituaries: NYT, 8–23–29; Newport, R. I., *News,* 8–23–29)

LISTINGS OF RESIDENTS

City directories list Edson Bradley at 1328 Connecticut Avenue from 1909–12 and again from 1916–22. There were no listings for 1913–15.

The *Elite List* shows the Edson Bradleys at 1328 Connecticut Avenue from 1909–17. In 1909 The Reverend and Mrs. Herbert Shipman were also listed. Before building their house, the Bradleys lived at Stoneleigh Court (1905–06).

1500 New Hampshire Avenue, N.W.
The Leiter Residence

The house was situated to the north of Dupont Circle, at the convergence of Nineteenth Street and New Hampshire Avenue. It was located in Square 135, on old lot 1. Lot 2 and part of lot 3 were also included in the property, which was later called lot 4. The house was demolished in 1947; the site is now occupied by the Dupont Plaza Hotel.

STATEMENT

The Leiter residence was built on the south end of a combination lot, 2/3 acre in size. The landscaping, apparently developed from plans sent by Frederick Law Olmsted, Senior,* was enclosed by a balustraded limestone wall. Though the main entrance faced on New Hampshire Avenue, a semicircular balcony and porch projected from the first and second stories overlooking Dupont Circle.

Rearing like a great stratified dinosaur, the Venetian accented Roman revival building of brick and stone rose in layers. The raised basement was rusticated and broken forward to support two story colossal pilasters capped by architrave, false parapet and, incongruously, a third story. Despite delicate ornamentation, the effect produced by the additional story was ponderous.

Brick ordinarily tends to reduce the monumental aspect of construction more often associated with limestone. Light, buff-colored material combined with pilasters and stone columns, balconies and porches can be employed to distract slightly from the visual impact of a structure overwhelming in size. In this instance, Ionic columns and multitudinous windows maximized the size by contrast, rather than visually reducing the scale of the whole.

HISTORICAL INFORMATION

Lot 1, Square 135 was sold to Mary T. C. Leiter in February 1891 by William Walter Phelps, who had also sold James G. Blaine the land for his house (Liber 1563 folio 443). The price was $83,276.53. The Leiters, who had been living in the Blaine mansion since 1883, selected T. P. Chandler of Philadelphia as their architect, and the building permit was issued 12 June 1891 (No. 2562). The permit described the house as three stories plus basement, 96 feet across the front and 75 feet deep. The height was to be 48 feet to the highest part of the wall and

*Refer to job number 1242, Olmsted Papers, Manuscript Division of the Library of Congress.

c. 1910
#2572, Columbia Historical Society Collection.

62 feet to the highest part of the roof. There was to be a tiled hip roof and a terra cotta cornice. The builder was J. E. and A. L. Pennock of Philadelphia, and the cost was estimated at $125,000.

In 1902 a permit was issued for the installation of a passenger elevator (No. 311, 8–18–02). A greenhouse, approximately 49 by 11 feet, was added in 1906, "built against (a) brick wall," according to the permit (No. 2908, 5–1–06). The tile roof of the house was removed in 1907 and replaced with red slate (Permit No. 2914, 3–25–07).

Sometime between 1891 and 1909 Mary Leiter acquired lot 2 and part of lot 3, Square 135; in 1909 she combined them into lot 4. In this year a two story brick addition was added to the rear of the house. The architect was J. H. de Sibour, a New York architect who had recently opened his office in Washington. The cost of this addition was estimated at $7,000 (Permit No. 4552, 5–25–09).

Mary Leiter's husband, Levi, died in 1904; she continued to live in the house until her death in 1913. Then her son, Joseph, and his wife occupied it until he died in 1932. Joseph willed the house to his son, Thomas, with the provision that Mrs. Leiter be allowed to occupy it during her lifetime (Will of Joseph Leiter, exemplified copy, filed 8–8–32). After her death in 1942 the house was leased to the Government for office use, then sold in 1944 to Dupont Plaza, Inc. for $190,000, subject to an indebtedness of $80,000 (Liber 8055 folio 437). The building was razed by Dupont Plaza, Inc. in 1947.

KNOWN ARCHITECTURAL DRAWINGS

Gates and gate posts. Wash drawing. Filed with permit No. 2562, 12 June 1891.

Plat, showing original house and configuration of 1909 addition. No measurements. Filed with permit No. 4552, 25 May 1909.

VIEWS

Exterior photographs

From northeast; New Hampshire Avenue portico: CHS, c. 1910.
Dupont Circle and Nineteenth Street facades: National Capital Planning Commission, T. A. Mullet photograph, building nearing completion, c. 1893; CHS, Proctor Collection, c. 1910; WDN, 7–11–47.
Dupont Circle and New Hampshire Avenue facades: National Capital Planning Commission, T. A. Mullet photograph; building nearing completion, c. 1893; *Inland Architect and News Record,* Vol. 3, no. 1 (Feb. 1894); National Archives, No. 66–G–9–23N–37, c. 1910.

ARCHITECT

Born in Boston and educated at Harvard, *Theophilus Parsons Chandler* (1845–1928) was associated primarily with the architecture of Philadelphia and the School of Architecture at the University of Pennsylvania, which he helped to establish and of which he was the first director.

After graduating from Harvard, Chandler studied in Paris at the Atelier Vaudremer. He returned to Boston to open his practice and then moved to Philadelphia in 1870. The Wanamaker residence at Twentieth and Walnut Streets and the Penn Mutual Life Insurance Company building at 1921–25 Chestnut Street (now demolished) are notable examples of his residential and commercial work in Philadelphia. Chandler was noted primarily for his ecclesiastical design. His church commissions included: the Swedenborgian Church at Chestnut and Twenty-second Streets and the Bethlehem Presbyterian Church on Broad Street in Philadelphia, the First Presbyterian Church in Pittsburgh, and Saint Thomas Episcopal Church in Washington, D.C.

Chandler was an early member and Fellow of the American Institute of Architects and one of the founders of the Philadelphia Chapter of the Institute. (Withey; George B. Tatum, *Penn's Great Town: 250 Years of Philadelphia Architecture,* Philadelphia: University of Pennsylvania Press, 1961, p. 118.)

BIOGRAPHIES OF THE RESIDENTS

Levi Zeigler Leiter (1834–1904) was born at Leitersburg, Maryland, a village on a tract of land just north of Hagerstown which an ancestor had purchased during the early years of the settlement of western Maryland. He was the son of Joseph and Ann (Zeigler) Leiter.

Leiter's rise from humble beginnings to a position of great wealth, while not quite a rags-to-riches story, is typical of that of many of the "self-made" men who dominated the American scene during the period of rapid expansion following the Civil War.

He began as a clerk in the village store, decided to move west, and became a peddler in Springfield, Ohio. He was attracted to Chicago, moved there in 1855, and took a clerk's job in a dry goods store. A fellow employee was Marshall Field. The two men eventually bought an interest in the store, but sold it to go into business with Potter Palmer, another dry goods merchant and a well-known name in Chicago affairs. Palmer soon retired, leaving Field and Leiter the owners of a prosperous and expanding business. By 1881, however, Leiter's interest had turned from the dry goods business to real estate. He was already a very wealthy man. His confidence in the vitality of Chicago caused him to invest heavily in the city's growth, thereby aiding it to recover from the tragic fire of 1871 and also greatly increasing his own fortune. His name is associated with the Chicago school of architecture as the builder of the first true steel skeleton building—William LeBaron Jenney's Leiter Building of 1889.

Leiter's interest in the civic affairs of Chicago was great. He was the second president of the Chicago Art Institute, was instrumental in providing a new building for the Chicago Historical Society (which had suffered severe damage in the fire), and gave large sums of money to the Chicago Public Library.

Levi Leiter also liked to travel and to collect fine books and manuscripts dealing with American history. The most valuable portion of this library was sold at auction in New York in 1933. (WH, 2–10–33; WP, 2–11–33; ES, 2–12–33)

Leiter came to Washington in 1883. He leased the Blaine mansion at 2000 Massachusetts Avenue (see text) for an annual sum of $11,500, the highest paid for a private residence in the city at that time (ES, 7–26–31). Then he built his own palatial residence, large enough to hold his library of thousands of volumes and to accommodate easily and elegantly the large number of people present when the Leiters entertained in the lavish fashion they preferred. Perhaps it was only Mrs. Leiter who liked to entertain;

Old CFA Files

Levi Leiter's obituary in the *Evening Star* (6–9–04) mentions that he cared little for social life and participated in it only to please his family.

Mr. Leiter was a member of many Chicago clubs and organizations, and in Washington belonged to the Cosmos and Metropolitan clubs. He was married to the former Mary Theresa Carver and had four children: a son, Joseph, and three daughters: Nancy, Marguerite (Daisy) and Mary Victoria. (DAB, NCAB)

Mary Theresa Carver Leiter (1844–1913) was the daughter of Benjamin Carver, a wealthy banker of Utica, New York and a descendant of John Carver, first president of Plymouth Colony (NYT, 3–7–13, 11:5). She was a school teacher, and she was also a woman of great beauty who aspired to become a leader of society. Mrs. Leiter was not a social success in Chicago, but when the family moved to Washington, built their impressive house and presented their three attractive daughters to society, her success was assured; from that time on Mary Leiter was someone to be reckoned with in Washington (ES, 6–9–04). The *Evening Star* source, incidentally, says that Mary Carver was "without a cent" when she married Levi Leiter, a direct contradiction to the *New York Times* reference above.

c. 1893
T. A. Mullett Collection
National Capital Planning Commission

All of Mrs. Leiter's daughters married Englishmen, and the two younger girls were married in the Dupont Circle house. The eldest, Mary Victoria, married George, Lord Curzon, who became Viceroy of India. The Leiters went to India to see their daughter after her marriage; it was at this time that Daisy Leiter met the Earl of Suffolk, whom she later married (ES, 3–7–13). A third daughter, Nancy, married Colin

Campbell, a colonel in the British army. Mr. and Mrs. Leiter made frequent trips to Europe to see their daughters.

Mary Leiter took a great interest in her husband's collection of books and manuscripts and spent much of her time cataloguing and arranging it. She was also very much interested in Mount Vernon and was a member of the group of women who were responsible for preserving the mansion (WP, 3–7–13).

Mary Victoria Leiter, Lady Curzon (c. 1871–1906) was the eldest daughter of the Leiters, a woman of great beauty and intelligence. She met her future husband during a trip to Europe, at a ball in London in 1890. He was thirty-one; she was nineteen. After a long courtship, mostly through letters, they were married in 1895. The reception was held in the Leiter house, and it was reported to have been one of the most brilliant ever seen in Washington (ES, 3–7–13).

Lady Curzon spent most of the remaining years of her life in India, where her husband was Viceroy. She was taken ill during a vacation in England in 1904 and never fully recovered. She died in 1906, leaving her husband and three daughters (ES, 7–18–06; 8–31–47).

Joseph Leiter, (1868–1932), Levi Leiter's only son, followed his father's example and entered the world of business and finance. He was born in Chicago and attended Harvard University; upon graduation his father gave him one million dollars to see what he could do with it. In only six years he had more than thirty million dollars worth of Leiter properties under his control (ES, 4–12–32). He was president of the Zeigler Coal Company in Illinois and of the Zeigler and Gulf Railroad Company, and a director of several banks and trust companies.

Leiter made one very expensive and well-publicized mistake in these early years, however. In 1897 he tried to corner the wheat market, dealing principally with the Chicago Board of Trade. The corner collapsed in 1898, and he was forced to sell his wheat at about half what he paid for it, resulting in a loss of at least ten million dollars, which was assumed by his father. Later business ventures made up most of the loss, however. He continued to manage the Leiter family's rich coal properties in Illinois as well as the Washington Gas Light Company, organized a combine of three street railway companies in Chicago, and even considered trying to buy the Great Wall of China to preserve it for future generations.

At the time of his death his income was estimated to be about one million dollars annually. He owned the Dupont Circle house and also built a mansion called the "Glass Palace" on the Virginia shore of the Potomac, near Langley. In addition to his management of the Washington Gas Light Company, Mr. Leiter was also a director of the American Security and Trust Company and a member of the Washington Board of Trade and Chamber of Commerce. He was a member of several social clubs, including the University, Metropolitan, Army and Navy and Chevy

c. 1893
T. A. Mullett Collection
National Capital Planning Commission

Chase clubs. Mr. Leiter was known as a sportsman. He was interested in horse racing and yachting, and at one time made a trip around the world on his private yacht.

Joseph Leiter was married in 1908 to Juliette Williams. They had three sons: John, Joseph and Thomas. Both John and Joseph died at an early age. The Leiters also had an adopted daughter, Nancy. (DAB; obituaries: WH, 4–12 & 4–21–32; ES, 4–20–32)

Juliette Williams Leiter (c. 1888–1942) was born in Fort McHenry, near Baltimore, the daughter of Colonel and Mrs. John R. Williams. She was educated at the Georgetown Visitation Convent in Washington and in later years was president of its alumnae association (ES, 10–30–42).

Juliette William's marriage to Joseph Leiter was one of the outstanding social events of 1908. After her mother-in-law's death in 1913, Mrs. Leiter carried

on the tradition of giving elaborate dinners and parties at the Dupont Circle house and originated the "Dancing Class," held on Friday evenings in the white and gold ballroom. She and Mrs. George T. Marye, wife of a former American ambassador to Russia, were rivals for social supremacy after the demise of the acknowledged leader of Washington society, Mrs. Richard Townsend, who reined from her mansion at 2121 Massachusetts Avenue, now the Cosmos Club (TH, 10–31–42). When the Duke of Windsor, who was the Prince of Wales at the time, was in Washington during World War I, he was entertained by Mrs. Leiter; during the Coolidge Administration Mrs. Leiter was presented at the Court of St. James.

Mrs. Leiter had other interests quite different from her role as a social leader. She designed play shoes for her children when she was unable to find what she wanted in the stores, and she was the owner of a fashionable dress shop, Francise, Inc., on Q Street near Connecticut Avenue. She was involved with many charitable organizations, particularly the Children's County Home, and in the years just before her death worked as a volunteer cashier at the Soldiers, Sailors and Marines' Club at 1015 L Street, N.W.

Mrs. Leiter was survived by a son, *Thomas,* and a daughter, *Nancy.* Thomas married Marion Oates of Montgomery Alabama. They had a daughter, Mary Victoria, but were divorced in 1956. Mr. Leiter died in 1958 (ES, WP, 4–27–58). In 1940 Nancy Leiter married Charles Thomas Clagett, a member of a family long distinguished in Maryland and Virginia. The wedding took place in the Leiter mansion. (ES, 12–6–40). The Clagetts now reside in Washington.

LISTINGS OF RESIDENTS

City directory listings are not included for this house as the Leiters were the only owner/occupants, with the exception of the short period during World War II when it was leased to the Government for offices.

Social registers list the Leiters at 1500 New Hampshire Avenue from 1896 until Mrs. Joseph Leiter's death in 1942. In 1894, previous to moving into their new house, Mr. and Mrs. Levi Leiter were listed with Mrs. Phoebe A. Hearst at 1400 New Hampshire Avenue.

1511 New Hampshire Avenue, N.W.
The Hitt Residence

The house was situated to the northeast of Dupont Circle on the east side of the Avenue. It was located in Square 136 on lots 15 and 16 (original lot 3). Parts of original lot 4 were also included in the property originally. The house was demolished in 1970.

STATEMENT

The free-standing Hitt residence faced west on New Hampshire Avenue. John Russell Pope, whose international reputation far exceeded that of most architects working in the capital, designed the center hall structure of three stories and concealed attic. The attic parapet (which seemed to reduce the actual building height), along with the first floor string course, visually compressed the structure by stressing horizontals. Though the limestone facade was George III, its strength (unlike some works by Robert Adam) was not reduced to seeming fragility by delicate ornamentation. With the exception of the mid–17th century English dining room, the interiors were more noticeably Adam.

HISTORICAL INFORMATION

Robert R. Hitt came to Washington in 1881 and sometime within the next year or so bought the land for the house his widow was to build years later. He bought lots 15 and 16 (original lot 3) in Square 136 at some as yet undetermined time—probably from Peter Campbell, who had subdivided lot 3 into lots 15 and 16 in December 1880. It is known that Hitt had this property by August 1883. In this same year he bought subdivisions of original lot 4 in three different parcels: lots 7, 8 and 9 from Robert Frey at al (Liber 1036, folio 49); lots 12 and 13 from Charles Payson (Liber 1042 folio 302); and lot 14 from Jesse V. N. Huyck (Liber 1043 folio 269).

Nothing was built on this property until after Mr. Hitt's death in 1906. At that time Mrs. Hitt decided to build a house on the site. She chose John Russell Pope as her architect, and the building permit was issued 14 July 1908 (No. 183). The house was described on the permit as a four story structure, approximately 85 feet across the front and 86 feet deep, faced with Indiana limestone. The back building was to be approximately 26 feet wide, 40 feet long and

54 feet high. There was to be a flat tin roof and no projections. Estimated cost was $125,000, and the builder was George A. Fuller. The house was completed in approximately one year (September 1909). There was an electric passenger elevator in the house (Permit No. 2366, 12–23–08). No records of any alterations during the period of the Hitt occupancy (until 1949) have been found.

In 1951, two years after Mrs. Hitt died, her son, William F. R. Hitt, sold the house to the Pan American Sanitary Bureau (Liber 9418 folio 83). It was converted to office use and then sold again in 1965 to the American Council on Education (Liber 12477 folio 266). It was occupied by the Council until it was demolished in 1970. An office building was erected on the site.

KNOWN ARCHITECTURAL DRAWINGS

Ground floor and first floor plans: *The Architecture of John Russell Pope*, Vol. II, introd. by Royal Cortissoz, New York: William Helburn, Inc., 1928. Pl. 92.

Site plan: Samuel Howe, *American Country Houses of Today*, New York: Architectural Book Publishing Co., 1915, p. 309.

VIEWS
Exterior photographs

New Hampshire Avenue and Dupont Circle facades: *The Architecture of John Russell Pope*, (*op. cit.*), Pl. 90; Samuel Howe, (*op. cit.*), p. 306; MLKW, undated photograph.
Detail of entrance:
Samuel Howe, (*op. cit.*), p. 304.
New Hampshire Avenue facade:
Samuel Howe, (*op. cit.*), frontispiece.

Interior photographs

The Architecture of John Russell Pope, (*op. cit*): dining room, ground floor stair hall, Plate 90.
Samuel Howe, (*op. cit.*), first floor stair hall, p. 305; library, p. 308; dining room, p. 310.

ARCHITECT

John Russell Pope: see text, 3000 Massachusetts Avenue, N.W.

BIOGRAPHIES OF THE RESIDENTS

Sallie Reynolds Hitt (c. 1844–1949), wife of Robert R. Hitt and builder of the house, was born in Lafayette, Indiana. She came to Washington when her husband was appointed Assistant Secretary of State in 1881.

The Hitts lived at 1507 K Street, N.W. for many years; it was while they were living there that Mrs. Hitt gained her reputation as one of the city's social leaders. Guests were often their neighbors: Senator Eugene Hale of Maine, Senator Nelson Aldrich of Rhode Island, Senator Stephen B. Elkins of West Virginia and Senator (later Secretary of State) Philander C. Knox of Pennsylvania. Mrs. Hitt's favorite way of entertaining was evidently a novelty for Washington at the time: buffet suppers and teas served on the wide porches of her house (ES, 2–1–49).

After her husband died in 1906, Mrs. Hitt built the house on New Hampshire Avenue. In spite of the size and elegance of her new house, Mrs. Hitt did not entertain as frequently as she had during her husband's lifetime (WP, 2–2–49).

The Hitts had two sons, both of whom lived in the Washington area. The elder was *R. S. Reynolds Hitt* (c. 1877–1938). He was in the diplomatic service from 1901–1914 and served as minister to Panama and later Guatemala. He married Edith Romeyn Gray, daughter of Judge John Clinton Gray of the New York State Court of Appeals. They had a son, Robert R., and a daughter, Edith Elizabeth. At the time of her father's death in 1938, Edith was married to Andor de Hertelendy, a secretary in the Hungarian diplomatic corps, and was living in Europe. Robert was a stockbroker in New York (ES, 4–17–38).

Sallie and Robert Hitt's younger son was *William F. R. Hitt*. He married Katherine Elkins, daughter of Senator and Mrs. Stephen B. Elkins of West Virginia. They were listed in the *Elite List* for 1916 and 1917 as living with Mrs. Hitt at the New Hampshire

1970, Jack E. Boucher

Avenue house. Katherine Elkins was prominent in Washington society and an ardent horsewoman. The couple made headlines when they were divorced in Paris and remarried in Washington two years later. Katherine Hitt died in 1936. William Hitt was living at their estate in Middleburg at the time of his mother's death.

Sallie Hitt lived to be one hundred and five years old. She died at her New Hampshire Avenue home, and the funeral services were held there.

Robert Roberts Hitt (1834–1906), husband of Sallie Reynolds Hitt, spent his youth in Illinois and entered politics as a young man; in 1858 he reported the Lincoln-Douglas debates. In 1874 he was sent to Paris as the first secretary of the American legation, a post he held until 1881, acting part of the time as chargé d'affaires. He was appointed Assistant Secretary of State under James G. Blaine in 1881, and in 1882 was elected as a Republican to fill the vacancy of a deceased Congressman. *The National Cyclopedia of American Biography* says that he served through 1893; the *Biographical Directory of the American Congress* reports that he served until his death in 1906.

Representative Hitt was constantly urging the improvement of the diplomatic service while he was in Congress and was also strongly in favor of increased friendship and reciprocity with the other American republics. He was appointed by McKinley in 1898 as a member of a commission to establish a government in the Hawaiian Islands. He was a member of the World's Fair Committee and did much to bring this fair to Chicago in 1893. He was associated in this endeavor with three other men mentioned in this book: Thomas B. Bryan (1205 Vermont Avenue), Owen F. Aldis (1347 Connecticut Avenue) and Robert S. McCormick (3000 Massachusetts Avenue).

LISTINGS OF THE RESIDENTS

City directories list the following tenants:

1910–1948 Mrs. Sallie R. Hitt
1954–1965 World Health Organization, Pan American Sanitary Bureau
1969–1970 Offices of various educational associations

Social registers listed Mrs. Sallie R. Hitt from 1911 until the time of her death.

1913 Massachusetts Avenue, N.W.
"Stewart Castle"

"Stewart Castle" was situated to the northwest of Dupont Circle at the convergence of Massachusetts and Connecticut Avenues. It was located in Square 113, on lot 26 (old lots 24 and 25). The house was demolished in 1901, and the site is now occupied by the Dupont Circle Branch of the Riggs National Bank.

STATEMENT

Of particular importance to the Stewart residence was that both the floor plan and lot shape were pentagonal. The major elements (pentagon, octagon and circle) were boldly stated (from the photographs note the lack of obtrusive chimneys). The building, which faced east, had a mansard roof, circular entrance tower on axis with Dupont Circle, and octagonal lantern. In addition, there was a projecting conservatory along Massachusetts Avenue, pavilions flanked the entrance tower, and pavilions with semioctagonal bays flanked the balcony along Connecticut Avenue. At the northeast extended a raised basement, two story service and ballroom wing.

The notion that detail is the measurement of "Victorian" architecture is reasonable for the Stewart residence (French Third Empire) and the Hopkins-Miller residences, but inaccurate when ascribed to those structures where detail becomes incidental to the brutal power of structure (2000 and 2122 Massachusetts Avenue). For the Stewart house, the relation of ornament to structure was neither obstructive nor competitive. Rather than a flood of superfluous decoration, the ornament was suggestive, seeming to define, as simply as possible, structural components: floor, bay, sill, lintel and building outline. The effect was a balance between wall surface and ornament, horizontals and verticals. A smooth stucco background rather than a pattern of brick was indicative of this balance. Though the actual pigments are not indicated, the illustrations show tonal differences between stucco wall, stone ornament and fishscale roof.

Like the chimneys which lacked sufficient mass or detail to distract from the major building elements, the carriage porch was a fragile ornament. It was, after all, only a shelter for temporary activity demanding little or no structure (a marquise or awning is as effective and can be equally appropriate).

HISTORICAL INFORMATION

Senator William M. Stewart built his "castle" on land acquired in 1873 from his friend and real estate partner, Curtis J. Hillyer. All Square 111 was purchased and the deed recorded in the name of Stewart's wife, Annie E. F. Stewart (Liber 731 folio 348). Although there is no way to date the structure exactly—it was built before the date of existing permits—accounts from the period usually give 1873 as the date of construction. It appeared on the tax books in 1875 with an assessed valuation of $65,000. An 1879 newspaper article stated that the cost of the house was about $80,000 and of the furnishings not much less. Supposedly, much of the furniture, carpets and lace hangings were made to order in Europe. (ES, 12–31–79) The "castle" also housed the Stewart's collection of painting and sculpture.

Apparently the Stewarts lived in their house only for short periods of time during the twenty-six years they owned it. On 30 December 1879 the house was badly damaged by fire. Newspaper accounts stated that the fire originated in the furnace but did not break out until it reached the roof, destroying most of the upper part of the structure. Damage from the fire was estimated at $15,000. (ES, op. cit.) A newspaper article written in 1891 implied that the roof was rebuilt in a style different from the original. It said: ". . . turrets and pepper-boxes, spires and fancy chimneys were blotted out by a mansard roof, and only the great spiral staircase, the ballroom, and two of the salons retain their former beauty and proportions." (Chicago Inter-Ocean, 1–25–91) However, in the city directory for 1875, facing page 321, is a full page advertisement with a drawing of a house on Massachusetts Avenue showing "Stewart Castle" in the background. Although the size is small and the rendering sketchy, the roof and general lines of the building appear to be very much the same as in post-fire illustrations.

The Inter-Ocean article also stated that the Stewarts did not repair the damage immediately, that "for many years the ruins stood patched into dryness by tarred felt." Indeed, the permit to repair the 1879 fire damage was dated 2 November 1882 (No. 621). At the same time a brick addition was built at the rear of the house. The estimated cost for both the

c. 1893
F. B. Johnston
Huntington Library

addition and the fire damage repair was $20,000. The architect was Robert I. Fleming.

In 1883 Mrs. Stewart subdivided Square 113 into lots 26–38 (Office of the Surveyor, Liber 12 folio 6). In that year she sold all the lots except lot 26, the site of the "castle." (Liber 1031 folio 181; Liber 1032 folios 52, 70, 72; Liber 1033 folio 125, and Liber 1037 folio 454.)

From approximately 1886–1893 the house was leased to the Chinese Government. In 1894 Mrs. Stewart was attempting to sue the Chinese for damage to the furniture. The result of the suit is not known. (ES, 1–20–94)

In 1899 Senator Stewart sold the house to Senator William A. Clark of Montana (Liber 2433 folio 101). In 1901 Clark razed the building and according to the *New York Times* (4–24–09, 7:3), planned to build his own house on the site. Apparently there was a disagreement over the plans, and he built his house in New York instead. The property remained vacant until Clark sold it in 1923, and the Dupont Circle Branch of the Riggs National Bank was built on the site.

There are no known architectural drawings of "Stewart Castle."

VIEWS

Exterior

From southwest:
George Washington University, Wright Collection, undated photograph. (A reproduction of this is in *Records of the CHS*, Vol. 48 (1971–72), p. 349.)

c. 1893 office (?)
F. B. Johnston
Huntington Library

From southeast:
H&M, p. 312, print, c. 1885; CHS, photograph attributed to W. H. Seaman, c. 1889, The Henry E. Huntington Library and Art Gallery, San Marino, Calif., Frances Benjamin Johnston photograph (No. 1927), c. 1889–1901; ES, 3–21–01.

From Connecticut Avenue and N Street, N.W., looking north with "Stewart Castle" in the distance:
The Commission of Fine Arts, photograph, c. 1885.

Interior

Frances Benjamin Johnston photographs in the Henry E. Huntington Library and Art Gallery, San Marino, Calif. These were taken when the Chinese Legation was occupying the building, c. 1889–93.
Ballroom (No. 1926); drawing room (?), (uncatalogued); library (?), (No. 1925); Chinese woman holding child, room unidentified, (No. 1924).

ARCHITECT

Although there is no building permit for "Stewart Castle," *Adolph Cluss* is generally thought to have been the architect. The *Evening Star* article on the fire of 1879 (12–31–79) says: "Mr. Cluss was the architect of the building," and recent research has also credited Cluss with the design.*

Adolph Cluss (1825–1905) was born in Heilbronn, Germany, and was educated in architecture and civil engineering in his native country. He came to the United States in 1848 and settled in Washington in 1853. After working for the Coast Survey, Navy Yard Ordnance Laboratory and the Supervising Architect of the Treasury, Cluss returned to the Ordnance Laboratory during the Civil War where he worked with his close friend, Admiral John A. Dahlgren.

It was at this time that Cluss and Joseph Wildrich von Kammerhueber entered and won the competition for the design of the Wallach School (1862). This was the first of Cluss's many school designs, the Franklin School at Thirteenth and K Streets being the most widely known. Others were the Seaton, Cranch, Sumner, Jefferson, Curtis and Henry schools. At the World's Fair in Vienna Cluss exhibited an elaborate model of Franklin School and received a "medal for Progress" in school architecture. He also won prizes at international exhibitions in Philadelphia (1876), Paris (1878), and New Orleans (1884).

His reputation enhanced by his successful design for Wallach School, Cluss began to receive an increasing number of important commissions. The Calvary Baptist Church at Eighth and H Streets, N.W., the Masonic Temple at Ninth and F Streets, N.W., the rebuilding of the old Smithsonian after it was damaged by fire, the Department of Agriculture building on the Mall (now demolished), and the Concordia Opera House in Baltimore were some of the projects in the office of Cluss and Kammerhueber during the 1860's.

Kammerhueber died in 1870 and Cluss practiced alone until 1876. During this period he designed both Center and Eastern markets, as well as two blocks of row houses; one at Connecticut and K Street, N.W. (Shepherd's Row), and another on the north side of K Street between Fourteenth Street and Vermont Avenue. "Stewart Castle" was also designed at this time. In 1872 Cluss was appointed a member of the Board of Public Works and was involved in the vast municipal improvement schemes initiated by "Boss" Alexander Shepherd.

After a brief period of collaboration with Frederick Daniel (1876–77), Cluss entered into partnership with Paul Schulze. From 1877–81 the firm worked on the design of the National Museum, now known as the Arts and Industries Building. At the same time Cluss supervised the reconstruction of the old Patent Office, which had been badly damaged by fire in 1877. Other commissions from this period were the Portland Apartments at Thomas Circle, now demolished, (1883); the Army Medical Museum and Library, also demolished, (1885); and Caldwell Hall at Catholic University (1887).

Cluss retired in 1890 and spent the next five years as an inspector of Federal public buildings throughout the country. He died in Washington in 1905 at the home of one of his daughters, Lillian Cluss Daw. Another daughter, Anita, was an accomplished harpist; a third married H. S. Lathrop, a marine engineer. Cluss also had four sons, all of whom died at an early age. His wife was the former Rosa Schmidt of Baltimore.

An interesting non-architectural fact about Adolph Cluss is that he was a friend of Karl Marx and an early subscriber to Marxist political theory. The two men met in Europe in the 1840's and carried on a correspondence for some time after Cluss moved to the United States.

BIOGRAPHIES OF THE RESIDENTS

The only owner-occupant of the house during its relatively short life was Senator *William Morris Stewart* (1827–1909). Senator Stewart was born in Lyons,

New York, but moved to Trumbull County, Ohio, when he was six. He went back to Lyons to attend a preparatory school and supported himself while he studied. With help from a friend, and money saved, he was able to enter Yale. He studied there until 1850 and then left for California to join the gold rush—to mine, prospect and build canals. He constructed one canal along the side of a mountain with levels he had made himself. In 1852 he began to study law, and in 1854 he was named attorney general of California.

The discovery of the Comstock Lode in 1860 gave Stewart a chance to prove his ability as a lawyer. He moved to Nevada as soon as the lode was discovered and was retained by the original claimants to argue the "one lode" theory; that is, that the Comstock Lode was one, not many parallel lodes, and that it was the property of those who first claimed it. The resulting mining litigation and Stewart's victory for his clients greatly increased his stature in the West. He was an ardent supporter of the Union at this time and was active in the controversies over whether Utah and California should remain loyal. When Nevada achieved statehood in 1864, Stewart was elected its first Senator. He was re-elected in 1869, but at the end of his term did not run again. One source states that the reason he did not seek re-election was that his fortunes had become somewhat impaired (NCAB). Perhaps the building of his "castle" had something to do with this. Stewart and two friends, Curtis Hillyer and Thomas Sunderland, had invested heavily in real estate during this period; they were known as the "California Syndicate" because each of the men was associated with that state. Land was cheap in the Dupont Circle area when Stewart first came to Washington, and he was the first of a succession of wealthy men to build a fine residence in that part of the city.

As a Senator during this difficult post-war period, Stewart proposed a plan of reconstruction which offered universal amnesty and suffrage. It was not adopted. As a member of the judiciary committee during the Grant Administration, he was instrumental in drafting the Fifteenth Amendment to the Constitution. Establishment of Federal Government mining laws also concerned Senator Stewart. Non-action by the Government from the time the mines were opened in 1848 until the first law was passed in 1869 had resulted in a confusing mass of local law. Legally, all the miners were trespassers, but Stewart argued that the Government's failure to act immediately had created equities and natural rights that could not be ignored.

When he left the Senate in 1875, Stewart returned to his law practice in the West, recouped his fortune, and was again elected to the Senate in 1886. He served

---

* Tanya Edwards Beauchamp, "Adolph Cluss: An Architect in Washington during Civil War and Reconstruction," *Records of the CHS*, Vol. 48 (1971–72), p. 349. A biography of Cluss is in Withey; his obituary is in the ES, 7-25-05.

Wright Collection (undated)
George Washington University, D.C.

eighteen years, and during this period he was identified with the silver controversy, directing his efforts towards the remonetization of silver. As a delegate to the Republican national convention in 1888, he drafted and secured a silver platform in the party's platform. When his party did not show sufficient interest in supporting his silver policies, he switched to the Silver Party and was re-elected to the Senate in 1893 and in 1899 as a member of that party. He endorsed Williams Jennings Bryan in 1896, but in 1900 switched back to the Republicans and supported McKinley. (DAB)

In 1902 Senator Stewart's wife was killed in an automobile accident in California. In 1905 he married a widow, Mary Agnes (Atchison) Cone. He retired from the Senate when his term expired in 1905 and returned to Nevada. Stewart had made and spent several fortunes. Much of his wealth went to charitable and educational institutions, and he was one of the first trustees of Stanford University. Senator Stewart died in Washington in 1909. The city lost an im-

Drawing Room, c. 1893
F. B. Johnston
Huntington Library

Ballroom, c. 1893
F.B. Johnston
Huntington Library

pressive figure—over six feet tall, with a long silvery beard and frequently sporting a wide-brimmed Western hat, William Stewart more than lived up to the title bestowed upon him: "The Silver King." (Obituary: NYT, 4–24–09, 7:3)

Senator Stewart's first wife was *Annie E. Foote,* whom he married in 1855. She was the daughter of Henry S. Foote, ex-governor of Mississippi and later a Senator. They had three daughters. Mrs. Stewart was described in 1898 as "a lady of fine intellect and accomplishments, master of several languages, widely travelled, and possessed by inheritance and training of the social tact and sagacity that so well befit the wife of a public man." (NCAB)

It was said that during one of the family's European trips, Mrs. Stewart saw a Rhenish castle that caught her fancy, and that it inspired the design of her own "castle." During the short periods that she actually lived in the house, Annie Stewart entertained lavishly. A Washington society book of 1895 mentioned a "brilliant Cinderella dance" for about two

hundred young people, and also described the interior of the mansion:

> The Stewart Castle, one of the earliest of the grand residences of the city, and which has been the scene of so many elegant entertainments, was opened this Winter in pristine magnificence, the first entertainment being a dinner given by Senator and Mrs. Stewart. Few houses in Washington afford more conveniences for entertaining. The drawing room is rich in gold ornamentation; the spacious ball room has been fitted up with prettily cushioned seats rich in Chinese embroideries. The imposing hall is both unique and beautiful, while the reception room at the end of the entrance is of brilliant color, warm and rich in its effect, the furniture being upholstered in red and the walls in red also. This beautiful mansion was erected in accordance with the design of a castle which Mrs. Stewart admired in her travels abroad. (Ida Hinman, *The Washington Sketch Book, A Society Souvenir.* Washington: 1895, pp. 103, 105.)

William Andrews Clark (1839–1925), who purchased "Stewart Castle" only to raze it, was born near

Connellsville, Pennsylvania. His family left Pennsylvania for Iowa, and Clark studied law at Iowa Wesleyan University. Like Stewart, he moved west when the mining boom began. He settled in Montana and by 1884 was president of the state constitutional convention. In 1898 he was elected to the Senate as a Democrat. Questions raised in the Senate regarding possible corrupt campaign practices caused him to resign his seat. He was promptly appointed to fill the vacancy caused by his own resignation, but did not qualify. He was elected again in 1901 but served only one term; he was not a candidate for re-election.

Out of his extensive copper mining, banking and railroad interests, Clark built one of the great fortunes of the period. He had a private railroad car, noted for its seemingly inexhaustible supply of bourbon and champagne. An allied project of one of the several Western railroads owned by Clark was a town called Las Vegas.* Clark maintained offices and a palatial residence in New York City. In this residence he displayed his fine collection of art, a collection which

---

* Lucius Beebe, *Mansions on Rails,* Berkeley, Calif.: Howell-North Press, 1959, pp. 102–103.

---

was given to the Corcoran Gallery of Art after his death in 1905. (BDAC, DAB)

LISTINGS OF RESIDENTS

The city directories listed Senator Stewart only infrequently at "Stewart Castle" during the period 1873-1901. If there were other residents they are unknown, as the directories were indexed by name only at that time.

1875 William M. Stewart, Connecticut Avenue corner Massachusetts Avenue.

1885 William N. Stewart, Dupont Circle corner Massachusetts Avenue

1886–1893 Chinese Legation, Dupont Circle

1896–1899 William M. Stewart, USS; 9, 13, or 8 Dupont Circle. The different numbers on Dupont Circle are confusing. The *Elite List* always lists the Stewarts at No. 8.

Social registers list:

1889–1893 Chinese Legation, Dupont Circle corner Massachusetts Avenue

1896–1899 Hon. and Mrs. William M. Stewart and daughters, 8 Dupont Circle. In 1898 a Miss Fox is also listed.

2000 Massachusetts Avenue, N.W., The Blaine Mansion

The building is on the south side of Massachusetts Avenue, N.W. where the Avenue and P Street converge at Twentieth Street. It is located in Square 95 on lot 1.

It is owned by Samuel Spencer, Violet Spencer Thoron and Roger Cortesi and has been converted to office use.

HISTORICAL INFORMATION

The Blaine house is on a site different from the one originally chosen. In letters written to her children, Mrs. Blaine at first mentioned a site on Sixteenth Street near Scott Circle. In fact, plans had

been prepared and the site graded when Mr. Blaine changed his mind. Mrs. Blaine wrote to her son, Emmons, in May 1881:

> . . . your Father . . . has conceived a sort of disgust with the Sixteenth Street place, on account of the vicinage of stables, and although he has had that immense tract graded, is not going to build on it, and fastening his affections on a lot on Massachusetts Avenue, P and Twentieth Streets, he comes upon the surprising fact that Mr. Phelps is the owner thereof . . . (1)

William Walter Phelps was a friend of the Blaines. He agreed to sell them the land (Liber 1213 folio 113) and the building permit was issued in June 1881 (No. 1379). The Blaines chose John Fraser as their

c. 1890
Columbia Historical Society

architect. The Sixteenth Street site was sold to Senator George H. Pendleton, who built on it in the same year.

The first floor plan of the Blaine house is described by Mrs. Blaine in a letter to her daughter, Margaret:

> This new locale gives us a frontage to the east on Twentieth Street, drawing rooms and dining on P Street, and library and hall and reception room on Massachusetts Avenue. (2)

The Blaines moved into their new house in December 1882. Period books on Washington and on Mr. Blaine give numerous descriptions of the house. As the interior has been so drastically altered, a few of these descriptive passages are quoted here to give some idea of how the house looked originally:

> The spacious halls and stairways were wainscoted, finished and ceiled in oak; the drawing room, the dining room and the library were finished in solid mahogany; and the chambers were finished in poplar and pine. The great charm of the house was that each and every room, large and small, had its open fireplace, some of them surrounded by beautiful mantelpieces, with carved wood and mirrors. (3)

Another description of both exterior and interior:

> It also appears that he (Blaine) likes plenty of light, for the number of wide window openings, filled only with broad sheets of plate glass, sixty-four in all, it is stated, attracted some wonderment at the time.
>
> On the eastern, or Twentieth Street front, is the main entrance, up a double flight of stone steps with polished brass railings. On the north side is an ample porte cochere, above which is a large stained glass window, lighting the staircase within. On the west front is a wide piazza, commanding the gorgeous sunsets known to this latitude.
>
> The main hall might be called baronial in its dimensions. It has panelings and ceilings of oak, the latter supported on polished oak columns with richly carved capitals. The stairs are massively built in oak, decorated with carvings, and the whole is set off by the great fire-place which fronts the visitor as he enters, and gives a home-like glow to the scene.
>
> To the right is a small reception-room, and to the left the large parlors and drawing-room. In the rear is the library, opening on the piazza before mentioned. It is finished in mahogany . . .
>
> On the other side of the hall is the dining-room, also finished in mahogany. (4)

There seems to be some discrepancy in the descriptions of where the dining room and library were located. Mrs. Blaine, in her letter to Margaret quoted previously, has the dining room on the P Street side and the library on Massachusetts Avenue; the descrip-

THE JAMES G. BLAINE MANSION.

View from Northeast, (20th Street) c. 1884
Picturesque Washington.

tion just quoted has them in just the reverse locations. At present, the southwest room (P Street) is lined with mahogany bookcases.

The new house proved to be too large and too expensive to maintain, and after the first year the Blaines spent very little time in it. In 1883 they leased it to Levi Leiter, the Chicago millionaire who had been a partner of Marshall Field; he lived in it until his own house on Dupont Circle was completed in 1894. (See text, 1500 New Hampshire Avenue.)

In 1891, according to the *Evening Star* (1–1–91), a fire caused damage estimated at fifteen thousand dollars. Fire loss was confined to the third floor, but water damage to woodwork and papering throughout the house was extensive. Jacob Myers of Philadelphia was the contractor hired to repair the damage (Permit No. 1411).

In 1898 the house was leased to George Westinghouse; he purchased it in 1901 (Liber 2537 folio 483). The only documented change he made in the building was the installation of a passenger elevator in 1903 (Permit No. 2770).

Mr. Westinghouse died in 1914. His son owned the house for several years but did not live in it and apparently made no changes. In 1920 the building was sold to Henry B. Spencer (Liber 4458 folio 320). In 1921 he converted it to an apartment house for three families with servants' rooms on the top floor (Permit No. 4132). The main staircase was removed, a passenger elevator installed and other significant interior changes made. The porch on the west side and the entrance steps on Twentieth Street were removed at the time of this remodeling. A four story glass enclosed addition was built on the northwest corner, and a one story brick addition added to the southeast corner. At this time also, one story commercial spaces were added on P Street. There were to have been seven stores—three abutting the house and the other four occupying the vacant part of the lot west of the house. Only those abutting the house were built. While permit No. 4132 does not specifically mention all these changes, they can be seen on the architect's drawings. George N. Ray was the architect for this work.

In 1944 the exterior was altered by the removal of the top section of the chimneys (Permit No. 266520).

The last major changes occurred in 1948 when the interior was converted to professional office use (Permits Nos. 313843 and 314827). In 1949 the part of the lot west of the house was graded to sidewalk level on P Street and paved to provide parking for doctors and patients (Permit No. 315482).

1. Harriet S. Blaine Beale, ed., *Letters of Mrs. James G. Blaine,* Vol. 1, New York: Duffield and Co., 1908, p. 201.
2. *Ibid.,* p. 205.
3. Ben: Perley-Poore, *Perley's Reminiscences of Sixty Years in the National Metropolis,* Vol. 2, Philadelphia: Hubbard Brothers, 1886, p. 462.
4. H. J. Ramsdell, *Life and Public Service of James G. Blaine,* Philadelphia: Hubbard Brothers, no date, pp. 173–75.

KNOWN ARCHITECTURAL DRAWINGS

Site plan. Ink on linen. Filed with permit No. 1379, 8 June 1881.

> Plat/showing the position of the house/carriage road, footpaths, etc./RESIDENCE OF/HONORABLE JAMES G. BLAINE/20th street and Massachusetts Avenue/Washington, D. C./Scale 8 feet to an inch.

Surveyor's plat, with drawing of proposed 1921 additions. Recorded on microfilm with permit No. 4132, 20 January 1921.

Stores: show window projections. Recorded on microfilm with permit No. 4132, 20 January 1921.

> DRAWING SHOWING PROJECTION OF/SHOW WINDOWS ON STORES FOR MR. H. B. SPENCER AT/1500 20th STREET, N.W., LOT 1. SQ. 95/Geo. N. Ray, Architect 1147 Conn. Ave./1–19–21.

Remodeling, 1920: plans for all floors and elevations of Massachusetts Avenue, P Street and west facades. Eight blueprints.

> These prints, prepared by the office of George N. Ray, are in the possession of Mr. Samuel Spencer, one of the owners of the building.

1970, Jack E. Boucher.

VIEWS

Exterior

P Street and west elevations:
> J. W. Buel, *The Authorized Pictorial Lives of James Gillespie Blaine and John Alexander Logan,* New York; N. D. Thompson and Co., 1884, p. 259, print.

From northeast, primarily Massachusetts Avenue facade:
> JWM, p. 241; print, c. 1884; Perley-Poore (*op. cit.*), p. 463, print, c. 1886.

From northeast, primarily Twentieth Street facade:
> H&M, p. 306, print, c. 1885.

Twentieth and P Street elevations:
> CHS, Proctor Collection, photograph, pre–1900; MLKW, photograph, c. 1905.

Interior

Theron Clark Crawford, *James G. Blaine—A Study of His Life and Career,* Edgewood Publishing Company, 1893. This book contains four interior photographs, titled as follows: "Blaine at Work," p. 536; "Dining Room in the Blaine Mansion at Washington," p. 568; "Mr. Blaine's Library in His Washington Home," p. 572; and "Drawing Room in the Blaine Mansion at Washington," p. 609.

It is questionable that these photographs were taken in the house at 2000 Massachusetts Avenue. The free-standing columns in the drawing room and details in the dining room and library are similar, but after close first-hand examination of the interior several discrepancies become apparent. The lower ceilings and other architectural details in these photographs suggest that they may have been taken in the Seward house on Lafayette Square, an early building which Blaine had remodeled extensively before he moved there in 1889.

The remodeling of this house was done by "Willie Camac," according to Mrs. Blaine's letters (*op. cit.,* Vol. 2, pp. 237, 240). This was most likely William M. Camac of the Philadelphia firm of Furness, Evans and Company. Camac had been with the firm as far back as 1871 at least. From 1867–71 John Fraser, the architect of the house at 2000 Massachusetts Avenue, had been a partner in the firm (at that time Fraser, Furness and Hewitt); so it is not unlikely that the interiors of the two Blaine houses would have similar characteristics.

ARCHITECT

The life and career of *John Fraser* (c. 1825–1903) is not easy to trace, and many questions remain. Possibly the first known example of his work is a design for the Washington Monument, submitted by a John Frazer, c. 1849. This misspelling of his name was not unusual, and the bell tower design showed elements not unlike those used by Fraser throughout his career. (1)

Fraser worked in Philadelphia for many years; from the 1850's there are at least four buildings attributable to him: the Burnett, Sexton and Swearingen Store, 1854; (2) the L. J. Levy and Company Department Store, 1855; the remodeling of the Pine Street Presbyterian Church, 1857; and the B. J. Farnham residence, 1858. For a period of at least two

8 June 1881
D.C. Permits, National Archives

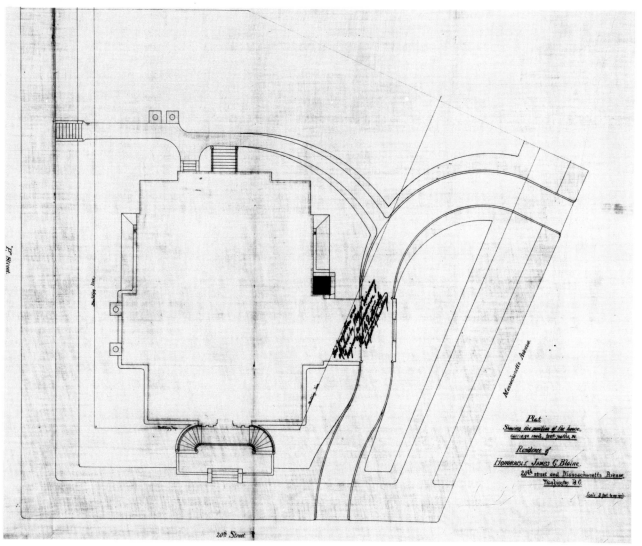

Plat
Showing the position of the house, carriage road, foot-paths, &c.
Residence of
HONORABLE JAMES G. BLAINE
20th street and Massachusetts Avenue
Washington, D.C.

years, 1858–59, Fraser was a partner of a civil engineer, Andrew Palles.

In 1861 John Fraser was one of nineteen architects who signed a charter for a Pennsylvania Institute of Architects. This organization never really became active, probably because of the disruption of the Civil War. In 1869 the Philadelphia Chapter of the American Institute of Architects was formed, with John McArthur, Jr., John Fraser, Frank Furness, George Hewitt and Henry A. Sims listed as the organizers. (3) In 1863 Fraser had an office at 424 Walnut Street. In that year he received an important commission: the design of a $200,000 building for the Union League Club of Philadelphia. By 1867 he had entered into a partnership with two former employees, George Hewitt and Frank Furness. The firm of Fraser, Furness and Hewitt, with office at 430 Walnut Street, lasted until 1871. (4) The most important building to come out of this partnership was the Rodef-Shalom synagogue of 1869, now demolished. (4,5)

In 1871 Fraser opened a Washington branch of his firm at 515 Seventh Street, N.W. Sometime during that year the firm was asked to submit a design for a building for the Pennsylvania Academy of Fine Arts, but in September 1871 the firm was dissolved. Evidently the dissolution took Fraser somewhat by surprise, and he wrote John Sartain of the Academy asking for an extension of time for submitting designs. (6) What transpired next is not known, but the building was ultimately designed by his former partner, Frank Furness.

It seems that Fraser remained in Washington until 1890; he was no longer listed in the city directories after that year. The listing retained the Philadelphia address at 430 Walnut Street until 1875; the Philadelphia directory showed him at this address as late as 1878. It is apparent that Fraser kept up his ties with Philadelphia while he was in Washington, as well as those with Riverton, New Jersey, a town near Philadelphia which was his family home. In 1878 he designed the Calvary Presbyterian Church in Riverton. Also, he is listed in the Philadelphia social register through the 1880's. In the Washington city directories a home address is seldom given. In 1872–73 the house address given was 1208 K Street, N.W., and from 1874–75 the listing read, "boards National Hotel."

The 1890 Washington listing for Fraser read, "John Fraser and Son, 1333 F." Richard Derman, whose thesis on Fraser has supplied much of the information on the architect's activity in Philadelphia and Riverton, says that the firm of John and Archibald A. Fraser remained in existence until 1902, even though New Jersey death records show that Archi-

bald Fraser died in 1895. The last listing of the Frasers in the Philadelphia *Blue Book* showed Mr. and Mrs. John Fraser and Miss Julia Fraser living in Riverton in 1903. Mr. Derman reports that there is no record of Fraser's death in the New Jersey State Archives. Perhaps the family moved to another state; in any case, John Fraser was by then an old man, and it is unlikely that he was still practicing architecture.

Buildings in Washington which can be documented in publications or in the building permit file of the National Archives as the work of John Fraser are:

1877   Residence for Lewis Clephane, 1225 K Street, N.W. (demolished) *American Architect and Building News,* Vol. IV, No. 141 (7 Sept. 1878), plate; Walter Clephane, "Lewis Clephane, a Pioneer Washington Republican," *Records of the CHS,* Vol. XXI (1918), p. 276.

1879   Residence for John T. Brodhead, 1500 Rhode Island Avenue, N.W., permit No. 2491, 14 June.

1880   Residence for Senator Donald Cameron, Scott Circle, N.W., Permit No. 1253, 16 April. (demolished)

1881   Residence for James G. Blaine, 2000 Massachusetts Avenue, N.W. Permit No. 1379, 8 June.

1881   Residence for B. F. Grafton, 1701 Massachusetts Avenue, N.W. Permit No. 1380, 8 June (demolished)

1881   Residence for Senator VanWyck, 1800 Massachusetts Avenue, N.W. Permit No. 73, 22 July. (demolished)

1884   Store for A. Saks and Company, Seventh Street and Market Space, N.W. Permit No. 585, 25 September. (demolished or incorporated into Kann's Department Store)

1974, Great Hall

Buildings in Washington which may have been the work of Fraser:

Vernon Row, 945 Pennsylvania Avenue, N.W., c. 1873 (demolished). A commercial row mentioned as being "the plan of architect Fraser," in G. A. Townsend, *Washington, Outside and Inside,* Hartford, Conn.: James Betts and Co., 1874, p. 583. Illustrated in JWM, p. 19.

Residence for Anthony Pollok, 1700 I Street, N.W. (demolished) and residence at 1424 Q Street, N.W. These two houses probably date prior to 1878 as there are no building permits for them. They are stylistically close to the Vernon Row commercial building and the Clephane house. The Pollok residence had a side porch very similar to the one on the Clephane house. It is illustrated in JWM, p. 245.

Residence at 1622 Massachusetts Avenue, N. W.(demolished). Interior wood trim was very much like that on the porte cochere of the Blaine house.

1. Henry Van Brunt, "The Washington Monument," in *Architecture and Society: Selected Essays,* William A. Coles, ed., Cambridge, Mass.: The Belknap Press, 1969, pp. 202–203, Pl. 113.
2. Winston Weisman, "Philadelphia Functionalism and Sullivan," *Journal of the Society of Architectural Historians,* Vol. XX, No. 1 (March 1961), p. 8, Fig. 10 and note 15.
3. George Champlin Mason, "Professional Ancestry of the Philadelphia Chapter," *Journal of the AIA,* Vol. 1, No. 9 (Sept. 1913), pp. 382–384.
4. James O'Gorman, *The Architecture of Frank Furness,* Philadelphia: The Falcon Press, 1973, pp. 31–32 and Catalog 2: Rodef Shalom.
5. George B. Tatum, *Penn's Great Town: 200 Years of Philadelphia Architecture,* Philadelphia: University of Pennsylvania Press, 1961, pp. 107–109. Pl. 106: Rodef Shalom.
6. Archives of the Pennsylvania Academy of Fine Arts. Letter from John Fraser to John Sartain, 5 Oct. 1871.
7. Richard Derman, *John Fraser: Nineteenth Century Architect,* a thesis written under James O'Gorman, University of Pennsylvania, 1971.

BIOGRAPHIES OF THE RESIDENTS

James Gillespie Blaine (1830-1893) was born at West Brownsville, Pennsylvania, the son of Maria Louise (Gillespie) and Ephraim Lyon Blaine. He entered Washington College in Pennsylvania when he was thirteen, and although his education there was of a limited nature, it was thorough in the classics, English and mathematics. He began to teach in Kentucky as soon as he graduated. He wanted to study law, however, and accepted another teaching position in Philadelphia so that he could study and teach at the same time.

In 1851 Blaine married Harriet Stanwood of Augusta, Maine, and with the aid of her family was able to purchase an interest in the *Kennebec Journal* and establish himself in the journalism field. Augusta re-

View from Southwest (P Street)
c. 1884
BMEL, James G. Blaine

mained his home except for the time he spent in Washington.

Blaine's career in journalism led to an interest in politics. He came from a family of Whigs, but soon abandoned the old party and persuaded a group of Maine voters, united by their opposition to the Kansas-Nebraska bill, to refer to themselves by the new Western name, Republican, thus introducing the name to the East. Blaine was, in fact, one of the founders of the Republican Party and was a delegate to the first national Republican convention in 1856. He saw the new party as one which would carry on the Whig philosophy as well as oppose slavery.

In 1858 Blaine was elected to the state legislature of Maine and served three terms. He was elected to the House of Representatives in 1863 and became Speaker in 1869. In 1876 Blaine moved from the House to the Senate and remained a Senator until 1881.

During these years in Congress Blaine's reputation grew. His skill as a public speaker, his generally level-headed reconstruction policies, and less admirably, his feud with Representative Conkling of New York brought him increasing national attention. Conkling was a supporter of Grant; Blaine led the group opposed to Grant, the "Half-Breeds," as they were called. Also, Blaine drew attention because of the taint of scandal attached to his name. Favors received from the Little Rock and Fort Smith Railroad resulted in the famous Mulligan Letters controversy; it was this more than anything else which cost him the Presidency in future years.

In 1876 Blaine's name was placed in nomination for the Presidency at the Republican national convention by Robert Ingersoll, who referred to him at one point as the "Plumed Knight," a name which stayed with Blaine the rest of his life. Because of the Mulligan affair, however, Rutherford B. Hayes received the nomination; the convention feared that those Republicans who were outraged by the scandal would turn to the Democrats if Blaine were nominated.

Blaine lost the nomination again in 1880 to his friend, James Garfield. With Garfield's victory he was offered and accepted the post of Secretary of State; he resigned, however, soon after Garfield's death, which opened the Presidency to Chester Arthur, a friend of Conkling's.

1970, Jack E. Boucher

In 1884 Blaine was finally nominated by his party; but his past association with wrongdoing, some of his decisions made as Secretary of State, and a statement made by one of his supporters calling the Democrats the party of "rum, Romanism and rebellion," alienated many people, including the large Irish Catholic vote in New York. He lost the election.

Blaine took a long trip to Europe in 1888 and was not a candidate when the next convention met. He threw his support to Benjamin Harrison who, when elected, chose Blaine as his Secretary of State. The relationship between the two men became strained, however, and Blaine resigned before the next convention. Harrison was nominated and Blaine was reconciled with him; but failing health prohibited him from taking an active part in the campaign, and in January 1893 he died at the age of sixty-two.

Blaine will be remembered for his oratory and his personal magnetism, but he made definite long lasting contributions to American foreign policy as well. He increased the ties of the United States with South America by presiding over the first Pan-American Congress and by promoting the theory of reciprocal trade treaties. He also secured a treaty with Great Britain concerning seal hunting in the Pribilof Islands, and raised the question of protection for migratory and ocean wild life.

Mr. Blaine was also an author, his most important publication being the two volume work entitled, *Twenty Years of Congress, from Lincoln to Garfield,* published in 1884–86. (DAB, NCAB; Obituaries: NYT, 1–28–93, ES, 1–27–93; WP, 1–28–93)

Harriet Stanwood Blaine (1927–1903) from Augusta, Maine, was teaching in Kentucky when she met James G. Blaine, a fellow instructor. The two were secretly married in 1850, but as there was some doubt regarding the legality of that marriage, another ceremony was performed in Pittsburgh in 1951. (DAB)

Mrs. Blaine is of interest in this study especially because of the two volumes of letters to her children which were published by her daughter, Harriet Blaine Beale. In these letters she discussed the plans for the new house, the change in site, and also the only major festivity to take place in the mansion while the Blaines lived in it—the marriage of her daughter, Alice, to Colonel John J. Coppinger. The letters reveal, too, the gradual realization that the new house was not what the Blaines needed at that time in their lives, a time when their large family was rapidly growing smaller as the children left home. In a letter to her daughter, Margaret, written in April 1883, she said: "How does it happen that the large mansion and the large family came in different portions of my life?" (Beale, *op. cit.,* Vol. II, p. 95)

Sometime in 1883 the Blaines leased their new house to the Levi Leiters. In 1885 the city directory showed them living at the Windom house on Scott Circle (See text, 1601 Massachusetts Avenue). The *Washington Post* (1–28–93) mentions that they spent a winter there, then rented the old Marcy house on the west side of Lafayette Square. In 1889 they leased and remodeled the Seward house on the east side of the Square; but instead of bringing Mrs. Blaine the happiness she expected, the house brought only tragedy. In January 1890 her son, Walker, died; this was followed in only two weeks by the death of his sister, Alice Coppinger. Emmons Blaine, another son, died in 1892, and Mr. Blaine died early in 1893. Mrs. Blaine left the house in 1894; it was torn down in that year and the Belasco Theater built in its place. The site is now occupied by the Court of Claims building.

The *Elite List* for 1895 showed Mrs. Blaine and a daughter living at Seventeen Dupont Circle. This was the home of the Reverend and Mrs. John A. Aspinwall. No further listings have been found in later *Elite Lists* or in city directories. She sold the house at 2000 Massachusetts Avenue in 1901 and died in Augusta, Maine, in 1903.

Four of the Blaine children married prominently. *Emmons Blaine* married Anita McCormick, the daughter of Cyrus McCormick, inventor of the reaper, in 1890. (NCAB) *Margaret Blaine* married Walter Damrosch in 1891. He was a conductor and composer who became known to millions of school children during the 1930's through the music appreciation radio broadcasts he produced for the public schools. (NCAB) *Harriet Blaine* married Truxtun Beale, the son of Edward Fitzgerald Beale, in 1894. The elder Beale was a navy man, Indian fighter and diplomat who, in his later years, was the owner of Decatur House on Lafayette Square. Truxtun Beale's grandmother was Emily Truxtun, a daughter of the famous Commodore. (DAB) The Blaine-Beale marriage was short-lived, however; it ended in divorce in 1896. *James G. Blaine, Jr.* married Martha Hichborn. She was the daughter of Admiral Philip Hichborn. Chief of the Bureau of Construction and Repair, and a descendant of Paul Revere. (DAB) Martha's brother, Philip, was married to poet Elinor Wylie, before she left him for Horace Wylie. (See text, 1205 Vermont Avenue.) The Blaine-Hichborn marriage also ended in divorce.

Levi Leiter: See text, 1500 New Hampshire Avenue, N.W.

Architrave and shutter.

George Westinghouse (1864–1914) was born in Central Bridge, New York, one of ten children of George and Emiline (Vedder) Westinghouse. His father was a manufacturer of farming implements. At the age of fifteen young Westinghouse had invented and built a rotary engine. After serving in the Civil War (he joined the army at the age of sixteen), he went to college for a short time, but left in order to devote all his time to inventing.

In 1869, before he was twenty-three, Westinghouse had received a patent for one of the most important of his inventions, one which would revolutionize railroading: the air brake. He organized the Westinghouse Air Brake Company, and as he began to work with and refine his invention he saw the advisability of making all air brake equipment standardized and interchangeable, from car to car and railroad to railroad. Westinghouse was one of the first manufacturers to apply this theory of standardization to industrial equipment.

From the air brake he went on to the development of a complete switch and signal system for railroads and, in 1882, formed the Union Switch and Signal Company with headquarters in Pittsburgh.

From 1880–90 Westinghouse took out more than 125 patents in the fields of railroad equipment, apparatus for the transmission of natural gas, and the transmission and utilization of electrical power.

In the mid–1880's he turned his attention towards developing a practical alternating current system and formed the Westinghouse Electric Company for this purpose. When it was ready, many electrical experts criticized the high voltage system as being dangerous. The controversy raged for years, but by 1893 Westinghouse was building the generators to supply electric power for the Columbian Exposition in Chicago. Later, his company built the first ten generators for transmitting the power of Niagara Falls electrically, and supplied the dynamos for the elevated and the subways in New York City, the Paris Metro and the Metropolitan Railway in London.

Mr. Westinghouse's inventions and companies continued to multiply until at one time the combined capitalization of his companies was about $200,000,-000; he employed 50,000 people.

Westinghouse received awards at home and abroad almost too numerous to mention. They included the Order of Leopold from Belgium, the Order of the Crown from Italy, the Legion of Honor from France, and the Edison Gold Medal from the American Institute of Electrical Engineers. He was a member of many professional and social organizations, and was admired for his integrity and tireless enthusiasm as well as for his scientific and manufacturing achievements.

In 1867 Mr. Westinghouse married Marguerite Erskine Walker. They had one child; a son, George Westinghouse, Jr. (sometimes referred to as George Westinghouse, 3rd) who married Violet Brocklebank, daughter of Sir Thomas and Lady Brocklebank of Irton Hall, Cumberland, England. (DAB, NCAB; Obituary: WP, 3–13–14, 3:6)

Marguerite Erskine Walker Westinghouse (1842–1914) was born in Roxbury, New York, and was educated at the Roxbury Academy. She exhibited a talent for sculpture and produced some notable pieces. Her artistic aptitude found further expression in the design and decoration of Erskine Park, the Westinghouse "cottage" and its gardens in Lenox, Massachusetts; and at Solitude, their home in Pittsburgh. Mrs. Westinghouse had a fondness for white which was revealed most strongly at Erskine Park, where there were rooms with walls and ceilings of white tufted satin, and driveways of white marble. (1)

Mrs. Westinghouse entertained frequently and extravagantly in her houses in Washington, Pittsburgh and Lenox. In her Washington home she gave a reception for the Society of Electrical Engineers in 1899 which was referred to in a book on Washington as "the finest reception ever given in a private residence in Washington. (2) For this reception a temporary frame structure, 59 by 44 feet, was erected in the yard. (Permit No. 1449½).

While Mrs. Westinghouse's favorite color was white, she was evidently fond of pink, too. A newspaper article described Mrs. Westinghouse and her Washington parties in this way:

> She was rather a small, dainty woman, with soda-water blond hair, and she was inordinately fond of pink. Pink satin ribbon, five or six inches wide, was festooned across the front of her refreshment table, a long table at one side of the dining room wall with smashing big bows at intervals, and American Beauty roses everywhere, perfuming the air.

> This was the usual decoration at her at-homes, and the refreshments were as elaborate as the setting. How the guests crowded in to get her lobster a la Newburgh! (WHT, 4–24–38)

Mrs. Westinghouse was also active as a board member of several hospitals in Washington and Pittsburgh. She was a member of many organizations, among them the National Geographic Society, the National Society of Fine Arts and the American Red Cross.

Mrs. Westinghouse lived only a few months after her husband. She died at Erskine Park in June 1914. (NCAB; Obituary, NYT, 6–24–14, 11:5)

---

1. Cleveland Amory, *The Last Resorts,* New York: Harper and Brothers, 1952, p. 29.
2. Allen B. Slauson, Ed., *A History of the City of Washington—Its Men and Institutions,* Washington: The Washington Post Company, 1903, pp. 407–08.

Pilaster capital.

Henry Fitzhugh (1867–?) was born in New Orleans, the son of Charles Lane and Emma Fitzhugh. He was a steel manufacturer who moved to Washington in 1921. He was married to the former Betty C. Poe. They had four children: John Danty, Henry J., Charles C. and Louise. He lived at 2000 Massachusetts Avenue in 1926. (WWNC, 1923–24)

Emily Crane Chadbourne was the daughter of Richard Teller Crane of Chicago, president of the Crane Company, manufacturers of pipes and pipe fittings. She was the divorced wife of Thomas Lincoln Chadbourne, a corporation lawyer who was a director of more than a score of corporations, including the Brooklyn-Manhattan Transit Corporation, New York Rapid Transit Corporation, Wright Aeronautical Corporation and Mack Trucks, Inc. She lived at 2000 Massachusetts from 1929 until 1932. (NCAB, Crane and Chadbourne)

Francis S. Whitten (c. 1881–1950) was a graduate of the Naval Academy, but retired from the Navy in 1911 to enter business. He became a partner in an investment firm in Wilmington and later was president of the Columbia Graphophone Company. After his retirement he engaged in the real estate business in Miami and Nassau. He was married to the former Katherine Lewis. They had one daughter, Mrs. Francine Lunn. The Whittens lived at 2000 Massachusetts Avenue from 1930 until 1932. (Obituaries: ES, 5–12–50, 17:4; NYT, 5–13–50, 22:6)

APPENDIX

Chain of Title:

1885   Deed 9 May, recorded 18 October 1886; Liber 1213 folio 113
William Walter Phelps et ux, Ellen S., (of New Jersey) to Harriet Stanwood Blaine (of Augusta, Maine)
". . . Original Lots One, Two and Three of Square Ninety-Five . . ." For $60,000.

1889   Deed 8 April, recorded 9 April; Liber 1384 folio 32
Harriet S. Blaine et vir, James G., (of Maine) to Samuel M. Bryan
". . . all of original lots . . . (2) and . . . (3) in Square . . . (95) . . ." There is a covenant with this deed which says that "no building or buildings of any kind or character shall ever hereafter be erected or constructed on any portion of that part of lot . . . (1) in said Square (now owned by the said Harriet S. Blaine) which lies North of a line drawn due West to the West line of said lot from the North Eastern corner of said lot (being

the corner formed by the intersection of Massachusetts Avenue with the West line of Twentieth Street) and this covenant and stipulation shall at all times hereafter, and forever be deemed taken and construed as a covenant running with the title to said lot . . . (1) and as forever binding the same in the hands of the present or any future owner . . ." Also, that ". . . no stable . . . shall ever . . . be built . . . on any part of lot . . . (2) . . . within the distance of forty feet from the division line of said lots one and two . . . and this covenant . . . shall at all times . . . be deemed . . . as a covenant running with the title to said lot two . . ." For $50,000.

1901   Deed 25 April, Liber 2537 folio 483
Harriet S. Blaine (of Augusta, Maine) to Marguerite E. Westinghouse (of Pittsburgh, Pa.)
". . . All of Original Lot . . . (1) in Square . . . (95) . . . subject however to the covenants . . . in Liber 1384 folio 32 . . ." For $150,000.

1914   Estate of Marguerite Westinghouse. Administration No. 21288.
Entire estate left to her son and only heir at law, George Westinghouse, Jr.

1919   Deed 13 January, recorded 23 January; Liber 4136 folio 420
George Westinghouse, Jr. et ux, Evelyn Violet, (of Pittsburgh, Pa.) to G. O. Mitchell (of Arlington, Mass.)
Lot 1 in Square 95 subject to the same covenants as above.

1920   Deed 14 December, recorded 28 December; Liber 4458 folio 320
Gladys O. Mitchell (of Arlington, Mass.) to Henry B. Spencer
$90. in Internal Revenue Stamps affixed. The rate before 1 July 1940 was $.50 per $500, making the price approximately $90,000.

1956   Will of Henry B. Spencer. Administration No. 90,649.
Property left to Samuel Spencer, Violet Spencer Thoron and Louise Spencer Cortesi.

1958   Will of Louise Spencer Cortesi (of New York City). Exemplified copy. Her share of property left to her husband, Roger Cortesi.

Building Permits

No. 1379, 8 June 1881. Permit to build.
Owner: James G. Blaine
Architect: John Fraser
Builder: Robert Davidson Company
Estimated cost: $48,000
No. 1411, 14 January 1891. Permit to repair or alter.
Owner: J. G. Blaine
Estimated cost: $15,000
Permit signed by: Jacob Myers, 1315 Sansom Street, Philadelphia, Pa.
"To make general repairs and restore damage caused by fire."

No. 1449½, 22 April 1899. Permit to repair or alter.
Owner: Mrs. J. G. Blaine
Occupant: George Westinghouse
"to erect a temporary frame structure 59'–2" x 44'— one storey high to be removed on or before May 24, 1899—conditional on consent of adjoining owners at 20th and P Sts."
"To be used for convention of electrical engineers"
No. 2770, 26 December 1903. Permit to erect passenger elevator.
Owner: George W. Westinghouse
"To install one passenger electric elevator, 3'–2½" x 5'–2"
No. 4132, 25 January 1921. Permit to repair or alter.
Owner: H. B. Spencer
Architect: George N. Ray
Contractor: George N. Ray
Estimated cost: $50,000 (Repairs, $30,000; Addition, $20,000)
"It is proposed to alter the present building so as to be suitable for 3 families with quarters on the top floor for their servants. Each stair and staircase is to be fireproofed; and stores are to extend under the present building as well as extended outside the building as shown. The plumbing is to be modernized as indicated and required."
". . . build new addition for 7 new –1– story stores, and make other repairs as per plans on file—8 projections for show windows."
Projections: 8 show windows. Projection: 3 feet; widths: one 9'–3", four 10'–0", one 9'–9" (20th St. side), one 14'–0", one 24'–9".
No. 645, 26 July 1921. Permit to install passenger elevator.
Owner: H. B. Spencer
Estimated cost: $3900.
No. 126317, 14 August 1929. Permit for trans. (transformer?)
No. 140008, 20 February 1931. Permit to repair or alter.
Owner: Henry Spencer
Estimated cost: $51
"To repair cement steps at 2000 Mass. Ave., N.W. on ground"
No. 215987, 27 August 1938. Permit to repair or alter.
"Randall H. Hagner has permission to replace rotted window frame and (illegible) with new on rear of building."
Estimated cost: $150
No. 266520, 31 January 1944. Permit to repair or alter.
Owner: H. B. Spencer
Estimated cost: $250
"Remove tops of chimneys about five feet (4 in dangerous condition). Repair arches over windows where dangerous."
No. 9013, 26 April 1946. Plumbing permit.
No. 291534, 10 January 1947. Permit to repair or alter.
"Randall H. Hagner Co. has permission to remove roof of old porch on east side of house and repair floor of porch."

No. 36479, 20 October 1948. Plumbing permit.
No. 313843, 3 December 1948. Permit to repair or alter.
Owner: Henry B. Spencer
Architect: Maurice S. May
Estimated cost: $3,000
"Install several stud non-bearing partitions in 1st floor, plastering and painting. See first floor plan of original application on file."
Filed with No. 313843: Letter from Mr. H. B. Spencer to the Engineering Department, Department of Building Inspection dated 12–3–48 asking for permission to proceed with installation of new partitions while possibility of overloading certain brick piers and walls in basement is being considered.
No. 314827, 24 January 1949. Permit to repair or alter.
Owner: Henry B. Spencer
Architect: Maurice S. May
Mostly illegible—further alterations to convert building to office use.
No. 315482, 23 February 1949. Miscellaneous permit.
Owner: Henry B. Spencer
Estimated cost: $2500
"To grade sidewalk level on P St. and pave so as to permit private parking for doctor and patients. Install sidewalk drain."
No. 39728, 3 March 1949. Plumbing permit.
No. 39729, 3 March 1949. Plumbing permit.
The following permits are concerned solely with repairs or alterations to the stores at the rear of 2000 Massachusetts Avenue, N.W. (2001–2005 P Street, N.W.):
No. 6793, 6 February 1925
No. 8100, 11 April 1927
No. 143186, 27 May 1931
No. 166802, 5 October 1933
No. 167515, 31 October 1933
No. 167592, 2 November 1933
No. 167643, 4 November 1933
No. 168084, 23 November 1933
No. 199767, 25 February 1933
No. 240672, 14 February 1941
No. 305792, 27 April 1948
No. 31376, 12 May 1948
No. 2504, 15 May 1948
No. A-51049, 31 July 1953

1970, Jack E. Boucher.

Listings of Residents

City directories list the following tenants:

1883 James G. Blaine, 20th corner P, N.W.
1884–1887 Levi Z. Leiter, 1500 20th N.W.
1888 No listing for either Leiter or Blaine
1889–1893 Levi Z. Leiter, 1500 20th N.W.
1898–1915 George Westinghouse, except for 1904 and 1907–13 when his name is not listed. Addresses given are 1500 20th St., N.W.; Blaine House, Dupont Circle; or Mass. Ave., corner 20th, N.W.
1916–1917 Jules Maillet, translator Pan American Union; 1500 20th, N.W.
1918–1919 United Service Club of America, 1500 20th St., N.W.
1920–1921 vacant
1922–1925 Japanese Embassy (address from this time on is 2000 Mass. Ave. N.W.)
1926 Henry Fitzhugh
1927–1932 Mrs. Emily Chadbourne
1930–1932 Francis Whitten
1933–1935 vacant
1936–1941 U.S. Rural Electrification Commission
1942–1945 Public Health Service (1944-45 listing from telephone directory)
1948– First floor: medical offices
Second floor: Spencer and Whalen, attorneys (Spencer, Whalen and Graham after 1969)
Third floor: American Short Line Railroad Association

Social registers list:

1898 Mr. and Mrs. George Westinghouse; Dr. William A. Stewart; Mr. Leon DeLaval (a French engineer and associate of George Westinghouse); Mr. Alexander G. Uptegraff (Mrs. Westinghouse's secretary)
1899–1901 Mr. and Mrs. George Westinghouse; Dr. William A. Stewart; Mr. Alexander G. Uptegraff
1902–1910 Mr. and Mrs. George Westinghouse; Mr. Alexander Garden Uptegraff (except for 1905–07).
1911–1914 Mr. and Mrs. George Westinghouse, Mr. George Westinghouse, Jr.; Mr. Alexander Garden Uptegraff.
1915–1916 Mr. Alexander Garden Uptegraff
1927 Mr. and Mrs. Henry Fitzhugh, Mr. J. D. Fitzhugh
1931–1935 Mr. and Mrs. Francis S. Whitten
1933–1935 Mrs. E. Crane Chadbourne

Note: The address is given as Blaine House through 1907; from 1908–21 it is 1500 20th St., N.W.; and thereafter 2000 Mass. Ave., N.W.

STATEMENT:

The "Blaine Mansion," one of the earliest great houses on Dupont Circle, was actually designed to face west across 16th Street, one block north of Scott Circle. For this reason the house as built has little regard to the avenue or its site. Nevertheless, it dominates the west end of the circle and functions as the lock to the upper reaches of Massachusetts Avenue. At the front, a triangular park formed by 20th, P and the avenue seems part of the private grounds to the house.

The stylistic inspiration for the building is indefinite, though there are obvious elements of Romanesque, Gothic and Renaissance details which provide character. The massing, an almost severe outline, gives the structure a brooding strength. The interior, apparently altered after a fire in 1891 and extensively remodeled for apartments in 1921, is characterized by large central spaces with peripheral chambers.

SITE:

Orientation: The building faces east on a trapezoidal lot measuring from respective sidewalks 124'–6" on 20th Street (east); 157'–5" on P Street (south); 120'–0" on Massachusetts Avenue (north); 100'–0" on the northwest; and 89'–6" on the west. A store addition (part of the 1921 renovations) on P Street breaks forward from the basement.

Paving: From the avenue there are three concrete risers with cheek walls and semielliptical concrete drive to the carriage porch. At the west, a second drive which connected the avenue with P Street has been destroyed.

Landscaping: The structure sits on a lot which is slightly higher than the surrounding streets. Grass and planting survive on the north side. Plantings are used in place of the 20th Street entrance stairs, and the P Street store addition has obliterated the former south garden. The west garden and drive were graded and paved for parking.

EXTERIOR:

Dimensions: The two and one half story structure (38'–0" to cornice) has a raised basement and three and one half story towers, 54'–0" high. The irregularly-shaped building has three bays on 20th Street, seven bays on P Street, five bays on the west, and six bays on Massachusetts Avenue. It measures approximately 86'–4" deep by 71'–4" wide.

Foundations: concrete footings and slab.

Structure: brick bearing walls and wood joists and rafters, except where remodeling has introduced steel.

Mechanical: The Otis elevator (800 pound capacity) in the service core west of the central hall is wood-panelled. A second elevator was recently installed in the north entrance hall.

Walls: brick. Two bands of rubbed brick separate the basement and first floor and emphasize most window sills. Molded brick courses are used to stress tower window lintels.

Mantel, 1970
Jack E. Boucher

Stoops: The pedestrian entrance on 20th Street is now a window and balcony. There were four risers from the sidewalk to a landing (with cast and wrought iron rosette railings) flanked by curved stairs which rose to the entrance stoop. The undercarriage is brick. The nine risers and their treads were sandstone. The railings were similar to that of the landing. Only the stoop and its railing remain.

Porches: The painted wood carriage porch on Massachusetts Avenue has brick pylons topped by molded cornices and sandstone crowns. The cluster columns supporting the roof are chamfered, beveled, turned and ornamented with applied jigsaw panels. Above a dado (formerly rosette railings) are glass panels, added in the 1920's, which screen the porch stair. The hipped roof had a tin crest, since removed. Jigsaw spandrels which formed segmental arches between the cluster columns have also been removed.

Several of the brick pedestals which supported the floor for the west elevation porch were incorporated into the kitchen and conservatory extensions.

Doorways and doors: Entrances were at each tower. The 20th Street entrance had a decoratively panelled double door and a semicircular transom window (now a fanlight). The doorway, flanked by stylized paired pilasters with shared Tuscan caps supporting double brackets, has terra-cotta sunflower panels and rosette stops capped by a staggered architrave, a rosette frieze and a cove cornice with cavetto end mounts. The arch spandrels are terra-cotta as is the leafy soffit of the entablature architrave.

The design of the original carriage porch entrance is not known. A cyma architrave frames a double door and its rectangular transom window. The west tower is closed by additions.

Windows: The segmentally-headed, double-hung windows have sandstone sills and peaked, brick lintels.

Cornice: The entablature has a molded brick achitrave, a corbeled brick frieze, and a cyma and ovolo, pressed tin cornice.

Towers: At the second and third floors of the north tower (the fenestration altered in 1921), the recessed tripartite windows have dado panels separated by Ionic columnettes supporting a rosette frieze, the lines of which are carried around the building. Between the two floors are a pair of terra-cotta Gothic panels. Above the third floor is a segmentally-headed Gothic frieze. The entablature is corbeled and the hipped slate peak capped by a decorative tin crest. The brick dormer has a double window with a muntin colonnette, a peaked segmental head, corbel ornament and a gable with tin finial.

The second and third floors of the east tower have recessed double windows with muntin colonnettes. The floors are separated by a terra-cotta frieze on line with the building cornice. The frieze acts as third floor window sill. The tower corners form pylons which rise, corbel capped, to the first ridge of the mansard roof. The tower has a hipped slate peak with a tin crest, a brick dormer facing 20th Street, and two oculus dormers of pressed tin, one facing north and the other south.

Dormers: The pressed tin dormers have double-hung windows flanked by scroll-buttressed, roll-panelled pilasters which support a plain frieze and a gambrel fishscale hood with a pressed tin spike.

Skylights: The hipped tin roof has four skylights. The first two illuminate the servants' quarters and the remaining two light the elevator shafts.

Chimneys: The seven chimneys are not as originally built. The more conventional rise from the roof directly above the cornice at the southeast, northeast, northwest and southwest, and share a string course with the dormer windows. The remaining chimneys at the north, south and west protrude from the walls at a point between the first and second floors. They share the rubbed and molded brick courses on the building facade. All chimneys are brick with corbels, chamfers and molded courses, having inset plain and Gothic terra-cotta panels. In 1944 the bulbous caps were removed and the chimneys closed with sandstone slabs.

1921
Second floor plan
Courtesy of Samuel Spencer.

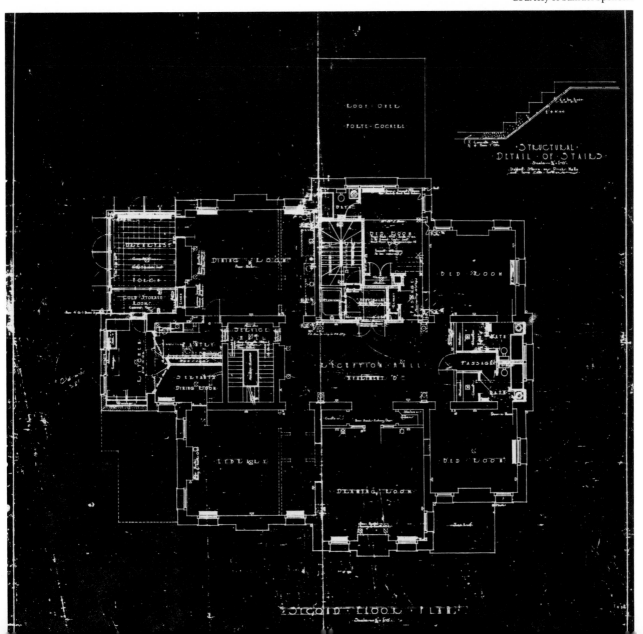

Jack E. Boucher, 1970

1921
First Floor Plan
Courtesy of Samuel Spencer.

PLANS:

According to the 1921 alterations (note plans) the three principal floors were made similar in plan. The design is essentially a central longitudinal hall surrounded by peripheral chambers with an entrance vestibule and stair at the north and a service core at the west.

SPACES:

The following details are common throughout the first floor. Elements individual to each space are described by chamber.

Flooring: 2¼″, oak.
Walls: plaster.
Cornice: plaster bead and cove.
Ceiling: 15′–0" high, plaster.
Doorways: 8′–3½″; single doors, 7′–0″.
Windows: 11″ jambs; panelled and louvered shutters with original brass hardware.
Hardware: brass door handles and knobs.
Heating: hot water radiators.

NORTH VESTIBULE:

This was formerly the stair hall. The original staircase was removed and a smaller enclosed stair and elevator installed in 1921.

Flooring: cast stone in black and white diamond pattern.
Baseboard: 4″, wood with cyma cap.
Chairrail: 3′–1″ high, wood.
Walls: The west wall has a recessed rectangular panel. The east wall has three recessed panels with semicircular heads centered by medallions.
Ceiling: The ceiling is divided into three panels outlined by dentil and bead courses and framed by beams with anthemion and palmette sides.
Lighting: There are four, two-light, reed and tassel, brass sconces with Bacchus figures.

LIVING HALL:

The 20th Street vestibule with flanking window benches was destroyed in 1921 to accommodate a larger space for a dressing room and bath. The new partition incorporates the old panelling. Other changes occurred at the pilasters and segmentally-headed archways.

Baseboard: 8½″, wood.
Dado: wood with two rows of panels.
Chairrail: 4′–1″ high, wood with reeding.
Walls: Panelled pedestals, possibly altered, support decorative pilasters which have cast iron, variant capitals. Matching columns were removed.

Ceiling: divided into three bays by panelled beams supported on pilasters. Each bay is outlined by roll, cavetto, fascia and ogee mouldings.
Doorways and doors: Most doors have been replaced. Centered at both the north and south walls is a segmental archway, 7′–1″ wide by 9′–8″ to the spring, closed and pierced by a door opening.
Chimney: projects 1′–1½″.
Hearth: 5′–7″ wide by 1′–7″; tile.
Firebox: 2′–5″ wide by 2′–6″ by 1′–1½″ deep; cast iron.
Mantel: wood cut to resemble stone. Tudor arch flanked by pedestals with Ionic columns which support an ovolo shelf of shells and dragons; 6′–2″ wide by 4′–6½″.

DINING ROOM:

The room was partitioned to accommodate a corridor from the hall to the new kitchen. The new wall incorporates the old wainscot and doorway.

Baseboard: 10″, wood.
Wainscot: 5′–7″ high, reeded vertical panels below a row of shorter panels capped by a reeded cornice.
Doorways and doors: mirror-paned; reeded architraves, wood.
Chimney: projects 1′–3½″.
Hearth: 4′–2″ by 1′–6½″; tile.
Firebox: 2′–6″ wide by 2′–6″ by 1′–1½″ deep; cast iron wreath, ribbon and flambeau back panel.
Mantel: 4′–2″ wide by 3′–5½″; wood, Tudor arch opening with leaf spandrels and double ovolo architrave.
Overmantel shelf: wood, with brackets; 6′–9″ wide by 4′–11″ high.

Dining Room, 1974

LIBRARY:

The alteration plans call for new doors to the drawing room with various changes to all three doorways. Indications are that the west windows overlooking the veranda were also changed. The ceiling was apparently replastered, eliminating the ceiling fixtures.

Baseboard: 5″, wood.
Wainscot: 4′–10″ high, three rows of raised panels capped by a lip moulding. Built-in bookcases of the same height and design break forward 1′–2½″ from the north and south walls. The bookcases are divided into bays by reed and guilloche pilasters with rosette capitals.
Doorways and doors: double doors to service area and drawing room, mirror-paned. Cased opening to hall. Rosettes center overdoor panels.
Chimney: projects 1′–4″.
   Hearth: 4′–2″ by 1′–6½″; tile.
   Firebox: 2′–6″ wide by 2′–7″ by 1′–0″; brick.
   Mantel: 4′–2″ wide by 3′–5″; wood, Tudor arch opening with leaf spandrels and double ovolo architrave.

Drawing Room, 1974

DRAWING ROOM:

The space is partitioned into an office and two smaller chambers. The opening to the southeast room is closed (a bathroom addition connects the two). Except for the mantels, the parlors are similar in style and detail.

Baseboard: 8½″, wood.
Walls: single flush panels in fascia and cyma mouldings.
Chimney: projects 1′–2″.
   Hearth: 4′–10″ by 1′–1″ deep.
   Firebox: closed.
   Mantel: wood; pilasters support a glyph frieze broken forward as figures over either pilaster. Shelf: 5′–4″ wide by 4′–1½″.

LIVING HALL (Second Floor):

Baseboard: 8½″, wood with scotia cap.
Dado: wood with vertical panels, painted.
Chairrail: 4′–0″ high, wood with reeding.
Cornice: cyma.
Doorways and doors: The segmentally-headed archway to the vestibule of the south room is 7′–1″ wide by 9′–8″ to the spring. The vestibule walls have closets. A French door 8′–3″ high opens into the south room.
Hardware: The French door has handles.
Chimney: 1′–1½″ deep.
   Hearth: 5′–0″, tile.
   Firebox: brick.
   Mantel: wood; Tudor arch opening, plain spandrels and molded shelf: 5′–0″ wide by 4′–3″.

SOUTH ROOM (Second Floor):

With the exception of the living hall, the details and style are typical of this floor.

Flooring: 2″, oak.
Baseboard: 6″, wood with cyma cap.
Walls: applied panel mouldings.
Cornice: bead, plain frieze, cavetto, ovolo and cove terminated by a bead.
Ceiling: 14′–0″ high, plaster.
Doorways and doors: single doors having flat panels in an ogee moulding within fascia and ovolo architraves.
Windows: Reeded pilasters support a plain frieze and a cyma, corona and ovolo cornice.
Hardware: brass mortise locks, escutcheons and knobs with inset rosettes.
Chimney:
   Hearth: 6′–0″.
   Firebox: cast iron.
   Mantel: cast iron surround. Wood; crossette architrave supports dentil, corona and ovolo shelf: 6′–1½″ wide by 4′–5″.
   Overmantel: applied moulding.

1520 Twentieth Street, N.W.

The house is on the southwest corner of Twentieth and Q Streets, N.W. It is located in Square 94 on lot 28 (parts of original lots 2 and 6).

Originally a private residence, it is owned by the Republic of Colombia and used as a residence for the ambassador.

PREVIOUS STRUCTURES ON THE SITE

Tax books show that the first structures on this site were erected c. 1873–74. These were three frame houses, built on the Twentieth Street side of the property. They were owned by William S. Graham, August Grimm and John O'Brien. According to the Hopkins map of 1887, the house on John O'Brien's lot was a double house, and a permit for repairs indicates that it was a two story frame with gables. In 1878 George F. Graham received a permit to build two brick dwellings (two story) on Q Street, one of which was eventually included in the 1520 Twentieth Street property. There are no permits for razing the frame houses; presumably this was done when the present house was built. The one brick dwelling was not razed until 1910.

HISTORICAL INFORMATION

The house at 1520 Twentieth Street was built by Thomas T. Gaff. Mr. Gaff bought parts of lots 2 and 6, Square 94, in 1903 (Liber 2714 folio 278; Liber 2714 folio 375). In 1904 he combined these lots to make lot 26. A building permit for the house was issued 20 September 1904 (No. 588) with the New York firm of Bruce Price and de Sibour as the architects. In 1910, four years after the house was completed, Gaff bought another section of lots 2 and 6 (Liber 3334 folio 166), and razed the brick dwelling on the property (Permit No. 2441). In 1911 he combined lot 26 with his new property to make lot 28. In that year he was granted a permit to enclose the new section with a brick wall and make a yard. A door and two windows were cut into the building to give access to the yard (No. 5401).

Mr. Gaff died in 1923 and left the house to his wife. In the same year she deeded it (with all the furnishings) to her daughter, Zaidee Langhorne (Liber 5401 folio 313). Mrs. Langhorne leased the house during the 1920's, then lived there briefly (1932–35) before leasing it again to the Grecian Legation (1935–37). In 1938 it was leased to the Colombian Embassy and sold to the Colombian Government in 1944 (Liber 8052 folio 567). There are no permits for any alterations during this period.

Apparently many of the original furnishings were left in the house by Mrs. Langhorne. A considerable number of pieces are there today, some of them bearing the names of European dealers who sold them to the Gaffs. A portion of Mr. Gaff's library also remains in the house. Two very fine Aubusson carpets, which belonged to the Gaffs, are now in the house of the President of Colombia.

In 1945 Colombia added a garage on the west side of the house where the yard had been (Permit No. 281396). This is the only significant change in the house since Colombia has owned it. At this writing, the building is undergoing some repair and restoration work.

KNOWN ARCHITECTURAL DRAWINGS

East elevation (20th Street). Ink on linen. Scale: ¼″ = 1′. Filed with permit No. 588, 20 September 1904.
    T. T. GAFF, ESQ., WASHINGTON, D.C. / Bruce Price and de Sibour, Arch'ts. / 1133 B'way, N.Y. / Dec. 21, 1903 / Revised June 29, 1904.

North elevation (Q Street). Ink on linen. Scale: ¼″ = 1′. Filed with permit No. 588, 20 September 1904.
    RESIDENCE FOR T. T. GAFF, ESQ., WASHINGTON, D.C. / Bruce Price and de Sibour, Arch'ts. / 1133 B'way, N.Y. / Dec. 21, 1903 / Revised June 29, 1904.

Plat showing projections beyond building line. Ink on linen. Scale: ¼″ = 1′. Filed with permit No. 588, 20 September, 1904.
    T. T. GAFF, ESQ. / 20th ST. WEST & Q ST. NORTH / Bruce Price and de Sibour, Architects / 1133 Broadway, New York / Aug. 5, 1903.

VIEWS

Exterior

Twentieth Street facade:
    Selections from the Work of J. H. de Sibour, Architect, Washington, D.C. Washington: Edward F. Gruver Co., bookbinder. Private publication, property of Mr. Jay R. L. de Sibour, grandson of J. H. de Sibour.

c. 1905 J. H. deSibour office book

SS, 12–9–45, Gravure section, p. 2.
Q Street facade and partial view of Twentieth Street facade:
  ES, 11–25–44, drawing by Helen Gatch Durston.

Interior
Photographs: SS, 12–9–45, Gravure section, p. 2
  Entrance hall and stairway, dining room, main drawing room, and sitting room off main hall. Prints from these negatives are in MLKW.

ARCHITECT

Jules Henri de Sibour (1872–1938), the son of Vicomte Gabriel de Sibour and the former Mary Louisa Johnson of Belfast, Maine, was born in France. His obituary in the *Evening Star* (11–4–38, 1:3) stated that he was descended from Louis XVI. When a young boy, de Sibour was brought to the United States where he attended St. Paul's School in New Hampshire and Yale University. In 1898 he married Margaret Marie Clagett, daughter of Mr. and Mrs. William H. Clagett of Washington, D. C. They were to have three sons: Henri Louis, Jacques Blaise, and Jean Raymond.

In 1899 de Sibour went to Paris to study architecture at the École des Beaux Arts. One year later he returned to the United States and began practice in New York City. He was listed in the New York city directories in 1901–02 at 1133 Broadway. He was taken into a partnership with Bruce Price, noted New York architect, in 1902 or 1903. Bruce Price died 28 May 1903, but the firm of Bruce Price and de Sibour continued to be listed until 1908 (at 1133 Broadway through 1907; in 1908 at 527 Fifth Avenue). From 1909–11 the listing read "Jules H. de Sibour." In

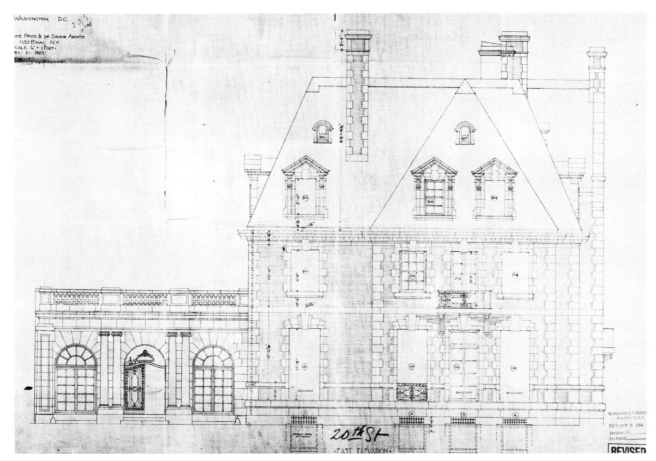

1903, D.C. Permits, National Archives.

1908 or 1909 de Sibour moved to Washington. The listings in the Washington city directories for 1908–09 read "Bruce Price and de Sibour," but after that they were in de Sibour's name only. His office was in the Hibbs Building through 1922, in the Edmonds Building in 1923 and 1924, and in the Investment Building from 1925–38.

Jules Henri de Sibour was one of the National Capital's most successful and prolific architects during his thirty years of practice here. His designs in Washington, D. C. include the Wilkins, Hibbs, F. H. Smith and Investment office buildings; the Chevy Chase and University clubs and the Riggs Theater and Office Building. In addition to the house at 1520 Twentieth Street he also designed the French Embassy (2221 Kalorama Road, N.W.); the Wilkins residence (Peruvian Chancery, 1700 Massachusetts Avenue, N.W.); the Moore residence (Canadian Chancery, 1746 Massachusetts Avenue, N.W.); and the Stewart residence (Embassy of Luxembourg, 2200 Massachusetts Avenue, N.W.). The most outstanding example of his work surveyed to date is 1746 Massachusetts Avenue, N.W. (Withey)

BIOGRAPHIES OF THE RESIDENTS

Thomas Trueman Gaff (1854–1923), the builder of the house, was born in Aurora, Indiana, the son of James Wade and Rachel (Conwell) Gaff. James Wade Gaff was in the distilling business in Aurora and later in Cincinnati, where the family moved when Thomas was a young boy. The elder Gaff was associated in the distilling business in Cincinnati with Charles Fleischmann. He was also a partner in the Cincinnati Dry Dock Company and a vice president of the Niles Tool Works.*

Thomas Gaff attended Harvard University for two years and then left to study chemistry at the Universities of Leipzig and Gottingen. Later he was awarded a degree from Harvard as of the class of 1876. Young Gaff continued his studies abroad until 1879 when he was called back to Cincinnati by his father's death to take charge of the family businesses.

* Information on the Gaffs in Cincinnati furnished by J. Richard Abell, Head, History and Literature Department, The Public Library of Cincinnati. Other sources: NCAB, WWNC (1921); Obituary: ES, 1–18–23.

He succeeded his father as vice president of the Niles Tool Works, a company engaged in the production of heavy machinery. In 1899 this company was consolidated with the Bement-Niles Works and the Pond Machine Tool Company to form the Niles-Bement-Pond Company, with headquarters in New York City and branches throughout the country as well as in London. Gaff was elected vice president of the new company and held this office until his death. He was also associated with Pratt and Whitney while in Cincinnati and was active in civic and cultural affairs. He was involved in a real estate venture in that city with a native of Cincinnati and later Washingtonian and neighbor: Larz Anderson (See *Massachusetts Avenue Architecture,* Vol. 1, 2118 Massachusetts Avenue, N.W.). In 1897 Gaff moved to Washington, and in 1905 Secretary of War Taft appointed him a member of the commission to approve the land appraisals for the Panama Canal construction.

Gaff was not just a businessman, however. He was possessed of considerable mechanical ingenuity, having invented a tachometer, a circuit controller and a two cycle oil burning engine. When not involved with his business, Gaff traveled frequently and enjoyed sailing and reading. He read Greek, Latin, French and German well. In his library, still in the house, are numerous, beautifully bound (and well-used) books in foreign languages: Viollet-le-Duc's *Dictionaire du Mobilier Francais,* Homer in both French and Latin, Goethe's works in German, H. Taine's *Les Origines de la France Contemporaine* and many others, as well as books in English on a wide variety of subjects.

In 1883 Mr. Gaff married *Zaidee Ellis* of South Carver, Massachusetts. She was the daughter of Matthias Ellis and Sarah (Forsyth) Ellis. The Ellis family was well known in Boston and Lenox as well as in Albany and Newport. Sarah Forsyth Ellis's journal, found in the library at 1520 Twentieth Street, mentions also that the Ellises moved from Boston to New York in 1866, and that they bought a house at 60 East Thirty-fourth Street. Little else is known about Zaidee Ellis Gaff, except that she was a member of the Chilton Club in Boston and the Colony Club in New York, and she had a home in Bermuda where she died at the age of ninety-three, 6 January 1955. (Obituaries: ES, 1–7–55; *Boston Herald,* 1–9–55, 45:2.)

The Gaffs had one daughter, Zaidee Ellis Gaff. She married Dr. Cary Duvall Langhorne, who, according to the *Evening Star* (1–7–55), was a cousin of Lady Astor. He was the son of John Duvall Langhorne and Ann Catherine (Tayloe) Langhorne of Lynchburg, Virginia and Washington, D. C. The Langhornes lived in Washington and at St. Bride's Farm in Delaplane, Virginia.

Mr. Gaff was a member of the Metropolitan Club, Chevy Chase Club, Cosmos Club, University Club and the Columbia Historical Society.

When the Republic of Colombia leased the Gaff house in 1938, the *Evening Star* (9–27–38) said, "A tradition of hospitality dating from Mr. and Mrs. Gaff's day has been maintained by a succession of interesting tenants." Biographies of these tenants follow:

Peter Goelet Gerry (1879–1957) occupied the house from 1924 to 1925. Gerry was born in New York City, the son of Elbridge Thomas and Matilda (Livingston) Gerry. His father was the founder of the New York Society for the Prevention of Cruelty to Children, the first society of this kind in the world. His great-grandfather was Elbridge Gerry, signer of the Declaration of Independence, delegate to the Constitutional Convention, member of Congress, governor of Massachusetts and vice president of the United States under James Madison. (DAB)

Gerry graduated from Harvard in 1901, studied law and began practice in Providence in 1906. He became interested in politics, was a delegate to the Democratic National Convention in 1912 and 1916 and was elected to the House for one term, 1913–15. Although defeated for re-election to the House, he ran for a seat in the Senate in 1916 and was successful. He served in the Senate until 1929 and then again from 1935 to 1947. He was a conservative Democrat and consistently opposed New Deal policies.

In 1910 Senator Gerry married Mathilda Scott Townsend of Washington, D. C. She was the daughter of Richard H. and Mary Scott Townsend, who built the house at 2121 Massachusetts Avenue which is now the Cosmos Club. (See *Massachusetts Avenue Architecture,* Vol. 1) This marriage ended in divorce in 1925. A year later Senator Gerry married Edith Stuyvesant-Vanderbilt.

In addition to his political activities Senator Gerry was also a newspaper publisher. He bought *The Providence News* in 1921 and the *Providence Tribune* in 1929. He merged the papers and published them until 1937.

Senator Gerry was vice president of the American Humane Society. In Washington he was a member of the Metropolitan Club. (WWNC, 1923, 1926); Obituary: NYT, 11–1–57)

The next tenant at 1520 Twentieth Street was **Dwight Filley Davis** (1879–1945). He lived in the house from 1926 until 1929. Davis was born in St. Louis, the son of John Tilden and Maria (Filley) Davis. He was a graduate of Harvard (1900) and the Washington University Law School (1903).

While in St. Louis he was active in civic affairs and was a member of many boards and commissions. He was also a member of the Board of Overseers of Harvard University from 1915–1921 and later from 1926–1932.

In 1916 Davis became a member of the War Relief Committee. He entered the Army in 1917 and served as a Lieutenant Colonel in France where he received the Distinguished Service Cross for bravery under fire. Later he was honored by France with the rank of Commander of the Legion of Honor. In 1921 he was named director of the War Finance Corporation, and it was in this year that he moved to Washington.

Davis was named assistant Secretary of War in 1923, and while acting as Secretary became involved in the Billy Mitchell controversy over aviation. It was Davis who finally alleviated this difficult political situation for President Coolidge by bringing about Mitchell's court martial and resignation. In 1925 Coolidge named Davis Secretary of War, a post he held until 1929, when he was made Governor General of the Philippines. He remained in this position until 1932, when he resigned.

Always involved in the politics of the Republican Party, an economic conservative and a foe of the New Deal, Davis nevertheless accepted service under Franklin Roosevelt when the United States entered World War II. He was named director of the Army Specialist Corps, an organization formed to commission men with special scientific or professional skills who were unable to meet the Army's physical requirements. It was at this time that he was promoted to Major General.

In addition to his public service, General Davis was also director of the Lehman Corporation, investment bankers; and chairman of the board of trustees of the Brookings Institution. Perhaps his name is most often associated with tennis, as being the donator of the Davis Cup. A top notch player at Harvard, he donated the cup in 1900, the year of his graduation, as an international tennis trophy.

Davis married Helen Brooks in 1905. They had four children: Dwight F., Jr., Cynthia, Alice Brooks and Helen Brooks. Alice made her debut at 1520 Twentieth Street; she married Roger Makins, later British ambassador to the United States (See 3100 Massachusetts Avenue). Cynthia married William McChesney Martin, chairman of the Federal Reserve Board from 1951 to 1970.

Helen Brooks Davis died in 1932 and in 1936 Davis married Pauline Morton Sabin, widow of Charles H. Sabin, president of the Guaranty Trust Company of New York. The second Mrs. Davis was very active politically and socially in Washington. She is remembered for her fight against prohibition, her interest in modern art, and her volunteer work for the Red Cross. She died in 1955. (Obituaries: ES, 12–28–55; WP, 12–29–55)

Dwight F. Davis: WWNC (1926, 1929, 1938); obituary: NYT, 11–29–45.

From 1930–31 the house was leased by **Claudius H. Huston** (1876–1952). Mr. Huston was born in Harrison County, Indiana. He was the son of a Presbyterian minister, Dr. Columbus DeWitt Huston, and Margaret Eleanor (MacRae) Huston. He worked as a country school teacher to pay for his education at Valparaiso University and later taught at Chattanooga Normal University. He opened a business school in that city, was encouraged by his contacts with businessmen to enter industry, and within twenty years had become an organizer and officer of twenty manufacturing and finance corporations in the Tennessee River Valley. His special skill was in reorganizing industrial or banking companies that were having financial difficulties.

Mr. Huston's political career began in 1920 when he was named chairman of the Republican state campaign committee for Tennessee. He helped break the "solid south" when he won Tennessee for Harding in that year and was rewarded with the post of Assistant Secretary of Commerce. Mr. Huston and Herbert Hoover became friends, and Huston was instrumental in getting the presidential nomination for Hoover in 1928. From 1929–30 Huston served as Chairman of the Republican Committee. Continuing party disharmony finally brought an end to his political career in 1932.

His wife, the former Grace Jordan, whom he married in 1902, died in 1917. They had four daughters, one of whom married Fulton Lewis, Jr., the well-known radio commentator. (WWNC, 1921; obituary: NYT, 8–16–52)

The only *minister from Greece* to live at 1520 Twentieth Street was *Demetrios Sicilianos*. Before coming to Washington he had been an attaché to the Minister of Foreign Affairs (1902), chargé d'affaires in Paris, director of political affairs in the Ministry of Foreign Affairs, and Minister to Hungary (1932–35). Dr. Sicilianos was also an art historian and published works on Byzantine iconography, Byzantine churches and monuments in Constantinople and Ravenna, and on the painter, El Greco. (IWW, 1938).

Ambassadors from Colombia

Ambassadors who have lived at 1520 Twentieth Street are listed below, with a few selected biographical facts included.

H. E. Miguel López Pumarejo, appointed 3 October 1938, received part of his education in the United States: at Chestnut Hills and Worcester Academies and at Manhattan College in New York City. He was a member of the coffee firm of Pedro A. López y Cia., and was president of the Chamber of Commerce of Bogotá, Representative in the National Congress, rector of the law school of the Universidad Libre, and a member of the governing board of the Pan American Union. His son is currently the minister of the Embassy in Washington; and his nephew, Alfonso López, is now the President of Colombia. (WWLA, 1940; Embassy of Colombia)

H. E. Gabriel Turbay, appointed 1 November 1939, was a physician and at various times a member of the House of Representatives. A leader in the Liberal Party, he was Minister to Italy and Belgium, a member and president of the Senate, and Minister of Government and Foreign Relations. (WWLA, 1940)

H. E. Carlos Sanz de Santamaría, appointed 23 August 1945, was an engineer, and also received a Master's degree in economics from Georgetown University. He taught this subject in Colombia. He was mayor of Bogotá (1942); Minister of State and of National Economy, Finance, and Foreign Affairs. He was also the chairman of the Inter-American Commission on the Alliance for Progress. (DLACB)

H. E. Gonzalo Restrepo Jaramillo, appointed 8 February 1947, was a lawyer who was also Dean of the University of Antioquia and president of the Banco Alemán Antioqueño. He was both a Representative and a Senator, and on several occasions a Cabinet Minister (Minister of Foreign Relations and Minister of Defense). He was also the author of several poetry books and essays. (Embassy of Colombia)

H. E. Eduardo Zuleta Angel, appointed 6 September 1949, was a jurist. He taught law, was a magistrate of the Supreme Court of Justice (1934) and later president of the Court. He was Minister of Foreign Affairs (1948–49), Ambassador to Peru (1943–45) and Italy (1951–52) and president of the IX Inter-American Conference (1948). (IWW, 1954)

H. E. Cipriano Restrepo Jaramillo, appointed 22 May 1951, was a civil engineer trained at the University of California at Berkeley. He was superintendent of the State of Antioquia Railroad System, vice president and president of the Colombian Tobacco Company, and founder and first president of the Colombian National Association of Manufacturers. He was also Colombia's representative to several international conferences. One of his sons, Mr. José Luis Restrepo, resides in Washington, D. C. (Embassy of Colombia)

H. E. Eduardo Zuleta Angel, appointed 23 July 1953. (See above)

H. E. Francisco Urrutia, appointed November 1955, was an accredited correspondent of the League of Nations in Colombia from 1932–45. He was also professor of international law and diplomatic history at the Universidad del Rosario, Bogotá (1940–46), Ambassador to Argentina (1948–50), to the United Nations (1950–51) and to Venezuela (1952–53). He was also permanent representative to the United Nations (1953–57). (IWW, 1959)

H. E. José Gutierrez Goméz, appointed 1957, was manager of the Cali Agricultural, Industrial and Mining Credit Bank (1932–35) and of the Uribe Angel Laboratories (1935–46). He was a member of various economic committees and missions, delegate to the Ninth General Assembly of the United Nations (1952) and Ambassador to the Council of the O.A.S. (1957). (IWW, 1960)

H. E. Carlos Sanz de Santamaría, appointed 8 March 1960. (See above)

H. E. Eduardo Uribe Botero, appointed 20 June 1963, was a lawyer. He graduated from the University of Antioquia and later was a professor there. He was a Representative to the Congress from 1935–37 and from 1941–43, and was both Secretary of Government and Governor of the State of Antioquia. He was a member of the Liberal Party and was at one time Minister of Government. (Embassy of Colombia)

H. E. Hernán Echavarria Olozaga, appointed 6 January 1967, was a graduate engineer and also a student at the London School of Economics. He was the director of several companies and Minister of Public Works and of Communications. (DLACB)

H. E. Misael Pastrana, appointed 26 December 1968, was a founder and editor of *El Porvenir,* a civil law Circuit Judge (1945), and has held many government posts since. He was secretary of the Colombian Embassy at the Vatican (1947–49), private secretary to President Ospina Pérez (1949–50), counsellor at the Colombian Embassy in Washington (1950–52), Secretary to the Minister of Foreign Affairs in 1953, alternate representative to the United Nations (1954–56) and founder and vice president of the Corporación Financiera Colombiana in 1957. In 1960 he was Minister of Development and in 1961 Minister of Public Works and Finance. He was in private business from 1961 to 1965, but returned to government service and was Minister of the Interior (1966–68) before becoming ambassador to the United States. In 1970 he was elected President of Colombia, a position he held until August 1974. (IWW, 1974–75)

H. E. Douglas Botero Boshell, appointed 15 December 1969, received his degree in law and economics from the National University in Bogotá and did post-graduate work in London. From 1939–1944 he was with the Bureau of Commerce and Industry, Ministry of Economics. He was head of the Industrial Property Office and General Counsel of the Ministry. From 1952–57 he was a member of the Board of Directors of the National Telecommunications Corporation. In 1966 he was appointed Minister of Communications; in 1969 Minister of Government. The Ambassador has also been president of the National Federation of Wheat Millers and a member of the boards of the conservative newspaper *La Republica,* the Riopaila Sugar Refinery in Cali, and Colombia and AVIANCA Airlines. He is married and has four children. (U.S. Department of State)

H. E. Julio Cesar Turbay Ayala, appointed 29 April 1975, is the President-designate (Vice President) of Colombia and is expected to return to his country and run for President sometime before the term of the current President expires in 1978. Ambassador Turbay is the leader of the Liberal Party and President of the Senate. In the past he has held several important government posts, including Minister of Labor, Natural Resources and Foreign Affairs. He has also been Ambassador to the United Nations and to Great Britain.

The Ambassador is married to the former Nydia Quintero, and they have four children: a son, Julio Cesar, Jr. who is a lawyer and economist, and three daughters; Diana, Claudia and Maria Victoria. (Embassy of Colombia; WP, 5-4-75)

APPENDIX

Chain of Title

1903 Deed 7 March, recorded 6 May; Liber 2714 folio 278
George Lothrop Bradley et ux, Helen McH., to Thomas T. Gaff
". . . All those parts of original lots . . . (2) and . . . (6) in Square . . . (94) contained within the following metes and bounds: Beginning for the same on 20th Street . . . (60) feet South of the Northeast corner of said Square and running thence South on said Street . . . (30) feet, thence west . . . (120) feet, thence North . . . (30) feet and thence East . . . (120) feet to the place of beginning . . ."

1903 Deed 4 May, recorded 6 May; Liber 2714 folio 375
Charles Buchanan et al (Committee of the estate of John H. VanAntwerp, Albany, New York) to Thomas T. Gaff (of Barnstable, Mass.)
". . . All that part of original lots . . . (2) and . . . (6) in Square (94) contained within the following metes and bounds . . .: Beginning for the same at the Northeast corner of said Square and running thence South on 20th Street West . . . (60) feet, thence West . . . (120) feet, thence North . . . (18) feet, thence East . . . (32) feet, thence North . . . (42) feet to a point on North Q Street and distant . . . (88) feet from the place of beginning; and thence East on said Q Street . . . (88) feet to the place of beginning. Being the same land conveyed to said John H. VanAntwerp by deeds recorded . . . in Liber 1381, folio 88 et seq. and Liber 1379, folio 250 et seq. . . ." For $22,000.

1904 On 16 May Thomas T. Gaff combined parts of original lots 2 and 6, Square 94, into lot 26. Office of the Surveyor, Subdivisions Book 29, page 89.

1910 Deed 15 June, recorded 16 June; Liber 3334 folio 166
Mary Frances Parker to Thomas T. Gaff
". . . part of original lots . . . (2) and (6) in Square . . . (94) beginning for the same at a point in the North line of said lot . . . (6) . . . (88) feet West of the Northeast corner of said Square, thence running south . . . (42) feet thence West . . . (16) feet thence North . . . (42) feet to the North line of lot . . . (2) and thence East along the North line of said lots . . . (2) and . . . (6) to the place of beginning . . ."

1911 On 31 May Thomas T. Gaff combined the West two feet of original lot 6 and the East 14 feet of original lot 2 by depth of 42 feet and lot 26, Square 94, into lot 28. Office of the Surveyor, Subdivisions Book 43, page 152.

1923 Will of Thomas T. Gaff, Administration No. 30186.
All property, real and personal, left to his wife, Zaidee Ellis Gaff.

1923 Deed 6 August, recorded 15 December 1924; Liber 5401 folio 313
Zaidee Ellis Gaff (widow) to Zaidee Gaff Langhorne

". . . all those lands and premises . . . described in the following deeds . . ." (Lists deeds to Gaff from Bradley, Buchanan and Parker: see above.) ". . . All of the tangible personal property, including furniture and household furnishings now being in and upon said land and premises . . . now belonging to the party of the first part and whether acquired by her under will of her husband, Thomas T. Gaff, or otherwise . . ."

1944   Deed 16 December, recorded 29 December; Liber
        8052 folio 567
        Zaidee Gaff Langhorne to Government of the
        Republic of Colombia
        ". . . Lot 28 in Thomas T. Gaff's subdivision in
        Square 94 . . ." For $115,000.

Building Permits

No. 588, 20 September 1904. Permit to build.
Owner: Thomas T. Gaff
Architect: Bruce Price and de Sibour
Builder: Richardson and Burgess
Estimated cost: $100,000
No. 676, 29 September, 1904. Permit to erect builder's
shed.
No. 1868, 30 November 1906. Permit to repair or alter.
Owner: T. T. Gaff
Contractor: John Walker and Son
Estimated cost: $600.
"Remove brick face of wall on 20th and Q Street
fronts 4″ deep, replace by stone ashlar to depth of new
grade of parking"
No. 2441, 15 November 1910. Permit to raze brick
dwelling at 2006 Q Street, N.W.
No. 5401, 25 May 1911. Permit to repair or alter.
Owner: Thomas T. Gaff
Contractor: Charles H. Soran
Estimated cost: $1,000
"Alter vacant lot west side of building into yard attached
to 1520 20th St. as follows: Construct brick fence back
of building line 13″; excavate area in yard; Cut two
windows and one door; install yard and area drain."
No. 281396, 9 November 1945. Permit to repair or alter.
Owner: Colombian Embassy
Architect: C. W. Muth, Jr.
Estimated cost: $2000
Permit to build brick garage: 41′–0″ x 16′–0″ x 10′–0″
No. 5517, 28 November 1945. Plumbing permit.

Listings of Residents

City directories list the following tenants:

1909–1923 Thomas T. Gaff
1924–1925 Peter Goelet Gerry
1926–1929 Dwight F. Davis
1930–1931 Claudius H. Huston
1932–1935 Zaidee Gaff
1936–1937 Grecian Legation
1938 Mrs. Zaidee Langhorne
1939 Colombian Embassy

Social registers list:

1909 Dr. and Mrs. Cary D. Langhorne
1916–1917 Mr. and Mrs. Thomas T. Gaff. Miss Helena
        Elliott listed in 1916.
1927 Mr. Dwight Davis
1929 Mr. and Mrs. Dwight F. Davis, Miss Alice Brooks
        Davis and Mr. Dwight F. Davis, Jr.
1932–1934 Dr. and Mrs. Cary Langhorne

STATEMENT:

The residence at 1520 Twentieth Street is in the
late 16th and early 17th century French manner most
often associated with the school of François Mansart.
Reminiscent of a country chateau, the building would
seem more effective surrounded by terraces, balustrades, pavilions and a moat, as Chateau Balleroy.
Generally a competent design, the brick is too dark
and the double-hung windows incongruous in a
French facade.

Though the interior has both 17th and 18th century chambers, their eclecticism is coordinated, the
craftsmanship excellent. The unusually open plan
allows for a flow of space which results in several
visual surprises. The rooms are orientated toward the
most agreeable natural light according to function:
the office and drawing room on the east for morning
light, the ballroom on the west for evening light, and
the dining room on the north for diffuse, non-direc-
tional light. Details are of special interest; the stair
balustrade is similar to those of 1700 and 2200 Massachusetts Avenue by the same architect (Vol. I), while
service doors and movable walls are cleverly concealed.

SITE:

Orientation: the residence, which faces east on the south-
    west corner of Q and Twentieth Streets, has a lot
    measuring 90′–0″ on Twentieth Street by 120′–0″
    deep. A private lot 16′–0″ on Q Street by 42′–0″ deep
    breaks into the site.
Enclosures: on the south, the garden court and parking
    area share a brick, limestone-capped stepped wall 17′–
    10″ high. The wall is connected to the building vesti-
    bule by a brick and limestone screen which is pierced
    by a semicircular-headed limestone archway closed by
    wrought iron gates. A low decorative iron fence
    screened the parking area from the street (the middle
    portion was removed). The fence is divided into sin-
    gle panels by limestone pedestals for iron lighting
    standards with formerly clear glass globes (now
    opaque).
Paving: the parking area is concrete scored as Belgian
    block. The garden court has a brick and glazed terra-
    cotta terrace connected to the parking area by a flag-
    stone walk.
Outbuildings: a garden located west of the residence
    was displaced in 1945 by a one story attached garage.
Landscaping: the original English ivy has been removed.
    Hemlocks flank the vestibule. On Twentieth and Q
    Streets is a border of grass and clipped privet hedge.
    The garden court has azalea, dwarf spruce, aucuba
    and scattered ligustrum.

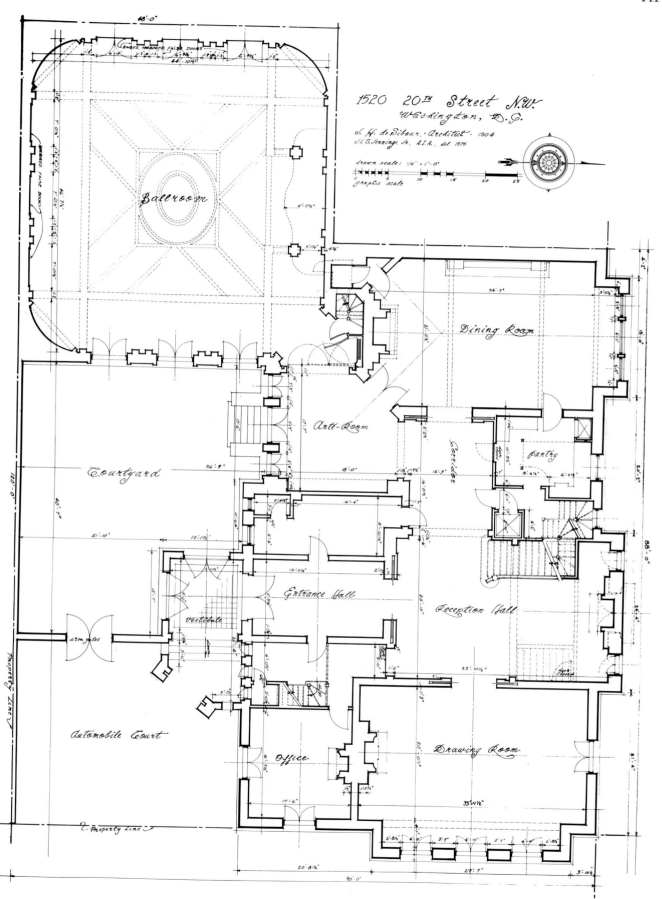

1520 20TH Street N.W.
Washington, D.C.

J. H. de Sibour, Architect · 1904
J.S. Jennings Jr, A.I.A., del 1975

drawn scale: 1/4" = 1'-0"
graphic scale

Ballroom

Dining Room

Pantry

Ante-Room

Corridor

Courtyard

Entrance Hall

Reception Hall

Vestibule

12'0 gates

Automobile Court

Office

Drawing Room

Property Line

Property Line

1971, J. Alexander.

EXTERIOR:

Dimensions: The residence, a raised basement structure of two and one half floors and attic, measures (southeast corner grade) 31′–6″ to gutter and 56′–3″ to roof ridge. The 55′–0″ east wall (20th Street) has a 4′–0″ projection and the 88′–0″ north wall (Q Street) two, 4′–0″ projections. The one story, 21′–0″ high, southwest ballroom wing measures 47′–0″ wide (west wall) by 50′–0″ deep (south wall). The 19′–3″ south vestibule projects 12′–0″.

Foundations: 1′–0″ square concrete footings and 1′–10″ thick brick foundations.

Structure: brick with steel beams and roof truss.

Walls: limestone base with block cap for two story Roman brick (limestone quoines) walls. The base cap acts as first floor sill. Limestone string courses continue the first floor balcony rail and the second floor balcony base. A limestone ground (similar to the quoines) frames the major openings.

Doorways and doors: vestibule double door of glass in iron frame with ornamented grille, ogee transom bar and semicircular light.

Windows: The basement windows are double-hung and protected by grilles.

The first story openings are French doors with transoms in block and keystone architraves; the second story openings are double-hung. The exceptions include the garden court French doors which have semicircular fans, the second story French doors (one overlooking 20th Street, the other to the south parapet), and (not including the east bay) the Q Street elevation.

On Q Street, the second bay French door has a fan-light (with scrolled keystone) and side-lights, the last bay has tripartite double-hung windows. The remaining windows are casement or double-hung of various sizes.

Areaways: third bay from east on Q Street; brick retaining walls and concrete stair. There are individual areas for basement windows.

Vestibule: The limestone base supports brick walls and a plain, limestone entablature with baluster parapet. The diagonal entrance facade is limestone, pierced by a semicircular-headed opening (with keystone), and covered by a wrought iron radial marquise (glass panels removed). There are five limestone risers to the "stoop" lighted by semicircular-headed glazed French doors overlooking the garden court.

Balconies: French doors have ornamented, wrought iron

Automobile Court

Entrance Hall.

balconies. First floor balconies are flush with the wall; Q Street and second floor 20th Street balconies are supported by ornamented limestone brackets.

Cornice: The vestibule and one story ballroom wing, connected by a one story projection, share a plain limestone entablature and baluster parapet. The main structure has a bracketed limestone cornice.

Roof: mansard with copper gutter and crest; slate on terra-cotta blocks.

Dormers: double-hung, set in limestone architrave with keystone; brackets support pediments. Semicircular-headed, double-hung attic windows.

Chimneys: There are six brick chimneys, five of which have limestone quoines, string course and cap.

ENTRANCE HALL:

Depth: 19′–9½″
Width: 11′–3½″
Height: 14′–0″

In contrast to the vestibule (a glass-enclosed porch) and the richness of the major interior spaces, the entrance hall is conspicuously stark. It is the means, both physically and transitionally, between the outside and inside. The materials and color hurry the visitor; there is no warmth in marble floors and still less charm when combined with plaster walls painted white. The only relief is the doorways and doors, the mellow wood a welcome invitation to discreet passage.

Flooring: cream-colored marble paving blocks.
Baseboard: 8½", cream-colored marble.
Walls: raised panels with corner rosettes.
Cornice: bundled reed.
Ceiling: cove with pulvinated floral border for central panel.
Doorways and doors: natural oak. 7'–6½" high single and pocket doors, raised panels; fascia and ogee crossette architraves. Entrance double door: 7'–11½" high to curved transom bar midpoint; glass in iron frame with decorative cast iron grille separated by bar from semicircular light; fascia and ogee architrave with scrolled key.
Hardware: brass knobs.
Lighting: four, three-light, shell, pendant, scroll-armed brass sconces, two with gas jets.

OFFICE:

Depth: 16'–3½"
Width: 15'–6"
Height: 13'–6"

The character of the chamber has been altered. The ceiling canvas (peeling slightly at one edge) is now concealed under tan paint. This, coupled with the 18th century mantel, the most delicate in the residence, would suggest the walls to have been papered or painted in a compatible manner. The present state of the space is apparently only a shadow of the former richness. Morning would have been the most agreeable time for this southeast chamber.

Flooring: oak, herringbone.
Baseboard: 6", wood with ogee cap.
Dado: wood painted white; raised panels.
Chairrail: 2'–6" high; wood, ovolo and fascia.
Walls: plaster painted white.
Cornice: fascia, ovolo and bundled reed.
Ceiling: plaster cove terminated by pulvinated gadrooning.
Doorways and doors: 7'–6½" high door to office vestibule, raised panels; fascia and ovolo crossette architrave.
Windows: 11'–6½" high French doors and transom lights; fascia and ovolo crossette architrave.
Hardware: brass. Oval door knob and espagnolette window bolts with rosette knobs.
Lighting: four, two-light (opaque glass-globed), spray and reed arm sconces (two of which have a gas jet).
Chimney: projects 1'–1".
  Hearth: 4'–7" by 1'–1½"; grey-veined cream marble with grey insets.

Office

Firebox: 2'–0" wide by 2'–0" by 1'–2½" deep; cast iron back panel and sides with rinceau surround.
Mantel: compact; receded columns flank panelled frieze and shelf, 4'–9" wide by 3'–8" by 1'–3" deep.

ANTEHALL:

The oak-panelled, L-shaped antehall to the Ambassador's office is detailed as the reception hall. The oak partition (partially removed) which screens the private stair is inset with a lead came and opaque glass transom. An original entrance from the reception hall has been closed (a heating duct partially obscures the doorway).

RECEPTION HALL:

Depth (from entrance to chimney wall): 35'–0½"
Length (from drawing room to dining room): 38'–2¼"
Height: 14'–0"

The hall functions not only as circulation space, but also as living room and reception hall. As the

Reception Hall, undated
Courtesy of Embassy of Colombia.

most important measure of the house, it is at once dramatic (the richly carved stair faces the entrance), inviting (an intimate chimney area) and baronial (sheer size and lavish use of material). The sobriety of style and mellow wood is a backdrop (or mediator) for the peripheral chambers. The bronze baroque chandelier, not original to its present location, more likely hung from an existing ceiling rosette over the stair well.

Flooring: oak, herringbone.
Baseboard: 7½″; ovolo and scotia cap.
Walls: three rows of raised panels in stiles and rails. Fluted Ionic pilasters support beams which section the hall.
Cornice: cyma, ovolo, cavetto and cyma.
Ceiling: flat panels divided by ribs.
Doorways and doors: 8′–10″ high pocket doors, raised panels; on a raised ground acanthus leaf pilasters support rosette crossettes of fascia architraves. 7′–6″ high concealed doors to pantry and cloak room.
Windows: beneath the stair landing and flanking the chimney are casement windows 3′–0″ from floor to sill with 1′–2″ deep jambs. Stair landing central French door with 8½″ riser, lead came and wood fanlight and recessed side casements 2′–6½″ from floor to sill.
Hardware: bronze. Door pulls and cremone window bolts.

Stair

Lighting: two, four-light, acorn and acanthus leaf, bronze 18th century sconces. One baroque, two-tier, sixteen-light, brass chandelier (perhaps originally over stair well). One, six-light, glass and brass finial drum lantern in side hall. Two, two-light, scallop shell, leaf arm and cherub, brass sconces on stair landing.
Chimney: projects 8½″.
    Hearth: 5′–10″ by 2′–0″; cast stone.
    Firebox: 4′–2″ wide by 3′–4″ by 2′–0″ deep; cast stone.
    Mantel: cast. Candelabra pilasters support rinceau frieze for shelf 6′–7″ wide by 5′–11½″ by 10½″ deep.
Furniture: bronze. Andirons, the left with Asian figure, the right with Negroid figure, both seated.

STAIR:

There are sixteen, 6½″ risers to the hall-width landing and thirteen, 6½″ risers to the second floor. The oak stair and second floor balcony railings are richly carved rinceau with floral baskets and dropped pendants at newels. The first floor newel is terminated by a scroll.

SECOND FLOOR HALL:

Floor: red carpet.
Baseboard: 7½″, oak; torus and cavetto cap.
Walls: oak; two rows of flat panels in stiles and rails.
Cornice: oak; ogee, ovolo, corona and ogee.

Drawing Room Mantel

Ceiling: 10′–9″ high, plaster painted white; coved. Center panel within fruit and flower pulvination. Pulvinated roundel for fixture over stairwell.
Doorways and doors: 7′–5½″ high, oak; raised panels. Panelled jamb; fascia and ogee architrave.
Hardware: brass. Ornamented oval and circular doorknobs with mortise locks.
Lighting: two, two-light, reeded arm brass sconces with milk-glass tulip shades, each outlet having gas jet.

Second Floor Hall

DRAWING ROOM:

Depth: 24′–1½″
Length: 35′–1½″
Height: 13′–10¼″

The combination of four French doors and an eastern exposure has resulted in an airy chamber (particularly bright in the morning), the physical character perhaps more reminiscent of a country house than one designed for the city. Though white with gold accent is used throughout, the original scheme (wall paper or fabric) would have been more vibrant with color and pattern. There is the further possibility that the applied wall moulding is not original as the profile does not exactly match the similar dado moulding. Attention is directed to the fine bronze-doré fixtures and hardware and, in particular, the similarity between the sconces and mantel "andirons." The chandelier, off-centered but on axis with the door and middle window, is not original to the room.

Flooring: parquetry covered with beige carpeting.
Baseboard: 8″, wood, ogee and bead cap.
Dado: plaster; panels of applied ovolo moulding.
Chairrail: 3′–0″ high; bead, fascia and ovolo.
Walls: wall-paper painted over; panels of applied ovolo moulding.
Cornice: plaster; fascia, talon and bundled reed.

Drawing Room

Ceiling: plaster, cove with gadrooning and bundled floral pulvination.

Doorways and doors: 8′–10″ high; fascia, cyma and backband architrave with crossettes and raised overpanel. Pocket doors; oak with raised panels.

Windows: 11′–6½″ high French doors with transom and 4½″ jamb; fascia, cyma and backband architrave with crossettes.

Hardware: door pulls with thumb-locks. Espagnolette window bolts with rosette handle cranks.

Lighting: four, three-light, urn and acanthus leaf French baroque sconces. One, two-tier, twenty-four-light, crystal bead, pendant and tear-drop chandelier, possibly 18th century Russian.

Chimney: projects 1′–5½″.

  Hearth: 6′–1″ by 1′–4½″; marble.

  Firebox: 2′–3½″ high by 3′–1″ by 1′–3½″ deep; cast iron with cherub back panel and lattice surround.

  Mantel: purple and grey-veined cream marble; consoles support guilloche frieze with tablet. Shelf: 6′–5″ wide by 3′–9½″ by 1′–5″ deep.

  Overmantel: mirror not original.

ANTEROOM:

Depth: (from hall to French door): 18′–0″
Width: 17′–7½″
Height: 13′–0″

The chamber alternates between the intimate and the public depending on whether the doors are open

Courtyard

Anteroom (to Ballroom)

NOW you . . .   See it . . .   And now . . .   You don't!

Ballroom

or closed. In consequence, the space can function variously as sitting room, conservatory or ballroom antechamber. As in the hall, the natural oak of walls and ceiling soaks up sound and is the means for a rich warmth and relaxing dignity. The room, as a sedate interlude between hall, ballroom and dining room, is enhanced by its comparatively small size, a southeast exposure (soft natural light in the evening) and a view with entrance to the private garden court.

Flooring: oak, herringbone.

Baseboard: 7½″; ovolo and scotia cap.

Walls: three rows of raised panels in stiles and rails.

Cornice: cyma, ovolo, cavetto and cyma.

Ceiling: flat panels divided by ribs.

Doorways and doors: 11′–1″ high folding doors with 1′–1″ jamb and 8′–10″ high double door (1′–7″ jamb) to dining room, raised panels; acanthus leaf pilaster capitals support rosette crossettes of fascia architraves. At hall; 12′–0″ high opening with beam on fluted Ionic pilasters.

Windows: overlooking garden court. French door with lead came and opaque glass fan-light, 10′–7½″ from floor to fan soffit, 7′–3″ floor to transom bar, 1′–2½″ deep jamb, and 7′–11″ high flanking doors.

Hardware: brass. Double door circular knobs, inset oval door pulls, cremone bolts with oval knobs at French doors.

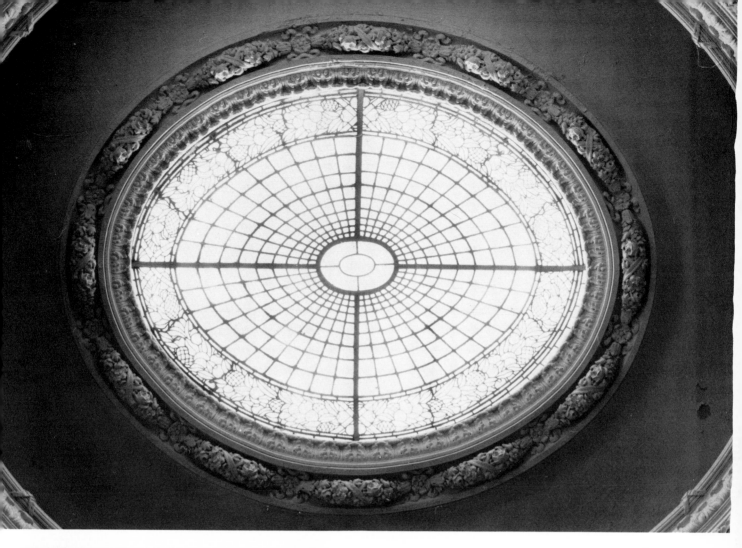

BALLROOM:

Width (from gallery wall): 44′–10½″
Depth: 46′–7½″
Height (at aisle): 14′–0″

The Edwardian chamber is astonishing in view of its size, richness and configuration. It is a two story vaulted and skylighted space with one story aisles. Movement is funnelled forward from the peripheral French doors (both real and false) and upward through the elliptical skylight. Whether the ingeniously designed folding doors are open or closed bears little on the impression received upon first entering. Painted white, the rich detail and space is in startling contrast to the sobriety of the hall and anteroom.

Flooring: oak, herringbone.
Baseboard: 8″, wood with torus cap.
Dado: wood; breaks forward 1″, raised panels.
Chairrail: 3′–0″ high; wood, ovolo and fascia.
Walls: plaster; ovolo panels with corner rosettes. The walls, each of three bays separated by fluted Ionic pilasters, are connected by a corner niche. The niches are spanned by segmentally-headed archways having crossette architraves and ornamented jambs and spandrels. Pilaster piers with brackets support the gallery for the cast iron orchestra railing.

Ballroom

Cornice: plaster; fascia architrave, floral frieze, egg and dart, bracket and cyma cornice. The entablature is carried across transverse beams.

Ceiling: plaster; derived from the quadripartite vault, in this case interrupted by an oval skylight suspended over a pulvinated occulus. The transverse beam over the orchestra gallery is interrupted by a semidome.

Doorways and doors: French doors (with fanlights) at east, west and south; 7'–3" to transom bar, 10'–6½" floor to soffit. Fascia and ovolo, crossette architrave with decorated spandrels. East doors open from garden court, view from mirror-paned west doors cut off by neighboring new building, mirror-paned south doors are false. In the northeast corner is a concealed door to the gallery alongside which the entire wall opens to reveal a pocket for the three-leaf folding doors from the anteroom.

Hardware: brass. Cremone bolts with oval knobs and floral tie-backs for drapes.

Lighting: eight, five-light, brass-armed, crystal finial and tear-drop sconces. One, three-light, tear-drop and bead crystal ceiling fixture.

DINING ROOM:

Width: 21'–11½" (wall to plaster wall)
Length (includes bay window): 38'–6½" (wall to plaster wall)
Height: 13'–3½"

The Tudor chamber has a northwest exposure for diffused evening sun. The character was altered when plaster-board was used to conceal the original ornamented ceiling. The elements are large scale (mantel, bay window, wainscot and beams) and would suggest a choice of furnishings similarly scaled for continuity and focus. The original design stressed a strong axis between the mantel and bay window. The in-

Dining Room

stallation of the Italian renaissance "sideboard" has interrupted this axis and further confused the scale. The artistry of carving as well as the type of oak, finish and "aging" would suggest the mantel to be originally from late 16th century England.

Flooring: oak, herringbone.

Baseboard: 6½"; stained oak, ovolo cap.

Wainscot: 7'–6" high; stained oak, two rows of raised panels with double fascia, ovolo and cyma cornice.

Walls: plaster painted white.

Sideboard (not original to room): stained oak. West wall "sideboard" (reputedly from Italy), 16'–4" long; cabinets with carved panels and 3'–10" high counter supports similarly carved splash panels, shelves, side cabinets and 8'–11" high cornice.

Cornice: stained oak; ovolo and fascia.

Ceiling: stained oak beams with gilded panels (similar to strapwork) divide decorated ceiling (now concealed under plaster-board).

Doorways and doors: 8'–10" high; stained oak; raised panels for pocket doors to hall and double doors to closet (safe) and ballroom anteroom, flanked by panelled pilaster architrave with Tuscan lintel. 6'–9" high wainscot door to pantry.

Windows: alcove bay of double-hung windows, 3'–1" floor to sill and 9'–6" sill to jamb.

Hardware: brass. Door pulls with thumb-locks and baroque doorknobs with 9" decorative escutcheons.

Lighting: four, four-light, acorn and acanthus leaf, 18th century doré sconces.

Chimney: two projections, each 9".

    Hearth: 5'–11" by 2'–0"; cast stone.

    Firebox: 4'–0" wide by 3'–9" by 1'–11" deep; brick with limestone surround and hood.

    Mantel: cluster columns and figure brackets support decorated Elizabethan frieze and shelf, 7–6" wide by 7'–6" by 2'–6½" deep.

    Furnishings: 3'–6" high bronze "andirons" each of a boy on seabull.

Dining Room Mantel

2025 Massachusetts Avenue, N.W.

The house is on the north side of the Avenue between Twentieth and Twenty-first Streets. It is located in Square 94 on lot 20.

Originally a residence, it is owned by the Church of the Saviour and used as a church.

PREVIOUS STRUCTURES ON THE SITE

Tax books show an improvement with an assessed value of $3,000 on lot H from 1872 until 1878. Part of lot H is now included in lot 20, but it is a small part; therefore it is doubtful that this improvement was on the site of the present house.

HISTORICAL INFORMATION

The house at 2025 Massachusetts Avenue was built by Samuel M. Bryan in 1885 on land that had been purchased earlier in the same year (Liber 1123 folio 101). W. Bruce Gray was the architect (Permit No. 260). Bryan made no alterations or additions to the house. In 1895 the house was sold to Bessie J. Kibbey (Liber 2011 folio 418). She added a third story to the existing back building in 1904 (Permit No. 2021).

There are no other documented changes until 1950, when the house was purchased by the Church of the Saviour (Liber 9157 folio 544). At this time a one story addition was added at the rear (Permit No. A 9855). Partitions were also added on the third floor at this time, and other changes made to convert the building from a residence to a church and offices.

There are no known architectural drawings of this building.

VIEWS

Exterior photographs

Massachusetts Avenue facade:
CHS, W. H. Seaman photograph, c. 1889, before house to west was built; ES, 4–21–51: MLKW has a print made from this negative.

ARCHITECT

Very little biographical information has been found on *W. Bruce Gray,* although he designed a number of buildings in Washington, including his own house at 1318 19th Street, N.W. A Washington commercial guide book of 1884 gives more information than any

c. 1889
W. H. Seaman
Columbia Historical Society

other source yet consulted. It states: "W. Bruce Gray is a native of New York, where he studied his art under the best masters, and has a thorough and practical experience of over fourteen years." (1) Ten years before the publication of this book the prize-winning design for a gate house in the First Junior Members' Competition of the New York Chapter of the Institute of Architects was published in the *New York Sketchbook of Architecture.* (2) The architect's name was William B. Gray—possibly the same man known later as W. Bruce Gray. This was in 1874; the guide book mentioned above says that in 1879 Bruce Gray established a partnership in Washington with Harvey L. Page, a native of this city, as the junior partner. City directories list the firm of Gray and Page from 1881 to 1885, with offices in the Corcoran Building. The two partners are then listed separately, with Gray having an office at several different locations in downtown Washington until 1901. The only other fact that has come to light regarding Bruce Gray's life is that he was a member of the Cosmos Club from 1887 to 1895.

Buildings in Washington by Gray, or the firm of Gray and Page, included: residence for J. Belden Noble, 1785 Massachusetts Avenue, N.W. (Permit No. 1586, 6–14–80); residence for A. M. Gibson,

153

Dupont Circle (Permit No. 650, 11–10–82); residence for Samuel M. Bryan, 2025 Massachusetts Avenue, N.W. (See text); residence for Jerome Napoleon Bonaparte, 1627 K Street, N.W.; residence for Charles T. Murray, 1343 Fifteenth Street, N.W.; residence for D. R. McKee, 1753 Rhode Island Avenue, N.W.; residence for C. E. Hawley, 1353 Connecticut Avenue, N.W.; residence of the architect (Gray), 1318 Nineteenth Street, N.W.; (3) residence for C. W. Needham, 1730 Sixteenth Street, N.W. (Permit No. 726, 12–26–93); Metropolitan Club, Seventeenth and H Streets, N.W. (not the building now on the site); and the First Baptist Church, formerly at Sixteenth and O Streets, N.W. Only the house at 2025 Massachusetts Avenue remains.

1. E. E. Barton, ed., *Historical and Commercial Sketches of Washington and Environs,* Washington: E. E. Barton, 1884, p. 96.
2. *New York Sketchbook of Architecture,* Vol. 1, no. 5 (May 1874), p. 1, Pl. XX.
3. See *Harper's New Monthly Magazine,* Vol. LXX (March 1885), pp. 520–533 for Noble, Bonaparte, Murray, McKee, Hawley and Gray houses.

BIOGRAPHIES OF THE RESIDENTS

Samuel McGill Bryan (1847– ?) was born in Cadiz, Ohio, the son of George W. Bryan and Susannah (Shidell) Bryan. Mrs. Bryan was a native of Frederick, Maryland. In 1862, before he was fifteen years old, Samuel Bryan joined the Eighty-eighth Ohio Volunteer Infantry as a drummer boy; a year later he enlisted as a soldier with the Eleventh Ohio Cavalry.

When the war ended, Bryan returned to Cadiz, where he was engaged in business for a brief period before being appointed to a position in the Treasury Department in 1867. In 1869 he was transferred to the Post Office Department, a position he left in 1872 to go to Japan and present to the Japanese Government his scheme for reorganizing its postal system. His plan was accepted, and he was appointed a special commissioner by the Emperor to negotiate postal treaties in Washington and in several European capitals. He was involved in this kind of work for the Japanese Government until 1878, when he was appointed a delegate to the Universal Postal Congress in Paris. He signed the resulting treaty and then returned to Japan to continue his work on the postal system there. When he left in 1882 he was decorated by the Emperor with the Order of the Rising Sun and presented with a gift of twelve thousand dollars.

Mr. Bryan returned to Washington in 1883, and in November of that year joined the Chesapeake and Potomac Telephone Company. In May 1884, when Bryan was general manager, the first underground telephone wires in Washington were laid in the vicinity of New York Avenue, Fifteenth Street and Vermont Avenue. The Chesapeake and Potomac was the first public service corporation to place its wires underground. (ES, 12–16–02; WP, 12–6–27)

Bryan later was appointed president of the Telephone Company, a position he held until 1899, when he resigned. An article in the *Washington Post* (2–19–99) said: "Pressing duties and engagements elsewhere have compelled Mr. Bryan to sever his ties with Washington. It will be our loss." No information has been found to indicate where Mr. Bryan moved after he left Washington.

Samuel Bryan was married in 1870 to Melissa Anna Shipley, daughter of John W. Shipley of Washington. (*Eminent and Representative Men of Virginia and the District of Columbia, of the Nineteenth Century,* Madison, Wisconsin: Brant and Fuller, 1893, pp. 63–64.)

Bessie Juliet Kibbey (1857–1949) was born in Washington, D.C., the daughter of William R. Kibbey and Juliet (Rokohl) Kibbey. Her grandfather was William Beckford Kibbey, one of the dominant financial figures in the capital. Kibbey had made his fortune in the leather export business in this country after leaving his native England against his father's will. He was not only prominent in financial circles, but also very much involved in the community and charitable affairs of Washington. (Proctor, *Washington, Past and Present,* Vol. III, pp. 131–33)

Kibbey's son, William, and his wife both died when their daughter, Bessie, was young; she was, therefore, raised by her grandparents. She carried on her grandfather's interest in charity and became one of the city's great philanthropists.

Miss Kibbey donated money for the city's first playground and was one of the original backers of the Washington Cathedral. When she died, she left $150,000 to the Cathedral for a carillon in the central tower to be dedicated to the memory of her grandparents.

Bessie Kibbey was a member of the board of governors of the Home for Incurables for fifty-five years; it was to this institution that she left her home at 2025 Masachusetts Avenue and other property, as well as $40,000 for the construction of a new wing to the Home.

(Mary Van Fossen Schwab, "As I Remember Her," *The Washington Diocese,* Feb. 1964, pp. 12–13; Obituaries: ES, 5–20–49, WP, 5–21–49; Will: ES & WP, 6–3–49)

The Church of the Saviour is an ecumenical church established in 1947 by N. Gordon Cosby of Lynchburg, Virginia, an ordained Baptist minister who was an army chaplain during World War II. He became dissatisfied with the practice of religion as he saw it and resolved to form a new church, evangelical in nature and based on a small, dedicated membership.

By 1947, Dr. Cosby and eight other interested persons were able to purchase a residence at 1707 Nineteenth Street, N.W. in Washington for use as a church. In two years the church had grown to the extent that this space was inadequate. When the house at 2025 Massachusetts Avenue became available in 1950, they purchased the building and remodeled it for church and office use.

At present the Church of the Saviour has close to eighty members and a Sunday congregation of about two hundred. It contributes to a wide range of missionary activities in this country as well as abroad. The church also sponsors a coffee house and has developed a farm in Maryland for use as a retreat and recreation center. (*The Church of the Saviour,* a booklet printed by the church.)

APPENDIX

Chain of Title

1885 Deed 21 April, recorded 22 April; Liber 1123 folio 101
August Miller to Melissa Anna Bryan, wife of Samuel McGill Bryan
". . . lot numbered . . . (20) in August Miller's subdivision of Square .. (94) as . . . recorded in the Office of the Surveyor . . . in Liber 13, folio 69 . . . containing 3847 80/100 square feet of ground . . ." For $9,720.

1895 Deed 29 May, recorded 31 May; Liber 2011, folio 418
Melissa A. Bryan et vir (Samuel McGill) to Bessie J. Kibbey
For $58,000.

1949 Will of Bessie Juliet Kibbey. Administration No. 73292.
Property at 2025 Massachusetts Avenue, N.W. left to the Washington Home for Incurables.

1950 Deed 20 February, recorded 8 March; Liber 9157 folio 544
The Washington Home for Incurables to Trustees of the Church of the Saviour
$66 in Internal Revenue Stamps affixed. The rate after 1 July 1940 was $.55 per $500, making the price approximately $60,000.

Building Permits

No. 260, 6 August 1885. Permit to build.
Owner: Samuel M. Bryan

Architect: W. Bruce Gray
Builder : John McGregor
Estimated cost: $40,000
No. 1219, 6 December 1887. Permit to build a private stable.
Owner: S. M. Bryan
Builder: M. R. Crandall
Estimated cost: $1,500
Note: the location given for this stable, "lot 64, Square 70, alley rear of Massachusetts Avenue, between 21st and 22nd," is crossed out and the lot and square of Bryan's house written in. There was an error in the lot and square numbers, or in the name of the Avenue, as Massachusetts Avenue does not run through or bound Square 70. The stable was probably located in Square 67, lot 3, on an alley between 21st and 22nd Streets, and P Street and Massachusetts Avenue. There is a permit for repair issued for a stable in this location with Bryan listed as owner. (Permit No. 901, 10–30–88) The deed for this land has not been found.
No. 2021, 24 June 1904. Permit to repair or alter.
Owner: Bessie J. Kibbey
Mechanic: S. H. Edmonston
Estimated cost: $2,000
"Construct a third story rear addition, 20 x 30 feet, on present two story building . . ."
No. A8812, 15 June 1950. Permit to repair or alter.
Missing from government files.
No. A9855, 7 July 1950. Permit for addition and repair.
Owner: The Church of the Saviour
Estimated cost: $14,500
"Build one three story brick addition to church and add stud and plaster partitions on 3rd floor, remove certain work, add enclosure (masonry) around basement stair and certain work as per plan." Note: only a one story addition was built.
No. A12354, 14 July 1950. Plumbing permit.

Listings of Residents

City directories list the following tenants:

1887–1895 Samuel M. Bryan
1896–1948 Bessie J. Kibbey
1954 Church of the Saviour Ecumenical

Social registers list:

1888–1895 Mr. and Mrs. Samuel M. Bryan. Mrs. Rebecca Shipley is also listed from 1889–91.
1896–1948 Miss Bessie J. Kibbey

STATEMENT:

The solid, dark building dominates nearby structures. There is no superfluous ornamentation to distract from the strong influence of tower, entrance portal and building height. Romanesque in detail, individual and linear elements are defined by boldly

1973

articulated materials and shapes.

The interior though more decorative is related in style to the exterior. The single greatest elements are the central living halls and galleried stair. Similar details used throughout unify the chambers.

SITE:

Orientation: The structure faces south on a lot measuring 60'–0" on Massachusetts Avenue; 55'–4" on the west (party wall); 51'–5" on the north (Que Street); 38'–6" on the northeast (party wall); and 40'–0" on the east (party wall).

Paving: From the avenue there are four concrete risers to a 10'–0" wide walk which is on axis with the front stoop.

Landscaping: The public sidewalk is banked by ivy, with grass, forsythia and various evergreen plantings bordering the building.

EXTERIOR:

Dimensions: The two and one half story building has a raised basement and a three story, 50'–0" high circular tower east of the Massachusetts Avenue entrance. The four bay structure measures 60'–0" on the avenue and 40'–0" in depth. A kitchen wing, parallel to Que Street, extends an additional 38'–6" along the northeast property wall.

Foundations: concrete footings and slab.

Structure: brick bearing walls and wood truss and rafter system.

Walls: The rusticated sandstone basement and first floor are separated by stepped courses of smooth stone which act as basement window lintel and first floor sill. The second floor common bond brick is separated from the first floor by a block string course. The second floor windows are flanked by sandstone quoines and capped by a sandstone string course. The brick walls extend above the building cornice to the transom bars of two half-dormers west of the tower.

Doorways and doors: The Massachusetts Avenue double door entrance is flanked by smooth sandstone dados with molded caps which support corner-indented, carved cushion-capital columns. The columns, recessed into the doorway jamb, support molded impost blocks and a semicircular arch of voussoirs. The sandstone tympanum within the arch is pierced by a stained glass, cusped oculus.

Windows: The basement double-hung windows have cast iron grilles and smooth sandstone lintels formed by the stepped string course upon which the first floor windows rest.

Sandstone first floor transom bars separate the clear glass from the stained glass. Over the sandstone architrave of the projecting west bay is a trabeated balustrade balcony.

The second floor is similar to the first floor with the exception of the double-hung, stained glass window over the entrance.

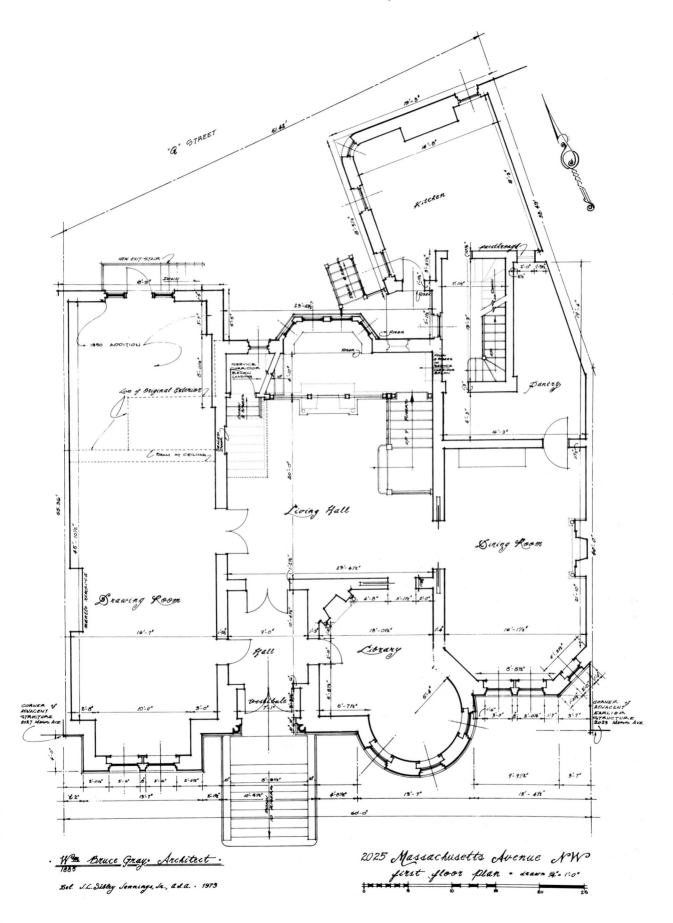

"a" Street

Kitchen

passthrough

NEW EXIT STAIR

1950 ADDITION

Line of Original Exterior

SERVICE CORRIDOR BELOW LANDING

Pantry

BEAM AT CEILING

Living Hall

Dining Room

Drawing Room

Hall

Library

Vestibule

CORNER of ADJACENT STRUCTURE 2027 Mass. Ave.

CORNER of ADJACENT EARLIER STRUCTURE 2029 Mass. Ave.

· Wᵐ Bruce Gray· Architect ·
1885

Del. S.L.Sibley Jennings, Jr., a.a.a. · 1973

2025 Massachusetts Avenue NW
first floor plan · drawn ¼"= 1'0"

Stoop: Ten brownstone risers with closed stringers and 10'–6" wide treads ascend over a basement areaway to the Massachusetts Avenue stoop. Seven risers descend to the basement entrance.

Porches: In the acute angle formed by the northwest wing, a wood stair rises to the kitchen porch. A concrete stair rises to the northwest building addition.

Areaway: Between the kitchen and northwest stairs, a brick areaway gives access to the basement.

Cornice: The continuous second floor lintel supports a beaded sandstone architrave, a plain frieze, and a corona and cyma cornice.

Roof: The slate roof has a central hip extended by depressed gables which have sandstone coping and copper flashing. The kitchen wing (on Que Street) has a shed roof.

Dormers: The two half-dormers have a sandstone architrave capped by a bead, a plain frieze and a corona band which supports a pediment centered by a patera. A sandstone bar, which carries the spring of the roof, separates the lower panes from lead came transom windows. The east bay wood dormer has a pediment with cusped fan.

Tower: The glazing is convex on each floor. The third floor windows have sandstone muntins and transom bars. A rusticated lintel course supports a bead moulding, a terra-cotta rosette frieze and a copper eave for the conical slate roof and copper finial cap.

Chimneys: There are five chimneys. Those visible from Massachusetts Avenue (one at the east gable, one west of the tower and one at the west gable) are cylindrical clusters of brick with sandstone caps.

PLANS:

From the first floor Massachusetts Avenue vestibule is the foyer, beyond which is the west end of the central living hall. East of the hall is the dining room; at the west is the former parlor; at the south is the library (east of the vestibule and foyer); and at the north is the galleried stair. North of the dining room is the pantry and kitchen wing, between which is a service stair.

The second and third floors have central living halls. The bedrooms are arranged in similar plan to the first floor, with the exception of an east service passage to the servants' quarters in the northeast wing and the recent office partitioning of the west rooms.

INTERIOR:

The first floor chambers are unified by a similarity of style and a repetition of general elements. Room shapes, types of window openings and certain details differ, however. The following items are common throughout.

Flooring: 2", oak, carpeted.
Baseboard: 1'–0" high, wood, reeded base with ogee cap.

Dado: wood, four rows of raised panels in stiles and rails.

Chairrail: 4'–7" high, fascia and chamfer.

Walls: plaster.

Ceiling: 11'–10½" high.

Doorways and doors: The 7'–11" high doorways are flanked by a molded architrave which supports a pulvinated frieze broken forward as rosettes at either end. Above each frieze is an ovolo, corona and cyma cornice.

Heating: The building has an American Radiator Company "Ideal" furnace. The "Balto" and "Wood Co." radiators are brass finished cylinders except where concealed behind wainscot registers.

FOYER:

The only difference between this and the living hall is the cornice which is a wood quarter-round above a picture moulding.

LIVING HALL:

The central living hall (as the most important space) connects all other chambers and capitalizes on changes in level. If left unpainted the dark woodwork would have been especially dramatic against the light from the prominent bay window on the stair gallery. The foyer is little different in detail though darker because of insufficient natural light.

Walls: Over the dado and facing the gallery is a built-in bevelled mirror.

Cornice: cavetto and block, plain frieze, ovolo and corona.

Doorways and doors: The doorway to the foyer is 8'–6" high. Over the dado paired plinths and pilasters with leafy capitals support an entablature having a fascia and cavetto architrave, a raised panel frieze broken forward as a rosette over each pair of pilasters, and an ogee cornice.

Lighting: Flanking the gallery alcove at the north are brass sconces with fluted milk-glass chimneys. The body of each sconce is a double ball of filigree attached to the wall by an arm.

Chimney:
    Hearth: 6'–1" by 1'–6", glazed tile.
    Firebox: 2'–8½" by 2'–7½" high, cast iron, dragon and wave back panel signed "Elihu Vedder, copyright 1882, Caryl Coleman."
    Mantel: 6'–9" wide by 5'–1" by 1'–6", tile surround, plinths support spiral columns with cushion capitals below a pulvinated rosette frieze (the continuation of the stair gallery) and an ovolo guilloche shelf.

Stair: The wood, U-shaped stair is carpeted. There are two risers east to a landing and seven risers north to the three bay gallery. At the west, there are three

Living Hall
1970, Jack E. Boucher

Firebox Back Panel
Jack E. Boucher

risers to a second landing and eleven risers south to the second floor. Beyond the gallery is a sitting alcove which projects as a bay window of lead came and stained glass. The base of the stair and gallery has raised panels. The panelled stringer is fretted. The balustrade has colonnette balusters (similar to the mantel columns) with arches. The gallery bays are separated by pedestals and dwarf columns with cushion capitals which support semicircular arches elaborated by drip mouldings. The dwarf columns are clustered at the gallery ends. The stair is open to the third floor.

LIBRARY:

The chimney and tower bow as principal elements are opposed to one another and set at diagonals to the chamber. The delicacy of run-plaster ceiling and walls combined with natural wood does not distract from the informality. Unfortunately the walls have been marred by a mural.

Walls: low floral relief, painted over with mural.
Cornice: floral ovolo and two bands of run-plaster reeding.

Library
1970, Jack E. Boucher

Ceiling: run-plaster, with border of repeated floral pattern overlayed by dogwood sprays.
Windows: The windows, similar to the doorways, have louvered shutters which fold into the jamb.
Hardware: The sliding door to the hall has brass pulls and recessed turn locks.
Chimney:
　Hearth: carpeted.
　Firebox: 2'–5" by 3'–0" high, fire tile.
　Mantel: 5'–0" wide by 4'–7", tile fire surround in thistle pattern, wood plinths with turned columns (tapered toward base) support fan frieze and plain shelf.

DINING ROOM:

As compared to the other chambers the dining room though more formal is similar in character in that the dark, quiet space is vitalized by devices such as a stained glass corner window.

Dado: At the north wall is a built-in buffet on spiral legs (splashboard removed).
Walls: The southeast and southwest corners are diagonal to the other walls.
Windows: southeast wall pierced by stained glass.
Hardware: brass door pulls to sliding doors.
Lighting: ceiling outlet for gas fixture.
Chimney: 1'–1½" deep.
　Hearth: carpeted.
　Firebox: 2'–5" by 2'–6" high, cast iron, acanthus back panel.
　Mantel: 5'–9" wide by 4'–10", tile surround edged by guilloche, wood pedestals with composite columns support frieze and cushion shelf broken forward over columns.

DRAWING ROOM

The chamber is entirely altered as a meeting hall. Sufficient evidence remains to prove that it was similar to the other spaces.

2122 Massachusetts Avenue, N.W.
Anastasia Patten Residence

The house was located on the south side of the Avenue between Twenty-first and Twenty-second Streets, N.W., in Square 67, on lot 13. The site is now occupied by the State House Apartments.

STATEMENT

When built, the Patten residence, which bordered the city limits at Boundary Street (now Florida Avenue) and Massachusetts Avenue, sat in a one and three-quarters acre private park. Rusticated sandstone facing for the raised basement was battered as if for a fortress foundation. Towers, windows and semi-octagonal bays were the vertical appendages of a monumental brick bulk. Dormers and slate mansard roof, unexpectedly squat, increased the impression of brooding vastness. Grey, tan and deep red earth colors added solemnity to an already forbidding aspect. The effect, desired or not, was one of great mass. Ornament was pressed brick (string courses, lintels, etc.), spare and light; an incidental foil. The brick cornice defined the building height in faint imitation of crenelated battlements.

HISTORICAL INFORMATION

In 1884 and 1885 Anastasia Patten bought the land for her house from William Sharon (former Senator from Nevada) and Jessie Adelaide Sunderland (Liber 1112 folios 50 and 53). The building permit was issued 5 February 1885 (No. 1137) with the architect's name given as Robert Fleming. The permit described a brick dwelling, three stories plus basement and attic, approximately 58 feet wide and 61 feet deep. There was to be a back building, two stories plus basement, approximately 25 feet wide and 30 feet long. At the rear of the property there was to be a two story brick stable, 28 by 30 feet. The estimated cost was $70,000. The assessed valuation in 1886–87 was $52,000.

Although the house was built on lot 13, the original property included lots 10 through 15. In 1901 the Patten sisters sold lots 14 and 15 to Isabel Anderson for the erection of the house at 2118 Massa-chusetts Avenue now belonging to the Society of the Cincinnati. (See *Massachusets Avenue Architecture*, Vol. I.) Mrs. Anderson paid $93,000 for the land (Liber 2583 folio 155).

In 1899 a stone porch and entrance steps were added on the east side of the house (Permit No. 1555, 5–4–99) and in 1909, a one story brick addition was added at the rear, adjoining the conservatory (No. 4717, 5–19–09). The sisters decided to add a tennis court in 1913 (Permit No. 5019, 4–19–13). From this time on only minor repairs were made to the building.

In 1944 the Pattens sold their house to Jerry Maiatico for $165,000 (Liber 8015 folio 6). They did not move until 1945, and the building stood vacant until it was razed in November 1947. Much of the furniture was sold at auction. A spectacular blue and amber Venetian glass chandelier, which had hung in the drawing room, was sold to an Evanston, Illinois, restaurant owner; the chandelier measured approximately 10 by 12 feet.

An article in the *Washington Daily News* (11–26–47), written at the time the house was razed, described the interior:

> The massive beauty of the old house is still visible—walls and ceilings of the downstairs rooms were panelled in oak or mahogany. Stained glass panels were in almost every window. A huge stairway with a beautifully carved balustrade twisted through the center of the house clear to the fourth floor. Wreckers have been working on the old house for nearly three weeks and scarcely have made a dent in it. They figure it will take at least two months more to finish the job—walls throughout the house are brick and 16 inches thick.

KNOWN ARCHITECTURAL DRAWINGS

Projection plan. Ink on linen. Filed with Permit No. 1137, 5 February 1885.
> Plan showing projections from Building Line/on Residence for Mrs. A. Patten/Mass. Ave. & Que Sts. N.W./Washington D.C./Scale: ¼″ = 1′/Stamped: Robert I. Fleming, Architect & Builder, Washington, D.C.

1909 addition: plan and elevation. Black line print. Filed with permit No. 4717, 19 May 1909.
> Addition to/2122 Mass. Ave./Miss Patten/Gormley-Poynton Co., Contractors

Evening Star, November 1940
Washingtoniana Room, Martin Luther King Library

VIEWS

Exterior

From northeast, showing Massachusetts Avenue facade and east elevation:
    MLKW; ES photograph, 1940.
From west:
    WDN, 3–28–46, p. 3.
From southwest:
    WDN, 11–26–47, p. 21. Photograph taken during demolition.

ARCHITECT

Robert Isaac Fleming (1842–1907) was born in Goochland County, Virginia, the son of John Malcolm Fleming of Aberdeen, Scotland. His mother was Eliza A. Robertson of an old Virginia family which also had its roots in Scotland.

At the age of nineteen Robert Fleming enlisted in the Confederate army as a corporal, fought in thirty battles, and by the end of the war had been promoted to the rank of lieutenant. After the war Fleming was appointed city engineer of Richmond. He stayed in Richmond only until 1867, when he moved to Washington and established himself as an architect and builder. He had no formal training as an architect; his education had all been in the hands of private tutors. In spite of his lack of training, Fleming was very successful and designed and/or built many residences and public buildings in Washington. Sources are confusing and contradictory in regard to differentiating between design and construction when discussing his work. In the following list of buildings associated with Fleming's name, an architect's name is given when it is known that Fleming was only the builder of the structure.

Non-residential: Kellogg Building, 1416 F Street, N.W., demolished; Howard University buildings; the British Embassy, 1300 Connecticut Avenue, demol-

1970, Jack E. Boucher.

ished; addition to the Shoreham Hotel, demolished; Department of Justice, demolished; National Safe Deposit Company (now National Savings and Trust), James H. Windrim of Philadelphia was the architect; All Soul's Unitarian Church, 14th and L Sts., N.W., R. G. Russell was the architect; Sumner School, 17th and M Sts. N.W., Adolph Cluss was the architect; Second District School.

Residences: Brodhead-Bell, 1500 Rhode Island Ave., N.W., John Fraser was the architect (see text); "Stewart Castle," 1913 Massachusetts Ave., demolished, Adolph Cluss was the architect (see text); Curtis J. Hillyer, 2121 Massachusetts Ave., demolished, now the site of the Cosmos Club; Anastasia Patten, 2122 Massachusetts Ave., demolished; Senator George Pendleton, 1313 16th St., demolished, J. B. Noel Wyatt of Baltimore is sometimes mentioned as the architect; Senator John R. McPherson, 1014 Vermont Ave., N.W.,* demolished; Senator Thomas W. Palmer, 1435 K St. N.W.,* demolished; Judge W. S. Cox, 1636 I St., N.W.,* demolished; J. A. Ashton, S.E. corner 18th St. and Massachusetts Ave., N.W., demolished; Robert I. Fleming, 1408 Massachusetts Ave., N.W., demolished.

Robert Fleming was a member of the District of

* These addresses are from the 1888 city directory.

Columbia legislature, a director of the Columbia Railroad Company and the Columbia Fire Insurance Company, and a colonel in the District National Guard. He was a real estate agent for former Vice-President Levi P. Morton, and at one time president of the Master Builders' Association. In this role he used his influence to better working conditions and to encourage organized labor.

Colonel Fleming was married in 1886 to Bell Vedder, a Washingtonian who was the daughter of Colonel Nicholas Vedder, chief paymaster for General Sherman. The Vedders lived at 1111 Massachusetts Avenue, N.W. Robert and Bell Fleming had two children, India Bell and Robert Vedder. Robert Vedder became president of the Riggs National Bank. His son, Robert W. Fleming, currently resides in the Washington area and is associated with the investment firm of Folger, Nolan, Fleming and Douglas. (John P. Coffine, ed., *Washington; Historical Sketches of the Capital City of Our Country,* 1887, p. 300; Proctor, *Washington, Past and Present,* Vol. III, pp. 62–63. Obituary: *American Architect and Building News,* Vol. 92 (1907), p. 90.)

BIOGRAPHIES OF THE RESIDENTS:

Anastasia Patten (? –1888), the builder of the house, was a native of Ireland, as was her husband, Edmond Patten. They went to California during the gold rush, and Edmond Patten made a fortune in the mining fields there and in Nevada. When her husband died, Mrs. Patten took their five daughters to Paris, where they were educated in the Convent of the Sacred Heart. She brought them back to the United States, decided to settle in Washington, and built a house in the newly fashionable Dupont Circle area. The girls made their debuts in the house, and Mrs. Patten began the tradition of lavish entertaining which her daughters carried on after her death in 1888. Mrs. Patten was known for her dominance, intelligence, outspoken manner and wit—qualities which were seen in her daughters as well.

Anastasia Patten's daughters were Mary, Augusta, Josephine, Edythe and Helen. Only two of the sisters married. *Augusta* married John M. Glover, a member of Congress from St. Louis. An article in *The Senator* states that the other sisters disapproved of Mr. Glover, and that this caused Augusta's estrangement from them.* While this may be true, it is also a fact that they accused Augusta of having received more than her share of their mother's estate, some of it during Anastasia Patten's lifetime. This is revealed in a bond made part of a trust relevant to certain other of Mrs. Patten's properties (Augusta and John Glover to Henry E. Davis et al, Liber 1535 folio 251, 28 October 1890). Augusta never returned to the Patten fold. She lived in St. Louis with her husband; they had one son, Edmund, who was killed in World War I. John Glover died in Colorado in 1926, but no date of death has been found for Augusta. It is known that she died some time before her sisters.

The other sister who married was *Edythe* (sometimes spelled Edith). She married General Henry Clark Corbin in 1901, after what was described as "one of the city's great romances." (TH, 7–17–46) She was married in the Patten house, and the wedding was attended by the elite of Washington, including the Theodore Roosevelt family. The Corbins traveled extensively during the short period of their marriage. General Corbin died in 1909; after his death Edythe returned to her old home to live with her sisters.

Mary (c. 1865–1946), *Josephine* (c. 1866–1945), and *Helen* (c. 1877–1946) never married. They lived together in the house at 2122 Massachusetts Avenue until Josephine died in 1945. They made their house a mecca for the prominent and influential of Washington, especially with their Sunday afternoon "at homes." Because of the Patten's Irish background and their dominance over the social scene, their house was called "Irish Legation" early in its history. To their "at homes" came diplomats, religious leaders, Presidents, politicians and leaders of society—everyone of any importance in Washington—providing the Pattens approved of them. They had strong likes and dislikes. From World War I on they despised all Germans; after the overthrow of the Czar they refused to set foot in the Russian Embassy. They had nothing good to say about Wallis Simpson or Edward VIII, but otherwise were strongly pro-British. They were friends of Alice Roosevelt and Mathilde Townsend. The Townsends lived across the street in what is now the Cosmos Club. (See *Massachusetts Avenue Architecture,* Vol. I)

The Pattens were devout Catholics; they had a private chapel in their house in which masses were often said by prominent churchmen. Cardinal Gibbons of Baltimore was a frequent visitor.

After Josephine died in 1945, Mary, Helen and Edythe moved to 1726 Massachusetts Avenue. Both Mary and Helen (better known as Nellie) died the following year. Edythe moved to 1911 R Street, where she lived with a companion until her death in 1959.

* Zan Zicka, "A Glimpse of the Patten Sisters," *The Senator,* 20 May 1939, pp. 14–15. See also: WTH, 11–4–40; TH, 11–17–45. Obituaries: Josephine Patten: TH, 4–1–45; Helen Patten: WTH, 7–17–46; Mary Patten: WP, 8–31–46; Edythe Patten: ES, 4–28–59.

LISTINGS OF RESIDENTS

City directory listings are not included for this house as Anastasia Patten and her daughters were the only occupants.

Social registers list the Patten sisters consistently beginning in 1891. From 1891–1894 a Miss Sarah Mason was also listed with them at 2122 Massachusetts Avenue.

2305 Massachusetts Avenue N.W.

This residence is on the north side of the Avenue just northwest of Sheridan Circle. It is located on old lots 14, 15, and 16, Block 11, in "Kalorama Heights"; now known as lot 59, Square 2516.

Originally a private home, it is owned by the Government of Chile and used as a residence for the ambassador.

HISTORICAL INFORMATION

Sarah Wyeth bought the land for her house in 1907 (Liber 3119 folio 313). The building permit was issued in 1908 (No. 426) with Nathan C. Wyeth as the architect, and the house was completed in 1909. Mrs. Wyeth lived in the house until her death in 1920. The house went to her son, Stuart, who sold it in 1922. It passed through several hands in that year. During the short time it was owned by Henrietta Halliday (Liber 4707 folio 249) a brick garage was built at the rear of the property (Permit No. 7969).

Mrs. Halliday sold the house to Harry Wardman late in 1922 (Liber 4876 folio 27); a few months later, in June 1923, he sold it to the Government of Chile (Liber 5017 folio 444). The Chilean Government made no major alterations until 1967, when a modern wing was added at the rear, behind the dining room. The two windows flanking the fireplace in this room were replaced by doors, giving access to the new wing. A swimming pool was also added. The architect for this addition was Hugo Errázuriz, brother of Mrs. Radomiro Tomić, wife of the Ambassador.

KNOWN ARCHITECTURAL DRAWINGS

Front elevation. Blueprint. Filed with permit No. 426, 4 August 1908.
    FRONT ELEVATION/RES. FOR MRS. SARAH S. WYETH/LOTS 14, 15, 16. BL. 11, KALORAMA HEIGHTS/Scale: 1/4" = 1'/Nathan C. Wyeth, Architect/1517 H St., N.W., Wash. D.C.
(Same blueprint filed with permit No. 2035, 24 September 1909.)

Projection plan. Ink on linen. Filed with Permit No. 426, 4 August 1908.
    PROJECTION PLAN/HOUSE FOR MRS. SARAH WYETH/N. C. Wyeth, Archt./No. 13/Scale: 1/4" = 1'-0"/Date: 7-28-08

Revised projection plan. Ink on linen. Filed with permit No. 2035, 24 September 1909
    REVISED   PROJECTION   PLAN/RESIDENCE

FOR MRS. SARAH S. WYETH/LOTS 14, 15 AND 16, BLK. 11, KALORAMA HEIGHTS/Dr. No. 43; Scale: 1/4" = 1'-0" Date: 9-15-09/Nathan C. Wyeth—Archt./1517 H St., N.W., Wash. D.C.

VIEWS

Photographs in the files of the Embassy of Chile, taken c. 1923:
    Exterior: Facade; rear elevation.
    Interior: Entrance hall, looking towards stair; entrance hall, from stair landing looking towards front entrance; southwest drawing room; southeast sitting room; dining room; library; bedroom.
Photographs in the *Sunday Star*, 8–19–45, gravure section, p. 2:
    Exterior: facade
    Interior: grand stairway, drawing room, dining room
Dining room:
    WP, 5–21–50
New wing:
    ES, 4–30–67

ARCHITECT

Nathan Corwith Wyeth (1870–1963) was graduated from the art school of the New York Metropolitan Museum of Art in 1889. He then spent ten years studying at the Ecole des Beaux Arts in Paris. After one year (1899–1900) as a designer with the Washington office of Carrere and Hastings, Wyeth joined the Office of the Supervising Architect of the Treasury.

From 1904 through 1905, he was chief designer for the Architect of the Capitol. There is evidence that Wyeth was involved in the design of the "old" Senate Office Building and the Cannon Office Building at the time. A photograph of a rendering of the "Terraces, Balustrades, and Approaches, Senate Office Building" indicates "Wyeth and Sullivan, Consulting Architects." Another rendering, "Office Building, House of Representatives, Washington, D.C.: B Street Elevation," is signed by Wyeth. Unfortunately, neither rendering is dated. (Files of the Commission of Fine Arts)

From 1905–1919 Wyeth maintained a private practice. In 1908, the year he designed the house at 2305 Massachusetts Avenue, he shared an office with William P. Cresson, who at the time was designing the house at 2234 Massachusetts Avenue for Henrietta

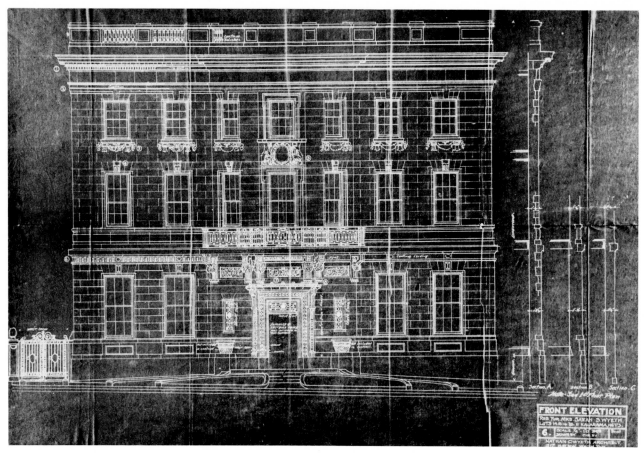

1908, D.C. Permits, National Archives

Halliday. At this point there is no evidence of collaboration between the two on either house. In addition to designing elegant houses for prominent people, Wyeth was commissioned to do the Battleship Maine Monument in Arlington Cemetery, the Tidal Basin Bridge, Key Bridge, the old Emergency Hospital and Columbia Hospital.

During World War I, Mr. Wyeth, as a major, designed hospitals for the construction division of the Office of the Surgeon General. After the war he became ill and spent several years recuperating in Switzerland. He returned to Washington to open his practice again, only to lose it during the stock market crash six years later.

From 1934 until his retirement in 1946, Wyeth was the Municipal Architect of the District of Columbia. Some of the public buildings he designed are: The Municipal Center; The Recorder of Deeds Building; the Georgetown Branch of the Public Library; Woodrow Wilson High School; and the National Guard Armory. (SS, 12–30–71; Obituaries: NYT, 9–3–63, 33:2; WP, 8–31–63, B 3:1)

BIOGRAPHIES OF THE RESIDENTS

Sarah Bell Stuart Wyeth (?   –1920) was the wife of John Wyeth of Philadelphia. He was the head of the chemical manufacturing firm then known as John Wyeth and Brother and now as Wyeth Laboratories, manufacturers of pharmaceuticals. John Wyeth was also a director of the *Philadelphia Record*. Mr. Wyeth died in 1907, and in 1908 Mrs. Wyeth built the house in Washington. The Wyeths had one son, Stuart, who was also a director of the *Philadelphia Record*. Nathan Wyeth, the architect of the house, was a cousin of Sarah Wyeth, according to an interview with Mrs. Nathan Wyeth in the *Sunday Star*, (12–13–70). (Obituaries, John Wyeth: NYT, 4–1–07; the Philadelphia *North American*, 3–31–07; *The Philadelphia Record*, 4–1–07. Obituary, Sarah Wyeth: *Philadelphia Public Ledger*, 12–23–20.)

Henrietta M. Halliday was the widow of Edward C. Halliday at the time she owned 2305 Massachusetts Avenue. He died in 1905, and in his will left her one hundred thousand dollars and a house at 1814

N. Street, N.W. (Admin. No. 12877) In 1908 she built the house at 2234 Massachusetts Avenue which is now the chancery of the Embassy of Ireland. It was designed by William P. Cresson, who at that time shared an office with the architect of 2305 Massachusetts Avenue. Both houses were built in the same year.

In addition to her own house, in which she apparently never lived, and the house at 2305, Mrs. Halliday also owned another piece of property on Massachusetts Avenue—the Wendell Mansion Apartments at 2339.

Mrs. Halliday died in 1923, approximately one year after she sold 2305. A letter filed with her will valued her estate at $1,930,870.57. (Admin. No. 30236)

Ambassadors from Chile

Ambassadors who have lived at 2305 Massachusetts Avenue are listed below, with a few selected biographical facts included where available.

H. E. Beltran Mathieu, appointed 27 November 1918. No information has been found on this ambassador.

H. E. Carlos G. Dávila, appointed 6 October 1927, was a journalist as well as a diplomat. He was the

c. 1923
Courtesy of Embassy of Chile.

editor of *La Nacion,* Santiago (1917–27); of *Hoy* (1931–32); and the director of Editors' Press Service, New York (1933–38). He became President of Chile in 1932 and subsequently retired. He was the recipient of honorary doctorates from Columbia University and the University of Southern California, and was an Official of the Order of the Crown of Italy. (WWLA, 1940)

H. E. Miguel Cruchaga Tocornal, appointed 18 September 1931, taught law at the University of Chile (1891–1900); was a deputy (1900–06); and among other government posts was Minister of Finance (1904–05), Prime Minister (1905–06) and Minister of Foreign Relations. He held several diplomatic posts: Minister Plenipotentiary to Argentina and Uruguay (1909–13); to Germany and the Netherlands (1913–20); and Ambassador to Brazil (1923–25). He was also a member of numerous commissions involving arbitration of legal questions. Dr. Cruchaga was President of the Senate and of the Chilean Academy of History, a member of the American Society of International Law and of the National Geographic Society. He was decorated by many Latin American and European countries, and he was an author, notably of the three volume *Droit Internationale* (1938). Dr. Cruchaga received an honorary degree from Georgetown University. (WWLA, 1940)

H. E. Manuel Trucco, appointed 17 October 1933, was a professor of mathematics and director of the Schools of Architecture and Engineering at the University of Chile. He was director-general of the National State Railways, a Senator (1926), president of the Radical Party, Minister of the Interior and Acting President of Chile (1931). (WWLA, 1940)

Senor Don Guillermo Gazitua, Counselor of Embassy and Charge d'Affaires ad interim, 16 November 1940. No biographical information has been found.

H. E. Rodolfo Michels, appointed 17 January 1941, was an engineer, owner of a gold mine and vice president of the Chile Exploration Company and Andes Copper Mining Company. He was the Governor of Coquimbo (1931–32), and a Senator in 1933. He was also the commissioner of the Chilean pavilion at the New York World's Fair in 1939. (WWLA, 1945)

H. E. Marcial Mora, appointed 5 October 1944, was a lawyer who held many government posts, including Minister of the Interior (1932), Minister of Foreign Affairs (1940), and Minister of Finance. He was also director-general of the post and telegraph

service. He was on the editorial staff of *La Nacion,* Santiago, president of the Banco Central de Chile (1939–40), a delegate to the United Nations conference in San Francisco in 1945, and president of the Radical Party. (WWLA, 1945)

H. E. Félix Nieto del Rió, appointed 27 January 1947, was a journalist and diplomat. He held many posts in the field of foreign relations: Consul General in the United States (1920) and Secretary of the Embassy (1921); director of the diplomatic department of the Ministry of Foreign Relations (1927–30); and Ambassador to Brazil (1933–38). A director of the *Revista Chilena* and the *Boletin de la Academia de la Historia,* he was also a founder and one-time president of the Comisión de Tratados de Commercio of Chile. He received many decorations and honors from foreign countries. (WWLA, 1940)

H. E. Aníbal Jara Letelier, appointed 24 February 1953, was a newspaperman. He was assistant director and manager of *La Nacion,* Santiago (1930); director of *Hoy* (1932–34); founder and director of *La Hora* (1935–39). In the early 1940's he was frequently in the United States as Consul General of Chile in New York (1939–43), delegate to the Maritime Conference in Washington and member of the Inter-American Development Commission, Washington. He was made an honorary citizen of New York in 1941 and was the civil aide-de-camp to Vice President Henry Wallace on his visit to Chile in 1943. (WWLA, 1945)

H. E. Mario Rodriguez, appointed 7 February 1956. No information has been found on this ambassador.

H. E. Mariano Puga, appointed 12 March 1957, was a lawyer who was educated at the Sorbonne and the University of Chile. He was a legal consultant for many American corporations, including Western Electric, RCA Victor, Parke-Davis and several film companies: United Artists, Warner Brothers, Republic Films and Fox Films. (WWLA, 1940)

H. E. José Serrano, appointed 16 July 1958. No information has been found on this ambassador.

H. E. Walter Muller, appointed 13 February 1959. No information has been found on this ambassador.

H. E. Sergio Gutierrez-Olivos, appointed 21 February 1963, is an international lawyer and diplomat who received part of his education at the Inter-American Law Institute in New York. He was a professor of law, Catholic University of Chile (1945–59) and director of that university's school of law (1951–54). Gutierrez-Olivos was a delegate to several international law conferences during the 1950's and 1960's, was Ambassador to Argentina (1959–62), and author of several essays on law. (IWW, 1974–75)

H. E. Radomiro Tomić, appointed 13 April 1965, is a lawyer, politician and diplomat. He was a member of the Chamber of Deputies during the 1940's and of the Senate, from 1950–53 and again from 1961–65. He was a founder of the Christian Democratic Party and a presidential candidate in 1970. He has published numerous political essays. (IWW, 1974–75)

H. E. Domingo Santa María, appointed 1 July 1968, is a civil engineer and politician (Christian Democrat). He was formerly a professor of physics at the Universidad Catolica, Santiago, and Minister of Economy (1964–67). (IWW, 1974–75)

H. E. Orlando Letelier, appointed 2 March 1971, was born in 1932 and educated at the Instituto Nacional de Santiago, O'Higgins Military Academy and the University of Chile. He was a director of the Student Federation of Chile from 1951 to 1952; president of the Centre of Art and Culture (1953–54); School of Law and Social Services, University of Chile (1953–54); economic adviser, Copper Department of Chile (now Copper Corporation), 1955–59; a member of numerous international conferences and one of nine experts who met under United Nations auspices to establish the Asian Development Bank (1964). He was with the Inter-American Development Bank (1960–70), was Minister for Foreign Affairs, Minister of Interior and of Defense (1973) and a member of the Socialist Party of Chile. (IWW, 1974–75)

H. E. Walter Heitmann, appointed 9 November 1973, was born in Santiago in 1917 and educated at the Chilean Military Academy and Aviation School. He became an Air Force officer in 1937 and retired as Brigadier General in 1972. Before becoming ambassador, Heitmann had been in the United States in 1956–57 when he was assigned to the Chilean Air Force Mission in Washington, and again in 1962–64 as the Air Attaché here. He is married to the former María Ines Rudolph. They have two sons: Carroll, a graduate of the United States Air Force Academy and Rutgers University; and Vernon, a graduate of the Air Force Academy of Chile. (U.S. Department of State; Embassy of Chile)

H. E. Manuel Trucco, appointed 29 April 1975, was born in Santiago in 1914 and lived at 2305 Massachusetts Avenue when his father was ambassador in the 1930's. He received his M.A. in economics from Georgetown University in 1937. From 1943–46

he was with the Office of the United States Coordinator of Inter-American Affairs and in 1946 directed the presidential campaign of Gabriel Gonzalez Videla. Ambassador Trucco was Under Secretary of Foreign Affairs from 1946–52 and Ambassador to Bolivia from 1959–62. In 1962 he was appointed Chilean Ambassador to the O.A.S., and since then has spent most of his time in Washington. He held this position until 1964 and then became special advisor to the president of the Inter-American Committee on the Alliance for Progress of the O.A.S. In 1974 Trucco was again appointed Chilean Ambassador to the O.A.S., a post he still holds.

Ambassador Trucco is married to the former Esther Saavedra. They have four children: two sons and two daughters. The Truccos have a special interest in Chilean artifacts and have brought many examples from their fine collection to the Embassy, where they are housed in the Chilean wing. (Embassy of Chile; U.S. Department of State; WP, 5–4–75)

APPENDIX

Chain of Title

1907   Deed 26 December, recorded 4 January 1908; Liber 3119 folio 313
George H. McFadden et ux, Emily B., (of Philadelphia) to Sarah B. Wyeth, widow, (of Philadelphia)
". . . Lots . . . (14) . . . (15) . . . and . . . (16), in Block . . . (11), 'Kalorama Heights,' as per plat recorded in Liber County No. 7, folio 34 of the Records of the Office of the Surveyor of the District of Columbia . . ." For $30,000

1922   Deed 11 April, recorded 27 April; Liber 4711 folio 234
Stuart Wyeth to James O'Donnell
". . . Stuart Wyeth, unmarried, only child and sole heir-at-law of Sarah Bell Wyeth, deceased, of Philadelphia . . ."
$100 in Internal Revenue Stamps affixed. The rate before 1 July 1940 was $.50 per $500, making the price approximately $100,000.

1922   Deed 29 April, recorded 8 May; Liber 4707 folio 249
James O'Donnell et ux, Emma V., to Henrietta M. Halliday
$135 in Internal Revenue Stamps affixed, making the price approximately $135,000.

1922   Deed 27 December, recorded 28 December; Liber 4876 folio 27
Henrietta M. Halliday to Harry Wardman et al
$150 in Internal Revenue Stamps affixed, making the price approximately $150,000.

1923 Deed 11 April, recorded 13 April; Liber 4950 folio 23

Harry Wardman et al to Frank Blumer

1923 Deed 12 April, recorded 4 August; Liber 5036 folio 128

Frank Blumer to Harry Wardman et al

1923 Deed 7 June recorded 14 August; Liber 5017 folio 444

Harry Wardman et al to the Republic of Chile ". . . subject . . . to a . . . deed of trust securing an indebtedness of $100,000 . . . which . . . . . . the party of the second part hereby assumes as part of the consideration for which this conveyance is made . . ." For $160,000

Building Permits

No. 426, 4 August 1908. Permit to build.
Owner: Mrs. Sarah S. Wyeth
Architect: Nathan C. Wyeth
Builder: John H. Nolan
Estimated cost: $75,000
Filed with No. 426: Special application for projections, 24 July 1908. One bay window: 4'–6" projection, 19'–0" wide.
No. 427, 4 August 1908. Permit to erect shed.
No. 704, 24 August 1908. Permit for hoisting engine.
No. 1697, 27 October 1908. Permit for engine.
No. 2346, 22 December 1908. Permit to erect storage shed.
No. 2035, 24 September 1909. Permit to repair or alter.
Owner: Mrs. Sarah S. Wyeth
Architect: Nathan Wyeth
Contractor: John H. Nolan
Estimated cost: $1,000
"To build marquise to front entrance" Iron: 9'–2½" x 10'–8"
No. 1711, 5 October 1910. Permit to repair or alter.
". . . Mrs. Jno. Wyeth has permission to build retaining wall 1'–6" thick, 13'–6" high."
Contractor: R. C. (?) Ballinger, 218 North 13th, Philadelphia, Pa.
No. 7969, 2 May 1922. Permit to build private garage.
". . . Mrs. H. Halliday has permission to build one brick private garage, 21'–6" x 18'–0" x 10'–0" "
Contractor: Harry Wardman
Estimated cost: $1,500

Listings of Residents

City directories list the following tenants:

1913–1920 Mrs. John S. Wyeth, or Sarah B. S. Wyeth
1921–1922 vacant
1923–1924 Mrs. Henrietta M. Halliday
1924–1925 Ziltram Mathieu
1926 Don Señor Beltran Mathieu, Ambassador E. and P., Chile
1927 Miguel Cruchaga, Ambassador of Chile

1928 Chilean Embassy

Social registers list:

1916–1919 Mrs. John Wyeth

STATEMENT:

Two of the three most significant aspects are the use of natural light in conjunction with siting and the logical arrangement of spaces in regard to function. Both are mutually dependent. The third element is the consistancy of style throughout. In the first and second instance there is a definite relationship between the individual space and its orientation to site as well as season. In the third instance, though each space differs in size and detail, the 18th century English manner prevails.

1970, Jack E. Boucher

SITE:

Orientation: The building faces south-southwest on a rectangular lot measuring 75'–0" (Massachusetts Avenue) by 100'–0" deep.

Enclosures: On the north property line is a 13'–6" high concrete and brick retaining wall.

Service buildings: The swimming pool is the site of a garage, constructed in 1922 and apparently demolished for the recent addition.

Paving: The driveways are concrete with limestone curbs. The entrance walk is concrete interrupted by three limestone risers.

Landscaping: At the street front, elm trees have been

replaced by box hedges. Hedges, crepe-myrtle and southern magnolia border the facade.

Rear patio: The flagstone terrace is asymmetrical with a swimming pool (22′–3″ long by 16′–0″) terminated by a semicircular east fountain. Bordering the brick party wall on the east are camellias; along the north retaining wall are lily-of-the-valley and English ivy; and by the brick kitchen wall are rhododendron and azalea.

EXTERIOR:

Dimensions: The three story plus basement structure, 50′–0″ from sidewalk to cornice cap, originally measured 62′–0″ wide by 47′–0″ deep with a west ell 21′–5″ wide by 14′–0″. Between the ell and the east wall is a 20′–7″ deep one story service wing. The central bow on Massachusetts Avenue is 20′–8″ wide by 5′–9″. O one story family room (added in 1967) measures 34′–0″ wide by 35′–0″.

Foundations: concrete footings and slab on fill.

Structure: brick bearing walls; steel beams.

Mechanical: (original) hotwater heating

Walls: Except for the street facade all original elevations are Roman brick (painted cream at rear facade). The street elevation granite plinth and flat-panelled limestone dado together "support" carborundum-finished, Indiana limestone walls. The facing is interrupted by a fret frieze which supports the base for the second and third floors. The base cap acts as window sill. The bow has rinceau panels over the entrance door and side windows, an oval cartouche with garlands and sprays over the central second floor window.

Doorways and doors: The double door entrance has a transom window with decorative iron grille. The limestone architrave is carved as a nailhead moulding.

Windows: All principal windows are double-hung with six-light sashes. The floor length second floor bay over the entrance allows access to the balcony.

The seven bay street elevation lacks architraves, except for the windows over the entrance which are crossetted. At the first floor the keystones have raised panels; at the second floor they are carved scrolls. The third floor sills rest on ornamented brackets and floral garlands. The casement windows flanking the entrance have ornamented grilles.

Stoop: The entrance stoop is granite. Over the entrance is a glass and iron, radial marquise on decorative iron consoles.

Balcony: In line with the base at the second floor is a limestone and decorative iron balcony supported on paired consoles.

Cornice: The street elevation has a limestone Corinthian entablature.

Parapet: brick, except at the street elevation which has a panelled limestone balustrade pierced over each bay with urn balusters.

Roof: nominally flat.

Chimneys: There are five Roman brick chimneys with limestone caps.

Addition: There are five redwood risers to the family room. The brick base for the addition supports a marble-bordered quarry tile floor and concrete piers. The piers, which terminate below the clerestory windows, support fir beams and an attic faced with concrete. The roof is built-up. Planters between the floor-length windows are screened by a wood trellis.

FLOOR PLAN:

The oval vestibule opens into the two story galleried stair hall. Flanking the hall on the right (east) is the sitting room adjoining the study, and on the left (west) is the salon adjoining the dining room. The study and dining room are connected by a one story pantry and kitchen wing which extends across the rear facade. The family room addition, which adjoins the dining room, has an entrance vestibule on the alley.

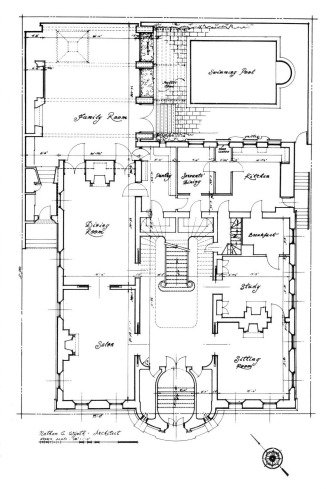

INTERIOR:

The following list includes those elements most common throughout the first floor public spaces within the original structure.

Floors: 2″, oak.

Ceilings: 14′–0″ (approx.) high; plaster painted white.

Doorways and doors: wood painted white; 8′–6″ high pocket doors; raised panels; 1′–5½″ deep jambs.

Windows: 10′–8½″ floor to reveal; 2′–1½″ floor to sill; 11½″ deep jambs; louvered and panelled shutters.

Heating: guilloche ventilator grilles on sills and, in conjunction with access panels, below windows.

VESTIBULE:

Width: 10′–0″

Depth: 13′–6″

Floor: grey mosaic with Greek-key border interrupted by six, 6″ grey marble risers to first floor elevation.

Dado (and first floor baseboard): grey marble.

Walls: plaster painted white; raised panels.

Cornice: wood painted white; double fascia with ogee and corona.

Ceiling: tray cove with center panel.

Doorways and doors: architrave at entrance double door breaks upward for swag panel. Iron and glass double door to hall with wreath, swag and rounded grilles.

Hardware: brass knobs and handles.

Lighting: bronze octagonal lantern.

STAIRHALL:

Width: 19′–0″

Depth: 32′–10″

Height (to second floor ceiling): 27′–1″ (approx.)

The Venetian window draws immediate attention. Originally the dark woodwork was unpainted and the impact of the single opening would have been more conspicuous. As likely intended, the eye is drawn up the stair, making movement the most characteristic aspect of the space.

First Floor

Baseboard: 6½″ wood.

Dado: raised wood panels painted white.

Chairrail: 2′–10½″ high, wood.

Walls: plaster painted white; panels of pale gold brocatelle in applied mouldings (not original).

Cornice: plaster; cove and run moulds.

Doorways and doors: oak-leaf and fascia, crossette architrave; acanthus ogee frieze; bundled oak-leaf cap; flat-panelled overdoor. Flanking the entrance door, and at the northeast beneath the stair are single 7′–5″ high doors with raised panels.

Stairhall, 1974

Venetian window: wood flat-panelled dado, spandrels and crossette architrave.

Hardware: brass door pulls and oval knobs.

Lighting: four, three-light, gilded metal sconces with garland and acanthus arms.

Stairway: wood. Fourteen risers north to mid-landing, paired flights of fourteen risers return to second floor. The closed stringers and flat-panelled stair and gallery soffits are reputedly mahogany (now painted). Cast iron balustrade and scrolled newels; wood handrail.

Gallery Floor

Floor: carpeted.

Baseboard: 7″, wood; double fascia and cyma extended over a fascia and guilloche frieze which is the depth of the gallery floor.

Walls: plaster painted white.

Cornice: wood painted white.

Ceiling: cove.

Doorways and doors: single doors; mirror-panelled; panelled jambs; crossette architraves. Doors over stair landing have decorative, cast iron flush balustrades with wood handrails.

Hardware: brass; ornamented oval knobs with mortise lock escutcheons.

Lighting: four, three-light, gilded rocaille sconces.

Stairhall, c. 1923
Courtesy of Embassy of Chile

Stairhall, c. 1923
Courtesy of Embassy of Chile.

SITTING ROOM:

Width: 19'–7½"
Depth: 18'–6"

From the hall the chamber is both characterized and dominated by a large percentage of window area to wall surface. Its location makes the space most susceptible to the seasons. In December, it receives sunlight especially in the afternoon when it would be warmest. In June, the room receives sunlight especially in the morning when the summer heat would be least noticeable.

Baseboard: 8", wood; cyma cap.
Dado: plaster painted white.
Chairrail: 3'–6" high, wood; bead and ogee.
Walls: plaster.
Cornice: plaster painted white.

Doorways and doors: raised ground for overdoor panel with corner rosettes, ovolo and cyma architrave capped by an egg and tulip cornice with drip mould.

Windows: raised ground for architrave similar to doorways.

Hardware: brass; door and window pulls, decorated oval knob with mortise lock escutcheon.

Lighting: two, five-light, flambeau and ribbon, gilded metal sconces with scrolled vine arms.

Chimney: 7'–5" wide by 1'–6" deep. Architrave surround as at windows and doorways.
    Hearth: 5'–0" wide by 1'–6"; white marble with pink-veined insets.
    Firebox: 2'–6" wide by 2'–4½" high by 1'–10"; cast iron with back panel wreath.
    Mantel: white marble; stop-fluted corners; panel frieze terminated by acanthus blocks; shelf, 5'–0" wide by 3'–8" high by 1'–1½".

Sitting Room, c. 1923
Courtesy of Embassy of Chile.

Sitting Room, 1974

Sitting Room, 1974.

STUDY:

Width: 15'–6"
Depth: 17'–5"

The chamber was very likely designed as a breakfast room. It is oriented to the early morning sun, as opposed to the dining room which receives the late afternoon light. As the smallest and most intimate of the formal spaces, its size is further predicated on the reduction of wall height by a coved ceiling, and floor area by glazed china closets. The mantel is unornamented so as not to distract from a central breakfast table.

Baseboard: 8", wood; ogee cap.
Dado: plaster painted white.
Chairrail: 2'–3" high, wood; cyma and block.
Walls: plaster. The door to hall is flanked by wood and glass cabinets with drawers below.
Cornice: wood painted white.
Ceiling: coved.
Doorways and doors: 8'–6" high single doors, raised panels; architrave on raised ground; carved overdoor panel flanked by consoles supporting cornice.
Windows: raised ground for achitrave as at doorways.
Hardware: brass; pulls, decorated oval knobs and mortise lock escutcheons.
Chimney: 6'–1½" wide by 1'–6".
   Hearth: 4'–11" wide by 1'–6"; white marble with yellow and grey-veined insets.
   Firebox: 2'–6" wide by 2'–4½" high by 1'–9"; cast iron wreath and ribbon panels.
   Mantel: white marble, raised panels below shelf 4'–11" wide by 3'–8½" high by 1'–2".

SALON:

Width: 27'–10"
Depth: 18'–6"

The most obvious physical characteristic of the chamber is the percentage of window area to wall surface. The room, though formal and dominated by the mantel, is bright with natural light, especially in the afternoon. The greens and yellows of drapes and wall fabrics help suggest early summer.

Baseboard: 8", wood; cyma cap.
Dado: plaster painted white.
Chairrail: 2'–10½" high, wood; bead and ogee.
Walls: plaster painted white. Peach and lime green damask panels in ogee moulding.
Cornice: wood painted white; Corinthian.
Doorways and doors: overdoor rinceau panel capped by frieze; crossette architrave; frieze flanked by scrolls supporting cornice.

Study, c. 1923
Courtesy of Embassy of Chile.

Windows: crossette architrave breaks upward for panel flanked by scrolls supporting cornice.

Hardware: brass door and window pulls.

Lighting: four, three-light, brass sconces with cornucopia arms.

Chimney: 7'–1" wide by 1'–6".

   Hearth: 5'–1" wide by 1'–6"; white marble with ochre insets.

   Firebox: 2'–6" wide by 2'–4" high by 2'–0"; cast iron lattice motif.

   Mantel: white marble Ionic columns support center tablet frieze and shelf, 5'–3" wide by 3'–11" high by 1'–5¾".

   Overmantel: mirror in ogee moulding.

DINING ROOM:

Width: 18'–6"
Depth: 27'–9"

With the exception of the chimney wall, the original natural woodwork (dado, cornice and doors)

Study, 1974

Salon, c. 1923
Courtesy of Embassy of Chile.

has been painted white. Though brighter in character, the chamber is perhaps less rich and warm. The narrow windows which flanked the chimney were replaced with wide openings to the family room.

Salon, 1974.

Baseboard: 9″, wood painted white; ogee cap.

Dado: wood painted white.

Chairrail: 2′–9½″ high, wood painted white; cyma and block.

Walls: gold brocatelle.

Cornice: wood painted white; Corinthian.

Doorways and doors: hall pocket door; cyma and double fascia architrave. Salon pocket door; overdoor panel; crossette architrave.

Windows: crossette architrave.

Hardware: brass door and window pulls.

Lighting: four, three-light, black enamel sconces with brass diaper and arms.

Chimney: 7′–9″ wide by 1′–8″; mahogany, flat panels; brass applique.

Hearth: 5′–1″ wide by 1′–6″; black stone with pink marble insets.

Firebox: 2′–11″ wide by 2′–4″ high by 2′–1″; cast iron, fleur-de-lis pattern.

Mantel: black stone, Ionic columns and pilasters with brass base, capital and frieze tablet for shelf, 5′–1″ wide by 3′–8″ high by 1′–2″.

Dining Room, c. 1923
Courtesy of Embassy of Chile.

Dining Room, 1974.

Dining Room.

Family Room, 1974

Family Room, 1974

Family Room.

FAMILY ROOM:

Width: 28′–5½″
Depth: 24′–4″
Height: 10′–3″

The family room is an addition, designed in the 1960's for a restricted site. A spacious area, it is also a foil for the formality of the original house. The casual atmosphere is perpetuated through the use of simple materials (rough plaster walls, light wood ceiling, tile floor), warm color (white, tan, brown and orange) and a visual flow of space through the glazed east wall to the patio. This openness is enhanced by the skylight of stained glass, water reflections from the courtyard pool and the sculptural quality of the chamber, which together form an ever-changing display of light, shadow, color and shimmering reflection.

Floor: hexagonal, burnt sienna, quarry tile. Flagstone in street vestibule with four 6″ risers to family room.
Baseboard: 3″, fir.
Walls: plaster painted white, rough finish. Sculpted plaster partition, 18′–2″ wide by 9′–2½″ high, breaks forward for passage 2′–5″ wide containing cabinet recesses.
Ceiling: fir, 3″ tongue and groove with transverse lighting troughs reflecting pier spacing. "Lantern": plaster walls pierced for stained glass and capped by a vent for natural light.
Openings: glass in wood sash, 7′–0″ high, onto patio; overwindow clerestory. Decorative iron gates (ceiling height) replace original dining room windows. Semi-circular-headed splayed opening to street vestibule.

**Garden Facade with terraces
1974**

2929 Massachusetts Avenue, N.W.

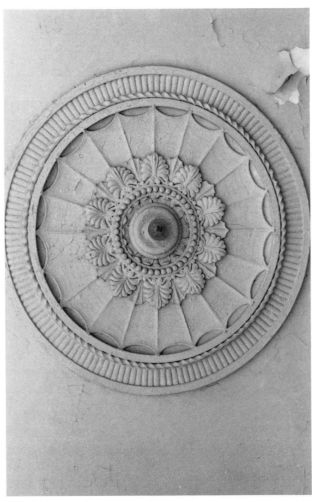

Loggia Ceiling Detail
1974

The residence at 2929 Massachusetts Avenue, N.W., is on the northwest corner of the intersection of Massachusetts Avenue and Rock Creek Drive. The property is located in Square 2198 on lot 808 formerly lots 11 and 12 which were part of a 1917 subdivision of lots 1, 2 and 3. (Subdivisions: Book 42, page 6, Office of the Surveyor.)

At this writing the property, owned by the Seafarer's Washington Building Corporation, is unoccupied and for sale.

HISTORICAL INFORMATION

This section of Washington, as with "Kalorama Heights," was an area of small farms and country estates. South of Massachusetts Avenue, between the park and Observatory Circle, was "Pretty Prospect," north of the avenue was an area known as "Massachusetts Avenue Heights." Recorded in the District of Columbia Office of Deeds (Liber 3949, folio 545) as part of James J. and Dorothy Flynn Richardson's Subdivision of "Massachusetts Avenue Heights," lot 12 (the site of the residence) was sold in 1917 to Mrs. John R. (Maie H.) Williams, mother-in-law of Joseph Leiter (1500 New Hampshire Avenue). In June of that year, Mrs. Williams' builder, Arthur L. Smith, filed permit to construct a $35,000 home (Permit 5361) designed by Clarke Waggaman (of the firm, Waggaman and Ray). In 1919 the firm was again hired for the northwest pantry and a

1974

southwest porch remodeling, now the ballroom aisle (Permit 473).

Lot 11, the garden north (rear) of the residence, was purchased (Liber 3949, folio 434), also 6 April 1917, jointly by Mrs. Williams and Maria H. Day who owned neighboring lot 13 (corner of Massachusetts Avenue and 30th Street) and in 1918 (Liber 4068, folio 68) acquired from Mrs. Williams the western five feet of lot 12 and the ten by twelve foot southwest corner of lot 11. In 1921 (Liber 4591, folio 490), Maria H. Day sold her interest in lot 11, minus the corner, to Mrs. Williams who in 1922 deeded both lots and residence to Count Lãszló Széchényi for $150,000 (Liber 4725, folio 182).

Count Széchényi, then Minister Plenipotentiary to the United States from (Royal) Hungary, with his five daughters and American wife (Gladys Vanderbilt), hired in 1923 the architect, Alfred Cass, to design the gardens and corresponding north portico, veranda and stairs (Permit 5436). Aside from a portable and expensive playhouse (Permit 2265) the most important alteration was made in 1927 when George Ray was hired to produce plans for the ballroom addition (Permit 537). With a greatly enlarged first floor, the house met the requirements of an embassy. In 1938, the Count signed the property over to his wife, Countess Gladys Vanderbilt Széchényi, perhaps to avoid any difficulties the growing war in Europe might have incurred (Liber 7269, folio 545).

Though the 17 April 1950 issue of the Washington Daily News states that the ballroom ceiling collapsed the previous year, there are no available permits for repair. It should be noted, however, that the present plasterwork compares little with that of the aisle or bow ceilings.

Countess Széchényi died in 1965 leaving her estate to her daughters and relations. Maintained as a private home until her death, the residence was sold in 1966 to the Seafarer's Washington Building Corporation, a subsidiary of the AFL–CIO (Liber 12639, folios 640 and 642). Their intention was to use the structure for opulent receptions, meetings, and committee chambers and, in fact, had caused several unfinished alterations (including a basement stair in the ballroom aisle) before learning that local zoning regulations enforced residential usage. The residence and grounds are in need of general repairs.

ARCHITECTS

Clarke Waggaman (1877–1919), born in Washington, was the son of Thomas Ennals Waggaman, a prominent real estate investor and founder of the

former Waggaman Gallery in Georgetown. Waggaman senior, bankrupted in 1907, is considered one of the first to introduce Millet and Corot to the United States. He also is credited with donating the last parcel of land for Rock Creek Park.

The younger Waggaman studied law at Georgetown and Catholic Universities before going abroad. He never practiced his profession and was only informally educated in architecture before returning to Washington in 1907. While still abroad he met Grace Knowlton, then a student in Paris, and in 1900 the two were married. Grace Waggaman financed her husband's architectural career.

As a successful and prolific designer of residences throughout the city and most especially in the vicinity of R Street and Connecticut Avenue, Waggaman in 1917 entered partnership with George N. Ray. In that same year he was elected to the AIA. Though he is almost entirely associated with domestic design, Waggaman collaborated with deSibour on the Montgomery Country Club. He was survived by a son, Colonel Wolcott Clark Waggaman (who may have designed a hunting lodge for Countess Széchényi in Hungary), and a daughter, Mrs. W. F. Holtzman (N.Y.T., 10–24–43; Legare). (A.I.A. Journal, v.8, April 1920; W.S., "Rambler," 2–22–20. Most information was received during an interview between Tanya Beauchamp (The Landmarks Committee at N.C.P.C.), J. L. Sibley Jennings, Jr., A.I.A. (N.C.F.A.) and Colonel Wolcott Waggaman: 11–28–73.)

KNOWN ARCHITECTURAL DRAWINGS

Site plan. Print. Scale: 1″=30′
Filed with Plat Book 59, page 436, 26 June 1922.
Ballroom addition site plan. Ink.
Filed with Permit No. 537, 20 July 1927.
Garden portico and steps site plans (2). Pencil and ink.
Filed with Permit No. 5436, 26 December 1923.

VIEWS

Exterior

From northeast:
  W.T.H., "Mansions and Memories," 12–31–39.
From southeast:
  W.P., "Office Use South for Mansions," 12–26–73, S.:B8.

Interior

Library toward northeast:
  House and Garden Magazine, "House of Countess Széchényi, 2929 Massachusetts Avenue," July 1940, Sec. II.

BIOGRAPHIES OF THE RESIDENTS

Count Lâszló Jeno Maria Henrik Simon Széchényi (1879–1938) was the youngest of four sons born to Count Emerich Széchényi, Austro-Hungarian Ambassador to Berlin, a leading participant in the Austro-German alliance and close friend of Bismarck. Count Lâszló, a cavalry officer as a young man, was wealthy in his own right though his wife entered into possession of nearly $15,000,000 upon her marriage. Before World War I, the Count's estates consisted of two castles, 20,000 acres, and extensive wheat, corn and blooded cattle farms. His brother, Count Dionys, was than head of the family (N.Y.T., 7-6-38).

Count Széchényi, a man of great charm and energy, arrived as Minister to the United States in 1922. Shortly thereafter he was offered the Crown of St. Stephen, but the number of contenders deterred the possibility of anyone occupying the throne of Hungary (W.D.N., 7-6-38). Before leaving Washington in 1933, he was honored with a four year scholarship at Georgetown University for the Hungarian student of his choice (W.H., 3-20-33; N.Y.T., 7-6-38; W.P., 7-6-38).

The diplomat's life was hardly uneventful. In 1927 he was challenged to a duel by Archduke Leopold of Hapsburg (then in Hollywood), an event which proved to be a publicity stunt. A 1928 auto accident destroyed the Count's left eye. The organization of a "magnate group" for speculative purposes collapsed during the Balkan trouble netting the Count $7,000,-000 in losses (N.Y.T., 7-6-38).

The Count was survived by five daughters: Gladys, who wed Christopher Guy Heneage Finch-Hutton (Viscount Maidstone), Alice (died 1974), who wed Count Bela Hadik of Hungary, Cornelia (died 1958), who wed Eugene B. Roberts of Washington, Sylvia, who wed Count Anthony Szápáry of Hungary, and Nandine, who wed A. Talbot Peterson of New York (W.P., 6-2-35; W.P., 7-6-38; N.Y.T., 1-30-65).

Countess Lâszló Széchényi (1886–1965) was born Gladys Moore Vanderbilt, daughter of Alice Gwynne and Cornelius Vanderbilt the second, and, great-granddaughter of Commodore Vanderbilt (W.E.S., 1-30-65). She was educated at Chapin and Brearley Schools and upon returning from her European sojourn married Count Lâszló Széchényi in 1908. The two met in Washington where he was an attaché at the Hungarian Legation. The wedding was held in the Vanderbilt mansion on Fifth Avenue, a New York residence since destroyed (N.Y.T., 1-30-65).

After the First World War, which had caught the family in the Austro-Hungarian Empire's struggle against the Western powers, the Count and Countess devoted their time to relief activities, a service for which both were decorated. With the separation of Hungary from Austria in 1921, Count Széchényi was sent as Minister to the United States from Hungary, a post he held until 1933 (N.Y.T., 1-30-65).

With the death of her husband, Countess Széchényi returned from Budapest to the United States where she maintained a home in Newport (she inherited The Breakers from her mother in 1934), New York City and Washington. In 1948, The Breakers was leased to the Preservation Society of Newport for $1.00 per annum (N.Y.T., 1-30-65).

During the Second World War, Countess Széchényi was a volunteer for the American Red Cross and the USO, resuming aid to Hungary, hospitals and individuals with the War's end. A reserved person, the Countess was rarely seen in public during her later years, although she took interest in such activities as the Moral Re-Armament Movement (N.Y.T., 1-30-65; W.E.S., 1-30-65).

Countess Széchényi was the last surviving of her parents' children among whom were Mrs. Harry Payne Whitney, sculptor and founder of the Whitney Museum in New York, Alice Vanderbilt, Brig. General Cornelius Vanderbilt, Reginald C. Vanderbilt and William H. Vanderbilt who died while a student at Yale (W.E.S., 1-30-65; W.P., 1-30-65).

The Countess was a member of the Dames of Cincinnati, St. John's Episcopal Church on Lafayette Square, the Colony Club in New York, the Metropolitan Opera Guild, the Art Association of Newport, and the Sulgrave Club (W.E.S., 1-30-65).

Hans Sulzer, born in Switzerland in 1876, was minister to Washington during the First World War. During the Second World War he led economic missions to both Germany and Great Britain. From 1935 until his death in 1959, Sulzer, an industrialist, was chairman of the board for the American-based Sulzer Steel and Iron Works. He was also president of the Swiss Chamber of Commerce from 1935 to 1951 and headed the Swiss National Commission of the International Chamber of Commerce (N.Y.T., 1-5-59).

Doctor Hans Heinrich Dieckhoff (1884–1952), born in Strasbourg, studied at the Universities of Lausanne, Oxford, Munich, Berlin and Strasbourg. He was a career diplomat stationed in Tangier when the First World War reached Morocco. Before the outbreak of the Second World War, he served in Constantinople, Valparaiso, Lima, Prague, Washington and London. A brother-in-law of Joachim von Ribbentrop, Foreign Minister under Nazi Germany, Dr.

Dieckhoff hailed the annexation of Austria and was linked to the German-American Bund. In 1937 he was sent as ambassador to the United States where he proved popular despite the circumstances (N.Y.T., 3–22–52).

APPENDIX

Listing of Residents

City directories list the following tenants:

1920 Hans Sulzer
1921 Mrs. Maie Williams
1922–1930 Lâszló Széchényi
1931–1932 Hungarian Legation
1933 Hungarian Legation
    Lâszló Széchényi
1934–1937 Lâszló Széchényi
1938–1939 Hans Heinrich Dickhoff
1940 Vacant
1941–1942 Countess Lâszló Széchényi
1943 Ogden Phipps
1944–1965 Countess Lâszló Széchényi
1966–1975 Vacant

Social register list: (compiled from *The Elite List*)

1924 Count and Countess Lâszló Széchényi
1927 Same (absent)
1929 Count and Countess Lâszló Széchényi and Miss Cornelia
1931–1932 Count and Countess Lâszló Széchényi (Hungarian Minister) and Miss Cornelia
1933 Count and Countess Lâszló Széchényi and Miss Cornelia and Miss Gladys
1944 Countess Lâszló Széchényi (Gladys Vanderbilt), Miss Sylvia Széchényi, Miss Nandine (at Foxcroft)
1950 Countess Lâszló Széchényi (Gladys Vanderbilt)
1955 Same

Chain of Title

1917 Deed 6 April, Liber 3949 folio 440
The American Security and Trust Co., et al, Trs. to Maie H. Williams
". . . under a certain Deed in Trust from Corcoran Thom, Trustee, date February 3, 1911 (recorded Liber 3404, folio 11), . . .

Witnesseth, That the said parties of the first part, for and in consideration of $10.00, . . . do hereby grant and convey . . ., in fee simple, the following described land and premises, . . ., namely Lot Twelve in James J. and Dorothy Flynn Richardson's subdivision of Lots 1, 2, and 3, being in the Subdivision . . . known as "Massachusetts Avenue Heights," as per plat . . . recorded in Book 42, page 6, Office of the Surveyor . . .

In consideration of the execution of this Deed, the said party of the second part, for herself and for her heirs and assign, hereby . . . agrees to and with . . . (such covenants and agreements to run with the land until April 3, 1931 . . .): . . .

(1.) That all buildings erected, . . . shall be built and used for residence purposes exclusively . . . outbuildings . . . erected upon the rear of . . . said land.

(2.) The said described land . . . shall not be used . . . for any trade, business, manufacturing or mercantile purpose.

(3.) That no house shall be erected upon said described land which shall cost less than $15,000.

(4.) That any house erected on said . . . land shall be designated for the occupancy of one family . . . and that only one residence shall be erected upon said Lot 12."

1917 Deed 6 April, Liber 3949 folio 443
The American Security and Trust Company, Trustees to Williams and Day
". . . under a certain Deed in Trust from Corcoran Thom, Trustee, date February 3, 1911 (recorded Liber 3404, folio 11), . . .

Witnesseth, That the said parties of the first part, for and in consideration of the sum of $10.00, . . . do hereby grant and convey . . ., in fee simple, the following described land and premises, . . . namely: Lot 11 in James J. and Dorothy Flynn Richardson's subdivision of Lots 1, 2, and 3 . . . in "Massachusetts Avenue Heights," . . . recorded in Book 42, page 6, . . . Office of the Surveyor, . . .

In consideration of the execution of this Deed, . . . (as in folio 440)"

1918 Deed 22 April, Liber 4068 folio 68
Maie H. Williams to Maria H. Day
". . . Witnesseth, That the said party of the first part, for and in consideration of the sum of $5.00, . . . does hereby grant and convey . . ., in fee simple, the following described land . . . namely:

Westerly (5) feet front on Massachusetts Avenue by depth of (105) feet, of Lot (12) . . .

Also part of Lot (11) . . . described as follows: Beginning for the same at the southwest corner of said lot, and running thence east (20) feet, thence north (10) feet, thence west (20) feet, and thence south (10) feet to the point of beginning. Subject to covenants and restrictions of record."

1921 Deed 10 December, Liber 4591 folio 490
Maria H. Day to Maie H. Williams
". . . Witnesseth, That the said party of the first part, for and in consideration of the sum of $10.00 . . ., does hereby grant and convey . . . the following described land and premises . . ., namely: An undivided one-half interest in and to part of Lot (11) in James J. and Dorothy

Flynn Richardson's subdivision of Lots in Square . . . (2198), "Massachuetts Avenue Heights," as per plat recorded in Liber No. 58 folio 23 . . . described as follows: Beginning for the same on Rock Creek Drive at the most easterly corner of said lot and running thence Northwesterly along the Northeasterly line of said lot, . . . (150) feet to the most Northerly corner of said lot; thence Southwesterly along the Northwesterly line . . . (74.67) feet; thence Southeasterly parallel with and . . . (10) feet distant from the South-westerly line of said lot, . . . (150) feet to said Rock Creek Drive; thence Northeasterly along said Rock Creek Drive, . . . (74.67) feet to the place of beginning. Subject also, to the covenants to run with the land until April 3, 1931, from and after which date they shall cease . . ., that all buildings erected or to be erected upon said land shall be built and used for residences exclusively, . . ."

1922   Deed 22 July, Liber 4725 folio 182
Maie H. Williams to Count Lâszló Széchényi
". . . Witnesseth, That the said party of the first part, for and in consideration of the sum of $150,000 . . ., does hereby grant and convey . . . in fee simple, the following described land and premises, . . . namely: Parts of Lots (11) and (12), . . . described as follows: Beginning for the same at the intersection of the Northerly line of Massachusetts Avenue, with the Westerly line of Rock Creek Drive, and running thence North-easterly along said line of Drive, . . . (189.67) feet to the most Easterly corner of said Lot (11); thence Northwesterly, along the Northeasterly line of said Lot (11), . . . (150) feet to the most Northerly corner of said Lot (11); thence South-westerly along the Northwesterly line of said Lot (11), . . . (74.67) feet to the Northeasterly line of the part of said Lot (11), . . .; thence Southeasterly along said line of said part of Lot (11) . . . (20) feet to the most Easterly corner of said part of Lot (11) . . .; thence Southwest-erly parallel with said Rock Creek drive, . . . (115) feet to the Northerly line of Massachusetts Avenue, . . . (130) feet to the place of begin-ning."

1938   Deed 21 September, Liber 7269 folio 545
Count Lâszló Széchényi to Gladys Vanderbilt Széchényi
". . . Witnesseth, That for . . . ($1.00) and other good and valuable considerations the said party of the first part, does grant unto the said party of the second part, in fee simple, the following described land and premises . . ., namely: Parts of Lots . . . (11) and . . . (12) . . . in Square . . . (2198) . . ."

1965   Will 30 January, Administration No. 113,252
Gladys Vanderbilt Széchényi
"(2) I give, . . . to each of my daughters Alice

Hadik, Gladys Peterson, Sylvia Szápáry and Nan-dine Széchényi Eltz who survives me and to the issue taken collectively of my deceased daughter Cornelia Roberts . . . the following:
    (a) My residence in the District of Columbia, known at the date hereof by the street number 2929 Massachusetts Avenue, . . ." Filed with the will is a complete household inventory.

1966   Deed 14 July, Liber 12639 folio 640
Eugene B. Roberts, Jr. to The Seafarer's Wash-ington Building Corporation
". . . Witnesseth, That for and in consideration of the sum of $10.00, said party of the first part does grant and convey . . . in fee simple, the fol-lowing described land and premises . . ., namely: Parts of Lots . . . (11) and . . . (12) . . . in Square . . . (2198) . . ."

1966   Deed 14 July, Liber 12639 folio 642
Alice Hadik et al, devisees to The Seafarer's Washington Building Corporation
". . . Witnesseth, That for and in consideration of the sum of $10.00, said parties of the first part do grant . . . in fee simple, the following de-scribed land and premises, . . . namely: Parts of Lots . . . (11) and . . . (12) . . . Square . . . (2198) . . .
    Said land being taxed as Lot numbered . . . (808) . . ."

Building Permits:

No. 5630, 13 June 1917. Permit to build.
Owner: Maie Hewitt Williams
Architect: Clarke Waggaman
Builder: Arthur L. Smith, 1130 Woodward Building
Estimated cost: $35,000
No. 5631, 13 June 1917. Sheds.
Owner: M. H. Williams
Size: 8x10 feet and 12x20 feet
". . . two temporary storage sheds for new building . . ."
No. 1814, 20 December 1917. Elevator.
Owner: Mrs. J. R. Williams
Contractor: Otis Elevator Company
Estimated cost: $2775.00
"Install one electric passenger elevator (3'-4" x 3'-11")"
No. 473, 21 July 1919. Alterations.
Owner: Maie H. Williams
Architect: Waggaman and Ray
Contractor: J. R. Beall
Estimated cost: $4,000
"Remodel southwest porch and add northwest addition as per plan." Site plan indicates that this was the pres-ent pantry and ballroom aisle.
No. 5436, 26 December 1932. Garden Additions.
Owner: The Royal Hungarian Legation
Architect: Alfred G. Cass, New York City
Contractor: William P. Lipscomb Co., Inc.
Estimated cost: $19,000
"Build steps/small tool house/ and garden wall." Site

plan indicates that this is the north portico, the terrace over the vaulted areaway and existing service wing, and the stairs, fountain and garden wall.

No. 5437, 26 December 1923. Shed.
Owner: The Royal Hungarian Legation
"Build storage shed 12 x 26 x 11 feet on parking and sidewalk—store material on 7 feet of street."
No. 2265, 4 September 1924. Playhouse.
Owner: Count Lâzsló Széchényi, Hungarian Minister
Architect: E. L. Davis
Contractor: E. F. Hogson Co., Boston
Estimated cost: $3,000
"Build one portable playhouse in rear garden, . . ." 12 x 36 feet, wood.
No. 537, 20 July 1927. Ballroom.
Owner: The Royal Hungarian Legation
"Storage shed for ballroom addition." The actual permit for construction is missing, however, site plans, with the signature of George Ray, indicate the location and size of present ballroom.
No. 141543, 11 November 1931. Temporary exit.
Owner: The Royal Hungarian Legation
"Erect temporary exit for reception as per plan on file."

STATEMENT:

The entrance facade of this late Georgian residence is only apparently symmetrical. Large windows and the distinctive use of plasterwork reduce the chambers to a domestic scale, which becomes all the more dramatic as a foil for the ballroom addition. The ballroom, which adds 50% to the first floor area, is overwhelming in proportion and character to the earlier structure. The surrounding landscape of terraces and walls is softened by the basically informal planting arrangement of the English garden.

SITE:

Setting: The building faces south on two lots; the first, on which the structure stands, measures 105'–0" deep from the avenue property line and 130'–0" wide; the second measures 84'–8" deep by 150'–0". At the north elevation are the east automobile court and kitchen service court which are connected by a vaulted areaway beneath the terrace and portico. The ballroom has a private court to the English garden.

The terrace is quarry tile with limestone border. Limestone steps descend to a balcony (overlooking the garden) from which paired, semicircular, brick stairs with limestone treads descend to a herringbone brick landing and limestone fountain. Wide, limestone steps descend to the lower lawn.

Enclosures: Surrounding the English garden is a high, common-bond brick wall, with a gate to the ballroom, and terrace stairs on axis with the portico. An ornamental wrought iron gate opens out from the automobile court to the side drive.

Paving: The center section of the concrete drive is gravel. The automobile court and curb are concrete.
Landscaping: Surrounding a bed of azalea and ivy is the semicircular drive. At the entrance front are clipped hemlock bushes, spruce, dogwood and maple trees.

The English garden is divided into two areas with centered green-swards bordered with ivy and mature azalea, southern and saucer magnolia, hydrangea, forsythia, hemlock, spruce, rhododendron, oak, althea and holly.

EXTERIOR:

Dimensions: The five bay entrance facade and north elevation are 59–5". The four bay east and five bay west elevations are 53'–0". The one story plus basement ballroom pavilion is connected to the main structure by a hyphen, 6'–9" in width. The ballroom pavilion is 31'–7½" in width by 64'–6" in depth to the semicircular north wall.
Foundations: concrete footings and slab.
Structure: brick bearing walls; wood joists and rafters.
Mechanical: The Otis elevator has an 850 pound capacity. The oil furnace serves a hot-water heating system. A dumbwaiter connects the pantry and basement kitchen. Food warmers are heated by hot-water radiators.
Walls: The limestone-faced base supports common bond brick walls interrupted by limestone belt courses at the second floor elevation and third floor window sill. The first two stories of the central entrance bay are limestone and break forward four inches with the third floor belt course as a guilloche-decorated cap surmounted by half-engaged urns. The basement, first and second stories of the east and west elevations break forward four inches for the first three bays.
Doorways and doors: wood, flat-panelled double door entrance. The east elevation French door to the first floor balcony has a limestone fascia architrave. Over the recessed French door above the entrance is a cast stone fan. Second story glazed doors with transoms and semicircular balconies flank the north portico.
Windows: casement and double-hung windows with limestone sills and bonded brick arches. The exceptions to the above are the east elevation oval occuli which separate the first three bays of the second story. The ballroom pavilion has wrought iron window guards.
Loggia: There is a semicircular drive from the street to the limestone loggia of Tuscan columns in antis. The entablature frieze has alternating patera and decorated gouge plaques.
Portico: At the north terrace is a one and a half story, wood, semicircular portico of Tuscan columns which support urn balusters and rail. The entablature has a panelled soffit and denticulated cornice.

Stoop: At the ballroom bow three limestone risers to a
landing give access to the brick stair and stoop which
follow the curve of the wall. The stair has seven limestone risers and a wrought iron railing.

Balconies: All balcony railings are wrought iron.

Cornices: wood. Bead and cyma architrave; bracket
frieze, corona, bead and cavetto cornice. The ballroom
pavilion has a denticulated cornice.

Roofs: hipped, slate. The ballroom pavilion has a built-
up roof.

Dormers: There are segmented ventilators for the attic
and a penthouse for the elevator.

Chimneys: There are five brick chimneys with limestone
caps; three over the hipped roof, one projecting from
the north wall for the kitchen and one at the ballroom.

PLANS:

The loggia, vestibule, center hall and semicircular
stair are on axis. The vestibule is flanked by closets
and the center hall is subdivided by columns and
changes in floor elevation. To the right is the front
drawing room and rear library, and to the left is the
front dining room separated from the rear pantry
and service stair by a corridor connecting the hall to
the ballroom.

The second and third floors have peripheral
chambers on three sides of a central space divided into
the north stair hall and south storage facility. The
central third floor storage room contains a steep stair
to the attic.

The basement extends beneath the north terrace and
the west ballroom. Chambers used for storage, laundry
and servants' are arranged along two passageways
below the entrance and side halls. The furnace room
is beneath the drawing room and the kitchen is beneath the pantry.

VESTIBULE:

Width: 6'–0"
Depth: 8'–0"
Height: 12'–1"

Floor: white and grey-veined marble squares.
Baseboard: 6½", wood.
Walls: plaster, applied mouldings.
Cornice: wood painted white.
Ceiling: plaster barrel-vault with applied mouldings.
Hardware: brass, knobbed handles.
Lighting: brass cylindrical lantern at ceiling.

ENTRANCE HALL:

Width: 17'–5¾"
Depth: 33'–1½"

Detail Entrance Vestibule
1974

The dark, formal space has three distinct areas; the
entry, the hall and the semicircular stair, each having
its own floor and ceiling elevation. Apparently the desired effect was to draw attention by way of these
changes in height toward the staircase which, in turn,
carries the eye to the second floor.

Entry:

Floor: white and grey-veined marble squares with three
6½" oak risers to hall.
Baseboard: 6½", wood.
Walls: plaster painted white.
Cornice: wood painted white.
Ceiling: 12'–4" high, plaster painted white.
Doorways and doors: glazed double door 8'–6" high to
vestibule; fan light. Mirror-paned single doors 6'–8"
high.
Hardware: brass filigree on silver ground. Oval knobs
and rectangular escutcheons for mortise locks.
Lighting: two hurricane lamp sconces with tassels and
chimney caps.

Detail Entrance
1974

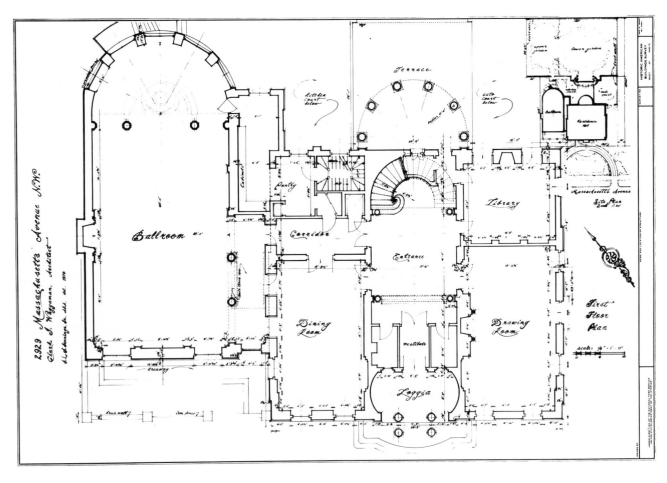

Entrance Vestibule
1974

Typical Hardware
1974

Garden Elevation
1974

Entrance Hall
1974

Hall:

Floor: 2″ oak with cherry and oak border.
Baseboard: 6½″, wood.
Walls: plaster painted white.
Cornice: Doric. Wood painted white.
Ceiling 11′–11″ high, plaster painted white.
Doorways and doors: flat-panelled mahogany double doors (7′–6″ high) and decorative plaster fans separated by ornamented transom bar.
Hardware: brass filigree on silver ground. Oval knobs and rectangular escutcheons for mortise locks.

Stair:

Semicircular, wood, left-handed, molded oak handrail. There are twenty-four 6½″ risers to the second floor and twenty-one risers to the third floor. The first three risers curve about the newel. The mirror-paned door beneath the stair opens to the rear portico vestibule.

DRAWING ROOM:

Width: 18′–11″
Depth: 32′–5½″
Height: 12′–1″

The Georgian chamber is formal without being entirely symmetrical. Large windows, with a southeast exposure, delicate ornament, and painted cream walls are elements used to create a light, airy chamber. The space is dominated by a richly detailed mantel with flanking mahogany doors.

Floor: 2″ oak with cherry and oak border.
Baseboard: 6½″, wood.
Dado: plaster.
Chairrail: 2′–2″ high, wood.
Walls: plaster with mouldings.
Cornice: plaster painted cream.
Ceiling: plaster painted cream.
Doorways and doors: recessed, mahogany doors similar to hall.
Windows: the double-hung windows, 8′–1½″ from sill to soffit, have fluted convex architraves, and, cyma and corona cornices. The chairrail acts as window sill and breaks forward with the dado. The central east bay is a French door onto a balcony.
Hardware: brass filigree on silver ground. Oval knobs and rectangular escutcheons for mortise locks.
Lighting: four, two-light, crystal, brass and enamel sconces.
Chimney: 12′–4″ wide by 1′–7″.
    Hearth: 1′–11″ deep, marble; black diamond insets on white ground.
    Firebox: 3′–6½″ wide by 3′–8″, cast iron flute and bead.
    Mantel: marble; white with green insets. Shelf: 7′–0″ wide.

Drawing Room
1974

Detail Drawing Room Cornice
1974

Detail Drawing Room Overdoor
1974

Dining Room
1974

Overmantel: recessed semicircular plaster arch.
Heating: The east wall windows have radiators behind
    dado registers.

LIBRARY:

Width: 18'–8"
Depth: 15'–0"
Height: 12'–1"

This is the smallest and most masculine of the
public rooms. Walnut panelling, green tile floors and
narrow windows were designed to focus attention
down and inward. With attention concentrated in
that direction, the contrasting white walls, cornice and
ceiling seem to blend together; their esthetic importance secondary. The intimate character results from
a space having an inward focus made more pro-
nounced with the manipulation of color, material and
light.

Floor: green 6" square tiles.
Baseboard: 4", wood.
Wainscot: 8'–3" high, walnut; four rows of flat panels
    in stiles and rails. The wainscot is furred out from
    the south wall for three bays of bookshelves.
Walls: plaster.
Cornice: wood.
Ceiling: plaster.
Doorways and doors: flat-panelled single doors 7'–6"
    high set in stiles and rails of wainscot.
Windows: casement; 8'–3" sill to soffit. The windows
    flanking the chimney have 2'–0½" high seats set in
    deep reveals. The wainscot continues into the reveal.
Hardware: brass. Mortise locks and decorative handles.
    Cremone window bolts with oval knobs.
Lighting: ceiling fixture removed.
Chimney: 5'–10" wide by 1'–4½".
    Hearth: 1'–5" deep; slate in oak surround.
    Firebox: 2'–11½" wide by 2'–10½"; fire tile painted
        black.
    Surround: 4'–1" wide by 3'–5"; black stone bolec-
        tion.
Heating: grille openings for radiators under window
    seats.

DINING ROOM:

Width: 17′–11½″
Depth: 29′–6″
Height: 12′–1″

While similar to the drawing room in scale and manner, the dining room has no mantel and little ornamentation to distract from a dining table centered in the chamber. With doors on three sides, the room becomes a circulation space in itself, which may be the effect desired in consideration of the adjoining ballroom.

Floor: 2″ oak with cherry and oak border.
Baseboard: 6½″, wood.
Dado: plaster.
Chairrail: 2′–2″ high, wood.
Walls: plaster with fascia and bead mouldings.
Cornice: plain entablature with picture mould and frieze.
Ceiling: plaster.
Doorways and doors: recessed, mahogany double doors similar to hall. French doors to ballroom.
Windows: 8′–1½″ sill to beaded 4¼″ deep soffit.
Hardware: brass filigree on silver ground as in drawing room. French doors have brass handles.
Lighting: outlines of four sconces indicate similar design to drawing room.
Heating: four exposed hot-water radiators.

CORRIDOR:

Width: 6′–11½″
Length: 18′–0½″
Height: 12′–1″

Floor: 2″ oak with cherry and oak border.
Baseboard: 6½″, wood.
Walls: plaster painted white.
Cornice: similar to dining room.
Ceiling: plaster painted white.
Doorways and doors: mahogany double doors similar to hall. The 6′–10″ high service doors are wood with raised panels in stiles and rails. French door to ballroom.
Hardware: brass knobs on single doors and French door. The double door has oval knobs and rectangular escutcheons of brass filigree on silver ground.
Lighting: two, two-light, oval-cartouche and reeded-arm brass sconces.

BALLROOM:

(Without the alcove)
Width: 28′–0″
Depth: 60′–0″
Height: 17′–0″

Ballroom Bow
1974

Airiness, a characteristic of this spacious addition, was contrived from the use of delicate ornament, high ceilings and many oversized windows. The extravagant size of the chamber, in direct contrast to the more domestic scale of the older house, is elegantly enhanced with Corinthian columns, crystal chandeliers and parquetry. As a space for entertaining large formal groups, the chamber is divided into three distinct areas: the entrance alcove and the garden bow, their ceiling height and detailing separate from the ballroom proper.

Floor: herringbone, oak.
Baseboard: 5½″, wood.
Chairrail: 2′–6″ high, wood.
Walls: plaster painted white. Corinthian columnar screens, responds and pilasters.
Cornice:
Alcove and bow: plaster painted white.
Ballroom: frieze with patera, and cyma and corona mouldings capped by recessed cove terminated by cyma moulding concealing lighting fixtures.
Ceiling: plaster painted white.
Alcove and bow: 14′–10″ high.

Ballroom
1974

Ballroom: coved, large central medallion for fixture (original, elaborately detailed ceiling collapsed in 1949).

Doorways and doors: The French doors have bead and scotia architraves with overpanels. The pantry door is 6'–8½" high and treated as wall.

Windows: floor length, double hung, 11'–0" high. Panelled jambs with recesses for drapes. At the bow one of the sashes raises for access to the garden stair landing.

Hardware: brass handles and corridor door mortise lock.

Lighting: two, three-light, gilded sconces in alcove; four, five-light, gilded sconces in ballroom. The bow has a tiered, crystal chandelier with six candles and sixteen concealed lights. The ballroom has a crystal chandelier with "Wedgewood" green placques at the bowl, sixteen candles and twenty-nine concealed lights.

Chimney:

Hearth: 1'–11" deep, slate.

Firebox: 4'–6" wide by 4'–0"; cast iron vertical flute and bead.

Mantel: grey marble with white decorative motifs: shelf: 7'–5" wide by 5'–5" high.

Overmantel: frame, removed (elaborate outline indicates design in 18th century manner, possibly for mirror).

Detail Ballroom Chandelier
1974

Detail Ballroom Mantel
1974

Detail Ballroom Cornice
1974

3000 Massachusetts Avenue, N.W.

The residence at 3000 Massachusetts Avenue, N.W. is on the south side of Massachusetts Avenue at the intersection of Whitehaven Street. The property is located in Square 2147 on lots 829 (the house), formerly parcel 52/11, and 6.

At this writing the property is owned by the Federal Republic of Brazil and maintained as the Ambassador's residence.

HISTORICAL INFORMATION

The McCormick villa was built on part of an estate called "Pretty Prospect," which was itself part of an older, much larger property, "The Rock of Dumbarton," northeast of Georgetown. (Oak Hill Cemetery on R Street is also a segment of "The Rock.") "Pretty Prospect" was already fragmented by 1889 when Calderon and Kate Carlisle sold their twenty-three acres in trust to Alfred Fleming, Issac Jackson and William Edmonston for $124,800. The trustees were given permission to subdivide the property so as to create squares, lots, streets and alleys. (Liber 1359 folio 449)

In 1907, the year of his retirement, Robert McCormick, former Ambassador to Russia and France, arrived in Washington with his wife, Katharine. Within the year Katharine Medill McCormick paid Alfred Fleming $29,970.34 for a triangular lot of over an acre (Liber 3118 folio 14). Though the early permits are missing for Square 2147, several sources, including Howe's *American Country Houses of To-day 1915,* agree that the house was designed by John Russell Pope about 1908 and the Brazilian government publication, *A Embaixada Do Brasil em Washington— Jan. 1935,* states the builder was William P. Lipscomb.

Katharine McCormick, a member of the famous and outspoken Medill-Patterson clan, was recently criticized for the character of her home (not necessarily its size). Her grandniece, Felicia Gizycka, who wrote with admiration of her grandmother's home at 15 Dupont Circle in the August 1970 *Washingtonian,* implied that the "distance" from the city center was an added detriment to a residence which "had neither charm nor warmth." To be sure, the house is aloof and may seem somber to those more impressed by frosting than content.

According to the 9 September 1934 *Washington Herald,* Katharine McCormick gave the house to her daughter-in-law, Ruth Hanna McCormick, sometime after the Senator's death. This is incorrect. In 1924 Mrs. McCormick deeded the house and, through a bill of sale, all its contents to her son, Senator Joseph Medill McCormick. (Liber 5157 folio 126)

The residence was only recently completed when in 1911 Mrs. McCormick bought adjacent lot 6 to the northwest of the original property for less than a dollar per square foot. It was over a half acre in size and, since never combined with the original property as one lot, may have been purchased for speculative purposes. (Liber 3468 folio 74)

In 1934, after Katharine McCormick's death, her former daughter-in-law (now Mrs. Ruth Hanna Simms) and General Charles G. Dawes (a personal friend), as trustees of the Senator's will (exemplified copy—1926), sold the house, with apparently considerable furnishings, to the Brazilian government for $200,000 (Liber 6824 folio 359). The 9 September *Washington Herald* states that several items of furniture originally belonging to Josephine de Beauharnais went with the estate. (At the time of this writing, the drawing room contains very fine French Empire pieces.) Lot 6 was not sold until 1942 when the Embassy bought the remaining property from Mrs. Simms and the General for $50,000. (Liber 7782 folio 137)

During the first year the Brazilian government was in residence, extensive renovations were made to the ground floor, including remodeling or elimination of service rooms, the enlargement of the library so as to accommodate the state dining room and the removal of the library fireplace. (Except for minor alterations, such as shifting the drawing room hall doorway, the first floor remains essentially unchanged.)

By 1935 a chancery had been built on Whitehaven Street southwest of the residence. Designed by Henry Francis Cunningham (in cooperation with Counselor C. de Freitas-Valle) as a one story "Early Federal" sprawl (WP, 11–11–34), the building has been destroyed for the new chancery (on lot 6) which was dedicated 2 October 1971 (WP). The construction of the new building on Massachusetts Avenue was subject to an agreement with the District of Columbia Government (Liber 12981 folio 6) based on points of completion though it seems apparent that the aesthetic appeal of the new structure by Dr. Olavo Redig de Campos (head of the Department of Building at the Brazilian Foreign Ministry) has proved successful.

Drawing Room, 1973

ARCHITECT

John Russell Pope, born 2 April 1874 in New York, was the son of Mary Avery Loomis and John Pope, artist and Associate of the National Academy of Design. He received his education at the City College of New York and earned an architectural degree at Columbia's School of Mines where he studied under Professor William R. Ware. In 1895 Pope won the McKim Roman Scholarship and, in 1896, the Schemerhorn Scholarship, together giving him two years at the American Academy in Rome. After graduating from the Ecole des Beaux Arts in 1900, he returned to New York where he worked for Bruce Price before opening his own office in 1903 (Withey; NYT, 8–28–37). It is noted that Pope and Jules Henri de Sibour (1520 20th Street) together worked in the offices of Bruce Price in 1902.

The office, famous for its internal organization (*The Architectural Record,* "Office Procedure," Feb. and Mar. 1931), produced in Washington alone such important structures as the Scottish Rite Temple, the National Archives Building, the National Gallery of Art, the Pharmaceutical Institute, Constitution Hall (DAR), the National City Christian Church, the Jefferson Memorial and the residences of John R. McLean, Levi P. Morton, Henry White, Robert S. McCormick, Irwin B. Laughlin, Mrs. Robert Hitt and George Hewitt Myers. Pope's work earned for him the 1917 Medal of Honor from the Architectural League of New York, the 1919 Gold Medal Award from the New York Chapter of the A.I.A., and a 1922 honorary diploma from the Jean Leclaire Institute (École des Beaux Arts). He became a Chevalier in the French Legion of Honor in 1924 and received honorary degrees from Yale (1924), Columbia (1929) and Syracuse (1932). In 1917 Pope, a member of the A.I.A. (1907), was appointed by President Wilson to the Commission of Fine Arts and later served Hoover on the National Board of Consulting Architects. From 1933 to his death in 1937, he was President of the American Academy in Rome and, in 1936, was awarded first prize by the Olympic Committee for the best athletic building (Yale gymnasium) of the year. (*The Architecture of John Russell Pope,* Royal Cortissoz, 1928; NYT, 8–28–37; NCAB)

Pope was an Honorary Corresponding member of the Royal Institute of British Architects and the Beaux Arts Institute of Design; a member of the National Institute of Arts and Letters, the International Congress of Architects, Alpha Delta Phi and the Sons of the American Revolution; and an Academician of the National Academy of Art. Pope belonged to a host of major clubs including Columbia University, Union,

Players, Century Brook, and Piping Rock in New York, Metropolitan in Washington, and Clambake in Newport. In 1912 he married the former Sadie Jones of Wilmington, North Carolina. Their surviving daughter, Jane London Pope, married Anthony B. Akers. (Withey; NYT, 8-28-37) Mrs. Pope died 7 May 1975. (WP, 5-8-75)

KNOWN ARCHITECTURAL DRAWINGS

Conceptual drawing of Whitehaven Street chancery. WP, 11-11-34.
Residence and chancery floor plans.
A Embaixada Do Brasil em Washington—1935.

VIEWS

Exterior:

Residence facade.
WH, 9-9-34.
Residence and chancery from Massachusetts Avenue, site plan, residence facade, driveway from entrance, chancery from Whitehaven Street, from garden, veranda detail.
A Embaixada Do Brasil em Washington—1935.

Interior:

Residence ground floor stair hall, ground floor dining room, salon mantel.
SS, "Gravure," 4-15-45.

BIOGARPHIES OF RESIDENTS

Robert Sanderson McCormick (1849–1919) was born at "Walnut Grove" farm in Rockbridge County, Virginia. His parents were William Sanderson McCormick, brother of the developer of the reaper, and Mary Ann Grigsby. The entire family eventually moved to Chicago where the manufacture of their machine would be more profitable. Soon after McCormick received his degree from the University of Virginia he was appointed (1892) Commissioner in London for the Chicago World's Columbian Exposition. His success with the British led to a diplomatic career, with his first position as Secretary of the American Legation at the Court of St. James. (WT, 4-17-19; DAB; WP, 4-17-19)

In 1902 McCormick became the first American ambassador to Austria-Hungary. As Ambassador to Russia from 1902 to 1905 he was instrumental in working out a settlement of the Russo-Japanese War, assuming responsibility for the Japanese interests. For his efforts, Czar Nicholas conferred on him the Order of St. Alexander Nevsky and the Japanese Emperor the Order of the Rising Sun. McCormick, who was the principal figure in the negotiations to admit the Associated Press into Russia, left in 1905 to assume the post of Ambassador to France (ES, 4-17-19; NYT, 4-17-19; DAB). It was during the retirement banquet given him in Paris that he advocated the necessity of a World Court to arbitrate both military and commercial disputes between nations.

Robert McCormick was married in 1876 to Katharine Medill, daughter of the founder of the Chicago Tribune. (WT, 4-17-19; NYT, 4-17-19)

Katharine van Etta Medill McCormick, wife of Ambassador Robert S. McCormick and daughter of Joseph Medill, founder of the Chicago Tribune, was born July 11, 1853. A precocious child, she was influenced by such personalities as Abraham Lincoln who was often a guest of the family. As a woman she was described in the *Washington Herald* (9-9-34) as "wise, witty, whose tongue could be sharp." Indeed, she could dominate conversation with agility not only in her native English but also in German and French. A great traveler, Mrs. McCormick was staying at the Hotel Trianon Palace at Versailles when she suffered a fatal heart attack. (*Chicago Tribune:* 7-5-32)

Funeral services were held at both the American Cathedral Church of the Holy Trinity in Paris and at the Chicago residence of Col. Robert R. McCormick, remaining son of Mrs. McCormick. She was, in addition, survived by a sister, Mrs. Robert R. Patterson (15 Dupont Circle, Vol. I) and three grandchildren by the late Senator Medill McCormick. According to the *Tribune* (7-26-32) Mrs. McCormick left an estate of $100,000 (as recorded by the Office of Wills, District of Columbia), the house at 3000 Massachusetts Avenue having been deeded in 1924 to her son, Senator Joseph Medill McCormick. (CT: 7-6-32, 7-17-32)

Senator Joseph Medill McCormick, born 16 May 1877 in Chicago, was the son of Katharine Van Etta Medill and Robert Sanderson McCormick. He was educated at Groton School in Massachusetts before graduating from Yale in 1900. Trained to eventually head the *Chicago Tribune,* he rose from a position of police reporter to the management by 1908 of all the departments within the *Tribune.* During this period, in partnership with Charles A. Otis, he bought the *Cleveland Leader* and the *Cleveland News*. (WES, 2-25-25; DAB)

Theodore Roosevelt was instrumental in McCormick's decision to abandon the newspaper business for a political career (ES, 2-25-25). In 1912 McCormick was Vice Chairman of the Progressive Labor Party, although by 1914 he had turned to the Republican platform (DAB). From 1918 to 1925 he was Republican Senator of Illinois, an office he held until his sudden death in 1925 as a result of an acute dilation of the heart which caused massive hemorrhaging. (NYT, 2-25-25)

The senator, responsible for the McCormick-Good Bill providing for the creation of the Bureau of the Budget, was a bitter opponent of the League of Nations and the Versailles Treaty (WES, 2-25-25; NYT, 2-25-25). In 1903 he married Ruth Hanna, daughter of Ohio Senator Mark Hanna. Their three children were Katrina, John Medill and Ruth Elizabeth. (DAB)

Col. Robert Rutherford McCormick (1880–1955), born in Chicago, was the son of Katharine Van Etta Medill and Robert Sanderson McCormick. His childhood was spent at preparatory schools in England and in America. He received his AB degree from Yale in 1903, and, in 1907, after winning his law degree from Northwestern University, he was admitted to the Illinois bar. In 1904 McCormick became a Chicago Alderman and from 1905 to 1910 he was the elected chairman of the Chicago Sanitary District Board. (EB; NYT, 4-2-55; ES, 4-1-55)

In 1910, the year his brother gave up interest in the *Chicago Tribune*, McCormick became responsible for the "family newspaper." After his tour in France, where he led the 61st Artillery Regiment during the War, he gained complete control of the *Chicago Tribune* (EWB). While abroad, he and his cousin, Captain Joseph Medill Patterson, collaborated on the development of the *New York Daily News*. In 1949, McCormick purchased the *Washington Times-Herald* from his late cousin's estate, Eleanor (Cissy) Patterson.* By 1953 the assets of the Tribune Company (of which Robert McCormick was President) were valued at $250,000,000 and included forest lands, paper mills, hydroelectric installations, shipping companies and WGN, Inc. (World's Greatest Newspaper) with both radio and TV networks. (NYT, 4-2-55; EWB)

McCormick was, in the opinion of the *New York Times* (a rival paper), "dogmatic, intensely partisan, unpredictable, vital, industrious and aristocratic," a

determined isolationist, and, as director (1937-48) of the Associated Press, particularly powerful in his opposition to Roosevelt and Truman as well as to the League of Nations, the World Court and the United Nations. (NYT, 4-25-55)

In 1915, while in London, McCormick married the former Amy Irwin Adams. Five years after her death in 1939, he married Mrs. Maryland Mathison Hooper (EWB). The McCormick's last home in Washington was at 2339 Massachusetts Avenue, while their permanent residence was the 1000 acre, twenty-five room estate called "Cantigny" near Wheaton, Illinois. (ES, 4-1-55)

Albert G. Simms (1882–1964), born in Washington, Arkansas, came to New Mexico in 1915 where he became prominent in law, banking, business and politics. His first wife, Katharine Atherton Mather, died in 1921; his second wife, whom he married in 1932, was Ruth Hanna McCormick, widow of Senator Joseph Medill McCormick. The two met while serving in the House, he as Republican of New Mexico (1929–31) and she as a Representative-at-large. (NYT, 12-30-64)

Alexander Brown Legare (1860–1943) was born in Charleston, South Carolina. Upon graduation from Annapolis in 1883 he was given an honorable discharge for lack of appropriate commissions. Legare was recalled at the outbreak of the First World War during which time he served in Naval Intelligence, rising to the rank of lieutenant commander. He was survived by his wife, the formed Grace Knowlton Waggaman whose first husband was architect for 2929 Massachusetts Avenue. (NYT, 10-24-43)

One of the most influential of the diplomatic representative from Brazil was *Carlos Martins* who distinguished his appointment by concluding the economic and military agreements which were to aid in the defeat of the Axis Powers during the Second World War. Born in Rio do Sul and a graduate of the University of Porto Alegre, Carlos Martins served in Paraguay, Vienna, Berlin, St. Petersburg, London, Paris, Amsterdam, Copenhagen, Ecuador, Panama, and Brussels before arriving in Washington (WP, 9-8-46). Maria Martins, wife of the Ambassador, is a noted sculptress best known for her dancers. She successfully exhibited both in New York and Paris (WDN, 9-23-40). Her daughter by a previous marriage, Lucia Fonseca, became a United States citizen in 1942. (ES, 9-29-42)

---

* The *Times-Herald* was sold in 1954 to Eugene Meyer of Meridian Hill in Washington. (NYT, 4-2-55)

APPENDIX

Diplomatic Representatives to the United States from Brazil: (1934-75)

State Department list:

10–02–34	Oswaldo Aranha
04–28–38	Mario de Pimentel Brandão
03–08–39	Carlos Martins
06–01–48	Mauricio Nabuco
06–12–52	Walther Moreira Salles
08–14–53	Sylvio Ribeiro de Carvalho, Minister Pleni-potentiary, Counselor of the Embassy, Chargé d'Affaires ad interim
10–20–53	João Carlos Muniz
07–18–56	Ernani do Amaral Peixoto
07–23–59	Walther Moreira Salles
09–02–60	Carlos Alfredo Bernardes, Minister Counselor, Chargé d'Affaires
10–18–61	Roberto de Oliveira Campos
07–09–64	Juracy M. Magalihães
10–18–65	Jorge de Carvalho e Silva, Minister Counselor, Chargé d'Affairs ad interim
02–02–66	Vasco Leitao da Cunha
06–30–68	Jorge de sa Almeida, Minister Counselor, Chargé d'Affaires ad interim
11–08–69	Celso Diniz, Minister Counselor, Chargé d'Affaires ad interim
02–20–70	Mozart Gurgel Valente
05–18–71	João Augusto de Araujo Castro

Listings of Residents

City directories list the following tenants:

1914 Vacant
1915–1917 Robert McCormick
1918–1919 Mrs. Robert S. McCormick
1920–1932 Mrs. Katharine McCormick
1933 Albert G. Simms
1934 Mrs. Katherine Legare
1935 Embassy of Brazil

Social registers list:

1916–1919 Mr. and Mrs. Robert S. McCormick
1920–1933 Mrs. Robert S. McCormick

Chain of Title

1889   Deed 28 January, Liber 1359 folio 449
Calderon Carlisle to Alfred W. Fleming, Tr. et.al.
"This Indenture, made . . . between Calderon Carlisle and Kate T. Carlisle his wife, . . . parties of the first part, and Alfred W. Fleming, Issac W. Jackson and William E. Edmonston . . . parties of the second part:

"Witnesseth, that . . . for . . . the sum of $124,800 . . . have . . . conveyed . . . all that certain . . . parcel of land . . . known . . . as and being part of . . . "Pretty Prospect" and heretofore "The Addition to the Rock of Dumbarton" and described as follows: Beginning . . . at the oak tree beginning of parts of said tract formerly belonging to Richard Parrott and afterwards to Benjamin Mackall and running thence North 2° East 42 perches to a road laid out 16½ feet wide thence with the meander of said road the five following courses and distances South 69° East 46 perches, thence South 80° East 7½ perches, thence East 16 perches, thence North 68½° East 20 perches, to the Northwest corner of land formerly belonging to Nicholas February and afterwards to Robert Peter Junior, thence South 47 perches to the Northeast corner of said land formerly Parrott's . . . , thence with said land North 85° West 72½ perches and thence in a straight line to the place of the beginning, containing 23 acres and 31 perches being the same land as was conveyed by Romulus Riggs to Robert Barnard by deed dated 29 November 1820 and recorded in Liber A.X. folio 484 . . . To have . . . said parcel . . . of ground . . . In Trust . . . for the following uses and purposes. First to hold said parcel of land . . . subject . . . to sale . . . hereafter granted in trust . . . the undivided shares . . . in said real estate to be (divided) in proportion to the amount of purchase money severally contributed by each, Second upon the further trust that said parties of the second part . shall have full power to subdivide said parcels of land into blocks and lots and lay off and dedicate streets, roads, alleys and ways and to sell, lease or incumber said parcel of land . . . as their discretion may deem most for the benefit . . ."

1907   Deed 15 October, Liber 3118 folio 14
Alfred W. Fleming, et.al. Trs. to Katharine Medill McCormick
"This Deed, . . . by and between Alfred W. Fleming and William E. Edmonston . . . and William H. Jackson, substituted Trustee by Deed . . . in place of Issac N. Jackson, . . . parties hereto of the first part, and Katharine Medill McCormick, . . . party of the second part: Witnesseth, That . . . for . . . the sum of $29,970.34 . . . do hereby grant and convey . . . in fee simple, the following described land . . . namely: Part of a tract of land called "Pretty Prospect," contained within the following metes and bounds: Beginning for the same at a point on the North line of W Street at its intersection with the South line of Massachusetts Avenue extended, and running thence along the South line of said Massachusetts Avenue extended, 46° 57′ West, 320 feet; thence at right angles to the Avenue, 43° 3′ West, 277.85 feet, to the North line of W Street; thence along

said W Street, South 87° 55′ East, 423.79 feet, to the point of beginning; containing 44,456 square feet of ground . . ."

1911 Deed 23 September, Liber 3468 folio 74
Alfred W. Fleming, et.al. Trs. to Katharine M. McCormick
"This Deed Made . . . between Alfred Walton Fleming (et.al.) . . . and Katharine Medill Mc-Cormick . . .
"Witnesseth That . . . for . . . the sum of $23,500 . . . do hereby grant . . in fee simple, all that certain parcel of land . . . known as "Norman-stone" and being part of the original tract called "Pretty Prospect" and now known as Lot 6 in William E. Edmonston and others, Trustees, Sub-division of Square 2147 contained within the fol-lowing metes and bounds: Beginning . . . at a point in the Southerly line of Massachusetts Avenue, distant 320 feet from its intersection with the North line of W Street; said point being the Northwesterly corner of the land now owned by Katharine Medill McCormick, and running thence Westerly with the Southerly line of Massa-chusetts Avenue 100 feet; thence Southerly and at right angles to Massachusetts Avenue 200 feet to the land recently conveyed to Moncure Burke by William E. Edmonston and others, Trustees; thence Southerly with said Burke's Line 123. 92 feet to the North line of W Street; thence East with W Street 20 feet to said McCormick's land; thence Northerly with said McCormick's line and at right angles to Massachusetts Avenue, to the point of beginning;—containing 25,094.52 square feet of ground, . . ."

1924 Deed 30 January, Liber 5157 folio 126
Katharine McCormick to Joseph McCormick
"Witnesseth, That . . . in consideration of the sum of $10.00, and other valuable considera-tion . . . does hereby grant . . . the following de-scribed land and premises . . . namely:
"Part of a tract of land known as "Pretty Pros-pect," Beginning for same at a point on North line of W Street at its intersection with South line of Massachusetts Avenue extended and run-ning thence along South line of said Massachusetts Avenue North 46° 57′ West 320 feet; thence at right angles to said Avenue South 43° 3′ West 277.85 feet to North line of W Street, thence along said W Street South 87° 55′ East 423.79 feet to beginning containing 44,456 square feet.
"Part of a tract of land known as "Norman-stone" now Lot 6 in William E. Edmonston's subdivision of Square 2147. . ."

1924 Bill of Sale 30 January, Liber 5157 folio 126
Katharine M. McCormick to Joseph McCor-mick
"This Indenture, . . .

Witnesseth, That in consideration of the sum of $10.00 and other valuable consideration . . . doth . . . sell . . . all of the furniture, pictures, draperies, rugs, tapestries, bric-a-brac, objects of art, and household furnishings of every kind, . . . about her dwelling house, situate and being num-ber 3000 Massachusetts Avenue. . ."

1926 Will, Administration Number: "Exemplified Copy"
Recorded in Probate court of Cook County, Illinois
Joseph Medill McCormick
"(5) I give, devise and bequeath all the rest, resi-due and remainder of my property, real, personal and mixed, of every kind and nature and wher-ever situated, to my wife and General Charles G. Dawes . . . in trust, to hold and administer the trust estate hereby created and to collect and receive all income, issues and profits thereof . . . I will hereinafter sometimes refer to said trust as my "Personal Trust Estate."
"(6) The Tribune Trust and my Personal Trust shall terminate at the expiration of (21) years after the death of the survivor of my wife and all my children surviving me, . . ."

1934 Deed 12 September, Liber 6824 folio 359
Ruth Hanna Simms, et.al. Trs. to United States of Brazil
"This Deed, made . . . between Ruth Hanna Simms (formerly Ruth Hanna McCormick) and Charles G. Dawes, as Trustees under the last will of Joseph Medill McCormick, deceased, . . . parties of the first part; and United States of Brazil, party . . . of the second part:
"Witnesseth, that for . . . ($200,000) . . . do grant . . . in fee simple, the following described land and premises . . . namely: Part of a tract of land called "Pretty Prospect," described as follows: Beginning for the same at a point on the North line of Whitehaven Street, formerly W Street, at its intersection with the South line of Massachusetts Avenue, and running thence along the South line of said Massachusetts Avenue, North 46° 57′ West, 320 feet; thence at right angles to said avenue, South 43° 3′ West, 277.2 feet to the North line of said Whitehaven Street; and thence along said Whitehaven Street, South 87° 55′ East, 423.36 feet to the place of begin-ning."

1942 Deed 13 August, Liber 7782 folio 137
Ruth Hanna Simms and Charles G. Dawes, Trustees to United States of Brazil
"This Deed, . . .
"Witnesseth, that for and in consideration of the sum of ($50,000) . . . do grant . . . in fee simple, the following described land and prem-ises . . . namely:
"Lot 6 in Square 2147. . ."

1969   Agreement 7 April, Liber 12981 folio 66
District of Columbia with Federal Republic of Brazil

"This Agreement, . . . between the District of Columbia . . . and the Federal Republic of Brazil. . .

"Whereas, Brazil owns certain real property . . . designated on the records as Lots 6 and 829 in Square 2147 . . . and

"Whereas, Brazil intends to develop such . . . property for embassy and chancery use in accordance with the plans approved in principle pursuant to Article 75. . .

"Whereas, said Article 75 requires that Brazil enter into an Agreement with the District. . . .

"Now, Therefore, in consideration of the mutual covenants and conditions herein contained . . . it is agreed as follows:

(1) Approved Plans: . . . Brazil covenants that it will use its . . . real property only for embassy and chancery purposes . . .

(2) Additional Time to Complete: If Brazil should fail to complete its part of the entire development (for reasons other than material causes. . .) within the time specified . . . it is . . . agreed that the Zoning Commission . . will consider upon receipt of . . . application, an extension of time. . .

(3) Future Conveyance: . . . Brazil, prior to . . . completion, will not convey the . . . property . . . without . . . agreement . . such conveyance shall contain a specific covenant binding the grantee, . . . to use for chancery and embassy purposes . . . and that no structural additions or alterations may be undertaken without . . . approval of the . . . Commission and Board. . ."

(4) Successors and Assigns: The application under Article 75 . . . was jointly filed by the Governments of Brazil, Bolivia, Great Britain and New Zealand, and recognizes the need to maintain the present character of the area between Whitehaven Street, Massachusetts Avenue and Observatory Circle. The Covenants contained herein shall . . . run with the land, shall bind . . . and shall inure to the benefit of the parties hereto and subsequent parties. . ."

Building Permits:

Permit cards by Square number, address or Subdivision are missing.

STATEMENT:

The residence is a study in aloof elegance. It is a rigidly powerful statement, symmetrical without superfluous ornament. The house sits toward the middle of its property away from Massachusetts Avenue. Its

1973

Loggia, 1973

c. 1935   Courtesy of the Embassy of the Federal Republic of Brazil

*Planta da propriedade adquirida pelo Govêrno do Brasil
podendo-se apreciar a collocação da Embaixada e da Chancellaria nos jardins*

evergreen and ornamental plantings suitable for a 15th century Italian palazzo or villa shield the building from view, opening only on the most dramatic occasion when seen from the direction of the city on Massachusetts Avenue.

Interiors in the manner of the seventeenth and eighteenth centuries are arranged about a central corridor and unified by similar floor, mantel, window and door designs. The service centers are at the north on Massachusetts Avenue.

SITE:

Orientation: The building faces southeast parallel with the Massachusetts Avenue-Rock Creek bridge. The triangular lot measures 320'–0" on Massachusetts Avenue; 423'–4" on Whitehaven Street; and 277'–10" on the northwest party line.

Enclosures: The retaining wall at the south increases in height with the elevation of Whitehaven Street from the avenue intersection to the house.

Paving: The serpentine driveway is asphalt with limestone curbing. The asphalt service road from Massachusetts Avenue gives access to the south service yard.

The wedge-shaped rose beds, which divided the 270 degree semicircular garden court at the southwest elevation, have been covered with concrete. Walkways and steps connect the entrance drive with the service road via the garden court.

Outbuildings: The chancery building at the southwest corner of the lot has been demolished. The single story, L-shaped structure was entered from Whitehaven Street. The colonnaded garden facade faced northeast (see photograph and site plan).

Landscaping: The landscaping shields most of the house from view. Except for turf at the entrance facade, along the driveway and at the rear beyond the service road, the structure is framed by dense evergreens including black spruce, southern pine, southern magnolia, hemlock and rhodedodendron. Additional color accents are indicated by beds of azalea, scattered dogwood and other small flowering trees.

EXTERIOR:

Dimensions: The four story plus basement structure is rectangular in plan with a five bay 87'–8" east facade and west elevation and three bay, 49'–9" north and south elevations.

Foundations: concrete footings, slab and basement walls.

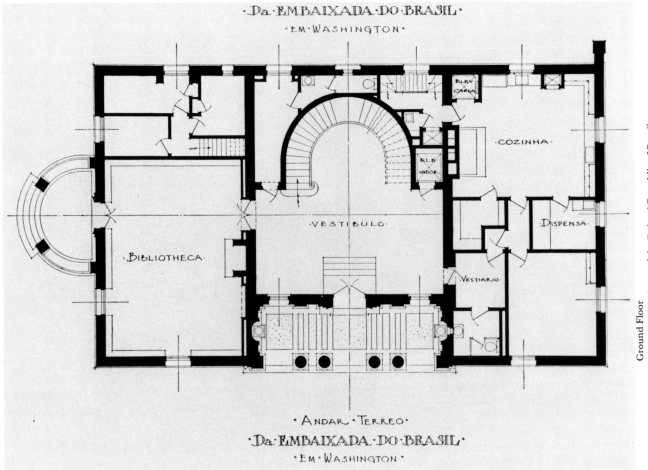

Ground Floor
Courtesy of Embassy of the Federal Republic of Brazil

Structure: brick piers and bearing walls, steel beams.

Mechanical: Otis passenger elevator; gas-fired boiler; recently installed combined central air-conditioning and heating system.

Walls: tightly bonded tan limestone blocks and corner quoines, carborundum finish. The building base is a low platform with torus cap. The base and rail of the first floor balconies are carried across the facade, breaking forward for the three bays over the loggia. A block string course acts as second floor sill and a cavetto and torus band serves as third floor sill.

Windows: All casement windows and French doors open inward.

The ground floor windows have iron bar grilles and panelled limestone architraves with sills and cornices supported on consoles.

The first floor shuttered windows have limestone, fascia and cyma architraves capped by a plain frieze and corona and cyma mouldings. Over the central window is a ribbon frieze broken by an oval escutcheon which rises above the second floor window sill.

The second floor shuttered windows have limestone, fascia and cyma architraves. The third floor or attic windows are without architraves.

Loggia: The ground floor loggia of two risers and a landing support pilasters and paired Tuscan columns. The end wall niches and the windows flanking the entrance door are semicircular-headed. The fascia and cyma doorway architrave is on a raised ground interrupted by consoles which support a dentil, corona and cyma cornice. The loggia ceiling is divided into panels by dropped beams with fret soffits.

Porch: The semicircular porch off the state dining room has Tuscan columns and responds which support a full entablature as base for the panelled balustrade of a first floor terrace.

Balconies: Panelled first floor balconies on scrolled modillions break forward from the central window at the Massachusetts Avenue elevation and the end windows of the entrance elevation.

Cornice: The structure has a cornicione, the smaller cornices delineating each floor in such cases replaced by plain string courses.

Roof: hipped; red clay tile.

Skylights: There are two principal skylights; one over the corridor, the other over a central bedroom which faces west.

Chimneys: There are four central chimneys of limestone with molded caps and a fifth chimney at the southwest which is both taller and narrower than the others.

Hall

Hall

GROUND FLOOR:

The centered loggia, entrance hall and semicircular stair are flanked by the powder and cloak rooms, kitchen and service stair on the right (north) and the state dining room on the left (south). Back of the principal stair is a service corridor.

HALLS:

The loggia, entrance hall and semicircular stair hall are an axial progression of spaces each having its own distinctive characteristic. The grand loggia is sculptured, having strongly defined surfaces and a Tuscan columnar screen. The seeming airiness of the elegant entrance hall is achieved by Corinthian pilasters, richly complex mouldings at cornice and ceiling, diffused light from the loggia, and the verticality of the stair hall. The dramatic stair hall is a plain, two story void with richly detailed cantilevered stair directing attention upward.

Flooring: marble; grey-veined black border on grey-veined white ground. There are four, 6″ marble risers from the entrance to the elevation of the hall floor. Eighteenth century altar balustrades of carved wood flank the riser well.

State Dining Room

State Dining Room

State Dining Room

State Dining Room

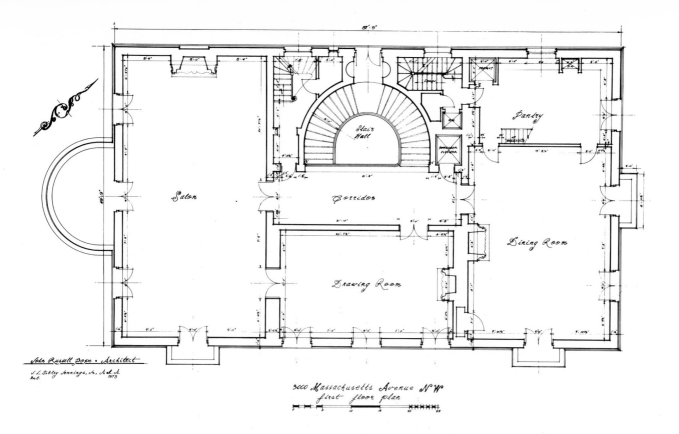

John Russell Pope · Architect
J L Sibley Jennings, Jr, A.I.A.
Del.   1973

3000 Massachusetts Avenue N. W.
first floor plan

Baseboard: 6″; grey-veined white marble.

Walls: plaster painted to simulate tan limestone blocks. Corinthian pilasters flank all openings.

Cornice: entablature painted white; plaster frieze.

Ceiling: plaster painted white; central sunburst within pulvinated oak leaves; rinceau and rosette border panels outlined by guilloche beams.

Doorways and doors: oak, flat panels in cyma moulding; wood architrave painted to resemble limestone. Single doors, 7′–7″. Double door to dining room, 4′–11″ by 9′–6″. Iron and plate glass entrance double door with fleur-de-lis in quatrefoil grilles; plaster ribbon and escutcheon at architrave.

Windows: semicircular-headed casement windows with wrought iron exterior guards.

Hardware: brass. Decorative double door handles (plain knobs and handles elsewhere); 1′–8″ high escutcheons; mortise locks; cremone window bolts with oval knobs.

Lighting: three, two-light, gilded metal, flambeau sconces; one twelve-light, silver-plated, mid-18th century chandelier; three, three-light, gilded metal, first floor corridor rocaille sconces.

Stair: The 5′–0″ wide semicircular stair has grey-veined white marble 6½″ risers, 10½″ treads at the closed stringer, and baseboard. There are sixteen risers to the landing, centered on the curved wall, and fourteen risers to the first floor. The cast iron, black-enamelled rococo balustrade has gilded embellishment. Over the landing is a semicircular-headed alcove with a flat-headed window. The alcove sill is grey-veined white marble, while the reveal has semicircular-headed niches with rocaille overpanels.

STATE DINING ROOM:

Length: 44′–9″   Width: 22′–7″

Three service rooms with basement stair and the original east library with its fireplace (now removed) were combined by the Brazilian government to form the present state dining room. The result is a space which seems excessively low for its length and width. Though dark, the chamber is made less oppressive by the introduction of a brilliant scenic wall paper depicting colonial Brazil.

Flooring: basket weave, oak.

Baseboard: 5½″, walnut.

Wainscot: 5′–6½″ high, walnut; flat panels. At the ends of the room the panels break forward 12½″ for cabinets. The wainscot entablature is oak with gesso duro ornament.

Walls: painted wall paper.

Cornice: painted white.

Ceiling: plaster painted white.

Doorways and doors: double door to hall, 9′–6″ by 4′–11″, walnut; flat panels; panelled jamb. Fluted pilasters with tobacco leaf capitals support entablature similar to the wainscot. The northwest pantry door, 7′–4″ high, is recessed into a wainscoted reveal.

Windows: wood casement, recessed in panelled jamb; south central French door to garden court.

Hardware: brass. Mortise locks with 1′–8″ high escutcheons. Cermone window bolts with knobs (decorated at original windows).

Lighting: fluorescent; concealed above door and window entablatures.

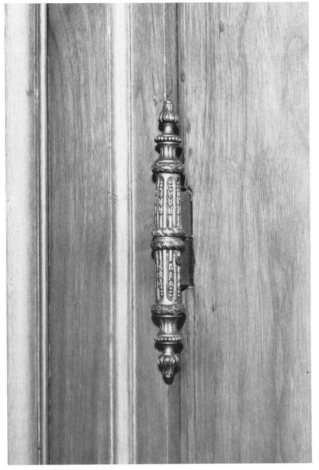

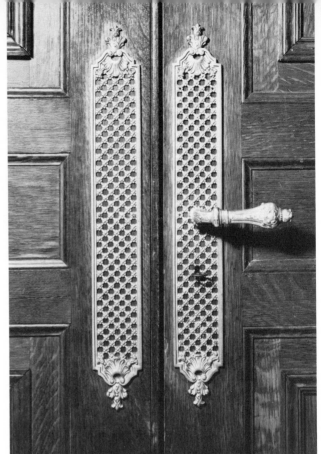

First Floor Reception Corridor

First Floor Reception Corridor

FIRST FLOOR:

About the central corridor is the principal stair on the west, flanked by the family stair and elevator; the pantry and family room on the north; the drawing room on the east overlooking the Massachusetts Avenue bridge; and the salon on the south. (See plans)

The central corridor is retained on the bedroom and servants' floors. There are service areas over the principal stair on these floors.

The following list includes those elements common to the main spaces on the principal floor.

Flooring: basket weave, oak.
Walls: plaster.
Ceiling: plaster painted white.
Doorways and doors: double doors, 11′–4½″ by 5′–0″, walnut; flat panels; panelled jamb; fascia and cyma architrave.
Windows: wood casements with French doors to balconies.
Hardware: brass. Door handles with mortise locks and 1′–8″ high escutcheons; cremone window bolts and knobs.

Family Room

Family Room

Family Room

FAMILY ROOM:

Depth: 32'–0"
Width: 24'–9"

Though the detailing is late 16th century English, the mantel is 18th century French in manner and may not be original to the room. The dark wood wainscot is a foil for the white walls and delicately ornamented cornice and ceiling. The northeast location affords a soft, natural light.

Baseboard: 5", walnut; quarter-round cap.
Wainscot: 5'–6½" high, walnut; flat panels.
Walls: painted white.
Cornice: wood and plaster painted white; grape vine frieze.
Ceiling: ribs and bosses.
Doorways and doors: three service doors, 7'–0" high.
Hardware: The northwest service door has a faceted glass knob.
Chimney: projects 1'–8".
  Hearth: 6'–0" by 1'–2½", purple-veined white marble.
  Firebox: 3'–7½" wide by 3'–5".
  Mantel: purple-veined white marble; consoles. Shelf: 6'–2" wide by 4'–0½".

DRAWING ROOM:

Depth: 17'–11"
Width: 30'–1"

This small chamber in the early Georgian manner (set with signed French Empire furnishings) has been altered by the relocation of the hall door and the more recent addition of green flock wall paper. The result, if less formal, is certainly more colorful especially with a purple marble mantel in the style of Louis XV.

Baseboard: 11", wood painted cream; cyma cap.
Dado: plaster painted cream; applied panel moulding.
Chairrail: 3'–3" high, wood painted cream; ogee cap.
Cornice: elaborate Roman Doric with triglyph and oak-leaf metope frieze.
Doorways and doors: doors painted cream.
Lighting: four, three-light, gilded metal rococo sconces; one eighteen-light, gilded metal Empire chandelier. There are two brass and green marble pedestals with bronze caryatids which may have supported branched candelabra.
Chimney: projects 8".
  Hearth: 5'–4" by 1'–3½", marble; grey insets on white-veined purple ground.
  Firebox: 3'–1" wide by 2'–9½", cast iron; 18th century group of people on back panel.
  Mantel: white-veined purple marble; consoles. Shelf: 5'–4" wide by 3'–10".
  Overmantel: mirror (not integral with wall); 18th century French manner, wood painted green with gilded ornament.

SALON:

Depth: 64'–9"
Width: 24'–10"

This florid chamber is an adaptation of Louis XV ornament scattered over heavier Louis XIV mouldings. The mantel width as compared to its height re-

Drawing Room

Salon

Salon

Salon

Salon

sults in its being squat. This same scale was used for the wall panels; their exaggerated width in relation to the room height is ponderous rather than rhythmic as the selected ornamentation would imply. The introduction of mirrors, however, creates an airy relief through repeated reflections.

Baseboard: 7½″, wood painted cream; ogee cap.

Dado: plaster painted cream; flush panels in reeded mouldings with gilded rococo corner ornamentation.

Chairrail: 2′–9″ high; fascia and ogee.

Walls: painted cream; flush panels in reeded mouldings with gilded rococo ornament. The north and south walls both have two mirror panels. The two nearest the east facade wall are opposite one another.

Cornice: painted cream with gilded ornament; cove.

Ceiling: painted cream with gilded ornament; rectangular bundled bay-leaf pulvination with semicircle at ends; two plaster medallions for fixtures.

Doorways and doors: painted cream.

Lighting: four, six-light, crystal sconces; two, twenty-light, crystal chandeliers.

Chimney: projects 1′–6½″.

 Hearth: 7′–7½″ by 1′–4½″, marble; maroon insets on grey and tan-veined ground.

 Firebox: 4′–9½″ wide by 2′–9½″, cast iron; 18th century allegorical scene.

 Mantel: grey and tan-veined white marble; consoles. Shelf: 7′–11″ wide by 4′–1½″.

 Overmantel: mirror in surround similar to wall mouldings.

3100 Massachusetts Avenue, N.W.

The Embassy at 3100 Massachusetts Avenue, N.W., is located in Square 2147 on the southeast corner of Massachusetts Avenue and Observatory Circle. The garden and original structure are on lots 38, 39 and 40. The new chancery is on lots 37, 43, 44 (now lots 824 and 825) and 45.

The buildings are used according to their original functions as residence and chancery.

PREVIOUS BRITISH LEGATION:

According to Constance McLaughlin Green *(Washington, Village and Capital—1800–1876)* the "Old" British Legation on Connecticut Avenue was the first foreign-owned legation in Washington. The 5 June 1930 *Washington Star* incorrectly wrote that the building was constructed in 1867. Deeds indicate, however, that the property remained in private hands (Jessie M. Bright) until at least 24 July 1872

when it passed to James M. Latta (trustee). More accurately, *The New York Illustrated Newspaper* of 25 December 1873 states, "Sir Edward Thorton is now building a magnificent mansion in the English style. It . . . will be, when completed, the most substantial building in Washington." Sir Edwin, Minister Plenipotentiary, took occupancy in 1876. With reference to the same article, the Legation was designed in the British Foreign Office and, according to John P. Coffine's *Washington: Historical Sketches of the Capital of Our Country—1887,* the American, Robert Isaac Fleming (arrived in Washington in 1867), was the contractor.

An Assessor's Returns Book (a "diary" used before entry into the General Assessment Book) gives no value for lot improvements until 1875–76 when $80,-000 was recorded. A June 1901 permit (No. 1941½) gave indication that a ballroom was added to the Embassy. (Great Britain's status as Legation was

Previous British Legation (Demolished)
c. 1901-03
F. B. Johnston, Huntington Library

Ballroom looking north toward Dining Room.
Note ceiling ventilator
c. 1901-03, F. B. Johnston
Huntington Library

Previous British Legation (Demolished)
c. 1900-1910
M. L. King Library

raised to Embassy in 1893—*The Washingtonian,* "With the Diplomats," Jan. 1930.) However, an article in the March 1889 issue of *Cosmopolitan* clearly stated, complete with illustration, that a ballroom of some size was part of the original structure. It was during Sir Esme Howard's stay in Washington that plans were approved for the new embassy at 3100 Massachusetts Avenue by the Foreign Office and the United States Commission of Fine Arts and, under his successor, Sir Ronald Lindsay, that 1300 Connecticut Avenue was destroyed (Permit Nos. 143200, 143297).

When new, the British Legation building stood in an area considered highly undesirable. There was nothing to recommend the site except delapidated Civil War barracks, brick yards and a few distant pigsties. The building, however, was a harbinger of things to come. The house was red brick with stone trim and slate roof. Its style was the whimsical "gingerbread" of the 1870's, adapting various elements from different cultural eras. Certain elements (as with the side entrance to the vestibule) are remi-

niscent of Furness or Fraser in the early 80's.* The structure is, as seen in photographs, "handsome" from the exterior and with reference to the exceptional interior wall papers and stencilling, impressive. As a postscript, attention is directed to the ballroom chandeliers which were re-hung in the new Embassy on Massachusetts Avenue.

HISTORICAL INFORMATION

An accurate historical study with a chain of title for the British Embassy must be based on conjecture and secondary information. Not only are deeds (except those for the new chancery site) particularly elusive (apparently purchase records are not immediately available from the British Foreign Office), but early permits for the Square are missing (refer to 3000 Massachusetts Avenue). In addition, it is

* Though it would seem safe to call the style "Victorian," it should be noted that other structures included in this volume (1601, 2000 and 2122 Massachusetts Avenue), and exhibiting a very different effect, have been similarly described.

Previous British Legation (demolished).
Drawing Room (SW Chamber) looking west to Ballroom. c. 1901-03, F. B. Johnston, Huntington Library.

Previous British Legation (demolished). Reception Room (SE Chamber) looking NW to Drawing Room (left) and Entrance Hall (right). c. 1901-03, F. B. Johnston, Huntington Library

understood that only rarely will a country extend the courtesy of filing permits to build. His Majesty's Government, however, both informed the President and presented plans for the new embassy complex to the Commission of Fine Arts in Washington.

The original site was lot 40, apparently a combination of lots comprising nearly four acres with access to Observatory Circle and 200 foot frontage on the avenue. According to the Baist Atlas the property, a parcel of 21.47 acres in a subdivision of "Pretty Prospect," was still in trust in 1903 and managed by A. Walton Fleming, W. E. Edmonston and J. H. Jackson (refer to 3000 Massachusetts Avenue). It is assumed the property was acquired after 1903 and before September 1924 at which time the project was brought to the attention of President Coolidge by the Secretary to His Majesty's Office of Works, Sir Lionel Earle.

Previous British Legation (demolished). Drawing Room (SW Chamber) looking east to Reception Room. c. 1901-03, F. B. Johnston, Huntington Library.

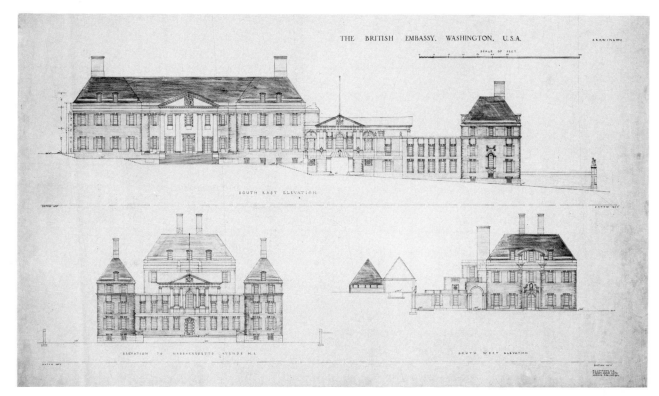

Elevation Drawing CFA Files.

The presentation to the Commission of Fine Arts 5 February 1927 (a meeting held in the New York City offices of William Delano) was perhaps two-fold: as a gesture of courtesy and because the site was adjacent to two federal reserves, Observatory Circle and Normanstone Park. Nine drawings were exhibited by J. Butler Wright, Assistant Secretary of State, on behalf of Sir Esme Howard, Ambassador from Great Britain. The design was received with general enthusiasm by Cass Gilbert. Thomas Hastings, Charles A. Platt, Louis Ayres, Milton B. Medary, Jr., Daniel Chester French, Herbert Adams and James E. Fraser. Chairman Charles Moore wrote: "It was the opinion of these gentlemen and the Commission that the architect (Sir Edwin Lutyens) had presented plans indicating a group of buildings appropriate to the uses intended, expressive of the dignity of the nation and imbued with charm." ("Minutes of the Commission of Fine Arts—Washington, D.C.")

According to Thomas Colquhoun, Property Services Attaché at the British Embassy, northeast lots 38 and 39, together an acre and having 200 foot frontage on the avenue, were given posthumously by Lord Lothian, probably in 1941. The lots became additional space for grounds originally designed by Lady Lindsay and subsequently altered and added to by various ambassadors (including Sir Patrick Dean)

interested in horticulture. The more recent plantings come from Kingsville Nursery outside Baltimore. Indeed, the grounds, because of their size, are of major importance in Sir Edwin's design. The British Embassy residence, more than any other study in this volume, is boldly "rural," letting the outside in.

The residence is in excellent condition and few if any changes were made until 1973 during the tenure of His Excellency, Lord Cromer. At that time, the interior was restored. A new heating and cooling system was installed as well as new kitchens and public facilities. The bedroom floor chimneys were closed and skylights incorporated in dormer roofs.

Lots 37, 43, 45, 824 and 825 are the present site of the new chancery completed about 1960. Since this parcel and structure will not be discussed here, information on the subject lots is on file at the Recorder of Deeds: specifically Libers 9933 (folio 302), 7623 (folio 19) and 9475 (folio 189).

KNOWN ARCHITECTURAL DRAWINGS

The Lutyens Memorial, the Architecture of Sir Edwin Lutyens, Vol. II: Drawings (1927)
Plate XCIII House and garden site
Basement of house-ground floor of chancery
Basement of chancery
Attic of house

VIEWS

The Lutyens Memorial:

Frances Benjamin Johnston collection (Prints and Photographs Division: LC):

E. B. Thompson purchase (MLKW) ca. 1932:

Southeast garden and portico
Complex from north on avenue
Complex from northeast on avenue

Miscellaneous:

Complex from northeast on avenue, 15 April 1931
    Collection of Commercial Photography Company,
    Washington, D.C.
Aerial from northeast, 14 August 1930
    Collection of Fairchild Aerial Surveys, Inc., New York
    City
Aerial from southeast, 1934
    Collection of United States Army Air Corps
Chancery courtyard, WP, 9–8–60
Southeast portico, WP, 3–28–54

ARCHITECT

Sir Edwin Lutyens (1869–1944), born in London, was the son of John Lutyens. Though his preparatory education was sporadic, he entered the Royal College of Art in 1885 and, in 1887, was apprenticed to the architectural firm of Ernest George and Peto. Six months later he left to open his own office in Sussex where he was greatly influenced by the works of Webb and Shaw. His stylistic maturity, which became apparent during the mid–1890's, is directly attributed to Gertrude Jekyll, the landscape gardener, who taught him the meaning of simplicity and directness. (EB)

Edward Lutyens' marriage in 1897 to Lady Emily Lytton (daughter of the first Earl of Lytton) and his introduction to Edward Hudson of the publication, "Country Life," led him to new and wealthy clientele. His commissions included (among others) Orchards, Godalming (1898), Deanery Garden in Sonnig, Berks (1901), Heathcote, Ilkley (1906), and Hampstead Garden Suburb (1907–09). In 1912 he was chosen to design the Viceroy's House for New Delhi, India (1913–30) which earned for him a Knighthood (1918) and a Knight Commander of the Indian Empire (1930). He was also responsible for the British School of Art, Rome, the British Pavilion, Paris (1900), the British Art Exhibition, Rome, the Office for the Anglo-Persian Oil Company, the Picture Gallery and South African War Memorial, Johannesburg. (NYT, 1–2–44; EB)

As a designer considered a modern successor to Christopher Wren, Lutyens received the 1925 Gold Medal from the American Institute of Architects. In 1924 he was made a member of the Royal Fine Arts Commission. He was given a honorary LLD degree from Liverpool University in 1928 and, in 1934, a Doctor of Civil Laws from Oxford. From 1932 Sir Edwin was an officer of the Legion of Honor and, from 1938, President of the Royal Academy. (NYT, 1–2–44; EB)

Lutyens, fellow of the Society of Antiquaries and honorary member of the Royal Scotish Academy, was to preside over the Academy Committee to draw up plans for rebuilding London. His clubs included Athenaeum, Burlington, Fine Arts, Beefsteak, and Savage. He and Lady Emily had one son and four daughters. (NYT, 1–2–44; EB)*

BIOGRAPHIES OF THE AMBASSADORS

(1929–1939)

Sir Ronald Charles Lindsay was born in 1877, the fifth son of Lord Lindsay, Twenty-sixth Earl of Crawford and first of the rank in Scotland. He entered the foreign service in 1898 and was given his first diplomatic post in 1900 when appointed Second Secretary to the British Embassy in St. Petersburg, Russia. From 1905 to 1907 he was on the staff of Sir Henry Mortimer Durand, then Ambassador to the United States. It was in 1909 that he married Martha Cameron, daughter of Senator Donald J. Cameron of Pennsylvania and granddaughter to Judge Sherman of Ohio. She and Sir Ronald's second wife were cousins. The first Lady Lindsay died in 1918 during the long siege of Cairo. (IWW, 1938; ES, 4–18–30; *Washingtonian*, 1–19–30)

The peak of Sir Ronald's career was perhaps as Ambassador to Turkey, although he was most popular in Berlin, the last post before his tour in Washington. Sir Ronald was a Knight Commander of the Bath, Knight Commander of St. Michael and St. George, and Commander of the Victorian Order. He

was military in bearing, spoke with dry humor and was fluent in the Turkish, German and Russian languages. (IWW, 1938; ES, 4–18–30)

Lady Lindsay was born Elizabeth Sherman Hoyt, daughter of Colgate Hoyt of New York and great-granddaughter of Judge Sherman of Ohio. General and Senator Sherman were her great-uncles. Lady Lindsay studied architecture at Columbia University and botany in Boston and England. She had designed gardens in Cleveland and on Long Island before her marriage in 1924 to Sir Ronald. Her activities in the American Red Cross included service in France during World War I. (WP, 1–22–34; *Washingtonian*, 1–1930; ES, 3–28—30)

(1939–1940)

The 11th Marquess of Lothian, was born (1882) Philip Henry Kerr, son of Major General Lord Ralph Kerr. His mother was the sister of the Duke of Norfolk. He left the South Africa of his early childhood to study at the Roman Catholic School in Birmingham and at New College, Oxford. He succeeded to the estates (28,000 acres) of his cousin, earning the titles Marquess of Lothian, Earl of Ancrum, Baron Long-Newton and Dolphingston, Viscount of Brien, Baron Kerr of Newbattle, Baron Jedburgh in Scotland, and Baron Kerr of Kersheugh in the United Kingdom. The family, which dates from 1357, was considered one of the wealthiest, though Lord Lothian was himself impoverished by inheritance taxes. As a member of the House of Lords he delivered his famous speech of 1937 which advocated resumption of token payments to the United States for war debts. Though educated in a Jesuit School, Lord Lothian became a devout Christian Scientist, a faith which acted as the chief bond of the Clivedon set of whom Geoffrey Dawson, editor of the London Times, and Lord and Lady Astor were members. It was because of this interest that Lord Lothian often visited Germany, which soon led to his introduction to Hitler, a man he strongly believed to be sincere. By 1938 he was to admit that "appeasement" had been a grave mistake. (WTH, "Merry-Go-Round," 3–29–39) This same religious belief hastened his death in 1940, a result of an uremic infection which is normally treated by a proper diet and medication. (WTH, 3–29–39; ES, 12–12–40; WDN, 12–12–40)

From 1906 to 1907 Mr. Kerr was Assistant Secretary of the Inter-Colonial Council of the Transvaal and Orange River Colony and Railway Committee of the Central South African Railways. In 1908 he became Secretary of the Transvaal Indigency Commission and, in 1909, editor of the *State,* a South African publication. He left the editorship of the

---

* A complete biography may be obtained from *The Lutyens Memorial, The Architecture of Sir Edwin Lutyens*, A.S.G. Butler with collaboration of George Stewart and Christopher Hussey, Charles Scribner's Sons, New York, 1950.

London Round Table, a post he held from 1910 to 1916, to become secretary to Prime Minister Lloyd George. He was political director of the *London Daily Chronicle,* a paper managed for Lloyd George, and author of sections of the Versailles Treaty. From 1921 to 1931, Sir Philip was director of United Newspapers Limited and in 1931 chancellor of the Duchy of Lancaster. He was appointed Parliamentary Under-secretary in the India Office in 1931, and succeeded to chairman of the Indian Franchise Commission a year later. (ES, 12–12–40)

Lord Lothian received his Washington post two days before Germany attacked Poland. As Ambassador, he launched a campaign to persuade the American people to take action against Germany, convincing President Roosevelt that American security depended largely on the British fleet remaining intact. Shortly thereafter Great Britain exchanged 99 year leases on eight Western Hemisphere possessions for fifty overage destroyers. As Secretary of the Cecil Rhodes Fund from 1925 to 1939, Lord Lothian was charged with selecting the American Scholars who would benefit by the program. (WDN, 12–12–40; WTH, 3–29–39)

Lord Lothian was buried at Arlington Cemetery. His heir, Peter Francis Walter Kerr, then eighteen, received along with the titles, his cousin's personal homes: Blicking Hall in Aylsham, Norfolk, and Monteviot in Ancrum, Roxburghshire. (ES, 12–16–40; WDN, 12–12–40)

(1941–1946)

Edward Frederick Lindley Wood, the First Earl of Halifax, was a shy, courtly and deeply religious individual. An austere personality was matched by a scholarly manner to which Sir Winston Churchill responded, deeming him "a man of light and learning whose friendship it is an honor to enjoy." (ES, 5–12–46) The negotiations between Lord Halifax and President Roosevelt during the conferences on international organization held at Dumbarton Oaks in Georgetown led to the Lease-Lend policy and 4.4 billion dollars in aid to Britain. Lord and Lady Halifax had three sons: the oldest is Captain (then) Charles Wood; the youngest, Lt. Richard Wood, lost both legs in 1943 during the African campaign; while Lt. Peter Wood was killed in October 1942. (ES, 5–12–46; ES, 1–26–46; ES, 4–29–43; WDN, 11–10–42)

(1946–1948)

Lord Inverchapel of Loch Eck, was born (1882) Archibald Clark Kerr, fifth son of John Kerr Clark of Crossbaskel in Hamilton, Lanarkshire. He was educated privately, entered the Foreign Office in 1906, and served in the Scots Guard during the First World War. Early in his career he was appointed Third Secretary to the Washington embassy, making his home in Georgetown. His first ambassadorial post was as envoy to the Central American Republics. It was in 1929, while serving his term, that he married the daughter of a wealthy Chilean. (ES, 1–26–46; ES, 5–5–46)

Before receiving his baronetcy, Lord Inverchapel represented Great Britain in Cairo, Berlin, Buenos Aires, Santiago, Washington, Rome, Teheran and Stockholm. As Ambassador to China from 1938 to 1942, he encouraged the development of the Chinese industrial co-operatives. His last post before coming to Washington was in Moscow where he was present at the Moscow Conference between Cordell Hull, Anthony Eden and Foreign Commissar Molotov. He was delegate at the Teheran, Yalta and Potsdam Conferences as well as at San Francisco for the formation of the United Nations. (ES, 1–26–46; ES, 5–5–46)

Lord Inverchapel, knighted in 1935, appeared on the New Year's Honor List of 1942 whereupon he was made Knight Grand Cross of St. Michael and St. George. In 1944, he was made Privy Councillor and in 1946 made a baron in recognition of his achievements in Moscow. Henry R. Luce, publisher of *Time and Life,* said: "Sir Archibald Clark Kerr is . . . the ablest diplomat. An aristocratic Scotsman, he is a power for liberalism." (ES, 5–5–46)

Marie Teresa Diaz Salas, the young wife of Lord Inverchapel, was described as one of the most beautiful women in Washington. She married Archibald Clark Kerr after her Santiago debut in 1929. The marriage was annulled in 1945, but the two were reunited in 1947. Between 1945 and 1947 Lady Inverchapel made her home in Greenwich, Connecticut, and New York City. In New York she worked for the Bundles for Britain Campaign and later as a nurse's aide at a New York hospital where she concentrated on polio, a disease which had confined her to a wheel chair for two years. (WTH, 9–7–47)

(1948–1953)

Sir Oliver Franks, born in Bristol February 1905, is the son of Robert S. Franks, Congregational Minister and noted professor of theology at the Congregational College of Bristol. For ten years he served as professor of philosophy at Queen's College, Oxford. In 1935 he arrived at the University of Chicago as a visiting professor and later accepted an appointment as professor of moral philosophy at Glasgow University. Before coming to the United States his position was Permanent Secretary of the combined Ministries of

Supply and Aircraft Production. Because of this work, which coincided with the War, he was knighted with the Order of the Bath. As chairman of the sixteen nation Paris Talks of 1947, he was instrumental in the development of the Marshall Plan. Married in 1931, his two children are Caroline and Alison. (ES, 11–28–48; WDN, 6–29–48; WP, 2–13–48)

(1953–1956)

Sir Roger Mellor Makins, born (1904) the son of Brigadier General Sir Ernest Makins, received his education at Oxford, earning in 1925 first class history honors. He joined the Foreign Office in 1928 and served in Washington from 1931 to 1934 before a tour in Oslo. From 1937 to 1940 he filled various positions in the League of Nations Affairs, arriving in New York as adviser at the International Labor Conference of 1941. During the war years Sir Roger served on the staff of the Resident Minister for West Africa (1942), and as Assistant to the Resident Minister at Allied Force Headquarters in the Mediterranean (1943–44). After serving as Minister at the British Embassy in Washington, he was appointed (1947) Assistant Under-Secretary from 1948 to 1952. While in Washington between 1945 and 1946 Sir Roger also served on the United Nations Interim Commission for Food and Agriculture. He was appointed Joint Permanent Secretary of the British Treasury after completing three years as Ambassador to the United States. (WWGB, 1955; WP, 1–6–53)

Sir Roger was made Knight Commander of St. Michael and St. George in 1949 and Knight Commander of the Bath in 1953. He and Lady Makins, married in 1934, have six children: twins, Mollie and Cynthia, Virginia, Christopher, Patricia and Dwight. The 500 acre family farm in Hampshire is "Sherfield Court." (WDN, 1–14–53) Lady Makins was born (1911) Alice Davis, the daughter of Dwight F. Davis, Secretary of War under President Coolidge and donor of the Davis Cup for International Tennis. (See text 1520 20th St.) Though raised in St. Louis, she graduated from Holton-Arms School in Washington, where she made her 1928 debut. (WDN, 1–14–53)

(1956–1961)

Sir Harold Caccia, born in 1905, received his education at Oxford. During the African Campaign in the Second World War, he worked on the Supreme Headquarters staff of General Eisenhower as a Foreign Office representative. Sir Harold was Deputy Under-Secretary for Foreign Affairs under Prime Minister Sir Anthony Eden, serving as a chief political adviser at international meetings. Previous to his post in Washington, he served as Ambassador to Austria.

Sir Harold and Lady Caccia (Anne Catherine) have three children: David, Clarissa and Antonia. (WP, 7–20–56; IWW, 1956)

(1961–1965)

Sir David Ormsby Gore was born in 1918 and studied at Eton and New College, Oxford. A conservative in Parliament, he served from 1951 as Private Secretary to the Minister of State for Foreign Affairs, Under-Secretary from 1956 and Minister of State for Foreign Affairs from 1957 to 1961. With the death of his father in 1964, Sir David became the Fifth Lord Harlech. While Ambassador to Washington, Lord Harlech received an honorary LLD from New York University. (IWW, 1964–65; ES, 2–19–64)

(1965–1969)

Sir Patrick Henry Dean was born in 1909 and educated at Rugby School, Gonville and Caius College, Cambridge. He was called to the Bar at Lincoln's Inn and from 1934 to 1939 had his own legal practice before becoming Assistant Legal Adviser in the Foreign Office. In 1945 Sir Patrick was made chief of the German Political Department and, in 1950, sent to Rome as Minister. He was briefly Senior Civilian Instructor for the Imperial Defense College and by 1953 had become Assistant Under-Secretary at the Foreign Office, rising to Deputy Under-Secretary in 1956. As Permanent Representative to the United Nations from 1960 to 1964, he seemed a logical choice to fill the post of Ambassador to the United States. While in America Sir Patrick received an honorary LLD from Columbia University (IWW, 1965–66; ES, 1–24–69; WDN, 1–30–69)

(1969–1972)

The Right Honorable John Freeman, born in 1915, was educated at Westminster School and Brasenose College, Oxford. Upon graduating Oxford in 1937 he worked as an advertising consultant, resigning for active duty in North Africa, Italy and Northwest Europe. Mr. Freeman rose from Financial Secretary to the War Office in 1946 to Under-Secretary of State for War by 1947 and finally Parliamentary Secretary to the Ministry of Supply, a prominent position from which he resigned in 1951. Though he retired from politics by 1955, in 1958 he became heavily involved in the publishing of the leftist magazine, "New Statesman." Returning from "retirement," he was appointed in 1965 British High Commissioner in India and Ambassador to the United States in 1969. (IWW, 1968–69) Mr. Freeman and his wife, Catherine, a former producer with BBC, have three children: Mathew, Thomas and Lucy. (WDN, 5–5–69)

(1972–1974)

George Rowland Stanley Baring, born 1918, is the first son of the Second Earl of Cromer. From 1931 to 1935 the young Viscount Errington was Page of Honor to His Majesty, King George V. He was educated at Eton and Trinity College, Cambridge, and from 1938 served as Private Secretary to the Marquess of Willingdon on his official visit to South America and later Australia and New Zealand. (WP, 1–17–74)

After the Second World War, during which time he rose to the rank of Lieutenant-Colonel and received the MBE, he left for America to study banking with the J. P. Morgan Company and the Kidder Peabody Company. He returned to England in 1948 as Managing Director of Baring Brothers. In 1953 Viscount Errington inherited his father's title, and, as a member of the House of Lords, accompanied the 1954 Parliamentary delegation to Brazil.

For two years (1958–60) Lord Cromer was head of the Treasury Delegation and the British Economic Mission in Washington and served as the British Executive Director of the International Monetary Fund, the International Bank for Reconstruction and Development, and the International Finance Corporation. In January 1961, Lord Cromer was appointed to the Bank of England as the youngest Governor since 1775. From 1967 to 1970 he was Chairman and Managing Director of the family banking firm of Baring Brothers. In 1971 Lord Cromer arrived in Washington as Ambassador from Great Britain, a post he held until 1974 at which time he returned to the Bank of England. (WP, 1–17–74; WSN, 4–14–74)

Lord Cromer married in 1942. The Countess of Cromer, Lady of the Queen's Bedchamber, is the Hon. Esme Harmsworth whose father, the Second Viscount Rothermere, was Chairman of the Associated Newspapers Limited. There are two sons and a daughter.*

(1974–

Sir Peter Ramsbotham is the younger son of a Governor of Ceylon, Viscount Soulbury. Sir Peter, a career diplomat, studied at Eton. Shortly after his marriage in 1941 he was stricken with polio. During the 1950's, he served four years in the United Nations. His last post before coming to Washington was Teheran, Iran. Of the three Ramsbotham children, Mary was paralyzed in a 1969 car accident. (WSN, 4–14–74; WSN, 5–10–74)

* Credit for much of the information is given to the Department of State, British Desk Office, Reference Biography Service.

(Demolished)
c. 1901–03
F. B. Johnston
Huntington Library

Both Sir Peter and Lady Ramsbotham were born in 1919. Lady Ramsbotham, the former Frances Blomfield, daughter of an army officer stationed in Cairo. She is related to Charles James Blomfield, who was Bishop of London for twenty years, and the Bishop of Limerick, her great-uncle and the father of poet Robert Graves. (WSN, 4–14–74; WSN, 5–10–74)

STATEMENT:

Two separate facilities with opposed activities (chancery and residence) are major factors in this design which reduces pedestrian access to a secondary consideration. The facilities are separated at ground floor by the residence drive and united at first floor by the Ambassador's study. The study which combines both activities spans the porte-cochere. A strong symmetrical axis further stresses the unity.

The architectural style is a distinctive and original interpretation of a limestone and red brick English country house: late 17th century from the avenue, early 18th century from the garden. The proportions and decorative elements verge on geometric art-deco rather than the classicism required of an 18th century building. A motif of circles within squares is applied throughout. The monumental effect is derived from massing. The design of compact blocks, with few distracting overhangs or projectons, is arranged on a series of platforms, each higher than the one before.

SITE:

Orientation: The chancery with the porte-cochere faces northeast on a 200'–0" square lot (measuring from the entrance gates.) The residence faces southeast on an irregular lot measuring 583'–11" at the chancery line, 17'–1" on the east, 583'–0" on the south, 145'–0" on the west, and 180'–10" on the northwest. The alley connecting to Observatory Circle is 52'–9" wide.
In 1941, the Marquise of Lothian donated (posthumously) the northeast garden lot which measures 200'–0" square. The polygonal north lot of the new chancery building measures 397'–5" on Massachusetts Avenue and 296'–0" on Observatory Circle.
Secondary buildings: The two story service buildings are concrete with Flemish bond brick exteriors, limestone trim and hipped slate roofs. The second floor is on grade with the service road. Ornamented

with limestone niches and pilasters, the garage rear wall terminates the south walk. At the swimming pool, brick changing rooms are separated by a limestone pergola of Tuscan columns.
Pavement: The entrance drives to the chancery and residence are asphalt. Asphalt was used to replace the center lawn of the chancery courtyard. The garden walkways are limestone bordered by brick retaining walls. At the portico, the main terrace has a geometric pattern of limestone and slate cut perpendicular to the grain.
Enclosures: The property is bordered by chain-link fences camouflaged with dense foliage. At the street elevation is a high wrought iron fence on a brick and limestone base. The pylons which flank the entrance gates are capped by urns at the chancery and lions and unicorns at the residence drives.
Landscaping: Due to size, the grounds are described by area. The areas are designated by the geometry of Sir Lutyen's terraces and walls and the lots comprising the property. Because of the numerous plantings, many of them are rare, a separate horticultural index has been made. Lady Lindsay, an American landscapist before she married Sir Ronald Lindsay, was responsible for much of the earlier plantings.

EXTERIOR:

Dimensions: The chancery is U-shaped, its courtyard 73'–10" wide by 75'–11". The central entrance pavilion (25'–9¾" wide, 23'–11" deep and 33'–7½" from finished floor to cornice cap) is flanked by two story hyphens, 27'–2½" from porte-cochere grade to parapet cap. The hyphens terminate at three and one-half story, raised basement wings, each wing 25'–8" wide, 40'–8" deep and 39'–6" from street elevation grade to cornice cap.
The porte-cochere and vestibules measure 52'–6¾" wide, 40'–6½" deep, and with the Ambassador's study, 32'–1½" from grade to cornice cap.
The residence, which faces southeast, is a rectangle of two and one-half stories, measuring 173'–8" wide, 62'–2" deep and 34'–0" from southwest elevation grade to parapet cap. At the northwest, the ballroom breaks forward 28'–8". The kitchen court is 35'–10" wide by 31'–8" deep.
Foundations: concrete footings and slab.
Structure: concrete floors and roof with steel beams and reinforcing; brick bearing walls; hollow tile partition walls.
Mechanical: Hollow ceilings contain heating ducts

c. 1934
U. S. Army Air Corps

and plumbing. The original Heggie-Simplex Boiler has been removed.

Walls: Flemish bond brick, reddish-brown; rubbed, gauged brick at building corners and windows; limestone trim.

The chancery base is limestone. There are recessed panels over all first story windows. Within the courtyard, the flush walls of the hyphens and wings are separated by ground story limestone blocks which simulate quoines, while the first story at the hyphens breaks back at a limestone belt course. The limestone first story of the pavilion is ornamented with Tuscan pilasters and half-engaged columns, a Doric entablature and a tympanum monogram of George V.

The porte-cochere ground story is limestone. There are bollards at the automobile entrances and flat arches with carved keystone capped by a pillow

Garden Pavilion

Detail, Chancery Court

Porte-cochere

and crown. Pilaster piers, which flank the vestibule openings, support beams for the concrete ceiling. The brick first story is ornamented with limestone Tuscan pilasters, a Doric entablature, and a brick tympanum with limestone monogram. Over first story niche(s) are urns, supported on a cornice which continues the Venetian window spring line. Brick pedestals for limestone lions are extended from the residence wall to straddle the pavilion roof ridge.

At the border of the residence drive a brick screen separates the chancery and porte-cochere from the residence grounds. There are limestone risers through semicircular-headed openings to the residence terraces. The screen is capped by urns which accentuate these garden entrances.

At the residence the brick base breaks forward four inches and upward for the first story window sills. The portico wall is limestone. The two story recesses for the portico and south entrance are defined with limestone pilaster bases and capitals.

Detail above Porte-cochere

Embassy Residence 1974

The south entrance capitals which lack pilaster bases carry Tuscan entablature blocks below pedestals which break into the roof and support a segmental arch as dormer. (see inside front cover)

Doorways and doors: The limestone pavilion entrance is rusticated and pedimented. Courtyard entrance to the wings is through glazed doors with limestone crossette architraves, flanking frieze consoles and pediment.

The glazed double doors for the porte-cochere vestibules are set in reveals and jambs separated from the wall by a deep groove. A "lintel," which is continuous across the wall, supports a cushion frieze and pediment.

The glazed double doors onto the portico are set in crossette architraves with keystones. The center opening frieze is flanked with consoles for a cornice drip mould.

The south entrance glazed double door is fanlighted and bordered with a limestone ribbon moulding and flanked by rusticated Corinthian pilasters for a broken-scrolled pediment. The scrolled keystone supports a monogram cartouche.

Windows: Generally all windows are six over six. The lip-mould sills and lintel keystones are limestone. Shutters are louvered.

Garden Entrance

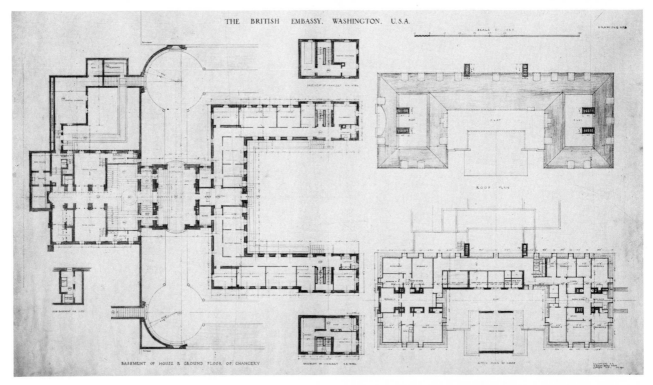

THE BRITISH EMBASSY, WASHINGTON, U.S.A.

Residence Garden Portico

The major exceptions include:

(1.)   basement casements set in segmentally-headed openings,

(2.)   porte-cochere oculi with limestone architraves and keystones set in brick recesses,

(3.)   a pavilion Venetian window with an exaggerated separation of side lights by half-engaged columns,

(4.)   porte-cochere first story Venetian windows, the central openings flanked with limestone pilasters for a semicircular arch and carved keystone,

(5.)   semicircular clerestory windows over the anterooms to the Ambassador's study and secretary's sitting room,

(6.)   and semicircular-headed stair windows at the chancery wings overlooking the residence drive.

Stoops: At the chancery wings are seven limestone risers to the courtyard entrances. The stoops have wrought iron railings. There is a limestone, 5½″ high platform (with curbstone gutter slots) to the chancery vestibule. There are four, 5½″ high limestone risers to the residence vestibule.

Portico: There are eight, 5½″ high, limestone risers from the rose garden to the portico. The risers are flanked by brick cheek walls. The portico floor is limestone and scaled slate squares set diagonally. A double row of limestone Ionic columns and pilasters support an entablature with cushion frieze and a roof with tympanum tablet depicting the British Royal Seal.

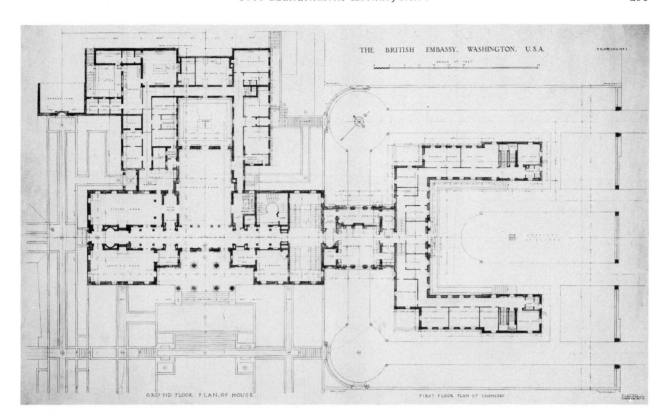

GROUND FLOOR PLAN OF HOUSE   FIRST FLOOR PLAN OF CHANCERY

Cornice: limestone. At the chancery wings corona, ovolo and fascia mouldings replace the block cap over the hyphens. The second story corona and cyma cornice is capped with a brick false parapet from which rises the roof. The shallow cornice at the residence is a cushion frieze between fascia courses capped with a parapet similar to that of the chancery wings.

Roof: slate, hipped, built-in gutters. The pedimented roofs are tin. Behind the east portico is an attic terrace with tin floor. The hyphen roofs are built-up.

Dormers: At the attic terrace are a glazed door (which breaks into the roof) and sash windows each divided by two mullions. The roofs for the double-hung, segmentally-headed dormers were recently pierced for skylights.

Chimneys: brick, limestone cap mouldings. The chancery wings each have one, the residence six, and the service buildings two. At the residence chimneys over the north roof are limestone monogram plaques of Charles V.

PLAN:

Access to the embassy is vehicular. Circulation is within the court and about the "U" of the chancery structure. The three principal axes are the east-west residence drive through the porte-cochere, the "pro-cessional corridor" which connects the three parts of the embassy (the chancery and court, the Ambassador's study over the porte-cochere, and the residence terminated by the swimming pool), and the east-west cross-axis of the terrace, ballroom and kitchen court.

ENTRANCE VESTIBULE:

There are two, 5″ risers from the side bays to the central bay.

Width: 35′–5″
Depth: 8′–0″
Height: 10′–8½″ (at double doors)

Flooring: limestone with center recesses for matting.
Baseboard: side bays—10″, limestone; plain.
Walls: tan limestone. Side bays have semicircular-headed niches with keystone and convex architrave of bound flowers.
Cornice: ogee, corona, cyma.
Ceiling: plaster painted white.
Doorways and doors: double doors, 8′–9½″ high, glazed; bead and fascia, wood surround; convex limestone architrave. Niches with semicircular-headed doors, 7′–11″ high, glazed. Semicircular-headed windows on stairrail. End walls with single oculi.
Hardware: brass door knobs.
Lighting: three, single-light, opaque glass, ceiling drum lanterns, matched.

STAIRHALL:

Width: 58'–2"
Depth: 20'–8"
Height: 26'–10" (from ground floor entrance)

The soffit of the double stair is cut from a shalow dome, 43'–9" in radius. The center span is a bridge between the Ambassador's study and the public rooms. At the ground floor, stone floors, walls and low ceiling, combined with indirect natural light, affects a crypt. At the first floor, the impression is reversed. Large windows admit morning and afternoon light, plaster walls and a high ceiling open up the space while crystal chandeliers add sparkle and delicacy. Attention is drawn upward to the brighter space and the Royal Portraits.

Ground floor:

Flooring: tan and black stone pattern. There are three, 5" risers to the stair platform.
Walls: tan limestone to first floor window sill.
Stairs: opposed stairs with thirteen, 5" risers to mid-landings and thirteen, 5" risers to first floor. The wrought iron, scrolled balustrade has a gold painted handrail.

First floor:

Baseboard: 7½", limestone.
Walls: plaster painted pale blue. Archways recessed 11½". Between the pilaster capitals are high relief friezes painted white on Wedgewood-blue ground.

Secretary's Sitting Room

Stairhall

Study Vestibule

Ambassador's Study

Cornice: wood entablature, 2'–6" high, painted white.
Ceiling: plaster painted white.
Archways: 11'–1" high to soffit.
Lighting: three, six-light, crystal chandeliers, matched.

STUDY VESTIBULE:

The study vestibule is part of principal axis.

Width: 8'–0"
Depth: 8'–0"
Height: 8'–4½" (to arch soffit)

Flooring: black and white stone squares.
Baseboard: 7½", wood painted white.
Walls: plaster painted pale blue.
Ceiling: plaster painted dark blue. Semicircular sphere.
Doorways and doors: double doors, 7'–6" high, gum-wood; raised panels; 8½" deep jambs; crossette archi-traves; semicircular pediments are recessed in 1'–2" deep archways.
Hardware: brass knobs with silver inlay.
Lighting: five-light, crystal chandelier.

Ambassador's Study (Demolished)
c. 1901-03, F. B. Johnston, Huntington Library

Ambassador's Study

Processional Corridor

Ambassador's Study

SECRETARY'S SITTING ROOM:

The Secretary's sitting room is painted white.

Width: 9'–10½"
Depth: 24'–4"
Height: 15'–0"

Flooring: pale gold carpeting.
Baseboard: 7", wood.
Walls: plaster. Breaks forward for chimney of Ambassador's study.
Cornice: 10'–4½" to cap; plaster.
Ceiling: plaster barrel vault painted dark blue, interrupted by Venetian window.
Doorways and doors: recently installed flush double doors, 6'–6" high.
Chimney:
    Hearth: carpeted.
    Firebox: 2'–7" wide, 3'–0" high; opening closed.
    Mantel: 3'–11½" wide, 3'–6" high; limestone, bolection architrave.
    Overmantel: plaster. Raised panel with shelf 6'–9" high.

Family Stair Hall

Sitting Room

AMBASSADOR'S STUDY:

The Ambassador's study is gum-wood, oil finish.

Width: 23'–10½"
Depth: 23'–10½"

The symmetrical space is centroidal. Attention, however, is initially directed toward the one large window, before which is the Ambassador's desk. The chamber is independent from the residence and chancery, though as the Ambassador's office, it is the link which connects them. The functional importance of the space is defined by its impressive scale and rich detail and material.

Flooring: beige carpet.
Baseboard: 10", wood.
Dado: see photo.
Chairrail: 2'–9" high. Carried across single doors and as bookshelf counters.
Bookshelves: 10'–3" high cornice cap at spring of window fan.

Walls: raised over panels. Carved panels at pilaster capital height symbolize power, wealth and knowledge.
Cornice: 15'–3" from floor to entablature soffit.
Ceiling: painted white.
Doorways and doors: raised panel double doors, 7'–6" high. Raised panel single doors 6'–6" high; wood cornice cap aligned with marble overmantel of similar mould.

Hardware: brass. Oval knobs with silver inlay. Hinges with acorn finials.
Lighting: sixteen-light crystal chandelier (eleven concealed lights).

Chimney:
Hearth: 6'–5" wide, 1'–9" deep; white marble.
Firebox: 4'–2½" wide, 4'–6" high, 1'–0½" deep; cast iron roundel of St. George and the Dragon. Electric "coalgrate" of pewter with aluminum reflector.
Mantel: 6'–11" wide, 6'–5" high; white marble with variegated inlay.

Ballroom

PROCESSIONAL CORRIDOR:

Width: 14'–2'' (at the galleries)
Length: 173'–8''

The corridor is the principal axis which unites the three segments of the embassy: the chancery, the Ambassador's study, and the residence. Within the residence structure the corridor is divided into five segments. These include the stairhall, the family stair gallery, the ballroom aisle, the dining and drawing room gallery, and the garden vestibule. The aisle and galleries, which reflect the ballroom in treatment, are similar in detail.

Flooring: black and white stone in diamond pattern.
Baseboard: 7½'', white marble.
Walls: plaster painted white. Corinthian pilasters painted white with wood columns painted to simulate marble. The frieze between the capitals is Wedgewood-blue, except where ornamented with high relief (as over archways) painted white.
Cornice: wood entablature, 2'–6'' high, painted white.
Ceiling: plaster painted white.
Doorways and doors: double doors, 10'–11'' high, gum-wood; raised panels; 10½'' jambs. Single doors, 7'–1'' high, gum-wood; raised panels; fascia and ogee architrave capped by cushion frieze interrupted by tablet and supporting pediment. Pocket door, 6'–11'' high, to circular stair; fascia and ogee architrave.

FAMILY STAIR HALL:

The family stair hall is tan limestone to second floor window sill.

Width: 20'–8''
Depth: 20'–8''

The tan limestone, circular stair is fitted into a square and lighted from the second floor. The lighting helps direct attention up through the "eye" formed by the stringer. Though all inside tread dimensions are the same, at the outside every fifth tread flairs to form a landing. Therefore, the stair is divided into eight sections of five, 5'' risers. The wrought iron balustrade has a metal handrail painted gold.

Second floor:

Baseboard: 7½'', wood painted white; ogee cap.
Walls: plaster; papered. Gold line with tan floral motiff on white ground.
Cornice: wood painted white; scotia, ovolo, corona, cyma.
Ceiling: plaster painted white; coved vault.
Lighting: plaster corner sconces with concealed light. Three-light, brass and opaque glass, ceiling drum lantern.

SITTING ROOM:

The sitting room (former library) is painted white.

Width: 23'–8''
Depth: 20'–8''
Height: 15'–0''

The informal chamber is best described as a morning room, since natural light comes from the east. There is no architectural center of interest. The plaster ceiling seems lower than in reality because the cove is unarticulated—therefore appearing to be flat above wood panelled walls. The view from the window next to the chimney is of the main stairhall.

Flooring: beige carpeting.
Baseboard: 10'', wood.
Chairrail: 2'–9'' high; breaks downward for window seats.
Walls: raised panels.
Cornice: 11'–9'' to cap.
Ceiling: plaster painted white.
Doorways and doors: double door, 7'–1'' high; raised panels; cable, fascia and ogee architrave. Glazed door to portico, in splayed jamb, similar to windows.
Windows: 10'–1'' to soffit; 1'–6½'' high window seats.
Hardware: brass. Door knobs with silver inlay; gargoyle hand-pulls at window sash.
Chimney:
    Hearth: 5'–10'' wide, 2'–6'' deep, white marble.
    Firebox: 2'–8'' wide, 3'–1'' high, 1'–10'' deep; cast iron back panel, monogram of George V.
    Mantel: 6'–1½'' wide, 6'–8'' high; slate surround; white marble bolection architrave.
    Overmantel: beveled, smoked glass mirror.
Heating: forced-air floor registers.

BALLROOM:

The ballroom is painted white with Wedgewood-blue as ground for ornamentation.

Width: 35'–2''
Depth: 49'–8''
Height: 17'–10''

The secondary axis is formed by the ballroom in conjunction with the portico and the kitchen court. The ballroom size is counterbalanced with French doors opening to garden vistas, columns which screen the space without inhibiting the effect of openness, and mirrors which in reflecting each other seem to create additional spaces. The plain ceiling is a foil for the rhythm of pilasters and rich texture of the frieze.

Ballroom (Demolished)
c. 1901–03, F. B. Johnston, Huntington Library.

Ballroom

Ballroom

Flooring: 2″ oak center, with 3′–8″ white marble border.

Baseboard: 7½″, white marble; plain.

Walls: Corinthian pilasters flank a pair of mantels and mirrored panels which alternate with double doors to the side halls and French doors to the court. A wood columnar screen (the shafts painted to simulate marble, the capitals painted white) separates the corridor. High relief friezes between pilaster capitals are punctuated by masks which are keystones for the side hall doors.

Cornice: wood entablature, 2′–6″ high, painted white.

Ceiling: plaster painted white; cove.

Doorways and doors: side hall double doors, 10′–11″ high, painted white with blue trim; raised panels; 1′–8½″ deep jambs. French doors to kitchen court.

Hardware: brass. Oval knobs with silver inlay at hall doors; handles to French doors.

Lighting: ten, three-light, crystal sconces. Two, similar, eighteen-light, crystal chandeliers flank one, two-tier, fifty-one-light, crystal chandelier.

Chimneys: flanked by wood pilasters (painted to simulate cream marble). Paired.

Ballroom

Dining Room

Dining Room (Demolished)
c. 1901–03, F. B. Johnston, Huntington Library

Dining Room

Hearths: 3'–8" deep; marble as in flooring border.
Fireboxes: 3'–4" wide, 3'–8" high, 1'–10" deep; cast
iron back panel, Royal Coat of Arms.
Mantels: 6'–11" wide, 6'–0" high; cream marble and
wood painted to simulate marble.
Overmantels: wood center tablet painted to simulate
marble. Over tablet cartouche breaks through cornice.
Heating: forced-air floor registers set in marble border.

SIDE HALL:

The side hall to ballroom and dining room is
painted white.

Width: 8'–8"
Depth: 18'–4"
Height: 12'–11½"

Flooring: 2", oak.
Baseboard: 7½", wood.
Walls: plaster with recessed panels covered in formal
white print on red ground interrupted by 2'–9" high
pedestals. Panel interrupts at baseboard continuous
astragal and cyma moulds. Pantry overdoor oculus of
enamelled glass and lead cames. Decorative plaster in
elevation drawing does not exist.
Cornice: scotia, corona, ovolo, corona and cyma.
Ceiling: plaster painted white.
Doorways and doors: double doors, 10'–11" high, gum-
wood; raised panels. Corridor door in jamb 3'–5½"
deep. Serving door, 7'–1½" high; raised panels.
Hardware: brass. Oval, paired-door knobs with silver
inlay; handle at serving door.
Lighting: three-light, crystal chandelier.

DINING ROOM:

The dining room is painted pale green with
white accents.

Length: 50'–3"
Depth: 20'–8"

Drawing Room (Demolished)
c. 1901-03, F. B. Johnston, Huntington Library.

Unlike the drawing room where informality and movement are encouraged, the function of the dining room is such that the participants are arranged in a formal, static position. They become a center of a linear (three chandeliers) design in which the massive mantel and columnar aisle screen also dominate.

Flooring: 2″, oak.
Baseboard: wood painted white; ogee cap.
Dado: raised panels. Breaks forward 1¾″ for openings and chimney wall.
Chairrail: 2′–9″ high.
Walls: raised panels; astragal at openings. The Ionic aisle screen is painted white. The aisle niches are 7′–7″ high to cornice cap.
Cornice: 12′–11½″ high; architrave painted green, cornice painted white.
Ceiling: plaster painted white; cove. Ceiling at aisle is 12′–5″ high.

Doorways and doors: double doors, 10′–11″ high, painted pale green with white accents; raised panels; ovolo architrave similar to windows. Serving doors, 7′–1¼″ high.
Windows: 10′–11″ high to soffit. Jambs, 1′–6½″ deep; flat panels. 1′–6½″ high window seats.
Hardware: brass. Oval knobs with silver inlay. Paired gargoyle hand pulls at window sash.
Lighting: three, eight-light crystal chandeliers, matched.
Chimney:
  Hearth: 9′–1½″ wide, 2′–11½″ deep. White marble.
  Firebox: raised 7½″ from floor. 5′–0″ wide 4′–9½″ high, 2′–9½′ deep; cast iron back panel, Royal Coat of Arms.
  Mantel: grey marble, free-standing Tuscan columns support Doric entablature shelf 9′–3½″ wide by 7′–2½″ high.
Heating: forced-air floor registers.

ANTEROOM:

Anteroom (to drawing room) is painted pale green. Mouldings and panels are similar in drawing room.

Width: 13′–11″
Depth: 9′–10″
Height: 15′–0″

Flooring: 2″, oak.
Baseboard: 11″, wood; ogee cap.
Dado: alternating raised and flat panels.
Chairrail: 2′–10″ high.
Walls: alternating raised and flat panels as at dado; astragal at openings.
Cornice: 12′–0½″ from floor to cap. Similar to south vestibule.
Ceiling: barrel vault painted turquoise.
Doorways and doors: double doors, 10′–11″ high, gumwood; raised panels. Jamb to hall is panelled.
Windows: 10′–11″ high. Plane of wall breaks back 6″ for 7″ deep jambs. 1′–6½″ high window seats.
Hardware: brass. Door knobs with silver inlay; gargoyle hand-pulls at window sash.
Lighting: five-light, crystal chandelier.
Heating: forced-air floor registers.

Drawing Room

Typical Hardware

DRAWING ROOM:

Width: 42′–8″
Depth: 20′–8″
Height: 15′–0″

An illusion is created which reduces the room scale. The chamber seems less high because of large, molded ceiling panels which, with the mantel and paired chandeliers, help divide the space into three

South Vestibule

Drawing Room

seating groups. The walls seem shorter and lower because of many large windows. The mantel and doors are nearly flush with the wall so as not to distract from but complement the illusion. The chandeliers, however, are too small; they focus attention on the actual scale of the room.

Flooring: 2″, oak.
Baseboard: 10½″, wood.
Dado: alternating raised and flat panels.
Chairrail: 2′–9″ high.
Walls: alternating raised and flat panels; astragal at openings.
Cornice: 12′–0½″ from floor to cap.
Ceiling: plaster painted white; border cove; pulvinated central roundel flanked by rectangular panels.
Doorways and doors: double doors, 10′–11″ high, painted pale green; raised panels and plain jamb.
Windows: 10′–11″ to soffit. Splayed jambs and 1′–6½″ high window seats.
Hardware: brass. Oval door knobs with silver inlay. Paired gargoyle hand pulls at window sash.
Lighting: two, eighteen-light, crystal chandeliers, matched.
Chimney:
  Hearth: 10′–8″ wide, 3′–2½″ deep; white marble.
  Firebox: raised 7½″ from floor, 4′–7½″ wide, 4′–5″

high, 2′–3½″ deep; limestone and brick with cast iron back panel, Royal Coat of Arms.
Mantel: white marble surround; polychrome yellow marble frieze broken by white tablet; flanking white marble pilasters support shelf 11′–6″ wide, 7′–2″ high.
Heating: forced-air floor registers.

SOUTH VESTIBULE:

Width: 12′–2″
Length: 31′–10″
Height: 15′–7½″

Flooring: black and white stone diamond pattern.
Baseboard: 7½″, white marble.
Walls: plaster painted white. Opposed semicircular-headed floor-length statuary niches painted dark blue and flanked by pilaster mouldings.
Cornice: 13′–4″ high from floor.
Ceiling: plaster painted white; coved vault.
Doorways and doors: double doors, 10′–11″ high, gumwood; raised panels; raised panel jambs. French door to garden with fan light and pilaster mouldings. Opposing archway to gallery.
Hardware: brass. Oval knobs with silver inlay. Hinges have acorn finials.

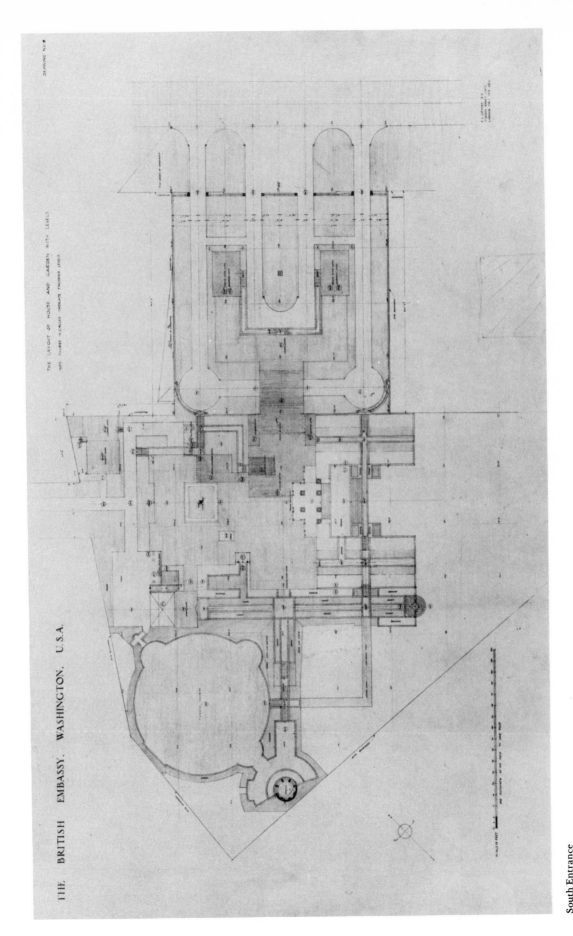

THE BRITISH EMBASSY. WASHINGTON. U.S.A.

South Entrance
3100 Massachusetts Avenue N.W.
Embassy of Great Britain

HORTICULTURAL INDEX

Plantings Listed by Area

Northwest Residence Drive:

Entrance gates: (building side) southern magnolia in bed of ivy bordered with clipped juniper; (turf side) purple beech.
Drive: climbing roses, hemlock, Japanese stewarta.
Porte cochere: ginko trees in beds of ivy and azalea.

Southeast Residence Drive:

Entrance gates: (building side) southern magnolia in bed of ivy bordered by clipped juniper; (turf side) holly.
Drive: holly
Porte cochere: ginko tree, beds of ivy and azalea.

Southwest Walk and Pavilion Court:

Walk: mock cherry, deciduous and evergreen azaleas, dwarf firs, aucuba, privet, Yoshino cherry, pink and white dogwoods, rose beds.

Axial Walk to Pool and Wild Wood:

Walk: ivy border with white dogwood, dwarf spruce and juniper, hemlock, Japanese spider maple. Juniper on retaining wall. Weeping willows in pachasandra beds indicate corners of tennis crosswalk and stairs.
Pergola: bordered by wisteria, dogwood, holly, hosta.
Pool: bordered by calla lilies, clipped hemlock, climbing roses, weeping Scotch elm, crepe myrtle.
Wild wood: mixture of day lilies, blue bells and daffodils with white dogwood, white pine, beech and butternut.

South Lawn:

(in pachasandra beds) azalea, andromeda, Japanese feather maple, mock cherry. Dogwood and oak on turf. (At property line) southern magnolia, roses, hosta, iris, azalea, blue spruce, forsythia, bamboo, dwarf firs, hardy thorn oranges.

Southeast Garden Terrace:

portico stair bisects terrace to form north and south parterre.
Building elevation: climbing roses and Japanese spider maples.
Stair to lawn: hemlock bushes.
Terrace set back: saucer magnolia.
North section: camelias and two mock cherry trees border rose beds.
South section: Japanese spider maples and two mock cherry trees border rose beds. Wisteria trees flank foot of stair to southwest walk.

Southeast Lawn:
at periphery in clockwise order of appearance.

South of terrace: Japanese pagoda tree, hydrangea, Japanese red maple.
North of terrace: climbing roses, oak, southern magnolia in low spruce bed.
Bordering residence drive: rose trellis fences off work space containing manure patch and cut flower beds of peony, calla lily, azalea, gladiola and geranium. Beds border green house.
Bordering Mass. Ave.: Chinese holly, spruce, southern magnolia, hydrangea, blue mountain cedar, Higas weeping cherry, dogwood, holly, red cedar, aucuba, willow oak, golden rain tree, honey locust, mock cherry.
Southeast property line (opposite portico terrace): hosta, dawn redwood, southern magnolia grove, azalea, American boxwood, white dogwood, Japanese stewarta, snowbell, hydrangea, mock cherry, forsythia, sugar maple, spindle tree, crepe myrtle, red Chinese maple, white birch, andromeda, fern, hemlock, red maple, pink dogwood, Chinese holly, rhododendron, purple beech, mountain laurel, white birch and leather leaf viburnum in daffodil beds, white birch and cherry trees in azalea bed.

On turf:

(in pachasandra beds) perfoliate beech, fern leaf beech, European weeping beech, copper beech, horse chestnut, Norway maple, red oak, Virginia pine, crepe myrtle, saucer magnolia, tulip trees, mock cherry.

Glossary of Architectural Terms
Pictorial

248

Plate 1

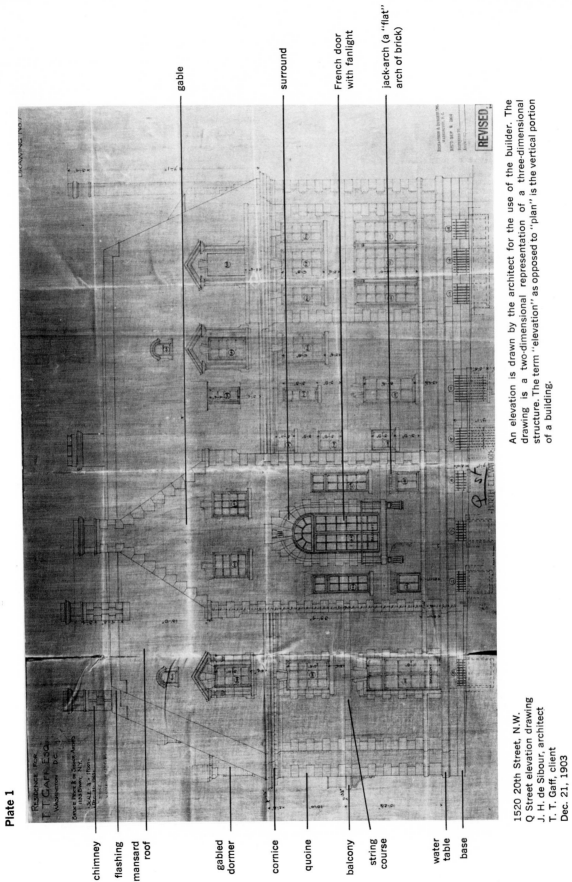

chimney
flashing
mansard roof
gabled dormer
cornice
quoine
balcony
string course
water table
base

gable
surround
French door with fanlight
jack-arch (a "flat" arch of brick)

An elevation is drawn by the architect for the use of the builder. The drawing is a two-dimensional representation of a three-dimensional structure. The term "elevation" as opposed to "plan" is the vertical portion of a building.

1520 20th Street, N.W.
Q Street elevation drawing
J. H. de Sibour, architect
T. T. Gaff, client
Dec. 21, 1903

Plate 2

half dormer —

common bond brick —

double-hung window with glass in lead cames —

rusticated (rough) — sandstone facing

semicircular-headed — voussoir arch (each stone is wedge-shaped and called a voussoir)

dwarf column —

cheek walls —

— string course

— tympanum

— spring stone (the line or stone from which the arch "springs")

— stoop

2025 Massachusetts Avenue, N.W.
Entrance facade detail

Plate 3

frieze with
glyph ornament —

frieze with
rinceau ornament —

radial marquise (canopy)
with opaque glazing —

transom window —

architrave with dog-
tooth ornament —

plinth —

— garlanded brackets

— limestone facing
(wet-rubbed finish)

— side window
with grille

2305

2305 Massachusetts Avenue, N.W.
Entrance facade detail

Plate 4

Flemish bond brick

Royal Escutcheon
(an escutcheon
is a shield)

broken-scrolled
pediment

keystone with acanthus-
leaf ornament

fanlight

transom bar (the "bar"
separates the door
from the light)

pilaster (Corinthian Order)
with shaft of smooth rusti-
cation

French door

plinth

3100 Massachusetts Avenue, N.W.
Southwest entrance

252

Plate 5

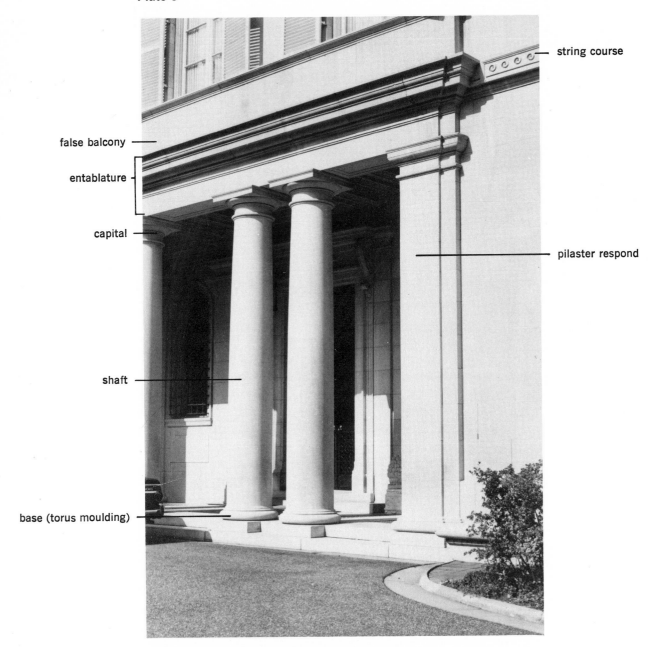

string course

false balcony

entablature

capital

pilaster respond

shaft

base (torus moulding)

3000 Massachusetts Avenue, N.W.
Entrance loggia: Tuscan Doric Order

The loggia as developed during the Renaissance is actually a portico "in antis." The "portico" is recessed into the structure flush with the building wall.

253

Plate 6

fret surround

coffer centered with rosette in patera

doorway architrave

niche

jamb

sill

tread

riser

3000 Massachusetts Avenue, N.W.
Loggia

Plate 7

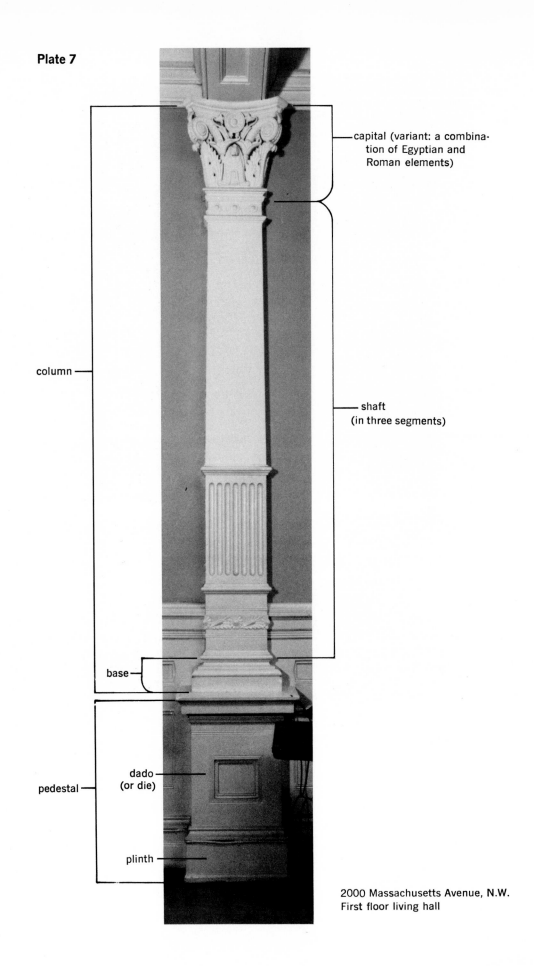

capital (variant: a combination of Egyptian and Roman elements)

column

shaft
(in three segments)

base

pedestal

dado
(or die)

plinth

2000 Massachusetts Avenue, N.W.
First floor living hall

Plate 8

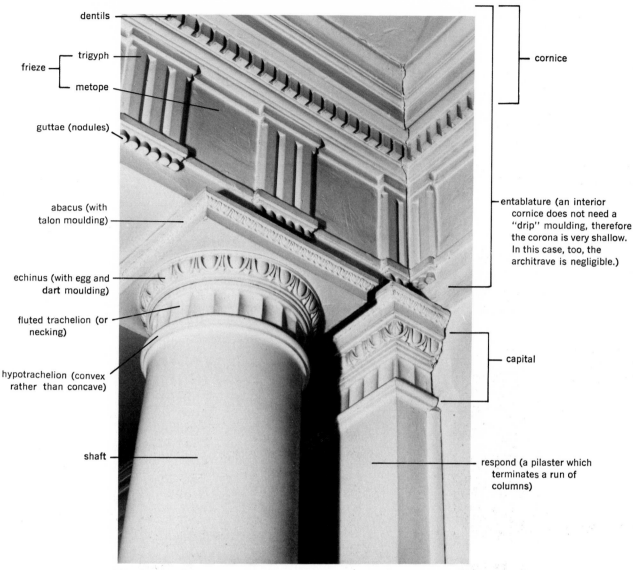

dentils

trigyph

frieze

metope

guttae (nodules)

abacus (with talon moulding)

echinus (with egg and dart moulding)

fluted trachelion (or necking)

hypotrachelion (convex rather than concave)

shaft

cornice

entablature (an interior cornice does not need a "drip" moulding, therefore the corona is very shallow. In this case, too, the architrave is negligible.)

capital

respond (a pilaster which terminates a run of columns)

2929 Massachusetts Avenue, N.W.
Entrance hall: A variant Order

Shown is a Tuscan column with a Roman Doric entablature. The column includes both the shaft and capital. The entablature includes the architrave, frieze and cornice.

256

Plate 9

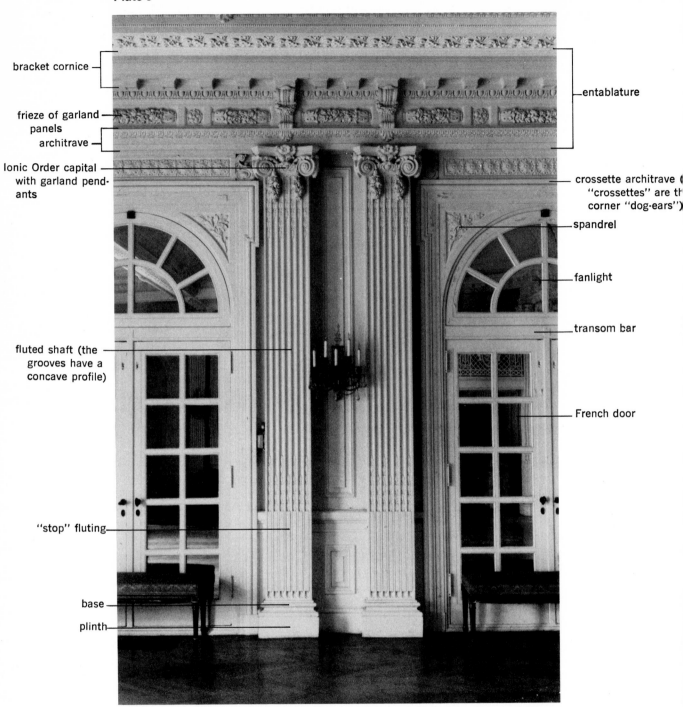

bracket cornice

entablature

frieze of garland panels

architrave

Ionic Order capital with garland pendants

crossette architrave ("crossettes" are the corner "dog-ears")

spandrel

fanlight

transom bar

fluted shaft (the grooves have a concave profile)

French door

"stop" fluting

base

plinth

1520 20th Street, N.W.
Ballroom west wall detail

Plate 10

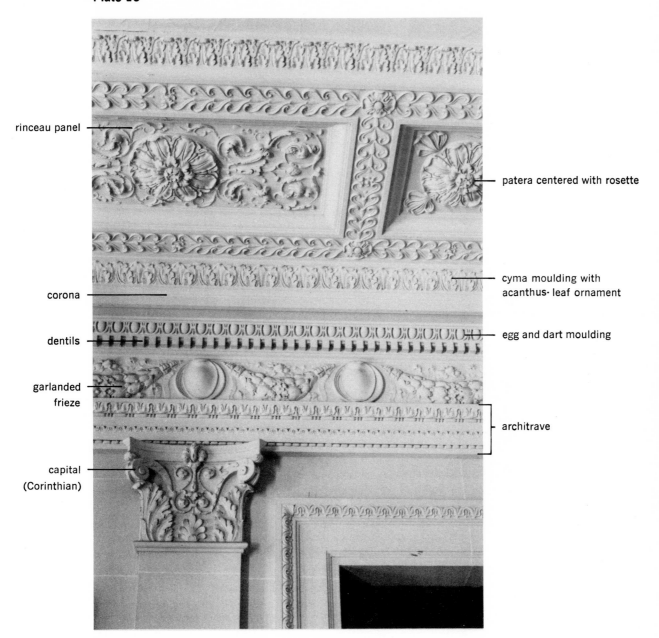

rinceau panel

patera centered with rosette

cyma moulding with
acanthus· leaf ornament

corona

dentils — egg and dart moulding

garlanded
frieze

architrave

capital
(Corinthian)

3000 Massachusetts Avenue, N.W.
Entrance hall cornice and ceiling detail

Plate 11

3000 Massachusetts Avenue, N.W.

Salon: mirror detail of applied Rococo
ornament

Plate 12

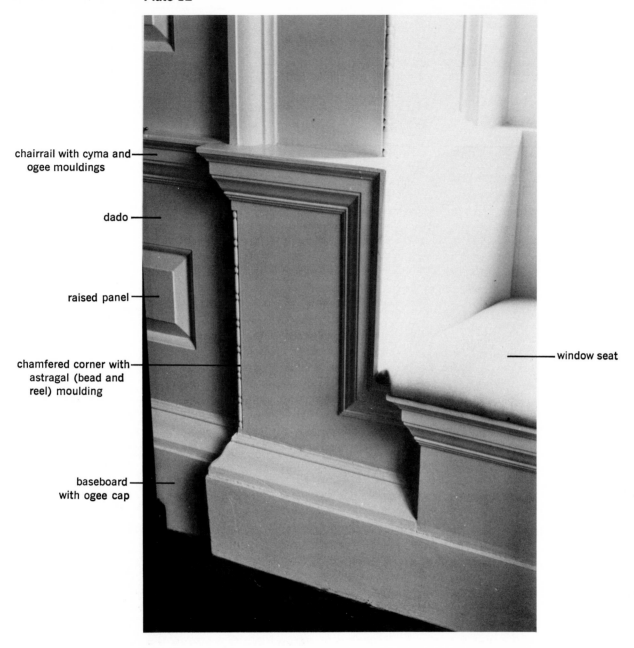

chairrail with cyma and
ogee mouldings

dado

raised panel

chamfered corner with
astragal (bead and
reel) moulding

baseboard
with ogee cap

window seat

3100 Massachusetts Avenue, N.W.
Dining room window and wall detail

Plate 13

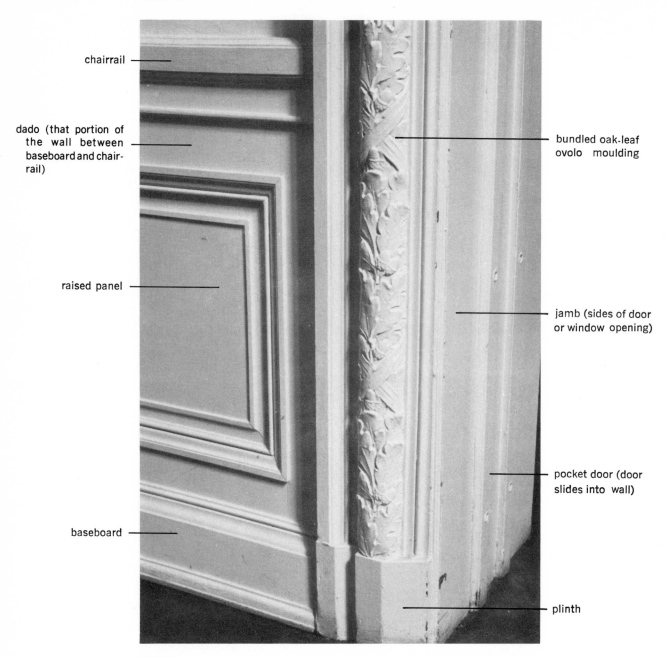

chairrail

dado (that portion of the wall between baseboard and chairrail)

raised panel

baseboard

bundled oak-leaf ovolo moulding

jamb (sides of door or window opening)

pocket door (door slides into wall)

plinth

2305 Massachusetts Avenue, N.W.
Stairhall doorway detail

Plate 14

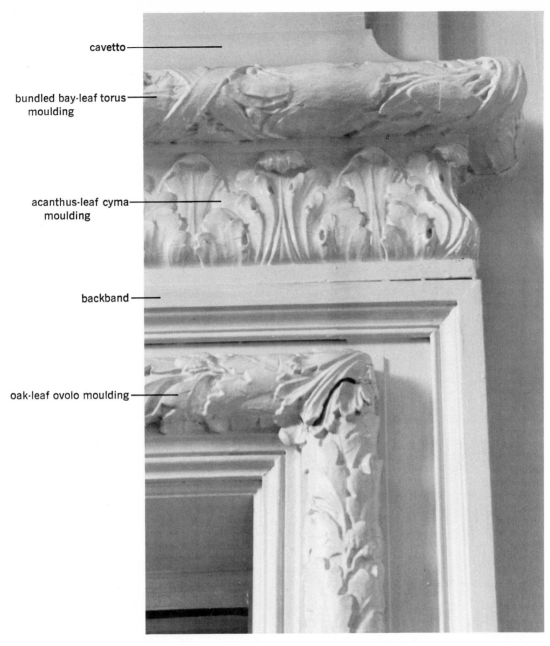

cavetto

bundled bay-leaf torus moulding

acanthus-leaf cyma moulding

backband

oak-leaf ovolo moulding

2305 Massachusetts Avenue, N.W.
Stairhall doorway detail

262

Plate 15

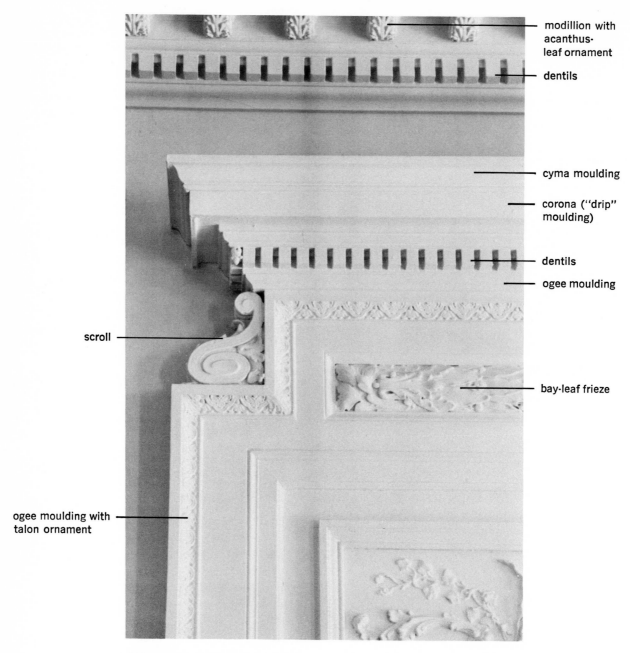

modillion with
acanthus-
leaf ornament

dentils

cyma moulding

corona ("drip"
moulding)

dentils

ogee moulding

scroll

bay-leaf frieze

ogee moulding with
talon ornament

2305 Massachusetts Avenue, N.W.
Salon overdoor and cornice detail

Plate 16

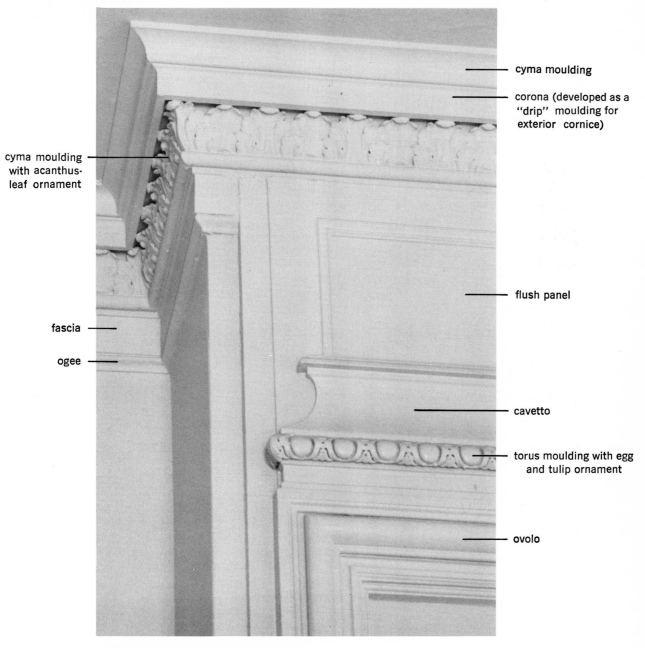

cyma moulding

corona (developed as a "drip" moulding for exterior cornice)

cyma moulding with acanthus-leaf ornament

flush panel

fascia

ogee

cavetto

torus moulding with egg and tulip ornament

ovolo

2305 Massachusetts Avenue, N.W.
Sitting room overmantel and cornice detail

264

Plate 17

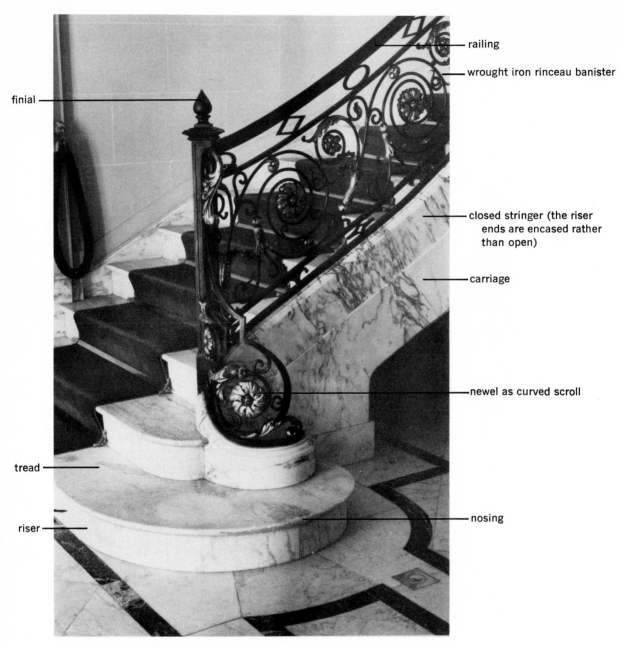

finial —

railing

wrought iron rinceau banister

closed stringer (the riser ends are encased rather than open)

carriage

newel as curved scroll

tread —

nosing

riser —

3000 Massachusetts Avenue, N.W.
Entrance hall stair detail

Plate 18

265

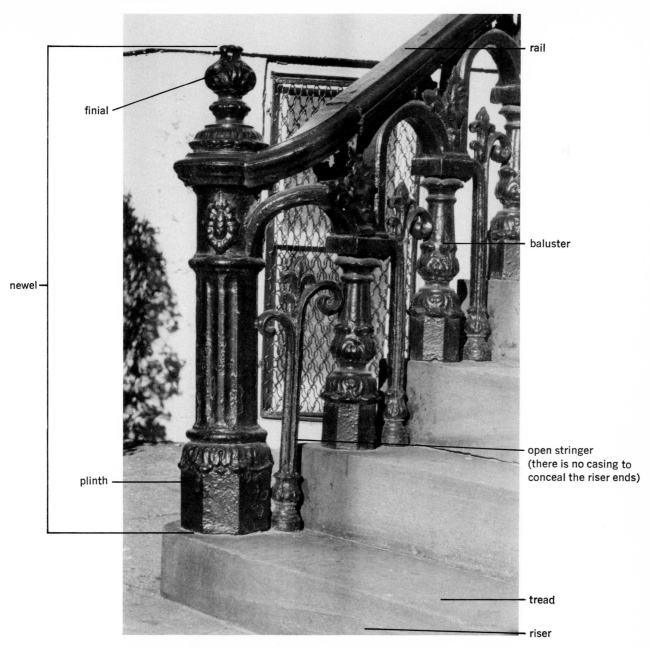

finial

newel

plinth

rail

baluster

open stringer
(there is no casing to
conceal the riser ends)

tread

riser

1013–15 L Street, N.W.
Entrance stoop on 11th Street

Plate 19

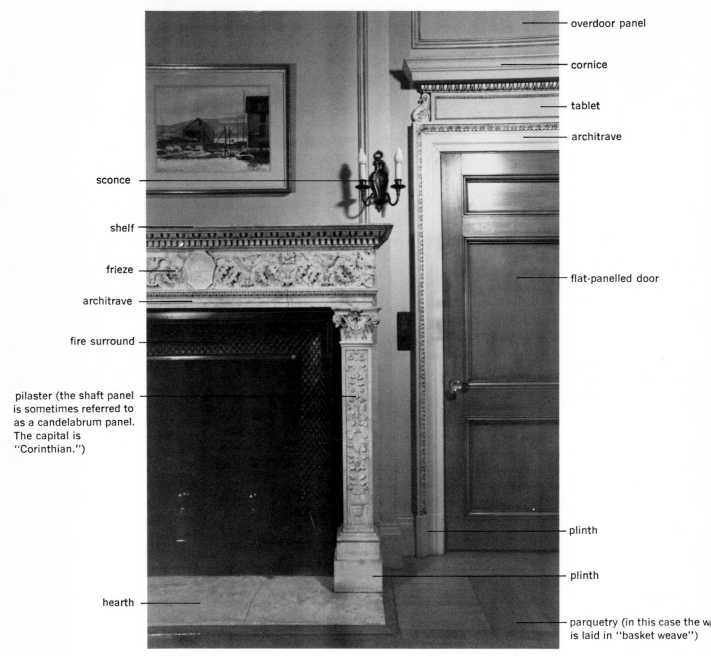

overdoor panel

cornice

tablet

architrave

sconce

shelf

frieze

architrave

flat-panelled door

fire surround

pilaster (the shaft panel
is sometimes referred to
as a candelabrum panel.
The capital is
"Corinthian.")

plinth

plinth

hearth

parquetry (in this case the w
is laid in "basket weave")

1500 Rhode Island Avenue, N.W.
Office mantel and doorway detail

Plate 20

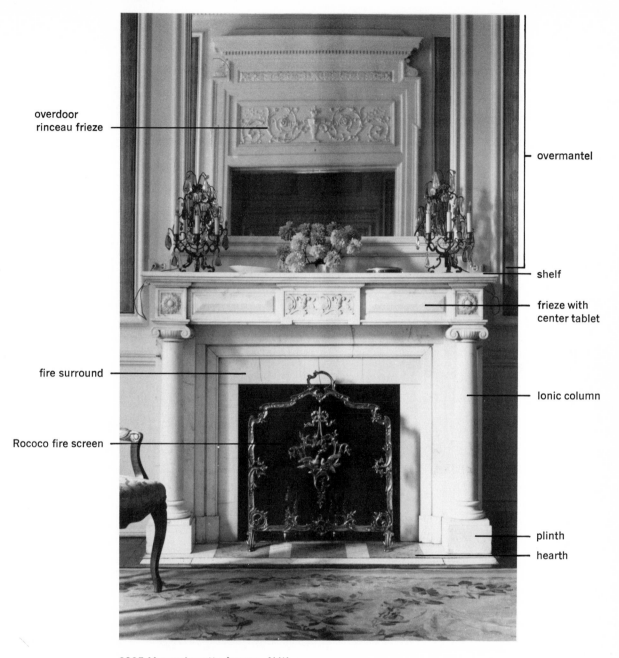

overdoor
rinceau frieze

overmantel

shelf

frieze with
center tablet

fire surround

Ionic column

Rococo fire screen

plinth

hearth

2305 Massachusetts Avenue, N.W.
Salon mantel

Plate 21

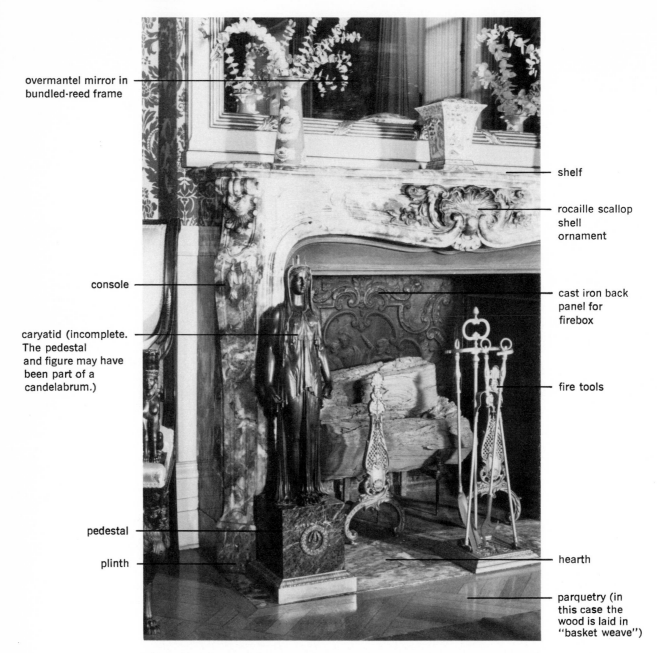

overmantel mirror in
bundled-reed frame

console

caryatid (incomplete.
The pedestal
and figure may have
been part of a
candelabrum.)

pedestal

plinth

shelf

rocaille scallop
shell
ornament

cast iron back
panel for
firebox

fire tools

hearth

parquetry (in
this case the
wood is laid in
"basket weave")

3000 Massachusetts Avenue, N.W.
Drawing room mantel detail

269

Plate 23

1500 Rhode Island Avenue, N.W.
Boardroom

Door knob with mortise lock escutcheon plate.

Plate 22

1520 20th Street, N.W.
Ambassador's Office

Oval door knob with bay-leaf ornament and oval keyhole plate for mortise lock.

Plate 25

3000 Massachusetts Avenue, N.W.
First floor dining room

Beaux Arts Classical door handle and mortise lock escutcheon.

Plate 24

2929 Massachusetts Avenue, N.W.
Library

Beaux Arts Gothic door handle with mortise lock.

Plate 26   **Plate 27**

000 Massachusetts Avenue, N.W.
alon

ocaille scallop shell hinge.

3000 Massachusetts Avenue, N.W.
First floor dining room
Cremone bolt for
French doors and
casement windows.

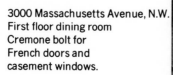

Plate 28

1520 20th Street, N.W.
Drawing room

Espagnolette bolt (two part:
crank and pull) for French
doors and casement
windows.

Inside back cover:
3100 Massachusetts Ave., N.W.
1974

2098 Albion x Birdin Lime Green